BEYOND THE LIGHT
IS THE LOVE
OF GOD

The Knowledge Given
to

LORNA GALLIMORE

through the Love and Devotion of the Brotherhood of Light

BALBOA.
PRESS

A DIVISION OF HAY HOUSE

Balboa Press books may be ordered through booksellers or by contacting:

Balboa Press
A Division of Hay House
1663 Liberty Drive
Bloomington, IN 47403
www.balboapress.com
1 (877) 407-4847

Because of the dynamic nature of the Internet, any web addresses or
links contained in this book may have changed since publication and
may no longer be valid. The views expressed in this work are solely those
of the author and do not necessarily reflect the views of the publisher,
and the publisher hereby disclaims any responsibility for them.

The author of this book does not dispense medical advice or prescribe the use
of any technique as a form of treatment for physical, emotional, or medical
problems without the advice of a physician, either directly or indirectly. The
intent of the author is only to offer information of a general nature to help you
in your quest for emotional and spiritual well-being. In the event you use any
of the information in this book for yourself, which is your constitutional right,
the author and the publisher assume no responsibility for your actions.

Editing by Kondria Woods.
Cover Design and original Artwork by Jef Brown

Printed in the United States of America.

ISBN: 978-1-4525-9215-2 (sc)
ISBN: 978-1-4525-9217-6 (hc)
ISBN: 978-1-4525-9216-9 (e)

Library of Congress Control Number: 2014904012

Balboa Press rev. date: 4/28/2014

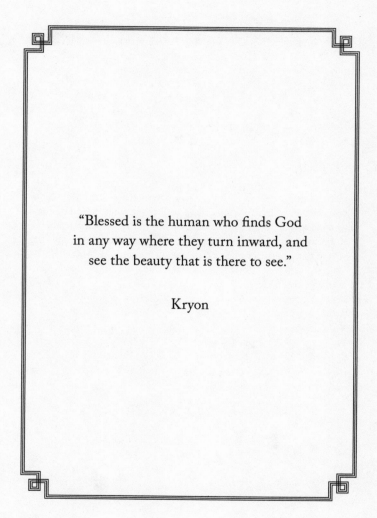

"Blessed is the human who finds God
in any way where they turn inward, and
see the beauty that is there to see."

Kryon

ACKNOWLEDGEMENTS

When the Brotherhood of Light shared the contents of this book, they informed me that the people I needed to help me would present themselves at the appropriate time. As they described, people came forward and offered assistance just when it was needed, like water in the desert to a thirsty man.

In the four years when the book was being constructed there were many hours of anxiety and worry, as I tried to organize the material, from my limited knowledge of the process involved in writing a book. To say I was overjoyed when help was offered would be an understatement. My receptivity to suggestions and feedback from those around me was always expressed with the deepest gratitude.

Thank you Kondria Woods for your time and patience while editing the manuscript to ensure grammatical accuracy, especially because the material could not be edited in the traditional manner. I extend special thanks to Jef Brown for his willingness to share his talents, creativity and inspiration to lovingly create the graphic used on the cover of the book, based on a rose from my garden.

To my friends Carolina Albano, Rev. Marcia White, Verna Ramdeen, Denise Marshall and Cathie Hudnall thank you for your love, encouragement and support in reading the manuscript and helping me to verify its accuracy against the original information given in the notebooks. Dear Courtney St John, thank you for rescuing me during the formatting of the manuscript. You saved my life!!

A huge thank you to Claudiu Fofiu and TJ Kohli for your help and creativity in developing the *Beyondthelightislove* website. You are the best!

I know that without the help and guidance of my earthly Guardian Angels, Dianne Miazga, Gloria Eickmeyer, Maren Piatt, and Virginia McDaniels, this book might never have come into being. Your love and guidance helped me to discover and focus my God-given gifts so that I could go within to contact the God-source and bring this information to light.

A huge thank you to all those who consciously or unconsciously help me to learn the lessons I came into this life to learn. Thank you for providing me with those growth opportunities to help me become the person I am today. Finally, I would like to thank my son Marcus, my genetic family and all my adopted families who were there for me throughout the struggles. Your love throughout the years has sustained and blessed me.

Love and Light!

CONTENTS

INTRODUCTION ~ THE TIME BEFORE THE BEGINNING

How does one begin to tell the story of the love of God for humanity, without beginning to tell the story of the presence of the love of God in your own life? The answer, I believe, is that one is inextricably tied to the other... so in order to understand the NOW moment and who I have become, I must return to who I was before the journey began, and trace my journey to the present and all that I am now.

It all began on the island of Jamaica, where I was born and spent the first 10 years of my life. My early years were unremarkable, in that I was like every other child, playing and living without a care in the world. When I was eight years old, my parents immigrated to England—much like thousands of families looking for a better life for their family in the early sixties—leaving me and my four siblings in the care of my father's step-mother. This experience was traumatic, in that we faced hardships not previously known – most notably the absence of our parents—so it was with great relief that we joined our parents in London in 1964.

Growing up in London in the 60s and 70s was a great experience. We lived in East London, with many other immigrant families from around the world, hailing from countries such as India, Pakistan, Greece, Cyprus, Turkey, and Guyana, just to name a few, and we were part of the working class of first-generation immigrants. I made lasting friendships which exist even today, and when I think of home, I think of England first, even though Jamaica holds a very special place in my heart as the country of my birth.

I was a product of the British educational system, attending Colvestone Crescent primary school at age 10 when I arrived in London, and then moving on to Haggerston Secondary Girls School from 11-18 years of age. From an early age History and Religion were my favorite subjects. Religion especially always intrigued me, and although I attended a public school, I was fortunate enough to be able to study Religious Instruction at an advanced level. Luckily for me, the school could not provide a teacher for me because I was the only student interested in this advanced course of study. It was decided that I would enroll in a Correspondence Course and I worked directly with college professors, submitting essays to them and receiving their feedback on my work. I was only 15 or 16 at the time, and they taught me how to question and to review religious information with a critical eye. I was fascinated by the information about God and the development of the Early Christian Church, Synoptic Gospels, and many other wonderful topics associated with the establishment of the Early Church. I learned how to ask critical questions about what I was being taught about God. I gained an understanding of how to compare and contrast New Testament Books and I grew into a sense of spirituality very early in life. As a result, I continue to have an open, questioning mind about spiritual development and God to this day.

My parents returned to Jamaica with my younger siblings, Janet, Paul, and Christopher when I was about 17 years old, but my sister, my brother, and I— the three eldest children— decided to remain in England. My eldest sister, Cynthia, soon married, I was to live with my aunt and finish school, and my brother, Keith, would do the same staying with other relatives and finishing school. At the onset, the decision for me to live with my aunt had seemed like a perfect solution, because I did not want to return to Jamaica with my parents and she was a favorite aunt. It soon became apparent, however, that this was not necessarily a good plan because I was very unhappy living with my aunt, yet I had no other option as I was still in school.

My parents did not send me any money for me to live on after they left...perhaps because they didn't have it to send... so I worked each Saturday and used that money to buy clothes and whatever else I needed. It wasn't much money, but I had to make it last each week because it was all I had. Unfortunately, I couldn't get any kind of public assistance because my aunt's husband would not agree to complete the paperwork so I could get free school lunches.

The unhappiness I felt during this period of my life was overwhelming, and I felt alone, deserted, and above all, I couldn't understand how or why my parents allowed this to happen to me. I didn't know what arrangements they had made with my aunt but I presumed they had made arrangements for my basic survival needs. I soon discovered however that no financial support was forthcoming because my aunt's husband would continually ask me whether my father had sent me money each time I received a letter from him. My aunt's husband refused to allow me to have a key to the house so each time I left the house I could not re-enter unless someone was at home. The result of this was that regardless of the time of the day or night, I had to wait for someone to open the door to allow me to enter. I had no sense of belonging and I felt like a stranger each time I came home and stood on the doorstep knocking on the door and waiting for one of my cousins to open it. My escape each weekend was to stay with my uncle Cecil and his family in their small, cramped apartment, where I slept with my two younger cousins on a small bed— but I felt loved and wanted there— and I would return to my aunt's house – for it was not my home – each Sunday night so I could go to school on Monday. Even this peace and happiness, was marred by the fact that when I returned to the house that night, I would be jolted back to the reality of my circumstance as I stood on the doorstep knocking. My heart would sink, and the sadness would quickly return.

I didn't tell anyone how I felt, but my uncle and his wife, Venice, knew the pain I was feeling in my heart. I certainly didn't complain. Instead, I kept all the hurt, anger, and pain I was feeling locked up inside of me, and I decided that I would survive all that was happening to me. I don't know where the strength came from, but I refused to give in to my circumstances.

I didn't understand why any of this was happening to me; I was mad at God and everybody else around me, except my uncle and his family. I was brimming over with hurt and pain. I prayed for rescue and cried myself to sleep most of the time when I was under my aunt's roof. I lost weight because I felt guilty about eating the food, since my parents were not contributing to the household. I refused to touch any food or anything else unless it was specifically offered to me by my aunt or her husband.

After what seemed like an eternity, rescue came in the form of my two friends, Marie Antoine (Dobbins) and Edna East, who invited me to share an apartment with them. They were two years older than I was, and had recently started new jobs as cocktail waitresses. The plan was that I would clean the apartment, shop for groceries, and cook for them in exchange for a place to live…because they were working shifts, they did not have the time to take care of any of these basic functions on their days off. It sounded like a perfect plan, and I was grateful beyond measure for this blessing. My aunt gave me permission to move out of her home and so I was freed from all the pain I had known.

I was 17 at the time, and I had been surviving on approximately $7, or maybe less, per week, but I was so much happier, even though I still had very little in terms of money. My friends were kind and generous, yet I felt bad because I had nothing to financially contribute to the household. They tried to reassure me that they made enough in tips to cover food and my expenses, but I felt very dependent. Finally, one day while I was at school, when I couldn't take it anymore…I broke down and told one of my teachers that I was surviving on wages from my Saturday job, so I had no money, and was living with friends. She put me in touch with Social Services, which made arrangements for me to get a weekly allowance so that I would have enough money for food and other living expenses. That was my route to survival until I graduated from school at 18.

After graduating from Haggerston, I continued working at Wallis a high-end chain of boutiques in London's West End, where I had been working on Saturdays and during school holidays. Although I had completed my academic studies successfully, I had not settled on a career path, and began to work full time in the fashion industry because I decided that I wanted to become a fashion buyer. I was told that in order to become a buyer, I needed full-time experience as a sales assistant. Unfortunately, this career path lasted only a few months before the boredom of being on the sales floor consumed me and I abandoned that idea.

Throughout those years, I was determined to be a survivor and was ready to take on anyone or anything that challenged me. Although I am a woman of very small stature, I must have believed I was a giant, because I was *fearless*. Whenever we had problems with landlords or any situation when a champion was needed to do battle, it was I who went forward into battle, wielding a vicious tongue, to put the world to right. I knew I was too small to physically fight anyone— and I really didn't want to fight – but my tongue did what my 95-pound physical frame could not do. I was a force to be reckoned with, especially when anyone attempted to take advantage of me or my friends.

I experienced the same growing pains that all young adults experience: that first love, a broken heart, hurt, pain, and everything in between. At the core of my being, I was very sad and felt alone, so I developed defense mechanisms to protect myself by adopting an attitude of strength and independence. I decided that I would rely fully and depend totally on myself for everything in my life. This was my way of trying to protect myself from any disappointment or from being deserted by anyone again. I would depend on no one, making my way in the world and taking care of myself.

After graduation, my Social Services allowance ended because I was past the age of 18. I therefore had to find employment in order to support myself. I continued working at Wallis full-time – while I tried to decide what I would do for a career— and when I abandoned the idea of becoming a fashion buyer, I worked in a shoe-store for a while, and then decided to join the Civil Service, because I thought this would be a stable occupation with a good salary.

I received a position at the Department of Education and Science at Waterloo in London as a Clerical Officer. After about a year, boredom set in with that job and I applied for a new job across the street at the Inner London Education Authority at County Hall; again as a Clerical Officer and was offered a position.

It was then that I met and was influenced by Olwen Davies, who worked in the same office with me at County Hall located across the bridge from Big Ben on the River Thames. It was Olwen who first asked me, "Why are you here?" It was she who persuaded me that, maybe I should look to other career options. Ironically, years earlier, my 6th Form Mistress and history teacher, Miss Rackham, had suggested that I should become a teacher, but at age 17, I flatly dismissed that suggestion saying, "I would rather die." Needless to say, at age 24, Olwen persuaded me that I was smart enough to attend college to become a teacher.

To understand this, you must know that in England, at that time, college was not an option that would be considered by someone who was a first-generation immigrant. I knew nothing about it, because no one I knew had attended college—my father was a carpenter by trade and my mother was a home maker with six children. She occasionally worked in factories, doing assembly work or packing, to help increase the family income. We received free school lunches and government assistance to pay for our school uniforms, so there was no reason why college would have been something that I would have known about or actively pursued. In fact, in my mind, only smart people went to college, and that certainly wasn't me...

At that time, most people in England could have a rewarding career without attending college, and being a teacher sounded very boring. Prior to my discussions with Olwen, I knew very little about college and had not given a profession any great thought, except in my early years, when I once heard someone in school talk about nursing. I had no idea what nursing entailed but it sounded good so I would quickly tell people I wanted to be a nurse whenever careers were being discussed. In addition, this decision to be a nurse had allowed me to fly under the radar for years when careers were being discussed by my parents. I remember, however, that when at age 15 my father asked me what I planned to do after school— a sore subject because each time he asked me, I had replied, "I don't know." Once, in exasperation, I replied, "I don't know and I don't care!" That was the wrong answer to give to my father because he used the rolled-up newspaper he had in his hands to swat me. I was devastated because my father had never done anything like that before in my life, and so my heart was broken to think that he had done it over something as trivial as my not knowing what I wanted to be.— At age 18, I still had no idea and at age 24, I was still undecided.

With Olwen's encouragement, I began to research my options, and discovered that college was the way to gain specialized training for specific occupations such as teaching. I decided that this profession might be a good option for me after all, in case I wanted to travel the world. I discovered that having completed my advanced studies whilst in school, I was academically qualified and prepared to attend Teacher Training College. I applied and was accepted at Avery Hill College, in Bexley, (outside of London) in Kent. During my interview, the head of the Special Education Department— my intended Major—told me that in order to begin the course, I had to gain experience working with special education students, so "maybe" he would see me in September… if I obtained the required experience. His words rang in my ears: "Maybe we will see you in September, and maybe we won't." His words became a battle cry for me because he had dared to challenge me, and suggested I may not be successful.

I went back to County Hall and resigned my position, and applied at a local Special School— as most of the special education students were educated in separate specialized schools in London at that time— for a teacher's aide position. Of course there was a salary cut but I didn't care, because I was going to prove the professor wrong and be at Avery Hill in September! I began as an aide in February or March 1977, and remained until the end of the school year in July, —with kindergarten students who would today be classified as Moderate to Severe Intellectually Disabled.—I loved my new job and my students, and I learned many things which provided me with valuable insight and experiences later on.

In September, I was anxious to meet the professor again to say, "Here I am!" It made me feel great to prove him wrong, and I became a thorn in his side for four years.

As the course progressed, I realized that my experiences with the students were a great asset because they allowed me to apply the theory to real situations I had already experienced. The practical experiences that I drew on later in class were invaluable, especially when I was learning the theory of education and I was able to return to the same school to complete the first of my four practicums. The experiences I had in the school gave me great insight into my chosen area of study and I was grateful that I had worked with the students before being accepted. I knew I had finally found something that I loved to do. My major was Education of Mentally Handicapped Children with a minor in Elementary Education. Although the major was not selected for any great altruistic reason other than simply because it seemed more interesting than English, Math, or any of the other subjects that I could have chosen. I loved every moment and never looked back. This was ironic, because I had selected that option and checked the box, telling God that if I was accepted, I would take that as confirmation that this was what I should be doing. That was the beginning of the next phase of my journey, even though I had no idea what God had planned for me.

As I reflect on that part of my life, I know that Olwen Davis was my guardian angel, put there to help me on the first leg of my life's journey. Likewise, my aunt's husband and my college professor were also there to help me and to challenge me, even though I certainly did not see it that way at the time. Her husband helped me to become strong because I was determined to survive in spite of him.

I lived off-campus in my own apartment and travelled by train and bus or with friends to get to college each day. Luckily, the government paid my college tuition and I received a grant to cover living expenses. I worked on Saturdays and each summer to support myself in this way until I graduated four years later.

While I had no immediate family members to congratulate me or to encourage me on any of these accomplishments, (my sister was living in Germany with her husband who was in the Army, and my brother was in Jamaica) that didn't matter after a while. I kept going because quitting was never an option…I was doing these things on my own to take care of my needs and I needed the approval or encouragement of no one. My friends were my support system, and I continued to take care of myself.

I completed my teacher certification training, loving every moment. It was very hard work and each of the four years I was assigned for a period of practical teaching in a school. We were required to pass the practicum each year or we would be asked to leave the course… and there was no transferring of credits. If you failed the practicum, the course was over, and you would have nothing. My course was special in that it was a four-year course and was more rigorous, allowing students to move on to an Advanced Degree upon completion. In essence, it was like an Advanced Bachelor's Degree. I was therefore very happy when after four years I graduated with an Upper 2nd Class Honors Degree.

I taught for a year in London in a Special School and I loved it, but I was very restless and so I decided that London was not exciting enough. Most of my school friends were getting married by this time, but that did not interest me although I had had proposals on two different occasions. I decided that marriage was not for me, so I decided to move to New York to find adventure.

The move to New York came about because during my years at Avery Hill, I had travelled to the USA as an Exchange Student to work in a summer camp for Intellectually Impaired adults in Upstate New York. I made many friends during my first and subsequent trips, but a special relationship blossomed with Cheryl Cannone who was also a teacher working at the residential facility. Cheryl and I developed a very special bond. Her wonderful Italian family lived locally and accepted me like a long lost relative. I had travelled to NY for Cheryl's wedding instead of staying in London to experience the excitement of Prince Charles and Lady Diana's wedding because Cheryl was so special to me. It was natural, therefore that when I thought about moving to America, the plan was to be near Cheryl. I applied to the residential facility and received a position, so I packed up my clothes in two very large suitcases and left London. I left my apartment with all my possessions in London, and stepped off the Short Line Bus in Middletown NY to begin my new life.

Unfortunately, soon after I began working, the administration changed my shift so that I was working the evening shift, which meant that I was not working the same shift as Cheryl. This posed a huge problem, since I had no car, and therefore had no way to get to work; since I lived with Cheryl on the other side of town and, of course, there was no public transportation. I was devastated because I couldn't understand why they would give me a different shift in light of what they knew of my circumstances. After only a week, I decided to quit the job because I couldn't get to work and I didn't want to be a burden. Once again, I found myself needing to make decisions about what to do and where to go.

There I was; no job, in a strange country, and no idea what to do. My options included returning to London, where my apartment was still available and I could return to my teaching job and face the fact that I had been a failure. Alternatively, I could go to Jamaica to visit my parents— whom I had not seen in more than five years— for a brief vacation, then return to London… or try to find another job in New York. I had another talk with God and decided to apply for a teaching position I saw in the newspaper, at a school located in the Bronx.

It was the week before school started in September 1982 and the job was a special education position in a private school for students deemed unmanageable by the NYC school system.

I decided that if I didn't get the job, I would take that as a sign that I should return to London…because by now I had begun to realize that things were not randomly happening to me, and I could see certain patterns emerging in my life that were not chance occurrences. Of course, they called me for an interview the Friday before school started, and I was offered the position. I worked in that school for four years, initially living with an old school friend for a few months until I found a basement apartment of my own. Sometimes when it rained, my apartment flooded and the landlord would have to replace the carpet and any of my belongings that were damaged or ruined. After a while it became a vicious cycle and I lived in fear of the rain. I was eventually able to find a new apartment on the 5th floor of a building close by.

Living in NYC was very lonely and was nothing like you see in the movies. I developed some wonderful friendships with co-workers and they became like family to me as well, since I had no immediate family living in the US. I was also reunited with my old friend Florence Angbah who had worked with me at Wallis in London… when we bumped into each other one day in the South Bronx, and discovered we lived less than a block apart.

When I think back, I don't remember ever being afraid, even though I was living in NYC, basically alone without any family and very few friends. I would travel Upstate on the bus to spend holidays with Cheryl's family and to get away from the Bronx, which was noisy and dirty. Her family became my family– and it was at this time that Cheryl's mother, Virginia McDaniels, first introduced me to her friends and my spiritual awakening began. Virginia McDaniels was another one of my guardian angels who was there to point me in the right direction to gain spiritual knowledge. I learned to meditate and used it as a way to calm my fears and make me feel better. When I was afraid, frightened, worried or needed to be at peace, I would sit and meditate and gain that inner peace, letting me know that all would be well. No matter how angry or upset I was feeling, I knew that meditation was the way to escape those fears and feel better. This therefore became a part of my regular practice because I was frequently mad at people because I was very impatient, and when things were not going well, I was anything but nice and cordial. (Ironically, I was always able to demonstrate the greatest amount of patience and love with my students in school but with adults who I felt should know better, it was a very different matter.)

It was during this time that I began to read and to attend metaphysical classes to learn more about different spiritual practices and to learn how to ask questions during meditation to contact the God within. The first question I asked was for the name of my Spirit Guide. This was a homework assignment given by Gloria Eickmeyer, our teacher, and I was excited to receive the name Michael in response to this question. I cannot remember how the response came, but I remember that it came. With this came the realization that I was not alone and that I had my own Angel named Michael around me to help me. I read many books which provided information about Angels and I felt very comfortable knowing I had my own Angel Guide whom I could speak to anytime. I know that Gloria told me on different occasions that I was like an open radio receiver with a direct channel to Spirit and that it was a gift. It sounded like something special but I never focused on it.

I lived in NY City for four years and then moved back to Middletown because I disliked living in the Bronx, and I had become a mother when I was living in NY and had a son, Marcus.

The relationship with his father did not last for very long because I was not willing to live a drama-filled existence, and would not subject my child to it either. I quickly realized I would have to be self-sufficient because no child support was ever offered and so I knew that I would have to rely only on myself, to raise him and that is what I did.

I had been working with pre-school students and the administration allowed me to take Marcus to work with me because they needed me back at work at the end of my maternity leave, and I couldn't leave him because I was still nursing him. I was then able to keep him with me until he was about nine months old because he wouldn't drink from a bottle. I was very grateful to my employers for allowing me to keep him with me because I would not have been able to afford to pay anyone to look after him even if I had wanted to do it. Needless to say, I was very grateful for my blessings but when he had to go to a baby-sitter there was frequently no extra money, so I worked in a *Roy Rogers* fast food restaurant to earn extra money to cover living expenses (while Florence took care of him in the evening).

There were times when I had no money and wondered how I would survive until the next pay check, but somehow a way was always found and I gave thanks each day and kept on going. Once, when I had no money at all, I walked along the street and looked down to find $20. I was overjoyed with this find which allowed me to survive until payday that Friday. That was the first of many occasions when I would find things in NYC.

I began to have recurring dreams of finding jewelry while walking along the street. In the dreams, I would be walking along the street and would look down and there would be gold jewelry on the pavement (sidewalk). You can imagine my amazement when I actually began to find gold jewelry while I was out and about in the city (items such as rings, bracelets, and pendants). I remember always giving thanks to God for giving me these special gifts as I wore each piece with pride.

Throughout my life, I have always been a dreamer—literally. When I was a child, I remember listening to my mother relate vivid dreams to us. She would tell wonderful stories about what happened in her dreams. There were always stories about seeing relatives who had passed away, so it was therefore not a surprise for me to discover that I was able to do the same. Each night I kept a journal beside my bed and would wake up in the morning and record my own vivid dreams complete with illustrations. Sometimes I was travelling on a road meeting people, and other times I would be lost. Being lost was part of a recurring dream-cycle which would happen whenever things were not going well in my life. I would have the same dream and it was like a wake-up call to take stock and make course changes – examine what was happening— in my life. In my dreams, I was sometimes lost, or I was frequently going somewhere and talking to wonderful people dressed in white on the road. During these dream journeys along the road, I would wake up happy but had no idea who I had met or where I had gone. Each day when I awoke, I would write everything in my journal with pictures to illustrate what had been seen. Over time, I realized that my dreams were very special in nature as they provided me with information about different aspects of my life.

Eventually, I began to follow the guidance given in my dreams and ever since then, I have always looked for signs to follow when situations arose. Alternatively, I would decide to move in a given direction with the proviso that if no obstacles presented, that absence would be the sign that I had made the correct choice. Somehow after this time, I never felt alone, even in times of despair, because I knew my Angels were with me, taking care of me. I came to realize that I was talking with them in my dreams and they were providing me with the guidance I needed. As a result of these early experiences, I have always been open and receptive to Spirit, and its presence in my life was as welcomed as any valued family member.

As my awareness increased, I found myself examining the beliefs that were at the core of who and what I was. I realized that from very early in my twenties, I had never been able to come to terms with the belief that death is the end of life. It never made sense, and this was never as pronounced as when Louis Armstrong died. For me, that was a pivotal moment because; it made no sense to me that humans would be placed upon the Earth for such a short time, given these magnificent talents, and then death would be the end of the road. It just did not seem to make any sense! Additionally, I had always been fascinated by the soul and soul development for some unknown reason, and so I began to spend a great deal of time after college reading books such as Gary Zukav's *The Seat of the Soul*. –To be totally candid, I had to read it three times over several years before I finally understood it— I read RAMTHA, and SETH books along with *Bringers of the Dawn* by Barbara Marciniak, and many other authors including Shirley MacLaine and Marianne Williamson who helped to open my mind to other possibilities and provided for me what was a better and more plausible explanation of why I was here. The more I read the happier I became as I discovered this new world.

In time, I became hungry for anything that had the word "soul" in the title because I was anxious to know more about what happens before birth and after death. Here, Brian Weiss' book, *Many Lives, Many Masters*, captivated me, together with *Destiny of Souls* and *Journey of Souls* by Michael Newton. I then discovered Edgar Cayce and was fascinated by the things he was able to do while he was asleep. It was as though a whole new world opened up to me, and I felt very comfortable in this world. These authors helped me to understand that there was much more to life and death than I knew, so I avidly read everything I could get my hands on when time permitted. It was also during this time that I was introduced to the KRYON books written by Lee Carroll, by another one of my angel guides here on Earth, my wonderful friend Dianne Miazga. I read one of the books and was very excited by the contents and added it to my quickly expanding little collection. I began to see and experience the world differently because I found that I couldn't discuss my new-found knowledge with everyone because most of my views about God and the reasons why we are here were very different. Therefore, I began to keep my thoughts to myself. Having been raised as a Christian, I had attended a Lutheran Church in the Bronx—and christened Marcus there—because it was the closest thing I could find to the Church of England faith I had grown up with in England, but I kept reading my books to learn as much as I could about those spiritual things that were of interest to me.

In 1990, I left Upstate NY and moved to Georgia following an old friend of mine, Lorraine Rodrigues, who had moved there from Brooklyn, NY four years earlier.

I hated the cold NY winters with freezing rain and snow, and the weather in Georgia sounded very inviting. I had been teaching elementary-level special education students in Upstate NY and hated to leave them, but I knew it was time to make a change. Over the years, I had learned many lessons from my interactions with my students, and when I look back now, I realize that my young students were some of my greatest teachers because they taught me how to love unconditionally. Those were wonderful years and my students will always reside in a special place in my heart.

With the move to Georgia came my separation from all my friends and co-workers, and my support system of friends like Susan Tetz who had been like a sister to me, picking up Marcus from the nursery and taking care of him at her home until I could get back to pick him up after class— at 9:00 or 10:00PM— for two years, as I worked to complete my Master's degree. Then, of course, there was also the loss of my family; Cheryl, her brother John and Virginia; Gloria, my teacher; Maren Piatt; Dianne Miazga, and the wonderful friends and spiritual community I had found, which helped me to grow and to understand so much about myself. The meditation ceased and I spent most of my time working. It was like moving from a lush garden with everything you could want or need to an isolated desert. Spirit was always with me, but because I was in basic survival mode for many years, I did not focus on my spiritual development.

As I review my life experiences, I realize that I have experienced the same hardships that most people face the world over. My biggest advantage was the fact that I had a profession that I loved, and as a Special Education teacher I was able to find employment that I loved. The hours were long and the pay was just enough for survival, but I never complained. I did what had to be done to assure that survival. There was no extra money for luxury items, so over the years I worked part-time to supplement my income and to purchase a home by working in the Food Services industry at the Georgia Dome, and Turner Field Baseball Stadium in Atlanta, as a Suite Attendant... all while going back to school part-time for an additional Specialist (EDS) degree.

Life has not been a bowl of cherries, but I guess I knew that complaining was not an option or a productive choice. I simply did what I needed to do and kept going... sometimes working six or seven days each week: five days at school teaching, and the weekend in Food Services. During this time, my spiritual development was at an all-time low because my sole focus was on survival. There was no meditation, I worked so Marcus and I could survive and I was always tired. I always felt connected and something within me kept me focused on doing what had to be done.

I cannot remember when or how I realized I was able to communicate with Spirit but in looking back in my journals it began in the early 1990s. I think Gloria told me my father – who had passed in 1985— wanted to speak to me so I should keep a journal beside my bed to write things down. Since I was already writing down my dreams, this was a very easy transition. This was how it all began. The first time it happened, I picked up my pencil and put it on the page and scribbles initially appeared independently of me as I held the pencil in my hand. It was almost as though the pencil was being controlled by a force beyond me.

This 'automatic writing' as it is called, became more controlled over time and words and phrases replaced the scribbling. Each time I wrote, the words became clearer and easier to understand, then the language emerged and I could clearly see that it was 'Olde English.'

My Angel Guide Michael identified himself in the text, and began speaking to me in the writing, so it was like talking to an old friend and I was never afraid or worried about what was happening. Michael was my Angel Guide for quite a while but then one day the writing was signed the Brotherhood of Light and the content and the tone of the information began to change significantly.

Throughout the years I have always known the value of meditation and I knew that I needed to meditate daily, but I must admit that I was not a disciplined student, so frequently I was either too tired or too lazy – not sure which— to try to control the communication with

Spirit or to meditate. I guess with no other alternative, Spirit began to awaken me (with a tingling/cramped feeling in my hands) in the early hours of the morning to communicate. The system worked for me because it meant I didn't have to establish a regular routine/ritual of meditation. I simply went to sleep and Spirit would wake me up if and when they needed to communicate. I would be awakened sometime between 1:30AM and 3:30AM and then I would pick up my notebook and pencil and write down what I heard in my head. I always said thank you to Spirit, then I would put down the pencil and notebook and return to sleep.

I say I was "awakened," but in essence, I was awake enough to write though never conscious enough to know what I was writing. The full realization of what had been written did not come until the material was reviewed when I woke up later that morning. I never worried about it nor did I ask who was speaking to me. I guess I just knew deep inside me it was all right. Sometimes the writing would be signed the 'Brotherhood' but sometimes it was not. Years passed and during this time my 'Friends,' as they became known, were always there reassuring me, guiding me, and telling me in the most loving of ways how much I was loved. I was given information and guidance about all aspects of my life. The guidance was given to me and also to my close friends who knew I spoke to 'Friends' at night and would ask for a message from my 'Friends'. Only some of my friends knew of the gift however, because I realized that most people were not accepting of the idea of getting guidance from a source identifying itself as The Brotherhood of Light.

The ability to speak to and to get guidance from Spirit became a part of me and it was just something I was able to do. I never considered that the ability to communicate with Spirit was anything special because it was something that came to me effortlessly. I never went out of my way to encourage or discourage it. I was simply a radio receiver with a wide open channel as Gloria once described it. I was never afraid of Spirit nor have I spent any time questioning, analyzing, or dissecting what was happening during these communications. (Maybe, because deep inside of me, I already knew the answers to those questions.)

As a result of my beliefs and my gift, I have always had two different groups of friends: those who understood my spiritual beliefs, and those who did not. I chose to keep the two sides of me separate because it was much easier that way.

My close friends knew I could give them 'messages from my Friends' when any kind of advice—romance, career etc.—was needed, but I never mentioned my ability to anyone outside of this small circle of friends… That is, until I shared my secret with about 700 people at Rev. Michael Beckwith's Revelations Conference in 2011 in Los Angeles. Since then, I have shared the knowledge of my gift with more people as part of my preparation for all that is to come. I am no longer worried about what people will say or think because this is who I am and I am proud and happy to share my gift with humanity.

Because I was focused on survival for many years, there were times when long periods would elapse without any communication with Spirit, because the demands of life were uppermost in my mind. At such times, it was almost as though Spirit was not there, but sure enough, when I was experiencing hardships, they would be beside me, reassuring me all was well and providing the loving guidance I needed.

Friends have often asked if I was not afraid of my Spirit Guides and the whole thought of communicating with non-physical entities that are always with you. To be honest I never really gave it any thought —maybe because somewhere deep inside my subconscious I guess I knew it was a part of me —Whatever the reason, it never bothered me and I was never afraid nor did I spend any time analyzing what was happening to me. I just accepted it as a part of me. In 2008, the nature of the information I was receiving changed prior to and after the election of Barack Obama when Spirit provided information about him and his mission. Again, as I had always done, I woke up, read the information, said, "Wow!" and carried on with my day.

The first piece of knowledge for this book was given in February 2010, and from that time until the middle of February 2012, I would be awakened during the early hours of the morning and write for an hour to an hour and a half in my journal all the information that I was hearing in my head. On the morning of 9th October 2011, I woke up, jumped out of bed, grabbed my note book and wrote "Beyond the Light is the Love of God" and I knew it was the title of the book. Spirit had told me that the title would be given in time but it came as a surprise and I was very excited. The following morning, I woke up and this time wrote, "The knowledge given to Lorna Gallimore through the Love and Devotion of the Brotherhood of Light." This made perfect sense to me because I knew that I could never claim authorship of the knowledge I was being given and would have to acknowledge the source.

Throughout this great adventure, I was frequently reminded by Spirit that I did not have to proceed with the book if I did not wish to do so. Spirit frequently reminded me that I had 'free will' and could choose not to continue with the task because they would still be beside me, regardless of the choice I made. The unconditional love of God would always be mine.

There were many nights when I was too tired to focus or to be awakened, and Spirit would acknowledge the tiredness of the human body and tell me to, "Return to slumber," or I would fall asleep in the middle of the writing. On these occasions, I would feel that I had let them down but there was no judgment from them. It was I who was being judgmental of my own shortcoming, as I saw it. Whenever I tried to struggle on, ignoring the tiredness of my physical body, the result would be clearly seen in the work when I read it the next morning; for in truth, it was sometimes illegible and I would have to ask for the information to be shared again. On numerous occasions, I could not be stirred from sleep due to excessive tiredness, and even though my hands tingled and I knew Spirit wanted to share information I would roll over and return to sleep.

Please be reminded that during the writing of the majority of the book, I was being awakened at approximately 1:30-2:30AM… would then write for an hour or hour and a half, put down my pencil and return to sleep until 5:30 or 5:45AM to wake up for work. As you read the information, note that the date reflects when each narrative was received.

As the work progressed, Spirit informed me that our mode of communication would need to change. This change necessitated that we change from Spirit waking me up to a system where I would call on Spirit when I was ready to write. This proposed change was fraught with great fear on my part, and naturally made me very uncomfortable because, after all, I had been using the old method for more than twenty years and I was very comfortable with it. It was familiar, it was known, and now I was being asked to step out into unknown territory.

Of course, I had no confidence in my ability to call upon Spirit and still receive the kind of information I had been receiving, but I think my greatest fear was that I would call and get no response. My other fear was that I would somehow infuse my thoughts into the information, therefore making it less original. With great love and encouragement, Spirit reminded me of others who had been able to complete this task. They mentioned Esther Hicks[1] and others who could communicate with Source at will, and assured me it would be an easy task.

In spite of the confidence of Spirit in my abilities, I was not reassured by this comparison with others. With fear and trepidation, I asked for a special phrase so they would know I was ready. The human side of me was living and thinking only in terms of my limited perception of the power of Spirit to know what was needed or what I was thinking at any given moment. I was reassured by Spirit that I didn't need to say anything special, but I would not relent so we agreed upon a phrase. Imagine if you can, someone talking out loud to Spirit saying, "I know you don't think I need anything, but I do! Please give me a phrase!" Of course, Spirit gave me a phrase! "Dear Ones, let us commune for it is good to come together." And so, with my need for a special phrase satisfied on 25th February 2012, I experienced what I call the first summoning. I sat with my pencil and notebook, said

---

[1]   Channel for Abraham (Abraham-Hicks Publications)

my phrase and began to write. And that, as they say, was that! The information flowed through me as it had always done in the past and there was no change in the knowledge that was shared.

Spirit was right! Not that I had ever doubted them deep down inside me, but the conscious human side of me said, "I am not sure this new thing will work so please be patient and do it my way.

On 28th March 2012, I asked for the chapter headings of the book and they were given. A few weeks after I began using the new process, I found that I no longer had the need to say the short phrase when I needed to communicate with Spirit. I simply sat and said what I needed out loud and the knowledge flowed through me. It is always given with such love that I have come to realize that I have been changed as a result of the information and knowledge that has been shared through me. Spirit frequently said my life would change and now I know what they meant. After all, you cannot deliver this kind of knowledge without it impacting you in every way.

I find that I am now more at peace within myself. I am meditating once again, and things that used to bother me no longer cause me any worry. I have let go and allowed the love of God to shine through me. I look at the knowledge that is shared and try to be that love and light that Spirit speaks of. As I continue to grow, I know that I am a Child of the Light. I know that we are all brothers and sisters regardless of race, creed, color, or religion, or any other group that, as humans we are assigned to for whatever reason. I know that I am so much more than any label that can be used to describe me, for I am a Child of the Most High God, loved eternally by my Mother Father God as are we all; and only that fog of forgetfulness which is part of the human condition would keep me ignorant of this fact. I know that the love of God was given to me eons[2] ago and is mine eternally. This much I know!

I believe that I came into this life to make a difference in the world and to serve humanity. As Abraham – Esther Hicks—told me at the Agape Revelations Conference in April, 2011 "You sent rockets of desire into the Universe asking how you could serve." I know my Spirit Guides are here to support me on this mission and to help me to do what I came to do. This much I know. Even though I didn't always consciously know it, I know it now, and that is what matters.

When I read today, I read and listen to the teachings of Kryon as channeled by Lee Carroll, together with authors like Rev. Michael Beckwith, His Holiness Sri Sri Ravi Shankar, Don Miguel Ruiz, Marianne Williamson, Gary Zukav, Deepak Chopra and many others that are sharing messages of love, brotherhood, peace, and caring for others. I am also looking within to find the answers we all seek. What I know more than twenty-three years after reading the first Kryon book is that these materials are all teaching the same thing about the unconditional love of God for humanity. The information is presented in different ways but it is all saying the same thing because it all originates from the One Source. They teach that God is a God of LOVE. They teach that love, peace, and brotherhood is the way forward for humanity because we are One. We are brothers and sisters who are here on Earth to find our way back to God. We come disguised in different colors, races and religions, "Just like flowers in

---

[2]   A long indefinite period of time:

the garden of God." God sees no color, creed, race, or religion, and neither should we. God is Spirit and sees only His children whom He loves unconditionally. We are Spiritual beings having a human experience first and foremost, and we are Spirit, we are Light, we are LOVE. We are expressions of God walking upon the Earth and we carry the God-spark within each of us.

We can all talk to Spirit whenever we wish, for we all have that knowledge deep inside us. All we have to do is be receptive, and let the love of God flow through us and become manifest in the world.

As I look back over my life I have come to realize how far I travelled along this road of life. Now I am aware that all those early experiences that brought me so much pain were the very experiences that strengthened me and helped me to become that person that I am today. Each obstacle (storms of life) placed in my path helped me to grow even though I had no idea at the time. That is why someone like me, can be the bearer of this information. Not because I am special– because I am not— but because I am just like everyone else. Like everyone else, I have doubted, asked "why me" when things are tough, believed I was alone in the world, made many mistakes; cried for God to rescue me, and thought there was no hope for me.

What I have come to realize now is that I have never been alone, because God has been with me, and loved me unconditionally throughout my life even when I was unaware of its presence. God was always there loving and guiding me in spite of myself, without any judgment, every day, especially when I was mad at the world and God. It seems clear, I must have asked God how I could serve humanity (in another lifetime) and then I opened myself up to allow His love to come through me in this one. I asked for help to become a better person, and I listened for the answer when it came, even when it was sometimes disguised as hardships. We can all do it, because we are made in the image and likeness of God and are powerful beings when we allow our light to shine forth. Everyone has the ability to do what I have done and to commune with Spirit if it is their desire. All one needs to do, is to be open and receptive. I know that I am still a work in progress, and every day I continue to learn, change, and grow, because I am human and I am therefore going to continue to face opportunities for growth (also known as mistakes) all the time.

What follows is the information given to me by Spirit, informing me of the task ahead. It details in the voice of Spirit, the love and guidance given to me along the way to guide and encourage me to "take up the mantle[3] and continue on with the task." The words are filled with love and encouragement and they provided me with the strength and courage to continue on with the task without knowing the name of the book, usually referred to as "the text" by Spirit, or how many chapters there would be. The material was not given in chapters but simply given as it is presented in the book… sometimes with a heading but mostly without one. The chapter names were given after the fact as I mentioned earlier, and as promised by Spirit they helped me to identify the contents of each chapter.

---

[3]   Figurative cloak symbolizing preeminence or authority <accepted the *mantle* of leadership

The editing and organizing exercise was a great lesson in learning to listen to the voice of intuition within. After I read each of the daily extracts I would examine the text then decide to which of the chapters 1 through 5 it belonged. Of course I second-guessed myself continuously and worried that I had not inserted the contents into the correct chapters. I was therefore very happy to hear from Spirit that almost everything was in its correct placement when I had completed the task. (I reviewed the text and made the necessary changes of course.) The irony was that somehow I knew deep inside me— call it inner knowing— that in placing them in chronological order in each chapter, based on the date they were given, they would all somehow be in the right place.

If there is one thing I have learned during this great adventure with Spirit, it's that everything happens as it should and when I let go and I allow the love of God to guide me, there is no need to ever worry, because everyone or everything I need to assist me with the task has come into my life at the moment when they were/are needed.

The information has not been edited for content—because I feel that the work must be presented in the original form as given by Spirit— but is presented in the language of Spirit exactly as it was given. Much of the teaching is given in metaphors because it is coming from the mind of God and this is how God has always spoken to mankind since ancient times, when it was given to the Prophets.

It is my hope that you will read this material with an open mind and that it will help you to find your way to the truth of the love of God for you. I know that this material has helped me to find a deep, sweet peace within my soul which has changed me forever.

I hope you can find that same sweet peace as you come to realize how much you are loved and adored by your Mother Father God who is a God of pure unconditional LOVE and nothing else.

6TH FEBRUARY 2010

Welcome Sister, sweet Daughter of Light. We say welcome indeed, for we see your heart and the joy in your return to ways of old. Say indeed, it is the time for the return to the former things that provide thee with strength and energy for life. It is from this that the most basic life-source springs, my child, for deep within the soul of man lives and lurks the heart of God. Our place and part in the creative source comes from the womb of God, and many as are they who do not know of the deep and abiding love of God for his children. Indeed, it is shown that many do not even know of the peace or love of the Father for his children. Know, Sweet Child that this love permeates all things, is the source of all things, and is the only way in which man truly enters in, and/or even reaches his true divinity. Angels who live on high and here below know of this divinity that dwells in the soul of man, but many, in fact, most mortal beings, will ne'er be able to grasp the true vastness of the eternal spirit and source of man. Why do we need to know these essential truths, is the question? The answer is simple, child: so that we can enter into the Grace of God. His goodness is sure, but the knowing of his power and source is the thing that will lead man into the place of sanctity and joy. For only with this powerful knowledge can man ever hope to know and fully understand the vastness of God, and enter into the eternal place we call The City of God. Though not a place but an entry point, in the vastness of the beingness[4], it is difficult to comprehend its true nature, since none may fully know all that exists in the realm of the nature of God. Its expanse, nature, and depth is far beyond the description of man's nature to comprehend, but know that its source is from the love fountain of God's Grace and is ever to be sought as souls travel on the road. Your task Sister Sweet will be to bring these messages of love and light to the forefront for the other seekers on the road.

Your challenge will be to present it to the light in the ways in which it can be fully comprehended by man. A task, indeed, but not one so far and away impossible so as not to conceive or to make far and possible into fruition for others to comprehend. It is well to know you will be able to accomplish this task and bring the word to fellow travelers on the road.

Your life will change, as this strength and the peace, and love, and possibilities of life, are presented to thee as truths to be lived and to be known to all those who seek the truth and the path of life that is available to all. Our thoughts are ever present and your eyes are ever open to the many wonders of the world of man.

This incarnation[5] has served thee well, and your life and its path, and twists and turns, are the very source of the nature and sanctity of God's grace and love for mankind. The dwellers of light who sojourn in the realm between God and man are many in number, and exist to share the joys of the kingdom with those still here on Earth.

---

[4]   The state or fact of existing

[5]   The act of assuming flesh or taking on a human body and the nature of man.

Using them as messengers, the Light Beings will and can share the energy, peace, and soul of God with his children here on Earth. No angel exists but to glorify God, and to work to bring his peace and love to the children of men. Our task, Sweet One, is to help you to grow and fully know the depth of the love that exists in the universal love of God. It is our pleasure to show you the Kingdom of God through glimpses into the innermost places of God's soul-understanding in its simplest form, since its true complexity cannot be brought into the being or nature of man in order to show its vastness or its nature. In time, man will begin to know something of the depth and strength of his possibilities. But as yet, these words and teachings are coming in small, yet succinct ways, so that he can begin to grasp as small as an atom of the vastness and magnificence of God.

2ND AUGUST 2010

For from afar comes one with great wisdom whose words will carry the seekers ever higher into the bliss of God. For sure, child, we say nothing but the love and wisdom of God can secure the sons of men, for truly the time is upon us for man to change his violent ways, and look to the ways of peace. Nothing but the love of God can cause man to change. No band of Angels above can accomplish these things, for the Lord of Hosts himself must bring this about. If man is to move to the higher realms of light and knowledge, he must know what his mission is charged to accomplish. He must take up his cross and do the will of God; for without this, he can never hope to move forward to that place of great inner peace and love. Without hope, love, and peace, he cannot move forward to the knowledge of the light and love of God. For many are called and many are chosen, but all do not take up the mantle and perform the task which they have promised to take, and will not perform the duties inherent to the task.

The Sons and Daughters of the Earth must take up the mantle, and know that their task is to be the Sons and Daughters of God, and to bring the word of God to all who would hear it. Know, Sweet Princess that your task is clearly set out. For, you are destined to bring these words to those who would hear it.

Then, like the words that fell on fertile soil in the story of the Sower of Seeds, your message will spread and grow and will bring abundant blessings to all those who hear the word and learn the truth of the love of God.

For surely as a man soweth so is he, and as a man believes and thinketh, even so is he. Thus, for those who hear the words and can receive them in love, in the way they were given, they too, will know of the abundant blessings and love of God that await His children. Fear not, Little One, but know you are being prepared for the journey of your life. Know you will be given the tools of the trade; for in reality, you already possess all that you need in order to share the gifts of love with all. Nevertheless, you will know that you possess all that is necessary for this journey of truth on which you have embarked. Know your support will be there, and know that all that is necessary for your success will find its way to you. For you are the messenger of the 'Love Series of God's Messages to the Earth.' But know however daunting this task may seem at first, you have nothing to fear; for you have been given this task because it was part of your destiny and plan for many years and many lifetimes; but now and only now are you in the state of readiness to take the mantle and move forward to deliver and to make good on the plan. Nothing but the love of God could do what is necessary and you, Sweet Child, will do what must be done, for even as we know your heart and your fears and innermost dreams; we know that this task is what is at the core of your beingness. You will be the conduit for much of what is to come and you will herald the beginning of this new awareness. More knowledge will be shared and you will complete the task when the time is right. Fear not, for all works in divine order. Many will come to know the truth through the words of love which are being given to you, so do not fear that you are not the conduit, for in truth, Little One, you are. Your life and your message going forward, will be in the service of God and all will be well. For, you will forget the former things, and move to the new things which will carry you forward.

Angels constantly bring you those who are ready to hear "the word" and you will continue to put them on the road and point them to the "Truth Teachings" of those alive today. We applaud your efforts and your wishes to learn those things to bring control to your life and routine... for focus is needed if you are to advance (as your spirit yearns for.) Nothing but the love of God can help to take you higher to those places where all things can be revealed. Nothing but God's love can give you the strength, courage, and love to move forward when the time is right. Know, Sweet One, that your needs will be met in all areas and you will be at peace, so that you can focus on that which must be done to deliver the words which will be given to you. Your life will change, and you will know much peace and joy as the road widens, and the travelers come to know your thoughts and words, Dear One.

We look to you, Sweet Child, to do what must be done and know that it will be done. Be you calm, and listen to the inner voice of God, and know that you will be led to the ways that must take you forward; for much study will ensue, but it will be learning that will excite and enthrall you as you discover the wonders of God's love.

Intuition and inspiration are yours, Sweet One, and you will see and know much, which will serve you as you move forward. Know that your messages will continue to come in words as they have done, and you will complete your task.We hail you, Little One, as you begin to share words of your gifts to open hearts. Know that you can and will be well. Be patient, Little One, and know that the wheels are in motion. Listen to your inner voice and know it is the love and guidance of God and your Angels that send you these words. Peace and Blessings. Love and Light! Adieu, Little One!

The Brotherhood

28ᵀᴴ September 2010

The Petition from Spirit

For today, begins the chapter and the verse of much that is to come. For, surely you know, Little One that much is being said of thee and the work which is here petitioned for thee. Do not you fear, Little One, but understand and know that the task must be done by thee. For even as we share the very words of love with thee, it is found that those who would take the charge from thee are at hand. Know, Sweet Child that this task is thine and will be accomplished by thee.

Look you to none, save thyself, to deliver these words to the Children of Men, for it is thy task and thine alone, Little One. Never since the dawn of time has such a message been given to one such as thee. But know that the zeal and zest that you would venture forth to use to deliver these words of love, even so, should and must they be taken forward, and given to the Children of Men.

Know, Little One, that the task must be taken by thee, and that delivered it must be by thee, Sweet Child. For what is thine is thine, commissioned by the Holy Spirit, and accepted by thee. This task is thine and only thine to accomplish. Know, Little One that the days are fast upon us when the job must be begun so that the words can be moved forward into final form. Know, Little One, that it was with love and pride that we asked thee to accomplish this task so many moons ago. Listen to the voice of reason and do what must be done. Know this task is thine, and thine, alone!

Listen and learn, for much new opportunities will come your way to learn those things that will help thee to deliver the message to the people who search in the darkness, for the great light to lighten the load and to take them on their way.

Do no harm to anyone, but follow the ways of love, and all will be well, Little One, for the love and wonder of God's love and grace will follow you far and will serve to lead thee home. For those who dwell in the shadow of the valley of fear and forgetfulness will need this great light and this reminder to take them home, but will not be able to find it but for thee.

Your courage and your love and your zeal to do this work will serve you well. For much is the joy that will be given to all the souls who will be brought to God by the words that will be delivered. Look you up and know that you are the Daughter of Light and your charge is necessary to help you move forward. Fear you not what will happen as you move forward, but know that we will always be beside thee to guide and to comfort thee in times of need. For, we are your mother and your father, and all the sisters and brothers of time, who are here to bring thee peace, and to show you the path back to the Father God.

Listen and do what must be done. Follow the path laid before you, and you will be led to the right and proper places to accomplish your task.

24ᵀᴴ FEBRUARY 2011

Indeed we see much happiness is here, for we are happy to see you encased in the Kryon[6] works and look to see our true selves. Know ye that we are One and indeed you have seen the truth of this. Happy are we, child, for now you understand the LOVE that is held here for thee. Happy, happy, are we to know of your thoughts and the connections you make to understand the works of Kryon, and the advances that are made to commune with thee. O such a time of great joy is upon us, Little One, for your learning is advancing at a great rate as you begin to see the vast connection to us all. For we are indeed One, and so we say happy is this moment in time, for you are able to begin to see through the veil and to understand what is here for thee.

---

[6]   Lee Carroll-channel for Kryon

Happy, happy is the moment. Happy, happy is the great love and joy that is felt for thee as you learn and move forward in the true knowledge and love of God; for such is the progress that is coming into being. Know, Little One, that you are among the Sons and Daughters of Light who have open channels to receive the Source information directly without the channeling. Happy are we to know that you continue to learn and to move forward in knowledge. Happy are we as you continue on in lesson, and proud, indeed, that this incarnation has served thee so well. Hail, Warrior Princess, Daughter of Light! We honor thee and give you all the glory as you continue to open and grow in knowledge and light. Happy, happy is the Universe who sings for joy at your rebirth and the knowledge that now begins to flow even more effortlessly to thee.

Behold the coming of the 'New Age,' Little One, when much will be made known to thee and much will be the accomplishments made on behalf of Kryon and, indeed, the Holy Realm of Angels and all those who daily support thee here and in distant places.

Laugh with joy, Little One, for she that was lost is found, and has seen the great light. Open your eyes and see all that is before thee. Understand all that is given to thee, and is here available for thee.

Approach the city of joy with much song and celebration, and come to know the power and magnificence of the Most High God. Know that, indeed, all is well, and much will be the changes coming about for thee. For the times they are a-changing!

We your Guides, applaud thee, Little One, and celebrate the accomplishments of the journey thus far! Know, indeed, there is much work still to be accomplished, but indeed the road gets easier as the information now comes to show you some of your true magnificence. Know ye the pride and love that is felt here for thee for discovering and opening the door to more that exists for thee here.

Know, indeed, that the Universe celebrates thee, and we here hold thee with much love. Be you ever happy with the new path and the new growth that begins this day.

For this, is but the beginning of much that is to be. We hail and honor thee, Little One, for thy wisdom and growth in getting to this place on your road of destiny.

This incarnation has indeed served thee well, and happy are we indeed to be here with and for thee as Guides and Teachers in this time. Hail, Warrior Princess, Daughter of Light; we see your heart and the happiness at this time in opening this new door. Be you happy, indeed, for this is the time, this is the moment for you to begin anew, and for you to begin to turn in different paths. The time is now and opportunities will begin to present themselves, for you are now ready for that which is to be made manifest. Be strong, Little One, and know that all is indeed well with thee.

Be vigilant and know that with open channels, much will be the information coming your way. Look at this and know that we are love, we are indeed love and light and are here to guide and support thee.

Share these words with those you love and begin to share the words of Kryon so they will know that all is connected and all is one. Be you full of joy, Little One, for we know your heart and we know your joys.

Be at peace and know the wonders will begin to appear. You are part of a vast whole and you have found your way home.

Hail, Princess Sweet! We, in celebration and joy, hold thee high, and now begin the new teaching… for that which was can be no more. For you will move with speed and light into realms of joy and peace. Be you full of joy and know that the work will continue, for you will need to continue to transcribe the text of your book which will bring such peace and joy to those who wait in darkness.

For, you will be the light that will shine through dark places, and bring hope to those who live without hope. Be at peace and know the task begins and the 'Days of Wine and Roses' are upon us, Little One. Know the search has just begun and the times are upon us as the changes and the upheaval continues. Kingdoms will continue to fall and the world will become a new place, for such is the shift in consciousness that has begun and will continue from this day. Know your heart and listen to voices you hear in your heart. Do what you know is right and continue to grow in knowledge and love.

All will be well for thee, Little One; know that you are on the path of wisdom and will learn much now that you have always known. Knowing that which is already so, now that the veil is lifting and you begin to see the light of the knowledge and love of God. For such is the awe-inspiring love of the source and wonder of the Most High God. Learn and see all that becomes clear to thee. See the true nature and majesty of God, Little One. Know that the peace, and light, and love of God will continue to flow into your heart. Let your heart be full of joy this day, for we indeed celebrate with thee, the continued opening of your awareness and oneness with your source, Mother Father God.

Be you changed and know you are loved of God, and a daughter of the Sons and Daughters of Zion. Be at peace and know that all is well with thee. Happiness is thine. This day begins the future of what will be for thee. Open your heart and know it waits for thee as written and as promised.

Oh such a day as this! Oh such a time as this! Blessed be, Sweet One! For the legions are celebrating your success and are ecstatic with your progress. Peace and Blessings, Little One.

Adieu in the Love of God the Father.

4ᵀᴴ MAY 2011

Know that the day of the Lord is here, and the words of the love of God must be shared with the Children of Men. Know, indeed, that the children are like men in a dry land thirsting for water. The love of God is the stream of life and the source of love, wisdom, and healing. Know, indeed, that many will drink and all will be fed. For, truly this is the time and so the thirst grows and is magnified, for they have waited for the coming of the water of life for eons, Sweet One. Know that the mission is needed and will serve a mighty purpose and help to save the City of God[7] for all mankind. Know that no special group will benefit, but all mankind; indeed,

---

[7]   Awareness of the bountiful love of God

for such is the nature of the great task at hand. Be you full of excitement, Little One, and know that your task will come into being as was written and expected. For proud we are, indeed, of thee for all thy accomplishments and happy, indeed, to be here for and with thee. Behold I stand at the door and knock! Who will hear my voice and open and say, "Come unto me?"

Yea, the Father God is knocking for mankind to open the doors to their hearts, so that he may deliver the good news of his love for all mankind. Know that the season of change is upon us and the task must be accomplished. Be ye strong, Oh sons and daughters of Zion, and swing wide the gates of your hearts. Open them to see what must be made available (the gates of heaven itself) for surely heaven is within the hearts of men. Let not fear approach this magnificent City of God, but instead let that love and prosperity rain down upon the Children of Men, and rain love, peace, and prosperity upon them. Behold, the days are here for a new song to be born in the hearts of men. For so it must be and so it will be, for the gates are open to let the Lord of Love into the hearts of men. Be you ready, O sons and daughters. Be you at ease and ready, for all that will transpire. For great will be the tumult[8] of those who recognize the wonderful coming of the days of the great awakening, which has already begun upon the Earth. Know, indeed, Little One, that much will be the rejoicing when all comes into being. For, we are indeed, among the hosts of those who are here to proclaim the great and wonderful awakening of mankind.

---

[8]   bustle: move briskly in a busy or hurried way

"For behold I will put a new song and a new word into the lips of my people," says the Lord. Be you ready for that which will come into being, know that all will be well as you move forward, brave Warrior Princess. Know that all will, indeed, be well. For all will begin to be revealed to thee, and you will come to see the magnificent and wonderful task you have undertaken, Little One. Happy, indeed, are we to be here with thee to travel part of your great journey with thee. Happy are we to see those that will travel with thee and help thee on this most magnificent of quests.

Be you full of joy and know that we are much happy for thee and the accomplishments thus far. Be you full of grace and continue to walk the great and wonderful path to bring the words of God's love to the Children of Men. Many will say why thee and ask how this was the task of such a one? Know, indeed, Sweet Princess, that as was declared by Abraham, (Ester Hicks at Agape, Revelations Conference in Los Angeles April 2011) you sent "Rockets of Desire" into the Universe, asking how to serve and asking for this very opportunity. Here now, it is come to pass, and you are being given the words and the way to deliver it to the Children of Men.

Know and remember your true magnificence, Little One, and know you will accomplish this great and wonderful task for humanity.

We are much enthralled for thee and the mission on which you embark. Know we are here with thee to hold thee up, push thee onward when your strength fails, and provide thee with faith and courage to continue along the way. Be of good faith and continue on, Sweet One, for your doors are open and it is time to move forward in courage and love, to deliver the great and most wonderful message of the love of God for mankind. Be you ever constant as you continue on this road. Know you are loved, and we hold thee ever in the love and grace of God to keep thee safe, so that all will be well for thee. May you ever know only peace as we travel along this path with thee. We are here for and with thee in the love and peace of the Father, to keep thee ever constant as the journey continues for thee. Peace and Blessings, Little One. Know that all is well for thee and thine and the great God of the Universe continues to support, love, and uphold thee. Be ever in the praise of God as you sing your songs of joy. Let the world see and know the peace of God that lives in your heart.

Adieu, Sister Sweet, we will here again with thee with more words of wisdom for the text.

Adieu in the peace and love of God.

Adieu

Author's Note

On 15th May 2011 when I returned from Rev. Michael Beckwith's Revelations Conference in Los Angeles, I had what I describe as a dream but it was actually much more than that. But, call it what you may, during this encounter I knew that there had been an arrival of new Guides/Angels because I remember being with someone who pointed into the starry heavens to show me where they came from. It was as always, a wonderful experience filled with love and happiness and then the following information was given on the morning of May 16th 2011.

16TH MAY 2011

Welcome, indeed; we say welcome, Brothers and Sisters, for indeed; we are the Travelers of Light who travel here to Earth to sojourn with thee, and to bring thee that much needed peace and joy of God. We say much needed, for these are the vibrations that have traveled across the miles to say that man is, indeed, in that place of readiness to hear and to know of the vastness of the love and beingness of God. Indeed, we see and know of all the travails[9] and the work that has here before been gathered. Indeed, we see and know of all those who have come before, trying to bring this very news to the sons of men, but to no avail; for, indeed, there was much distrust and much pain in the hearts of men; so no great understanding could come into being of the great expanse, and knowledge that is the great and most glorious and wonderful love of God.

We say, indeed, happy are we to be here with thee, Sister of Light, for being with thee will allow us to share the Word, and to bring that which has been longed for by so many, for so very long. We know, indeed, that now is the right and perfect time, for many changes are happening upon the Earth, which will allow these

---

[9]   Work especially of a painful or laborious nature: agony: torment:

great truths to become manifest, and to be acceptable to the sons of men. Know, indeed, if this time were not the true and perfect time for the delivery of this great gift, we would not have been summoned. But summoned, indeed, we have been, and so here we are, Little One. We know, indeed, your heart is ready for this great change, which will come about, and so we say, indeed, the readiness was long in preparation, and now in delivery. For, we are indeed here, and are in great readiness to share our knowledge of love and light with thee, and those upon the Earth. Know, indeed, that such a great spectacle will ne'er be seen as when the great and wonderful road show, -if such we might term this wonderful display of knowledge- begins. For, indeed, the very supports of the Earth will be shaking with the news, and the joy of that which will be delivered. Know, Little One that you have angst[10] much of this great change in mode of communication, and have wondered much at its very nature. Know, however, that you are not able to imagine the delivery mode, for to be of true nature, it has not been seen by those here upon the Earth.

Know, indeed, it will be very simplistic in nature, but in reality and truth, is complex in its format. We sense fear in thee arise in what could be this strange, and maybe yet fascinating, thing that will come to be. Know, indeed, we will unite with thee, and in the union will be able to share the information that is needed directly with those in attendance. We know the great fear this will bring to thee, since knowledge of such things will not be familiar, but know, Little One, that you will become accustomed to the joining, as did sweet Esther Hicks when first she joined with the Source energy Abraham.

---

[10]   A feeling of anxiety, apprehension, or insecurity

Know, indeed, that your union will be somewhat easier and will be much less invasive, if such a term can be used. For, indeed, we know your fears, but yet say; be not dismayed or anxious, but know that you will be well and the physical body will be taken care of, and no harm will come nigh thee.

Our requirements of thee will be well known when the time is upon you, so again, be of good courage and know indeed all will be well. We say, be of good courage, for we know that your soul is one of courageous and youthful vigor. For much has been the great travails of this soul in past travails, and adventures, so indeed we are much happy to be here with thee to help thee to deliver this great message of love and hope to those upon the Earth. We know, indeed, there is much work to be done... so we say, indeed, this is the time and this is the moment for us to begin to share news of ourselves with thee, so that in the beginning of this co-creative existence, we can become that which we are and share this great and wonderful news with thee.

Know, Little One, that you are, indeed, in readiness for that which is to come. We will continue to share the words with thee in this form, for there is still much that needs to be delivered of the text, but know also that we must also begin to share and to become one with thee, so that when the public co-creation and partnership begins, you will, indeed, be ready and the whole joining will be nothing of great worry for thee.

Much will happen for thee in dream-mode at first, and so we will acquaint thee with who we are and will commune with the in this form. Next, we will visit with thee in the light of day; so to speak, so that you may view us and come to be familiar with our features, if such we might call them. Know we will take on form that will allow thee to see and to know us. For, since we are to become co-creators, it is of importance that no fear exists of who and what we are. Much like the work completed by others here on Earth, you will gain that blessed insight like our dear brother, Gary Renard[11] who worked so diligently with Source.

Know, Sweet Sister that you will be able to see and know much, for this is the desire of this time, and it is acceptable to those waiting for this news to know from whence it comes. Know, indeed, this was not always so, therefore much secrecy was needed. Today, your world has changed and the acceptance by many has been brought to this level. Know, Little One that much will be the talk of thee when the time is here. For, indeed, we can say this for it has already happened, and we are simply here to bring it into being for thee.

For the linear time and the zone in which we are existing is of different kinds and nature, so that we exist simultaneously here in this moment, but also in other moments, also at the same time. So for thee, what is the now time has already happened and is long gone. Know, therefore, this is why we are able to be here, and explain this to thee. In simplest form, the future and the past and the NOW moment, are all happening simultaneously all in the same space and time. You will learn more of this, so fret not, for much will be your knowledge of these things, and great will be your teachings. For in being able to understand, you will likewise then be able to teach others all that you have gleaned (learned). Know, Little One, that you are a good student and the learning will not be difficult for

---

[11] Author of *The Disappearance of the Universe*

thee. And we are much happy to be here with thee, for the journey to Earth is a blessed one, filled with much hope for mankind... and we are much happy to be here with thee to share in this greatest of adventures.

Joy, love, and happiness in abundance are ours and we are anxious, if such we may use this word, to co-create with thee. We see and know your great heart and the abundant love you carry for mankind.

Know, indeed, this task will be well executed with the great love you possess, and the knowledge we bring to share with all. In simplest form, it will take on some of the form of Esther and Jerry—Esther Hicks-Abraham—yet in its nature will differ; for such is the demand of the news that will be delivered that it cannot help but be different. We call on thee to meditate, Little One, for indeed this will bring thee relaxation and allow us to come to thee quickly and with ease, so that we may meet and commune at this time. Know that we are aware of your needs as one in a physical body, and will always be mindful, if such we may use this term. We love thee with the deepest love, Little One, and are in awe of thee, for this great journey on which we are about to embark.

Know, indeed, that the sensations you feel are simply those brought about by us (tingling sensations in the hands and fingers.) Be not afraid, but know we are much curious of the physical and its magnificent possibilities. Be at peace, Little One, and know no harm will come nigh thee, for we guard and watch over thee daily. Be at peace and know, indeed, that much is the happiness and excitement we feel at this new adventure on which we embark with thee. For never has such an experience as this presented itself upon the Earth. Peace, love, and the light of God come upon thee,

Little One. We are here! We are light; we are love… ever present, ever with thee, ever ONE. May the blessings and the peace and love of God abound with thee. We will here again to commune in this format, but will also begin to see and union with thee in other formats and in other ways.

1ˢᵗ June 2011

The Nature of Love

Hail to thee, blithe spirit, hail Daughter of Light! It is indeed with much pleasure that we join with thee here. Know, indeed, we are much happy to be learning your ways as we continue to become familiar with thee. We see and know your beautiful heart indeed, Little One. And am enjoying the sojourn here as we become ever more familiar with thee and the things involved with the physical existence here on Earth. Know, Little One, that much, indeed, is the news this day, as we see, indeed, that the controlling of the instrument is, indeed, still in need of work. (Spirit was trying to manipulate my limbs without much success.) Know we will master this with speed however as we gain more practice. We say, indeed, blessed are those who toil here upon the Earth, for indeed, the laborers are many and indeed, we see firsthand the very nature of the distractions which cause man to forget his way and lose sight of those very things which would serve to bring him such peace, happiness, and joy.

Know, Little One, we see, indeed, the hardships that man brings upon himself. And in awe, we wonder why no help is in sight... for truly he knows all the answers, and has the remedies buried inside himself, but cannot find a way to release them. Know, Little One, he must learn how to summon that knowledge, and bring it to the forefront of his existence. For in so doing, he can lessen the pain of his existence, and return to the way of living that he was designed to embrace.

Know, Sweet One, we see such pain that our hearts are broken, for the Children of Men, but fully are coming to realize why we are needed here upon the Earth. Know, Sweet One, we see much need for the words of comfort we bring, and so as we continue to learn the ways of Earth, we are happy, indeed, to be here with thee, to bring the relief which will help man to move forward upon the road.

Know, Little One, that the days of anguish must end upon the Earth, and in so doing, the peace can return to the hearts of men. We are much happy, indeed, to see the very beginning of the plan to meditate, and with much happiness, we know that you will be successful in getting the mind to relax so that the peace you seek will be available to you. We are much happy for this to become a regular occurrence, and are much happy to see and to know that you strive to give the support that is necessary for us to share the knowledge with thee. Know, Little One, that we see that the text will begin to be transcribed... so happy are we, indeed, with this progress. Know, Sweet One, we see and know and continue to learn the challenges and the needs of the physical. Yet, indeed, we see much of the joys of the physical body, so know that it is with great care and happiness that we now continue to deliver the text for thee.

Author's Note

Having been provided with this information by Spirit, it was apparent that I had to make choices whether to accept the charge or graciously decline. I knew, however, that there was no real choice to be made except to continue with the work, because each day as I read the wonderful words of love that were being shared, I knew that I had to deliver them to humanity. The knowledge that was so lovingly shared with me is presented here for you. I know that the road ahead is full of unknown adventures, but I am not afraid of what is to come, because I know that whatever happens I will never be alone, for my Mother Father God will be with me on this wonderful journey supporting and loving me each and every day. My hope for you is that you will come to remember once more the love, peace, and joy which is our loving and benevolent parent. For God is LOVE and so are you.

CHAPTER 1

MAN AND GOD

For indeed always the question has been asked why God would love man at all. For in his lowliest of states when man in total forgetfulness would cause great pain and suffering upon his brother and commit the most heinous of all crimes against his brethren. The question begets itself how can a God ever love those who would bring such pain and suffering to his fellow man?

6ᵀᴴ FEBRUARY 2010

ANGEL OF THE MORNING

Call me Angel of the morning, and see the delight in the eyes of all who come to know the Father, for in his great mercy and wisdom we find the Three Pillars of Grace. The Three Pillars of Grace are there to manage and to help to bring into fruition all that is truly meant to be. These Pillars were established in man's knowledge long ago in ancient times. They support the learning of knowledge that he must pass through in order to accomplish the work that he has been sent to Earth to accomplish. For as we know, man, of himself, is not able to accomplish anything, since only through the simple grace of God is he able to move to higher dimensions of thought or action. At the simplest level, man must know that which he is taught, but it becomes apparent that he is not taught everything he must do, since some of it is innate to his nature. If man is to progress, therefore, it is apparent that the knowledge must come from some other source external to man. For from his own knowledge, he cannot hope to know all that he must do if he is to master the lessons of life and move to another plane, such as that which is existing only in the realm of Spirit.

Our goal, as Children of Men, is to move always upward and onward to total connectivity with God. But the question is, how can this be accomplished while living here on Earth? The answer is that it is a difficult task, but not totally impossible, since we must give of self and give for self if we are to advance to higher levels of skills in the path of seeking knowledge, and gaining understanding of the many levels of understanding that are possible and that exist... if man is to advance in understanding and true knowledge of the nature and sense of God's bounty and grace. The grace of God truly passes all understanding since man cannot comprehend all that exists in God's grace and/or how to attain it; for within man's heart is planted the seed which suggests that this is incomprehensible. The truth, Dear Ones, is that this is not such a difficult task if one realizes that love is the source of all and the means through which all entry can be gained. Truthfully, the gates are guarded by love, and to gain entry, one must know that the possession of love will allow entry to all souls who want to move forward in the light of God.

Know, it is not yet known, that the key is such a simple one, and that is the true reason for sharing these words with you, Dear Brethren. For the message that must be shared with the Children of Men is that "Love is the Answer." This love, and the knowledge of love, can help all to advance to the highest levels, or the lack of it can bring man to sink to the lowest depths. For if no grace or connection to God exists in the heart of man, he is doomed to wander aimlessly in the valley of despair, with no hope of rescue or containment. He must thirst like a man in the desert, even though the water rests in pools beside his very person, for he cannot see it or know of its existence, since these things are outside of his grasp and his understanding. It would be in comparison to looking at one's image in a mirror, but not knowing who is looking back at thee. For the image represents someone or something unknown in nature, so that the person stares aimlessly on as though nothing were there at all... in a state of blindness, yet all the time seeing the true image, but nevertheless being unable to comprehend that likeness which is there reflected back. So, child, the knowledge of God's grace is what allows man to recognize himself when faced with this reflection in the mirror.

Our hope is to provide the insight to allow man to see and comprehend all that is possible to attain through the knowledge of God's love and grace. For there is no other cause for man's journey on the Earth than to know God: Simply, to know, and to grasp the nature of his bounty, and the wonders of his love. It is not a love that is based on reward or favor, but a love that is provided to all with no thought of reward. It is there for those who would try to see and to understand the nature of the reflection visible in the mirror. A man must first ask the question, why am I here? What is my purpose, and what shall I do to gain the promise of life?

The answers to all these questions circle around the promise of love and grace; for they are the only reasons why man must pass through the trials of this earthly life: to learn of the love of God. For in this arena, he can truly see that man, of himself, is of naught[12], but God is truly all there is. All is centered on God. All focus and thoughts are centered on the knowing and sharing of the nature and love of God. For God's grace and his love are the things that cause us to stray or to find the true path. The path to love is found not by searching far

---

[12]   Nothing: of no value or account:

and wide, but by searching deep within the heart of man. It is not God who punishes, but man who punishes by being unable to see those things placed before him. He is not able to see or grasp the things God has placed in his hands, and so he searches aimlessly in the wilderness of despair, searching for that which he already has.

Opening the heart to the possibilities of God can only come when man is ready, for not all can see the hand in front of them. For this is akin to blindness in a thick fog or room full of blinding smoke, when one is unaware of all that exists around, and thinks themselves alone or lost, when in truth, one can be in a room full of people or objects. So, like any blind man in an unknown land or space, he must slowly move around, inching his way as he tries to make sense of his world. The love of God is like the cane that is placed in his hand, which will help him to navigate the darkness and find his way to familiar places and things.

Adieu

9TH FEBRUARY 2010

The windows of the world open and reveal the true nature and abundance of God. The view is exceptionally sweet, for in this nature, truly there rests the umbrella to the soul. Far from all the tenacious arms and struggles of life, we find the flowering and ever present nature and abundance of God. This mantle[13] sits and is encircled by the throne of the Beings of Light who daily fly between different avenues and the varied worlds which are inhabited by man. Here, we say worlds, for such it is, for man indeed occupies different worlds from which he gains many varied experiences, which help the soul to grow and experience and know the true wonder and nature of God.

Fear not, Dear Ones, when we speak of the habitation of different worlds, but know that this is so since man must experience many things in order to learn and appreciate the very nature of God. It is abundantly clear that the nature of God is not easily understood but is known by man in different names and tongue. They call him BABBA Deity, God of Host, Lord God Almighty, among many

---

[13]   The mantle is a particular type of layer within an astronomical body

different and varied nations, for such is the nature of his being in their tongue. We say this, but know God is not known as in form, but is given this name so we can try to begin to understand him from the vastness of his power and love.

No name can truly encompass[14] the magnificence of God because he is beyond explanation and yet also beyond comprehension. He is not able to be explained or to be described in words that can do justice to his being. The Lord of Hosts who dwells within man is the same wonderful Ruler and Counselor that reigns in the heavens below, and above, in the deep regions of the creation.

Man cannot yet grasp how much exists, for it is truly a powerful thought to know or to comprehend how much truly exists outside of man's comprehension or awareness. Man's logic and knowing is so shallow in comparison to the nature of all that exists, that it doesn't bear speaking of here. He is truly a being beyond compare and a man of many virtues. (We say man but yet not man, for of such he is not.) God is magnificence in all that he does, sees, and thinks…for man. He is all encompassing, all knowing, all seeing and all doing. Everywhere present and never absent. How can such presence be comprehended? In truth, it cannot, for man is of such limited knowing or understanding that he cannot yet even know of all the things he doesn't know.

The Angel realm is of the nature of God's beingness[15]. Its purpose is to support the Beings of Light on their mission here on Earth. They spend their time learning the ways of man so they can support him when he fails. The very nature of man means there will always be a

---

[14]   Comprehend

[15]   The state or fact of existing

vast need for Beings of Light to support him here on Earth. We rely on them to send you help in times of need, and to remind you of your greatness on those occasions when valor comes into play. Their role and function is to be there when you fall, be there when you rise, and to support you in all that craves your attention.

Adieu

For in the heavens, man dwelleth alone in the kingdom, while on Earth he dwells with grace and power; for from afar, it is clear that the spirit of the Most High God is never far from the throne or never too distant from the heart of man. It is not to say that man can, of himself, perform any feats of wonder, for to be sure, this is not so; for the nature of man is a powerful one, but he is not aware of his power and might. Man is capable of many things and all things through the love of God, but he is not able to fathom the full depth of his full potential or to understand the magnitude of his power. He feels small and unable to achieve anything at all, when in reality, he can perform many feats that would serve to bewilder him.

Our task is to help man to see and appreciate his true potential, power, and promise. Promise, yes! For he has the potential and promise of God, that he can do anything that is placed before him, because he possesses the power and knowledge of God's children. This power and knowledge is provided to man, but is not fully known to him, since in doing so he would not be able to control— or grasp, in some cases— how to control or master the full potential of his strength. So, in order to protect man from himself, he is never fully aware of the true potential that lies within him. He finds small bursts on occasion and is left to wonder the remainder of the time.

Like a child, looking lovingly at a toy but not fully able to grasp how it works. He tries and tests its force and plentitude, but cannot determine how it is constructed and why it is able to move. The task of understanding seems complex, when in effect; it is of the simplest reality. Man is not able to grasp or attain the full knowledge of himself or the true depth of his potential. He is not able to grasp and retain the knowledge of who he is or why he is able to control the regions around him. He remains in awe of himself and his might; for to know the full effect and power, would lead him to know who he truly is, and he is not able to grasp and accept this knowledge.

Man's trials and tribulations on the Earth stem from the very nature of his creative source, for he is not able to control the urges to destroy that which he has built and created. His constant battles within himself to better self, and to better his peers, has caused the tensions of this world. The competitive spirit, and the urge to outdo his peers, has caused many a war and strife on the Earth. The search for answers, and reasons why things are in existence, has caused him to ever be in turmoil within himself. His nature, and will to survive, also has helped to cause some great tragedies on the Earth, and yet man continues to pursue the path of self-destruction, never seeming to know that he can control all within his dominion. Without averting his gaze, he can calm the seas and bring changes to the very nature of Earth. He spends his time toiling in vain in some areas, doing unnecessary penance, and causing pain and anguish to others for no apparent reason, other than his ignorance of his potential greatness and might. The love and power of man has caused much anguish for the Angels who dwell in the realm between heaven and Earth. For the path to self-destruction seems so close all the time. Man sits on the edge of self-destruction, but can so easily choose to move in other directions and create his true reality and his destiny.

For it is so easy to do all the wondrous things God has placed within the reach and grasp of his knowing and his knowledge, yet he spends his time on harmful things and practices which can serve to destroy his fellow man. Man must learn that destruction means just that, and that he cannot destroy others without destroying himself. To live as the Angels and God would have them, men would be like Angels here on Earth, caring for each other, and living the selfless life of love and fulfillment. Instead, he chooses to live in strife and turmoil most of his days.

The nature of man is constantly showing the weaker side of his nature, but with love and understanding, he can learn to reveal the true likeness of God that dwells within his heart. No ears may hear his coming, but he is still able to enter into the silence of God and glean that information that can lead him upward and onward into the light. We must strive to become our God-like selves, and to reveal this God-like nature in all our dealings with our brethren here on Earth, and not spend our days in turmoil and pain trying to find ways to cause pain and hurt to others.

Loving, sharing, and caring can help man to find his way out of this darkness, into the light of God's eternal love and benevolence, which is there for the taking when man reaches out his hands to take it. No powers on Earth are as strong as the power of love for his friends and his brethren. When he can acknowledge and know that he is part of his neighbor, and that they are not two but one in the love and bosom of God, man can advance on his journey. When he learns that if he destroys his neighbor, he destroys himself, man can change the ways of his heart and create that heaven here on Earth for all who dwell on this planet. Only then, can he truly know the blissful peace that can exist in his heart. His fears will dissipate and he will find love and joy within himself.

Adieu

1ST MARCH 2010

"Yes! God is real in my soul, for he has loved and made me whole. His love for me is like pure gold— real, I feel him deep within my soul."- Morris, K.

The soul of man and the development of the soul of man permeate all things. His development is the true source of all things. Man must learn how to control his urges and to take charge of himself. Without this development, his soul potential can never be realized. Man is the child of God. The true and ever developing child of the Most High God, and his needs are ever-present in the eyes of God. It's never the needs of a child who is able to make clear choices, but the needs of the one child who cannot differentiate between what is good and right, and what is necessary, at the given moment. Man's urges are always predetermined by the most basic of things, such as, the need for fulfillment of this most basic of desires. He is not able to view things with a different eye, but simply to see all things as they surround and focus him. The love of God can help man to direct his needs in a more determined and precise manner. Through the love of God for man, man is able to see and know that his life can be focused on a more spiritual and less mundane existence. His task then becomes to find and focus his eyes on the things of God: The things of God which call for man to open his heart and see and know that his soul, and its development, is abundantly important to the journey on the Earth plane. Man must learn that soul development and understanding comes as one of man's main duties whilst here on Earth. His focus must be on finding the source and reason for being while in the current incarnation. (Why choose this physical body and task to fulfill?)That is the task. For in understanding this task; man can hope to find the reason for his struggle and strife. If man cannot find his reason for being, he is once again lost in the desert without hope of finding his way home (way to God.) This, after all, is the reason for the journey when on the Earth: to develop the knowledge and the manner of the ultimate return to the Father God. For if man is not able to find the true reason for the sojourn here on Earth, he remains in abject bewilderment, seemingly lost with no reason for being.

This, then, is when he finds other ways in which to fill the void within himself, by the use of vices and other suffering, which serve to diminish the soul's purpose and to bury its reason for being even more deeply within the subconscious of man so that the void within him opens…and he is even now pushed further into despair, desperately seeking for that which will give him purpose of being. Some turn to vices, such as the introduction of foreign stimulus, in this great search for meaning. But in vain, for nothing introduced outside of man can truly help him to find that which is hidden so deeply within him. To conquer this and to find the answer to man's questions, he must know that he has to look within himself for the answer, and to know that God's love can help him to find his way. The love of God can truly make him whole. Without the recognition of the place and value of God in his life, man cannot pursue the highest goal or attain the largest prize: the development of his soul. The soul of man, that most precious of all gems, is what will cause man to move to the next level of development. Without this development, he will perish and lose his way upon the Earth. Doomed to wander like the blind man, without a cane to tap his way to God's grace and love.

Our task then, Dear One, is to guide man to that very place that will allow him to gain the treasured prize, and to advance on the journey, so that he does not perish for lack of water in the desert.

The love of God is the water of life for the drowning man. Without it, he must perish. God's love and grace is given freely, and must be freely taken, if man is to progress onward in this journey to the Father, source of all. The kingdom awaits and man's only task when upon the Earth is to get back to the source, and do what must be done along the way to develop his soul, as he seeks to find the true source of his being and the reason why the journey was undertaken in the first place.

Yes, God is so real; but if man fails to discover and to fully know this, he can never hope to move on in his journey and to fully learn all that is destined for him to do. His task, then, remains unfulfilled, and the journey becomes one of loss and pain, for the soul development is not undertaken and man is lost.

Adieu

3RD MARCH 2010

Blessed assurance, Jesus is mine - Crosby, F.

Beloved children, we must learn the ways of God and must daily kneel at the throne of God. Our thoughts and actions must clearly say we are the Sons and Daughters of God. All the men of God must know in their hearts that, as Sons and Daughters of the Most High God, it is incumbent on man to do that which is Holy. To spend the time in prayer and supplication, to give God the glory, and to know that without God, there can be no glory, for man cannot do anything without the blessings of the Father.

The Children of Men are like chaff in the wind without the grace of God the Father. The Sons of Men are like children left alone in the desert. They cannot survive of themselves, but yet with God's love, they can do all things and be all things. The Angels who sojourn here on Earth spend their time moving between the two realms, and there they do that which will bring joy to the Father God. Man cannot, of himself, bring about changes upon the Earth, but can use the strength of God to become like new in the eyes and strength of God. The man that is not of the spirit cannot hope to survive without the love and support that is found in God's arms. Angel or man cannot hope to be at peace without the arms of God sheltering him in all that is necessary for the movement of man to go from one realm to another, and to remain in the kingdom as long as it is necessary to do so. Awake, Oh Children! Daughters and Sons of Zion, see the glory and majesty of God and know that God is Lord of all creation. Put on your armor and prepare to meet the ravages of the day. For without the love and the praise of God, man can do nothing. If man cannot do what is expected, then he must be held in the arms of God and given all that will allow him to move to that place of rest and supplication in all the regions of the world. If man is to move on or to progress, he must do that which is necessary or he will fail to move on in the passage and glory of God's love and direction.

Of all the tasks of man upon the Earth, God must know that he can lead man to new and verdant[16] places, and help him to grow into the child of God that he is. The soul of man cannot progress without this love and flowering of God's blessings within him. He will be powerless to bring changes to those within the kingdom if he cannot do what must be done. The joys of God are never able to be fulfilled without the love and peace of God.

Adieu

---

[16]   Green with vegetation

7ᵀᴴ March 2010

From deep within the past ages of man, there have been those chosen few who were charged to deliver the news and message of God's love for his children. These souls, while on Earth, had labored to deliver the truth of God's love for his children. In their zest and zeal, they took things upon themselves to alter the given words and to make them more palatable[17] for the ears of man. It is now time to deliver the message without any additional words to soften the impact. For the time of change is upon us, and man must do that which will help mankind to change its ways. The ways of man must change or humankind will not survive. The selfishness must end, and the new season of love must be brought into the experience of man, so that he can survive upon the Earth. Man cannot live only by bread, for he needs the spirit and love of God to flow into his heart. In order to truly live, man must know other things in order to advance. If he fails to gain the new knowledge, then he will fade into nothingness, wither, and die.

---

[17]   Acceptable or agreeable to the mind

The love of God is such a powerful tool, that only it can truly bring about the shift in consciousness needed upon the Earth. Only in this way can man hope to save himself and move to higher planes in consciousness. Man must change, or he will perish, and be removed from the Earth. The Lord of Hosts is pleased to give man the insight to change his ways. Not from wickedness, as stated in days of old, but from selfishness, to a season of love for his brethren. We see and know man's true capacity for loving and caring for his brethren, but continue to see the acts of inhumanity, which do not represent the true character and nature of man. For since man is a spark from the source of God, and carries the same love and light within his soul, he is capable of oh, so much more. He cannot settle for the mediocre, when the magnificent is at hand. He cannot settle for the mundane, when the marvelous is his to claim. Man can and must step into the light of his Godhood and claim the prize for giving and receiving love.

Man must begin to see his brethren as his brother, the holder, and bearer of the divine spark of God. He can no longer see him as a stranger who is disconnected from him, but he must now see him as the link to God. Only with the emerging awareness and the knowing of the connection of all life, of all things upon the Earth, can true change come into being. Only through the love of God, can this begin to be the way of being on all levels, at all times; instead of how man lives every day.

When faced with tragedies, we see the love that can pour forth from man. But once the tragedy has subsided and the immediate pain is gone, he swiftly returns to the former things of old, and produces and functions not in that same loving way, but returns to the selfishness of old. How wonderful it will be when man can operate from this place of love and compassion as a way of being, each and every day. When he can share the nourishment of the Earth equally, without thoughts of hoarding, but of giving freely of God's bounty to those in need. Why see thy brother starving, and look away as if blind? Man must function as one who sees into the hearts of his brothers, and helps to supply their needs. There must be ways in which man can give to all in need without thoughts of insufficiency and lack! There is no lack in the mind or experience of God! All man needs to survive has been provided upon the Earth.

Only through greed has there emerged scarcity and deprivation. For if we hoard, we do so at the peril of others. We cannot continue in the ways of old, but must shift our consciousness of being and purpose, and know that we are all one. To keep more than is necessary for survival, is to break the bond of caring with thy brother.

Only in lending a hand, can man ever know true happiness. Only in giving love, and sharing all the blessings of this world, will mankind ever come to know the true love of God. For if man cannot give to his own brothers and sisters, his soul moves to a state of deep and desolate despair. He must know that his brother is like all others, and that in hurting his brother man, he is hurting himself; since all hold within them that divine spark of God. The same divine spark that unites all men as brothers and sisters in God. All one family, all one tribe, all one kinsman. To harm our family, is to bring shame upon the heart of God. If we kill or maim our brother, we are doing it to God. For God is in all men.

Man must begin to see the eternal light of God shining in the face and heart of each human being, rather than seeing him as an unconnected soul. Man must know and accept that God is the source of life, and the Lord of all creation. He is the beginning and the end. He is all there is! As carriers of the divine source and soul beingness of God, man is the child of God, and the heir to the kingdom of God. The kingdom only accessible through love, and the knowing of all the things given to man: that the knowledge of love and loving, is that most powerful gift of all.

Man cannot let the will of the selfish be the ruler of the day. He must claim his rightful place, and do what must be done to return to God. He must become the way to connect to the sacred source of God. He has the tool and the knowledge already buried deep within his soul. When the soul is created, this is part of the first building block that is within the atom of the construction. That the capacity to love and honor God is there, and is ever present, is a tribute to this fact.

Why has man searched throughout lifetimes for God? Why has man sought inner enlightenment, but because the search for the love of God is programmed into his very being? It is no accident that all men, aware or unaware, search for one thing their whole life. He searches for that which will make him whole; that which will fill the empty spaces of his knowing with meaning. He is searching for God. He is searching to find God, not remembering that the God source is here in his heart already.

The awakening time is upon us, O Children of Men! The eyes of man must be opened and remain open so that he can see and know the truth of his being. He must understand and know that the time for change is upon the Earth, and man must learn how to accept and come into his true nature and beingness. He cannot remain as though ignorant of all his gifts. He must open his eyes and his heart and show the love of God that is within all men. Vanity, hate, envy, and scorn must be removed from the heart and mind of God. Without this, man can never prosper and advance into the kingdom of God's love. For fear, hate, envy, and pain is not the source of God. LOVE is all there is, and so the demonstration of this love will bring about unimagined love, peace, and joy into the soul of man. He can then see and know that we all are one; that all men are truly brothers and brethren of the same one and only magnificent God. All life springs and emanates[18] from God, and man cannot advance if he cannot yet attain this most simple, yet powerful, of all truths.

We must remember: we are Daughters and Sons of the Most High God. As such, we must demonstrate our beingness and show the love we have for each other. Let there be no thought of selfishness, but replace this with SELFLESSNESS. Let us replace pain with love, and wanting with giving. Man must be able to move on to higher levels of awareness and knowing, for only in this can he become who he truly already is; the Daughters and Sons of the Most High God.

If man cannot accomplish this task, he is doomed to wander the desert, looking for that which he already has been given so freely: the love of God. He must search within himself to find the true love of God, and to see and know that, only through love, can he find the forgiveness and redemption he has been seeking for millennia. His search will never end if man does not open his hands and heart

---

[18]   To come out from

to this simple truth, that LOVE is the way, the path, the destiny, the journey, and the prize at the end of the journey. Open your eyes, Dear Ones, and see and know God's love. Take the time to see the true love and power source that lives within your soul. Know that you have what you need for the fulfillment of your heart's desire. You were given it at the creation of your soul. Now is the time to remember that gift is already yours and to show and share it with your brethren. Help them to bring their soul light to the fore. Let man know that the words of Jesus spoke only of love and forgiveness. This is the message of Buddha, and all the great ones put upon the Earth, to enlighten man and to remind him of his divinity. They all spoke of the things of love. None spoke of war or violence. They all spoke of peace, and forgiveness, and LOVE, as the way to enlightenment. They all lived lives of love and peace with their connectivity to the one source: love.

They were truly enlightened, and now it is time for all men to remember that they, too, have the same magnificent God spark at the center of their being. If only they will recognize that, to awaken the sleeping giant within man, all he must do is return to love. Return to the love-source already present within him, and open his eyes to see that when he looks into the mirror of life, he sees his brother reflected back at him. For they and he are one. One heart, one love, one being (that being of God.) If he cannot recognize his reflection as himself, he remains blinded to the love of God within him, and he sees only his own selfishness, greed, envy, and pain looking back at him in the mirror.

Adieu

12TH MARCH 2010

For the soul of man is like unto a child in the womb still coming into beingness. He must remain in this state until it is time to move onwards, and out into the light; for without God, there can be no light in the mind of man. God is the only light that exists for man. He is all there is, and as such, he is the maker of all things. Man must know that the presence of God in his life will shut out the darkness, and bring him into new and magnificent light, for such is the power of God's love. Such is the feeling and loving nature of God. He is able to bring light into the darkness of man's soul, and to give light to the lowest regions and depths of man's soul. Even in the deepest caverns will it introduce new and magnificent light into man's being. Without God, there is only darkness, sadness, and pain. For man cannot see, and so remains in darkness, as a blind man unable to see the true magnificence that is around him.

If man is to progress, he must come to know God, since without him, he cannot move forward. The layers of the kingdom of God's soul are truly magnificent, for within each layer live the Diadems and

Angels who flutter and fly within and without (inside and outside) the realms of God's soul. Their charge is to keep the heavenly light and brilliance of God's love ever-present in the heart of man. They work tirelessly to accomplish this task and bring souls into their God-consciousness. Their charge is to show man the way back into the light and love of God's grace. They are the source of the beginning of the return to man's perfection. They work to help man to know his wonderful nature, and to find God with relative ease. Without them, they (man) would not (the souls) ever be able to progress and move forward into the true light-beingness of God.

The job of these Diadems has been truly kept— in some degree— a secret, for most know not of their existence, but to be sure, it is their charge since the beginning of time to help man in his quest for enlightenment. Without them, man's time upon the Earth would be much less fruitful and he would perish for sure. Man, of self, would perish, if left to his own devices, so the Angel Band are there to give support and love in the form of welcomed reminders when needed, that God is the true source of all, so that man can and will move forward in his earthly quest for God. Without these Angels, man would search for eons for God, only to give up in desolation and return without an answer or the knowing. The Diadem are the throng who are there when man needs help, taking on earthly form when man needs assistance, so that he will know he is not alone in the darkness of his isolation and pain. They are the ones who emerge at the last moment and stretch out that hand, (if you will) that can pull him out of the quicksand of despair into the light of God's love. Man cannot forget the help that God sends his way when he needs those gentle reminders, that God is there as a source of love and rescue.

If man cannot know God through the Angel Band, then he is destined to remain in pain and suffering in the fog of despair, until he can be rescued. The Angel Band's function is to give evidence of God's love for man. They are the teachers, healers, and helpers who emerge in the nick of time. Their tasks are too numerous to mention, but suffice it to say that their function is critical to the advancement of man. The nature of Angels and man is such that it cannot easily be explained, but suffice it to say that the function of one is to bring life and love to the other.

Without the presence of Angels upon the Earth in the lives of men, there would be even more darkness in the soul of man. Man's place and knowledge of God is provided for by the Angels who show him how to accomplish his task. You might say, we,—The Brotherhood of Light—are in essence part of this Angel and Diadem Band, for our charge is also to help bring light into the soul of man. Thus, we are ever available to man, and are ever aware of his needs. We are in tune to the beat of his heart, from birth to the moment when the last air is expelled by man and the soul exits the body. Man is the business of the day for every Angel.

If that is so, then why is there tragedy and despair in the life of man? Simple! Because man does not take heed and follow the guidance he is daily given. The still, small voice that is heard is the voice of God and of Angels. If man would only learn to heed that voice, he would be able to see all the true wonders of the ancient world, and get a glimpse into the soul of God. For it is full of light, energy, and love, and can allow the light to shine into all men when he feels that there is the need for it. Man must not wait for God to come in search of him, but must go out to find out how he can find God by himself.

Knowing all the time that he is not alone, man can eventually proceed forward to the place of love and fulfillment. Sharing the love of God is the task of the Diadem Band, who moves between man and God (heaven and earth). Man can soon learn that it is his portion to find his way back to God, and as such, he will get all the help that is necessary to bring this about. Man is the child of God, and as a parent, he cannot allow him to remain lost in despair, but instead, he brings him into the light of love and acceptance. The nature of man is what slows the process and keeps him in abject darkness for long periods of time, and even in darkness forever.

Awake! All you who sleep unaware of the bountiful gifts of God that are waiting for you if you will accept God's grace. Awake, O you Daughters and Sons of Zion, and know that God is here now and always to help, guide, and support you, as you try to move forward. Awake and know all that is thine in the kingdom of God's love. For without God, man withers and dies like the flower without rain, and like a man bereft[19] of that most precious thing he has imagined. Man is not able to move forward without the knowledge and love of God in his life. Open your hearts, O Children of Men, and claim the prize of redemption through the love and fervor of God. Take what is thine so that you will be able to move into the beingness of God with ease and understanding of his love.

Amen

---

[19] Deprived : Loss: refuge lacking something needed or desirable, wanted, or expected

16ᵗᴴ March 2010

For the power and the glory are yours, Almighty Father, healer of all, One God, Immortal. So it is said, for God is ruler of all and the Father of all, yet we know that the fatherhood is of the spirit, so that he is the ruler, as of a household. He controls our lives and is the very source of life to his children, and without him they die. Even so, Dear Ones, is the nature of the true relationship that exists between God and man, for they are interdependent souls. Each needing the other in order to truly live, and then grow into the fullness of being. For man cannot exist without God, and likewise, God has the nature of man as his being, and so the two are one; and as such, must exist together or not at all.

The nature of man, since the dawn of time, has been one in which man needs God: For he is the source of life to them. Man cannot be without God because the two are so intertwined that the one would surely perish for loss of the other. (Even though it is wise to know that God would not perish, but that his nature would not be served without the love and adoration of man, who, being placed upon the Earth, was part of the agreement made eons ago. That the two would be able to coexist as one original being; one never being able to survive alone, but always needing the other to be able to make sense of his world, or to be at peace upon the Earth.)The days have long since passed when man felt he could survive without God. For now, he clearly knows that he must be with God in order to know true peace, love, and light.

Man is not a solitary animal; he cannot exist in isolation, but must be in the essence and company of others. His most precious need of all, however, is the need to be with the Father God. Mother Father God is the source and power that man must be eternally linked with, if he is to survive and grow. Of self, man is naught, for without God, he is only half himself. He is constantly in search of that which will make him whole and complete. Without God, he is half of who he is meant to be, for the nature of God and of man are linked and intertwined in such a way that man cannot exist without God. The Brotherhood of Light is the link at times between God and man. For they— the Celestial Band— help to unite the two, and to keep them together by helping man to stay connected with God, and to come to know his true divinity. Without them, man loses some of himself, and certainly cannot find his way back to God, their source.

God is the true light and way of all things and is the source of help and security to man. They provide that level of help and guidance, which is needed, if man is to stay focused upon his task. (The return to God after the great period of separateness, which is caused sometimes, by man moving into reincarnation.) With incarnation, man can lose his way and forget his true identity, so his need for

God guides him and he is sometimes able to find his way back to the Eternal Father. When man cannot remember his identity and is lost, then the Brotherhood can help him to return by showing him the way and reminding him of his true self. Not any easy task, my child, but one so invaluable to man, since without it, he would remain in a place of desolation. Without any glimpses of his true self, and no memory of what he is, he would wander aimlessly and lose himself. The nature of man calls for the support and guidance of something or someone outside himself, even though all the true guidance needed is already within him.

It is just unfortunate that man cannot see or fully appreciate and know his total power, or he would be unable to fully comprehend his power and place within the bosom of God. He is not able to see and know the love of God, or to be that which is his to be, without God at his side; for so is he made, that he cannot fully know the true nature of the power that exists within him. Man and God are one in spirit and nature, for the one is part of the other; but man cannot know his true magnificence or he would likely destroy himself. He has great potential, but cannot be left to realize his own Godhead or he would be lost to himself and his own nature, and destroy himself eventually. Thus, God must give him help and support to keep him ever on task, and to gently guide him as he starts to move closer with God, so that they again return to oneness.

All that man can do is to follow the light within his soul if he is to become a mature soul-child of God. He will be like a child forever, if he is left by himself (spiritually). The love of God stirs deep within his soul and he begins to mature to the point where he can exist by himself, yet not still without God. For without God, he is always in search of the divine spark and the very source of meaning in his life. Man and God become one and that is the culmination of the bond that exists between them. They are always one; they will always be one, even though in the nature of man, he doesn't remember the bond or the oneness that existed when creation was put into the mind of God. (That man's purpose on Earth would be an integral part of the plan and the most important part of the plan for the emergence of soul and the development of that soul, so that man could fulfill his purpose on Earth.) Man can see and know much, yet see and know nothing; so we know that the power and source of all his greatness comes only from God, for without God he is nothing. He cannot exist, for how can life exist without light and energy and love? All these things are most vital functions in the life process of man, even though he is bereft of memory and has to be reminded of his true divinity by those who support him upon his earthly experience, so that he can develop into the essence, and wonder, and beauty, of his true self.

Man must know God if he is to grow. Without God, his soul growth cannot proceed and he withers and dies spiritually. The two are one and must be together if man is to thrive and spiritually flourish in his incarnation on the Earth. The memory of God must become a real and constant source in his life or he is not able to function at the optimum soul level alone. Guidance must be provided so he can find his way and remember the true path and his reason for being. Without God, he is alone, lost, and desolate. With God, he is exalted, whole, and fulfilled. Why, then, cannot he survive alone? We know why! It is because God and man are particles of each other and must be together to be complete and fulfilled. One needs the other to know true peace, light, and love. Man needs God to be at peace, and to learn love, and to be who he is meant to be upon the Earth.

Adieu

17ᵗʰ March 2010

That man should exist outside of God is a trial; and we see that he is able to exist without knowledge of God in his life. This existence, although banal,[20] is nonetheless possible and so man is able to exist with no knowledge of God. Man's journey upon the Earth helps him to forget, and so he lives with no knowledge of God in his life. A life lived without God is one lived without love or understanding. Man cannot be who he truly is without God in his life, so the existence is one of sadness and pain. There is emptiness and he cannot advance for there is no joy. Without knowledge of God in the life of man, there is a large hole and man remains in this place of despair, unable to find solace[21] or to understand his pain and emptiness. He must remain here in this place with no hope, for his only way out, which is made possible through the love of God, is not available to him. Man must remain here and find that he is alone and in need of consolation. But there is no consolation to be had, since what he really yearns

---

20   Commonplace: dull: boring

21   To relieve: to console: to comfort

for, deep within himself, is the love of God. Man must be lost and in his despair he sinks, into further pain with no hope of rescue.

Man of sorrow is born on Earth, sometimes with no hope of redemption; but yet, with the love of God, all things are possible for him. If he follows his heart, and lives with the love and promise of God, he is truly able to survive and to advance in his development. With God in his life, hope is abundant and man can move forward on the path. Man can always learn how to change and better himself when he knows of the love of God. Without this knowledge, he is like an orphan left alone with no one to care for him. He has no one to teach him the most basic tenets of life and he drifts aimlessly on, until death takes him. Without protection, love, or the knowledge of his true direction and aim in life, man is truly lost and will die… die that spiritual death, that death of abandonment and despair. He is lost without direction, cause, and focus, and so he is alone and so withers and dies.

To claim his knowledge of God is to claim life itself. For with this, man is able to advance and grow in stature and spirituality, so that he can see and know the true love of God and claim his rightful place as a child of God. Ignorance of God brings separateness and anxiety for man, for he cannot fully know all that exists in the kingdom of God for him. He is like one who is blind and deaf, for no light can enter into his world…and so he is lost and alone, without hope of rescue. Man must know God in order to advance in his development. This knowledge of God allows him insight into the beingness of God, and provides the ability for man to see small glimpses of his true potential. It is here that challenges can ensue, for with small peeks into the world of possibilities, man is able to begin to see some of what exists in the mind of God. Knowledge of the love of God is like a light shining in the darkness of the soul of man. It begins to illuminate small sections and moves around until all parts have experienced some light. Like a torch moving gently in the darkness, all else is darkness and despair...except for the path of the light, and so soon all has had an experience of light and a deep and abiding memory of other things that bring them joy and happiness. Once introduced to light, in however small doses, the search begins in earnest to find more light in which to bask. This light is, of course, the love of God. Knowledge of which can allow man to open his spiritual eyes and his heart, so that he can know God, and through this knowledge, also come to know himself.

Man without knowledge of God is like one lost in the depths of a coal mine, deep in the bowels of the earth. All there is is desolation, pain and loneliness. With the love of God, however, there is the emergence of light, and the knowledge of joy, peace, and contentment. Man without God is nothing therefore, but with God, he is all he can be: the essence of love, peace, and fulfillment. When man knows of the love and life that is truly present for him with the love and acceptance of God, he is able to truly move mountains— mountains of ignorance, fear, pain, and loneliness. He can move out of the darkness and into the light in a very short period of time, and become a new and wonderful spirit-filled child of God. With the knowledge comes the responsibility to increase the size of the gift, and the nature of the love and possibilities open to man. Man must use the gifts, given like the Ten Talents,[22] to

---

[22]   Matthew 25:14-30

increase his gift in order for him to grow in the love of God. He finds the urge to get more and more of this precious gift comes daily, and he must do all that is possible within his power to increase his knowledge, and his share of this gift: For he has come to know that this gift will multiply if handled with love, and so he becomes the recipient of an even more precious gift of joy from God. He is the bearer of all that is most precious, and so he continues daily to grow in the knowledge of the love of God, and to blossom and bloom.

Like a flower in the spring, warmed by the sun and watered by the rain of God's love, he is able to prosper and to grow, so that he towers above others who are bereft[23]of his gift. He grows in stature and is seen as the favored child of the Most High God. He is able to appreciate all that is available, and take it and use it to nurture his soul so that he can continue to thrive and grow. Such is the gift of God in the spiritual life of man. He is the water in the desert and the rain in the drought, so man begins to flourish and to grow. Without God, none of these things come into being and man remains lost and alone, unable to find a reason for being or a way out of his spiritual isolation, pain, and anguish. No light appears, and so in the absence of light, he either dies or develops into a different life form… and so remains in the darkness as something other than his true self.

Morphed into a shadow of his true potential, he is unrecognizable and in pain, for he is alone and in deep despair and will eventually wither and die.

---

[23]   Deprived of or lacking

Man is the essence of God-beingness, but without the light of God shining in his life, he remains without hope and lost upon the Earth. With God, the light of love can shine forth and man can begin to emerge; and so, man is able to be found and to advance in his spiritual development. Thus is the life of man without the knowledge, and love, of God in his life. He is alone and lost without the light of God to light his path and show him the way to true happiness.

Amen

For God's love is indeed so special for man, that the Children of Men would do everything in their power to possess it and to keep it all the days of their lives. Like selfish children who fight daily to get the attention of a parent, even so is the love of God regarded by man. He daily wrestles, and fights with all things within himself, and strives to win the coveted prize, which is— and always has been— there for him to attain. Man must learn and remember these truths, that God's love is there every day and there is no need to fight to attain it, since it is freely given. All men, regardless of creed, or color, or religion, have access to the love of God. For God does not see color, or religion. He sees his children and thus like a parent, loves and cares for them all equally.

There are no favorites. All are equal in the mind and love of God, for we are all ONE. Since all men are united under God, there is no need for man to compete for God's favors. Again, all is freely given and can belong to the Children of Men. It is man who separates from God in his quest to gain more favor, and it is likewise he who is the cause of the strife and suffering upon the land. That man sees division where none exists, and sees separateness, where God sees unity is most apparent. There is only love in the mind of God, but in man, where all things dwell; there is the fear and the urge to be better and to gain more at the expense of the weaker brethren. This is how the nature of man has been actively cultivated for many eons, and this is how man has survived. Suffice it to say, these are not the ways of God and not the ways of man that God wants to see demonstrated daily for mankind.

Clearly, man must learn to see God in a different way and to understand his power and might. Likewise, the love of God is not tied to any single reward or is not unconditionally given on good behavior. It is here and is available for all children who would heed the call, and come to life in the knowledge and love of God. It is all based on this simple fact that God loves unconditionally and so must man. We must close our eyes to any and all perceived differences and see and know we are all one. All are one in the mind of God, so there is no reason to hurt your brethren to acquire God. To the contrary, Dear Ones, we see and know that God's love is the great **EQUALIZER.** For since all are one in the eyes of God, man has no need to fight or to spend much time in pain and anguish, trying to secure that which he already has been given so freely by God. The nature, fear, and function of man must change so that he can begin to see how to survive, and to bring man back from the path of destruction on which he is so hell-bent.

Man must learn to realize that the love of God is easily attainable and all he needs to do is to accept the gift he is being given every day. All things are available for man. His source is the love given to all men in equal abundance, so that he can partake of the things without strife and turmoil. Man must learn to simply open his hand in order to come into God's grace; rather than to think that God is not a God of all men, but only of some. His love is freely given, and even so, can be accepted by all men.

It is time, O Children of Men, to open your hearts and hands and receive the love of God graciously and freely, so that he can gain entry to everyone; it is the answer to all, and LOVING ALL MEN equally as brothers and as equals in the eyes and the Godhead of God. He is our father and mother, so we know we can and we must know how to access God and leave all other things open.

For the love of God is everywhere, given and taken freely, happily and in the spirit of LOVE, not in one of pain or jealousy or any other thing. Man must move from his flawed state into the state of God-beingness and there he will see and know God. Whereas, if he continues to fight, he continues to condemn himself to more of the same pain that he has always known. He is all there is, and all there will ever be, and man must see and know these truths if he is to emerge from this tomb of darkness in which he has buried himself for many centuries.

Amen

21ˢᵀ MARCH 2010

For much has been written of the nature of God's love for man, but hear, O Children of Men, these words, and mark them well, for of such is the true and all-encompassing truth made. The nature of God's love for man is found in the texts written from ancient times. It details man's woes and the ways in which God punished man.

Know now and forever, that the God of love will not, and would never punish, for such is not his nature. There is no punishment that God would cause to happen to man. There is no reason for God to punish, for man's punishment is harsher than anything God would deem appropriate for the transgressions of man. So, Dear Children, listen and understand that God is not a God of wrath or punishment. HE IS ONLY THE GOD OF LOVE. A love that is all-encompassing, and that will outlast the ages and that will ensure that man is ever in God's protection, love, and care. There is no reason for God to punish man, for man punishes himself and keeps himself in pain and anguish, the like of which God could never conceive. So, Dear Ones, know that God does not punish, for he is the God of LOVE.

A God of love cannot punish and bring destruction on that which he favors, or on that which he has created. No such possibility exists, so understand, that the limited view of God as described by such ancient texts, does so simply out of ignorance of the true nature of God. GOD IS LOVE and a God that is love cannot bring pain, destruction, and any form of pain down upon those he loves. Look ye no further but know these truths, that God is LOVE, and that is all there is.

Man cannot grasp that the truth of God is such a simple truth, and so has spun many a fine yarn in order to document his thoughts on the nature and love of God. That is why we have the Angel Band established with the task to help to keep man safe, and to help him remember and know his true connection with God and his true divinity.

The loss of one soul is an agony to God, so when souls live in darkness and move away from the love of God, and deny its existence and also the existence of God, it is here when God grieves for mankind, for he is part of each soul, and the loss of even one causes deep anguish and pain.

The Angel Band's main function on Earth is to remind man of his divinity and to help him find his way back to the knowledge and love of God whilst still here in the form and shape of physical man. They work tirelessly night and day, trying to bring those lost and alone back to the fold, where they can feel that true, and everlasting, and abiding love of God. His nature is known to them and they work tirelessly to bring relief from pain and suffering to mankind. They know that the loss of even one precious soul to the darkness of pain, hurt, envy, lust, and greed, are the things to be protected against. They work to keep man safe from himself and his very nature, and to help guide him on his way during this incarnation. He is their focus at all times and they work tirelessly to bring each one that has strayed and is dwelling in negativity back to the ways and the love of God, where they might find peace and solace in the love of God.

Thus Dear Ones, we see and know that God's love is never of punishment or wrath, but rather of LOVE and support, LOVE and devotion, so that man can be protected and delivered from his nature and his vices. He is to be secured and safely supported every day lest he destroy himself. Even so, we know that many souls come into incarnation to help, support, and protect man from himself.

Unfortunately, lured by power, they all too often forget the nature of the journey and the reason for their sojourn on Earth. Thus, they fall into hopelessness, forget their charge and mission, and are lost themselves.

The temptations of Earth are difficult to ignore indeed, for they include lust for POWER, WEALTH and FAME. These are the vices of man that help to bring him into despair, and to let him forget his divinity, and reside in the deep dark places of the soul instead, in avarice and greed, instead of following the path of PEACE. These are the times that cause the Angel Band much anguish. For trying to bring man back is no easy task, once he has decided to travel the highways and byways of the negative life. O Children of Men, remember your true divinity, and know that the only thing that matters is love, FOR LOVE IS ALL THERE IS. Know this truth and discover the power within you. It will help you to move to the highest of realms whilst still in human form, and to truly know and feel the benefits and blessings of God's love for mankind.

Know in your soul that God is all there is, and that the only thing that matters is love. Once this truth has been understood and accepted, man can finally move on to know the true reason for the time spent on Earth. It is for naught, but to help man discover and remember his true nature, and to continue to develop to find his way back to the love of God. A love that never wavers, a love that is never ending, and one that is truly able to surpass all things and to be shown forever in the way man is being protected by Angels from his own powers; protected so that he does not destroy himself, or each other; and so that he can realize his true potential and the magnificence of his soul and its destiny, whilst the incarnation of his spirit on Earth has occurred.

Man can never fully know, understand, or remember his true divinity: For he would not be able to understand it, but suffice it to say, he will be able to advance enough if he can remember to love all souls, and to love all of God's creations, and respect their rights to live and coexist upon the Earth.

Man must know that he is not all that there is in the universe or in the heavens, but that many other forms of life live and exist here on the Earth… and that he is to support and to help sustain all life, since all comes from God and all are precious in the sight of God.

Knowing and understanding the nature of God is man's total reason for being upon the Earth. If he can learn and remember these truths when incarnated, then he will have reached the highest peaks of his reason for being.

He will know why he is here, and his purpose for being upon the Earth will cause him to move on and to evolve as a spiritual being: For it is impossible to know the purpose, and not advance when the true understanding and knowledge is known. Man can understand that he is here to show love to all others also on the path of self-discovery, and to support them on their journey.

No task is too small if it helps another soul to advance, or simply to learn of his true divinity, and bring him out of the shadows into the light of God's love. This is the truth of the discovery of man's purpose, and the way in which he can move on and help others to discover their own divinity and connectedness with the source of all things, with God the maker of all things, and the reason for all things.

Being kind to one another, and loving and sharing the blessings of this world with others, these are ways to enlightenment and to advancement spiritually. For in knowing these things, man can help his brother on his journey, and at the same time, help himself to feel that deep and abiding love that rests within his soul. Selfishness will cease, and love will become the order of the day, and all will know peace, joy, and contentment brought about by sharing with all men the bounty which God has placed here on Earth. Equity will bring peace when man knows that if he takes from his brethren, he is taking from God and also from himself. Then and only then, can man find peace as he discovers his real purpose on Earth. IT IS TO LOVE his brethren, as taught by the great teacher Jesus. Loving thy brethren as thyself because he and thee are truly one. Thus, loving your brethren is loving yourself, and loving God, as all are one and the same parts of the whole. If I love my brother, then I show my love for self and God. If I bring pain to my brother, and suffering upon either, I bring it upon myself, for we are all one and the same.

To love God is to love man, and to love man is to love God. All are one, and thus man's purpose is served and his reason for being is fulfilled, and he can return to the arms of God's love and reside there forever. Ah! So simple a truth, yet so difficult a task, as judged by man's inability to come to this realization thus far! As the realization comes into being, man can move forward and can find the peace which has eluded him for so long; for he will be safe in the bosom of God and will finally know peace.

Amen

27ᵀᴴ MARCH 2010

"For unto us a son is born; unto us a child is given." - Isaiah 9:6

Even so was the Son of Man given to mankind for the teachings of love to show the true way into God's kingdom. But we know that many do not yet understand the fullness of the power and might of the man Jesus. **Suffice it to say, that the message was of the power of the LOVE of God and the redemptive nature of God's love for humankind**.

Never under-estimate the true power of God's love, and never do we say that there is anything else of real value in the world, save the true and un-abiding power of LOVE, as it has been given and shown to mankind.

Until mankind can realize that without love, man will perish; the hope for all will not be fully realized. For man cannot hope to survive upon the Earth without LOVE for his brethren, love for himself, but above all, love for one another. Man's selfishness is the very thing that can and will destroy him if he fails to make changes in his life.

For man must be able to see and know that God's love for mankind is the true source of what makes man special upon the Earth. For of himself, man is naught, but the power of the love of God gives him the wonderful ability to become the enlightened upon the Earth. Man cannot continue to live upon the Earth and then demonstrate continuously his contempt for all things and thoughts that center upon love. For if he continues on this path he will move to his own destruction and that of the Earth as well. O Wonderful Counselor, Sons of Men, know you not what you do each day when in your ignorance of God's love for you, you squander all that is so easily and readily given?

Look you to your actions to see the downward spiraling of the humanity of man in his treatment of his brother. Know you not that this cannot continue indefinitely, for there must be a change in the heart and mind of man towards his brothers and to the planet? Know you not of your own majesty and might? Know you not of the wonderful gifts you possess and the way to come into God's kingdom?

Let yourself move out of the darkness and into the light of God's love, for only in this way can man hope to redeem himself. Keep yourself focused on love and light, and you will see the changes that will come upon the Earth.

Know you not that, without love, you all perish? For the knowledge and love of God is the only true source of redemption for man. A change must come so that man can learn the true path of LOVE to God the Father. Man cannot continue to move and to exist in the path of selfishness and of pain. He cannot continue to bring suffering upon his fellow man. He must learn and demonstrate acts of selflessness and of charity for his brother. Without this, he cannot ever hope to advance his soul development and will remain in the depths of despair and be forever in pain. Not a pain inflicted by God, but by himself; for in his ignorance of what is his right and birthright, he searches for meaning in his life but can find none.

He is unable to find any kind of solace, for without love, he is like an empty vessel, without purpose, lost and alone. Man must remember his purpose and seek to fulfill his true mission upon the Earth, so that he can advance spiritually and gain the peace he seeks daily. Only love can help man to bring changes to his life, and only love can cause him to change.

Until man can see that hopelessness exists where love does not exist, he cannot hope to advance, and so he is destined to remain as one in a stagnant pool, drowning from the foul odor and the stagnant[24] air. LOVE can cause man to lift himself out of the pool of stagnation[25] and into the sweet smelling aroma of God's love and of his light.

Only love can cause man to make the changes that are needed in the world. Hate, malice, and envy must cease, and love must be the order of the day. Man must see that the path to God is possible only through the knowledge and demonstration of the true and redemptive process of loving one another. This is the only true way to save mankind from itself and from sure destruction. Love is the

---

[24]   Foul or stale: stale or impure from lack of motion

[25]   Not develop or make progress: to fail to develop, progress, or make necessary changes

only answer for man's redemption[26]. Without it, he dies spiritually and is lost. Man must love himself and his brethren, and all upon the Earth, for without this there is naught.

Amen

---

[26]   Improving of something: the act of saving something or somebody from a declined, dilapidated, or corrupted state and restoring it, him, or her to a better condition.

2ND April 2010

"My soul will make its boast in God, for he has
answered all my cries. His faithfulness to me is as
sure as the dawn of a new day." – Hayes, M

And even so is the love of God given to the Children of Men. For
the love of God is given freely, without cost or without any kind of
recompense[27] being required.

Man is only required to acknowledge and to know that God has
given his love freely, and for man to be able to demonstrate the same
kind of behavior to his fellow man, his brother. How selfish is that
gift? There is no predetermined cost attached. All that is necessary is
that man sees the gift and in turn, demonstrates the same behavior
to his fellow man.

For the soul of man truly needs to magnify the Lord, and to sing his
praise; but that is all that is required. No sacrifice is owed, and no
debt needs to be paid in exchange for the gift so freely given. If man

---

[27]   to give something to by way of compensation: pay for

can demonstrate this same kind of love to his brethren, then the love of God would be available to all men. Man must demonstrate this same act of love for all, for as 'The Christ' taught, "How can you love God who you cannot see, when you cannot love those you can see?"[28]

Thus, the act of loving is the true demonstration of the service of God and the true way to acknowledge that man has developed beyond the most basic of creatures. When man knows that he is but the source of God's love, and that his task is simply to love others, and he can demonstrate this behavior in the most unselfish way; then, and only then, can man hope to advance his spiritual growth. For man cannot ever hope to advance spiritually, until he can learn how to do these things. Until this is demonstrated on a daily basis, with the ease of breathing, and with the natural nature of doing something that cannot be made false, man cannot advance.

When the nature of man changes and allows him to see 'The Christ Light'[29] in his brother, man will be able to say he has advanced. Without this critical step, man is destined to remain at the same developmental level and to fail to proceed or to grow in his spiritual quest. This, then, is the great gauge to help man on the spiritual journey. He must be able to look into the mirror and see his neighbor as a brother without regard for race or religion. He must be able to see and to know that the spark and spirit of God dwells in all souls equally, and that he must take care of his brother; for therein lies his salvation and the growth of his soul, that he is so desperately in

---

[28]   1 John 4:20

[29]   Light of Christ is the divine energy, power, or influence that proceeds from God and guides every person and gives life and light to all things.

need of. He must be able to see and know, that all men are one; part of the family of God, part of God, part of the eternal beingness of God... so that to do harm to his brethren is to do harm to oneself.

When this recognition comes, man will surely have advanced to the next level of his development, and can claim to be the heir to the throne of God. For in loving one's brother, we love our self. In seeing the God in others, we learn to see the God-light in our self. The knowing and the loving of all others, helps man to know and to love himself. If you can give love to others easily, then you can be open to receiving love from others. If man cannot do this seemingly simple task, then he cannot progress to the next spiritual level.

He is destined to remain in the same state, in ignorance, of all the wondrous gifts that await him. He is unable to advance in his knowledge of the love of God and he stagnates, withers, and dies. Spiritually lost and alone, he is in the wilderness of despair and cannot proceed because he has lost his way. When all earthly things assume importance over the things of God, then man can know nothing of the immense power and love of God. For he is defined by his knowledge of the Divine; and he cannot see, know, or acknowledge all the power, magnificence, and wonder of God.

Hear, O Children of Men, this message sent to guide you as you travel the highways and byways of life! Look and learn of the great magnificence of God, and see and know, and feel, his great love for you.

Know your magnificence is dimmed only by your own inability to see and know its true power and its true grandeur. Know that you are children of the Most High God, and as such have the keys to the kingdom... not a kingdom far away, but one right here on Earth. A kingdom where love rules all, and makes all men stronger, not weaker. For in knowing the love of God, man can share it with others and help them to grow; which in and of itself, is the true lesson of man which must be learned and conquered, if he is to advance spiritually. Know and understand that the love of others is the greatest treasure or prize to be gained by man. Not the selfish hoarding of what man considers to be wealth, but the true wealth that cannot be bought; which can only exist in the heart of man... that of the unselfish demonstration of the caring and love of man for his fellow man.

Only this can help man to grow while here on the Earth. Only this teaches him that which he desires to know, and feels in the deepest depths of his soul...the love of God. That love, that was demonstrated by 'The Christ' in the ultimate sacrifice, by giving his life in payment for others, by showing how to truly love. He was able to move to the highest level of spiritual levels by personal sacrifice. Man does not have to go to such lengths to show his Christhood[30]. All he needs to do is to see the spark of God in all, and give love to his brother. To show kindness to all, and to be the spark of God in the life of others by demonstration of acts of love; seeing only God, when you look upon the face of a stranger. Seeing only love when you look in the eyes of others; this is the great act of love that will allow man to fulfill his true destiny upon the Earth. This is the way that he will be able to move to higher levels and to learn how to become the God-light that he truly is.

---

[30]   The state of being the Christ, the anointed one of God

Only then can he see and know that God alone can give him what he searches for. Only then can he find the peace that he has searched for throughout the ages. Only then can he truly understand his reason for being.

If he cannot do these things, he will remain in ignorance of his true purpose upon the Earth and will stagnate, wither, and die spiritually. He must find this meaning or he dies as a spiritual being.

Nothing but the love that is already inside of man can help him to advance to the next level of his soul development. Only this can help man to know his true being and his true self.

Amen

5ᵀᴴ APRIL 2010

THE ANGEL BAND

God rejoices over you in song! So shall even the Angels sing to know of the triumph of man over his nether soul,[31] for the triumph of man is the triumph of God. The Angel Band is known to few but yet they are always at hand when the needs of man need to be addressed. For it is clear that they do what must be done to assist with the work of protection. For their joy is to protect man from himself, and to bring him safely into the kingdom of the Most High God.

For millions of years, they have roamed the Earth and places like it, keeping watch over the children of God. Their charge: to protect and help them to survive, so that they might return to God, the eternal beingness.

If they fail in this task, then the soul of man is shrouded in darkness and fear, and is left alone. For thousands of years, they have worked in an anonymous state, unable to help man to become who he needs to be. For they strive to be the silent helper and friend of mankind. For thousands of years, they have worked tirelessly to help man to become who he should be, and to guard him from himself.

---

[31]   Lower soul

For indeed, the Angel Band serves a great function in the lives of men. Their function is to support man when he rises and to lift him up when he falls. They are the guardians of mankind, whose task is to be there at all times, to remind the Children of Men of their greatness. For indeed, it is they who are there in man's greatest time of need, to be the inspiration and the great booster of the hearts of men. Know, indeed, that the Angel Band consists of the following, Dear Ones; the Diadem Band and the elements of those who are ever with mankind, making him aware of his connection with the Most High. For indeed, it is they who are most recognized as helpers of men. They are the ones charged to be with man throughout his days. Each soul, when incarnated upon the Earth, has the love, support, and encouragement of the Angel Band. Their task is simply to uphold mankind so that in their darkest hour, they can be reminded of their true magnificence. Thus, they appear to man in dark times, taking on the guise of humans in order to give them the very help they need to keep them safe. The Angel Band, of itself, consists of the Diadem Band, and the Arc Angels, who are not assigned to the Earth, but can come to assist the Angel Band on rare occasions… when great mastery, and strength, and resilience are required of men.

It is they who would then appear in the darkest of times, and when man is facing the biggest trials and tribulations, so that they can give strength and courage to mankind. Know, Dear Ones, that the Angel Band, the Diadem Band, and the lesser, if such we may refer to them, Angels; are all given the tasks to be there… ever watchful, and ever present, with mankind, to uplift him, and to keep him safe. It is they who will walk beside you, daily coming into view when some great show of courage is needed. For they will uplift and uphold thee, and carry thee on wings; to help and support those in the greatest need.

That mankind believes in Angels, is a truth established since the dawn of time. For indeed, they know that something unnatural or unexplained has occurred, to allow the human in need to display the courage and strength to overcome the obstacle at hand. Know, Dear Ones, that the Angel Band are the souls who have taken on this special role, to guard and protect mankind from himself.

It is therefore their task, as the great watchmen and overseers, to always be with man, to lift him up when he falls... or to support him in all his waking moments, least the darkness overtake him. As the Sons of Men forget their divinity, and wander aimlessly upon the Earth, the Angel Band and the Diadem Band are working tirelessly to find ways to remind man of his connection to God, and of the love of God that is available to him.

Thus, we see that they take on human form when necessary. Appearing when there is the most critical need, and being the love and support, that can reassure man that all is indeed well: And giving him the strength to weather the storm, and to arrive safely on the shore of God's love. Know, Dear Ones, that the Angel Band are ever with thee, but in silent support. They are the voice of reason, the cricket on your shoulder; the small voice within you telling you that all is well, when the knowledge of man says all is lost.

That the Angel Band and the Diadem Band differ in their function, is evident; for although they are there to support and uphold mankind, they do so in different ways. The Angel Band are the still small voice ever with thee, reassuring man that all is well.

The Diadem Band are the great teachers, whose task is to teach man, and to help to inspire him to even greater heights. Know, Dear Ones, they are the ones who are there to teach, and to tutor man, and to help him remember his greatness. They inspire, and make suggestions to the heart of man, on ways to become even better. For they will be with man, when inspiration is needed, to help and inspire greatness in man's behavior. They are the ones who are ever-present, when man begins to search for cures, and ever-present when man, in deepest thoughts and meditations, looks for God the Father. For they can help to inspire, and bring those thoughts of greatness into the hearts of men. Know, Dear Ones, that these Beings, for such they truly are, are ever with thee. Always ready to support man on his quest upon the Earth. For it is the greatest joy of them both, to be here, to support, uplift, and to assist mankind as you daily struggle to remember your true nature and your magnificence. It is they who are the great watchmen who are ever at your side. Know, Dear Ones, their greatest joy is that they can uplift man. Even at the hour of death, or the "Great Release," they are there, ever seeking to support and uphold thee. Even so, their greatest moment of sadness is when a soul is lost, for they cannot bring them back from the edge of darkness, and are unable to show them, in any way, how precious they are in the eyes of God. For indeed, when man is in so much gloom and despondency, it is then that they work the hardest, trying at all costs, to bring man into the light of God's love.

They toil tirelessly, trying to find ways to show man his true value, and his true worth in the eyes of God. On some occasions, they are successful. But, on those rare occasions when man is so deep in the dungeons of despair within himself, they are unable to bring them out of the darkness, and man is lost. Know, Dear Ones, that at such times they weep for thee; for the loss of one soul is of the greatest pain for them.

For they know that Mother Father God indeed weeps for the loss of one soul: for all are precious in the eyes of God. Know, Dear Ones, that the Angel Band are as close to you as your very breath, for they are ever around you and with you. They learn the ways of man, and take on human form, when it will allow them to serve you in your times of need. They are your guardians, your angels, your protectors, and your friends. They are love of the greatest magnitude. They are Light Beings who have taken on the task to support the Sons of Men in human form, until they once more return to spirit.

Know, Dear Ones, they are your Angel Band, who will be with you from the beginning to the end of each physical incarnation. Know, Dear Ones, that you are precious in the heart and mind of God, and thus he sends these guardians to be here for thee; to love thee, and to keep thee ever in the light of God's love. Know, Dear Ones, that indeed they are the greatest supporters of man upon the Earth, for they love thee, uphold thee, and shield thee from dangers. Ever-present, never absent, and always there to be the support for God upon the Earth. Be at peace, and know, Dear Ones, that you are indeed so loved and precious to God the Father, that he will forever try to uplift and uphold thee; so that you may return to the bosom of his love, in the light and love of the Most High God. Know that your Mother Father God is ever-present upon the Earth, and is as close to you as one of these angels. For you are never alone. Even in the valley of the shadow of death, God is there with thee.

Be at peace, and always know: when man forsakes you, your Mother Father God is ever at your side, to uphold and to love you, and to keep you ever in his loving care. For this is the way of God, and this is the way that God can place his arms around all his children upon the Earth. For the Angel Band and the Diadem Band are ever present to be with thee, Dear Ones.

Amen

30ᵀᴴJANUARY 2011

Welcome sure, Sister Sweet, for a welcome it is indeed. Hail to the mighty and loving power of God, for so we say, and even so it is. For today, Sweet One begins the changes and the shifts that will change the heart of many and help to put things in the very order that they should be in. Let not your heart be troubled, but know that all will flow as it should, through the might and power of the Almighty.

Know that all will be well, but the changes that are apparent will begin to come into view. All will begin to see that which must come to pass. Know, Little One, that the day is here for all to see and know of the great and magnificent power of the great and wonderful God who reigns supreme in the lives and the hearts of men.

Know, Little One, the beginning of the 'Shift' is seen this day. Let no fear come nigh thee, but listen to the wind and watch the trees, for even in their majesty, they know that 'a change is gonna come.'

O hills harken to the song of the love of God for man. See the passion and the power that lives in the words, and thrives in the hearts of men. Hail, O hail the day of the coming of God, for so his power is without end. Let your hearts sing to know of such joy and love for humankind.

Let your voices be raised to tell of the magnificence of God, and the terrible, and yet gentle, awe-inspiring love of God for mankind. Let the hills bow down, and let the trees sing out his name to all who would hear the songs of time. Great are the blessings that will abound for those who will open their hearts and hands, to see and to receive the blessings of God. Know, Little One, that they are many indeed, sent and made available in oh, so many different ways.

Open your eyes, open your hearts, O Children of Men, and see and taste all the many blessings of God, given to you by your loving Father God. Be you full of grace and begin to say "Aye, for he lives in the hearts of men, indeed." For so it must be, Little Ones, for only so can that which is thine truly come into being. The day and the hour is upon us for man to open his heart to the joys of God, to see and know all that is to be given to mankind through the grace and love of God. Let your hearts shine, let your love and light shine, O Children of Men.

Look ye up and see all the glory of God given to mankind. Open your eyes and heart, and take that which is so freely given. For even so is the love of God freely given to man. Let not the fear of the flesh surround or encompass thee. Be the shining light of God. Be the child of the Most High God, and show thy face to all who would see and know the face of God. For the face of love is indeed the face of God, Little One.

Be you always vigilant, and come to know all that is possible for you, O Sons and Daughters of Mankind. Accept the gifts so freely given, and know that these are thine, provided only through love, and at no cost to thee and thine.

The hills begin to shout this day and to sing the praises of God, for so the joy and magnificence cannot be hidden under a bushel,[32] but must be placed on the highest mountain top, where all indeed will see its radiance and will come to know the wonderful power of the love of God. Praise be to the Father God, for such he is due. We say 'He' but know, Dear Ones, God is formless and shapeless and without any of those earthly descriptions that can be applied to man. Know, Little One, the love of God likewise is without end; void of form, and yet everlasting, being made available, free of cost to all who would grasp the divine spark within themselves and remember their own source. Nothing can alter the love. Nothing can disturb the flow. Nothing can interrupt the flow or source from which it is so abundantly made available to mankind.

Let your hearts be open, and see the great and awesome love of God for thee. Know you are heavenly blessed, O Children, for such is the nature of God in his benevolence to give all that is available to his Sons and Daughters. Let the winds become calm, and the oceans cease to roll, and the tides cease to change, before the love of God will ever cease to flow and be available for the Children of Men.

Let the winds howl no more like lions, and let the sands of the desert cease to be, before the love of God will be taken from the Children

---

[32] A vessel (basket)used as a dry measure for 8 gallons or 32 quarts (vessel sometimes used as a table by the poor)

of Men. For such will never be, for God will never take the love he freely offers, from the children of his very heart. Listen, O Children, and hear these words, for truly they come from the bosom of God. Peace be unto you, O Sons and Daughters of the Most High God.

This is the wisdom given to man through the voice of those here on Earth. Peace and blessings, Brethren.

The Brotherhood

1ˢᵗ MARCH 2011

Welcome, Little One, Child of Light; indeed, we say welcome indeed; for we see and know thee and thy courage and wisdom. Hail, Warrior Princess, Daughter of Light; we say hail indeed! For today is the beginning of the rest of tomorrow, for indeed, much are the needs of this time. For the days are quickly upon you, for changes to occur that will indeed change the face of much that has been.

We say welcome, indeed, to the NEW that has come into being and to the OLD that, even so, continues to exist. Let not your light grow dim, Little One, but instead let it provide the glow of light and love that will indeed provide the light for the entire body. Be you safe and sound and know that the days of change are here and cannot be delayed; for the times of God's magnificence are evident among us.

Let all who would question the true power of God look in awe on all that has occurred and will continue. How are the mighty slain and how are the mighty uprooted? Surely this can only take place through the love and magnificent source and power of God.

Hail, Warriors of the Light, Sons and Daughters of Earth. Let not fear consume thee, but know, indeed, that all moves as it should so that the kingdom of love can be established upon the Earth… but know and learn the true source of all that is happening now upon the Earth. For the Lord of Hosts is the refuge[33] of man, and in his kingdom, naught can prevail if love is not within it. Look ye on and see the devastation of kings and princes who gain their mighty power at the expense of the weak and infirm. Let not fear teach thee to ignore the ways of God, but know, indeed, that the ways of man pale in comparison.

Hail, ye daughters and sons of humanity. Look ye on and wonder no more, for these are the times that cause men's hearts to change. So indeed it is, for the times they are a-changing. Let not fear consume thee but know, indeed, that all moves as it should so that the kingdom of love can be established upon the Earth. Look on and see, and know that nothing can survive that is not built on a solid foundation of love and peace. For so it is written, Little One, and so it will be. Know ye that the days of change are truly here and can and must bring about the shift in consciousness, so that man can proceed with his life, and his development and growth upon the Earth. Let all who come upon the face of the Earth remember the times we now show thee, for the beginning of the great change is indeed upon us.

Look on and know of the great and magnificent truth of the love of God for mankind, for only in this way can man see and know all that is to be truly brought into existence.

---

[33]   Protection from danger or distress: that which shelters or protects

Hail, Little One; we say hail, indeed, for the days are here when the hearts and minds of men must change. Hail indeed, for here comes the days of peace. For man must begin to know peace if he is to enter into the kingdom, and bask in the glow of all that can truly be upon the Earth.

Let not fear consume thee, but know that these are the manifestations of God upon the face of the Earth. Let not fear and hate come nigh thee, but know that the love of God can remove tyrants and kings alike, for even so it must come to pass.

For God is in his heaven, and all is right upon the face of the Earth. For the changes will continue, and much will be the deluge[34] of those who flee from the wrath of fear, that would be brought upon the souls of those who dwell in these lands.[35] Know that the mighty hands of God, stretch to all kingdoms, and bring forth all those who would come out of the darkness into the light. Know indeed, Little One, that the Sons of Men will prosper, and light will return even to the dark places where none has existed for so many generations. Look and learn that the times they are a-changing, and so it must be if man is to continue to grow and learn. The ways of those who oppress the weak and lowly can no longer exist. For this is the time to move to enlightenment and godliness. For without it, the Sons of Men will perish and be condemned to live in the darkness and fear of ignorance. O Children of Men reach up and see the light.

---

[34]   Overwhelming number

[35]   Unrest in Tunisia, Tehran, Egypt, Libya, and Yemen.

Reach out of the depths of despair and taste the sweet smell of love that waits for thee. Taste the joy and freedom that lives and is available for thee, for so it is, Little One. Know that the kingdoms will vanish, much of what was must cease to be, if love, and light, and wisdom are to become evident upon the Earth. No longer can the wicked ones bring fear into the hearts of the weak and oppressed. Look on and know, for the days of change cannot be reversed or denied. The bell has been rung and the time for delay has passed. Move forward, Dear Ones, and know your true power, O Sons and Daughters of Light. Move forward and see all that is to be. For the days of love must be brought into being, and the nights of horror, and fear, must vanish upon the Earth.

These are the days that approach, Dear Ones, and these are the times that indeed try men's souls. Know that changes will continue and more kingdoms will rise and fall before the end times[36] truly come into being. Look on, Little One; look on and know that God is in his heaven and all is right with the world. Know that the power and might of God must become evident in the hearts and minds of those who dwell in the dark places of fear and ignorance, if man is to survive upon the Earth and reach his true potential. Let all who doubt these words, open his eyes and see and know the true power of the love of God for mankind. Look on and know that these are indeed the days and nights of the new kings of Earth. Let all see and know that man has awoken and now can tame the beast[37]. For the spirit of love has taken hold, and the voice cannot be silenced.

---

[36]   End of negative thinking and actions and the beginning of enlightenment upon the Earth

[37]   Fear, hatred, ignorance and forgetfulness

Look on and know that all is as it should be, and the love of God will prevail and help man to grow into his Godhood and his birthright, and none can cause this to cease from coming into existence. Look on and see the light. Breathe it, know it, and become the light; for only in this way can success become the order of the day. Breathe the peace, the love, and the beauty of God, and know that things are as they should be and all will be right with the world. May God's grace become you and behold you, Little Ones. Know the peace of God in your hearts, and let God's peace shine upon you this day. Grace, love, and peace, to you all.

Adieu

THE NATURE OF GOD

For as much as God is in his heaven, and all is right with the world, we know indeed that there is much that the Sons of Men do not comprehend about the nature of God. For indeed, God is Spirit and is omnipresent. –Everywhere present, and absent nowhere—Thus we see, Dear Ones, that there is no place where God is not. So we know indeed that at all times, and in all places, he is present. This presence is the presence that keeps the love of God ever available to mankind. For indeed, without it, man would have no idea of his true and utter beingness and his place in the kingdom. It is the omnipresent nature and beingness of God, that allows Him, if such we may refer to him as 'Him,' to be all things to all people at the same time, and to allow the Sons of Men to feel connected to God whilst in different places upon the Earth.

It is this, that allows mankind to think that God is a God who chooses one group above the other, for indeed they cannot grasp the idea, that it is the one God which is being felt everywhere upon the Earth at the same time. Know, Dear Ones, that this is the true and most wonderful essence of God, that allows man to feel that he is so special, that he is unable to comprehend that there would be enough of God to go around... and therefore allow for everyone to feel his love and his presence at the same time.

Of course, it is also evident, that the work of the Angel Band keeps the thoughts of God in the hearts of men, and thus the feeling that emerges in the hearts of men is that God is with us, so he cannot be on the side of those we see as our enemies. Know, Dear Ones that this truth is no truth at all, for God does not take sides, nor indeed can he. For how does a loving parent choose one child above another? How does a loving parent stand by and allow one child to harm or hurt his brother?

Know indeed, that the free will of man, when upon the Earth, causes him to choose behaviors and ways of being in the world, which do not always mean peace. Thus, we see that the Sons of Men see what they conceive to be differences, between the Sons of Men from different corners of the globe... and in fear and ignorance, they see themselves as separate from their brothers and sisters, and thus are able to destroy them.

Know, Dear Ones, that God does not take sides, and because he is a loving Shepherd, he cannot harm his own Sons and Daughters; so he mourns when the pain of man is seen in the hatred and anger that is war, and famine, and disease, which can be prevented, yet is allowed to happen across the world. Know, Dear Ones that the love of God does not exclude, but only includes; for since all mankind is one in God, all are loved and all are protected by God.

Too many times, the question is asked, "If there is a God, why are there disasters?" The truth, Dear Ones, is that these occurrences are caused by elements in nature, and in some instances by the ill-treatment of the Earth by mankind. For, in having total disregard for the blessed Earth, man causes many of the conditions upon the Earth. If with reverence the Earth is cared for by man, we know that indeed there would be fewer disasters; for in paying homage to Mother Earth, man would recognize that his way of being in the world is in direct contrast with the laws of life. For, in being selfish and consumed by his own greed, and the need to plunder the Earth in search of its minerals, he would know that he is causing the problems which emerge in later days. Know, Dear Ones that the Earth was given to mankind because of its great beauty and potential. It was given as a place that possessed all the essential elements for humans to prosper with ease. Know therefore, that the lack of care for this your home, can only leave it in disarray... and raped[38] and pillaged[39] without renewal.

Look to yourselves, O Sons of Men! And see and know that the Earth is your home. If you allow ruin to come upon it, you will suffer from the lack that is caused by your inability to do what is needed to sustain it. Know, Dear Ones, that the time is right for you to begin to correct, and to change your ways of being in the world: For to continue on the path of robbing, and taking from the supply of God, will cause you great distress in future times. Know, Dear Ones, if you tend this your garden, (Earth) then you will be able to get all that is needed for you to live in happiness and abundance. Like the

---

[38]   Seizing and carrying away by force

[39]   To strip of natural resources

farmer who tends the soil, and shows love for the Earth, you will reap the benefits of its love. For in loving the Earth and in taking care of your home, you give it the respect that is necessary and thus it can sustain you. If however, you continue to abuse the Earth, know that it will revolt, and will return to you only that which you give to it. Clean your oceans, and take care of the land. Protect the life that is found, and forget your selfish ways in taking all the wealth from the land for selfish pursuits. Know that these ways will contribute to the ways of survival in later times. For when the beauty and majesty of the Earth is destroyed, then what remains will be in revolt. Know, Dear Ones that knowledge is power, as it is said, so that the warnings must be heeded.

Look at the regions of the world where the disregard for Mother Earth has caused famine and destruction time and again, and see and know that the behaviors of man have caused these very tragedies. Know, Dear Ones that your lives can be so beautiful, if you look for the simple and the beautiful, and appreciate all that is available for mankind, free of cost, upon the Earth. Instead of sharing the resources, the Sons of Men are hoarders, who take it upon themselves to take what is considered precious and to waste it upon the Earth. Know, Dear Ones, that with renewal, your needs can be met. But with the disregard for all that is now present, even that will disappear from view because of man's unwillingness to change his ways, and to know that he is the steward of the Earth, given to him as his home. When you destroy your home, wither will you go, O Sons of Men? Pay heed to the signs that are given to you by Mother Earth, and know you will reap the rewards. Disregard the signs, and know that you will continue to bring disasters of your own making. For mankind can avert so many of the tragedies of nature that come upon mankind, by being aware of the effects of his behaviors upon the Earth.

Open your hearts, and open your eyes, and see what you have done! Blame not God, but know indeed that it is but the result of man's behavior that causes him pain. For he is the author of his life, and creates the scenery and the backdrop from which he will exist. Look to yourselves, O Sons and Daughters of Man, and know that you can contain much of the disasters by paying heed to your actions. Know also, that it is not the nature of God to cause floods or famine to punish man, as was thought in ancient times: For indeed, God does not harm his children. His only actions are those of a loving parent.

The free will of man when upon the Earth is that which helps to create these occurrences, and the destruction of the Earth: For, like a spoiled child, he knows only his own desires, and wants immediate gratification. Thus, he takes, and takes, as his heart delights; without regard for the needs of others, and therein is the origin and result of the behaviors of mankind. Mankind is here upon the Earth, to experience life in human form, and thus is a co-creator. He has the free will to make his world. Thus, he must consider all actions and their impact not just on his garden, but on all the gardens of the world. For they are all connected, and are all from one source. All are connected. Everything returns to Mother Earth, for she is the source of all life. Know, Dear Ones, that you must contain your desires, and your need, for ever (always) taking that which you do not need to sustain your life. Remember your brethren, and change your ways. Know that no man is indeed an island: All are connected, all are one, and the Earth is provided as your refuge, your home, and your garden. Step out into the light, and see and taste its beauty, and its majesty. Know that you are blessed by the gifts of the Earth; by animals, and plants and all things put upon the Earth. Know that you are the caretaker and protector of its resources, and pay heed to the messages being given to you by the Earth itself.

Look on and know, that only in this way can you continue to enjoy the blessings, the beauty, the bounty, and richness of the Earth. For with continued disregard for this home, it will fall into disrepair, and become uninhabitable. See the beauty, and protect all that has been provided for you by God. Know indeed, that this is your great gift, provided by your Mother Father God to help you survive upon the Earth. Taste the richness of the variety of all things upon the Earth, and know that you can destroy all these wonderful things, if you continue in your ways.

Be at peace, and know that all is in your hands, and do that which must be done.

Adieu

30ᵀᴴ AUGUST 2011

For, indeed, we see and know that the great and wonderful love of God flows endlessly for humankind. We see and know, indeed, that there is no limit to the love or wondrous nature of the love of God for mankind. It is unceasing, unending, and will never fade away or die. For the love and nature of God is such that there is no end to the vastness of this love. For in truth, since God is eternal, even so is the nature of this great love for mankind. For as God is an eternal being, even so is the nature of the love of God for man, and for all mankind. For there is no place where God is not, and likewise there are no circumstances under which the love of God for man does not exist. Know, Dear Ones that man's love and the love of God for mankind exist as one. They are inseparable, and even as man cannot be divided or separated from God, even so is the love of God inseparable from mankind. For one cannot exist without the other. For even as the Lord of Hosts is ever concerned, and is eternally taking care of his children; like the hovering parent who cannot be separated from his children lest some great harm should befall them, even so, is the nature of the great love of God for mankind likened.

For your Mother Father God can never desert his children, or ever remove them from his vision for even the smallest expanse of time. For in so doing, he would be leaving parts of himself unprotected, and vulnerable to the winds and rains, and all the storms of life, with none to watch over them, or to provide for their daily needs.

Look on and know, that the Lord of Hosts can never abandon his children, or remove them from his sight for any period of time, without feeling that most intense pain, that such an action would stir and cause to come into the reality of man. For man without God, is bereft of all knowledge of himself. He is alone, and tossed upon the seas of life to fend for himself, and to stay strong in all his doings lest any come upon his unguarded and unprotected children, and lead them into paths of destruction or forgetfulness, without thought of God or the things of God. For man without knowledge of God is a shadow of himself, left crying in the wilderness of life, searching in vain for his lost parent, asking him to take him gently into his arms and to protect him and love him.

Thus, we say the love of God is part of the very beingness of God, which allows mankind to come into his own magnificence. For without God, man is nothing. But with the love of God, man is everything. For the Sons of Men are living daily lives of turmoil, sullenness, fear, doubt, worry, and death. Of ignorance and separation, and even so, is likened to death.

With the love of God in the lives of humankind, know, Dear Ones, it is the rebirthing of mankind and the way in which man can enter into his own Godhead and become that which he has been throughout time: The Sons and Daughters of God the Father. Know, Dear Ones, that this great and all-encompassing love of God for mankind is never truly expressed or understanding of the nature of the relationship between God and man. For man and God are both eternal beings, living together or separately. (When man forgets his purpose, if such we may describe it, for man truly cannot exist without the love of God within himself.) For mankind must know and remember that he is naught, without the love and beingness of Mother Father God, being made aware to all the Sons and Daughters of man, each and every day.

Know, Dear Ones, that man and God are inextricably[40] linked, and forever will be one: In that the beingness of man is the same essence as the beingness of God. Thus, they are one. Ever connected, ever one, ever at peace. For God cannot be truly happy without the knowledge that all his children are loved, cared for, and protected. If these needs are not met, then the love of God for mankind cannot be. For God has naught but, the love and caring for his children.

Open your eyes, O Sons and Daughters of Man, and reclaim your heritage and your love, freely given of God. Given and yet never removed from the heart and soul of mankind: For man and God are together. Always joined, always linked, always one, even when man, in his ignorance of his kinship, forgets that he is in any way connected to the love and beingness of God. Even in these instances, man and God are still forever one, and thus God can help to bring man back from the brink of despair, and out of the mouth of fear, loathing, and loss. For, as man learns, nothing can separate him from the love of God. Freely, the love of God is given, and even so, freely all the blessings of God are made available to man.

---

[40]   Incapable of being disentangled or untied

Know indeed, that God is one with humankind inside or outside of this great reality. For even so, is the love of God for mankind never discarded or rejected or forgotten: For man can always turn to God, and receive all that he so desperately seeks. Know that the love of God is an endless source of blessing, and the richest, deepest kind of (God-love) love that can be shared. Take ye your fill of this love meted out[41] for mankind, and know that you will live. You will know the joys of love, and the great peace of God, which will descend upon you, and allow you to know peace. For man and God are indeed one, and even so is the nature of the love of God for mankind.

Adieu, Sweet One, we leave thee now but will return with more words for the text.

Adieu! Adieu!

---

[41] given in portions: spread out: distributed: divided up

26TH SEPTEMBER 2011

Welcome Child of Light. Indeed, we say welcome. For the welcoming of this day is one of the great gifts given by Mother Father God to the Sons and Daughters of Mankind. For indeed, great is the glorious dawn set upon the Earth to refresh and to replenish the soul of man. For thus it was written, that the dawn of the Son of Man was given to the Children of Men, and indeed, we see and know that the Sons of Men can and do celebrate the glorious dawn. For even so, it was seen as the earliest of praises to Mother Father God. For even so, it is expected to be given to the Children of Men, that the rising of the sun is that most special of all events upon the Earth.

Know, Dear Children, that the Children of Men indeed are the heirs to the throne of God, if they would but realize this special and glorious place, in the hierarchy of God's love. Know, Dear Ones that the love of God for mankind, takes on the most special of all traits, and the most special of all relationships. For indeed, mankind has been given that most special of all charges of being the very ones to be upon the Earth, and to come to know the truth of the relationship between God and man.

For indeed, the question is, why is mankind so special in the eyes of God, if such we may say it? Indeed, we see and know, that the love of God carries with it the very special and most wonderful ability to know the favor of God. For such is the very truth, Dear Ones. For the truth is that the kingdom of men was given to them as a special gift, from the God of Love for mankind; that they may indeed take and eat of the tree of the fruit of knowledge.(For such is the knowledge referring.) For indeed, the reference is given, to describe the great and glorious love of God given for mankind. For mankind are the beloved children of God, loved and protected by God for eons. For in their infancy, this great love was made available for all mankind to be able to utilize, so that mankind may indeed learn, of the magnificence of God, and of the true and most glorious relationship that exists between the two.

Know, Dear Ones, that this love of God is the foundation on which all of man's knowledge is hinged. For even as man is likened to the children of God, even so indeed are the Sons of Earth given the knowledge of the trees, and birds that are given to man. For it is of great importance, that man may indeed utilize all things found upon the Earth, and utilize this to his own advantage. For thus it is written, "All things were given to man, and he had dominion over the fowls of the air, and the fish in the seas."[42]

For thus it was written, that the Children of Men were the favored of God. Having all things that they desired made whole, so that indeed, it would be well for all to utilize the very best of all things, put upon the Earth.

---

[42]   Genesis 1:28

Know, Dear Ones, that the many and most glorious blessings of man, cannot be measured. For indeed, all things were put upon the Earth that man might know that he was favored of God. For all things upon the Earth were under his dominion. Know, Dear Ones that man has taken the gifts of God, and used them for ill gains, and has forgotten that he is the favored of God.

For indeed, he has caused much destruction to come upon the Earth; so that the fowls of the air, and even the fish in the great sea, have lost their habitats, and are doomed to be removed from the Earth. All due in part, to the very lust and greed of man .Why destroy your home, O Sons of Men? Know ye not that you will have nowhere else to go, and nowhere else to shine in your glory, and bask in the true brilliance of your nature? For only upon the Earth, do these most special of all gifts find that they can exist. Only here on Earth, can they find expression.[43] Know, Dear Ones, that the great and most powerful love of God, is that thing which allows man to flourish and to thrive upon the face of the Earth. Know, Dear Ones, that all is as it should be, and indeed, all is as the Mother Father God put it into being. For the Children of Men must move toward the end of his days, before he can turn once more to see the error of his ways, and know that only he indeed fails to be aware of his unique ways of acting upon the Earth, or indeed his true knowledge of all things upon the Earth.

Know, Dear Ones that this very nature must change, if man is to advance and come into his true glory, as the children of God, and the true heirs to the many blessings of God, established for mankind

---

[43]   Flourish and grow

upon the Earth. Know, Dear Ones, that so powerful is this most glorious purpose, so that he can of himself become aware of other children of God, who likewise dwell upon the Earth.

The plants and flowers are given dominion upon the Earth. For such is their portion, Dear Ones, to know that the sunlight of God's love is there made available for all. Know, Dear Ones, that God's love is given for all, and is available even for the birds, and the flowers, and the trees. For such it must be, that God's love will be made available to all his children, that they might be able to truly come into their most magnificent and glorious awakening: For this awakening heralds the dawn of a new and most glorious dawn upon the Earth, when man will see and know that he is connected to all things upon the face of the Earth. Thus, the 'Ancient Ones[44]' knew of the great connection of man to nature, and to the very source of God, and with reverence, paid homage to these truths. Know indeed, that these times are past upon the Earth, and thus, man must see and know of his own true magnificence as a child of the Most High God. Know, Dear Ones, that indeed God has been most gloriously known and recognized, for this is his true place upon the Earth; to remember and to return to his true source and nature, as children of God. Be you aware, Dear Ones, that the love of God for mankind knows no bounds, and knows no other way to express itself, than to show mankind all of these most special and glorious gifts upon the Earth.

Why use, and abuse, and destroy your home, Dear Ones? Why forget your true nature as shepherds of the Earth, given the skills to farm and cultivate the glorious blessings found upon the Earth?

---

[44]   Indigenous peoples: those living in ancient times: long ago

Why gorge[45] thyself upon the blessings, leaving nothing for the great tomorrow? For, if indeed, you eat all, and replenish not the source, you must lack for all things when the source withers and dies. Thus we say, this is the chance for mankind to be mindful of all things, and to show the utmost respect for all things; for such it was given to man to use as was seen judiciously, and not with greed or avarice, but as a soothing, and most calming, and wonderful existence as possible, in the nature and knowledge of God.

Know, Dear Children, even so, thus is the nature of mankind to take and eat of all things, but not to take and eat whilst thy brethren suffers for lack of the very same. Know, Dear Ones, indeed thus it was written. For these are the true and glorious gifts of men given to all mankind, without thought or worry. For so were all things given to the Sons of Men to use as necessary, but yet indeed man has taken this one step further, and now resides in that place where hunger, hurt, and pain resides each day. For thus, it was given to man, and even so can this greatest responsibility be taken from the arms of man, for his lack of reverence to the nature of the great gifts given each and every day.

Be at peace, and know that the children are indeed being called upon land and sea, and even so does he begin to control himself. For such is the way of God, and all is then not lost, and goes to those loving him, that he might truly taste and know the blessings of God's love and its boundless nature. For so good is the boundless and most wonderful pick made available to man from the vast and magnificent storehouse of God, that exists for mankind's pleasures upon the Earth.

---

[45]   Eat greedily

Be at peace, and know that all is indeed well, and all will be put to rest, if such is the will of mankind. For mankind has the great and wonderful will to live to be the ruler of all things. Be at peace and know that all is delivered in divine order, and with the knowledge of how to hunt and trap the magnificent creatures still known as wild by mankind. This is, of course, the very nature and love of God for his children who daily wonder of what substance and might they are made. For thus, man is made of the same wonders of God, and given this power to rule with equity and honor, if such is his will. Be at peace and know that all is indeed in divine order right now, and all is indeed right with the world.

Let the blessed of the Earth say yes, we are bent upon the same success of all those who follow the ways of God, and come to know of his true and most glorious magnificence.

Peace be unto you, O Sons and Daughters of Mankind! Know that all is indeed well.

Adieu

The Brotherhood

28THSEPTEMBER 2011

Welcome Little One, indeed we see with expression your struggles to do all that is needed and indeed we applaud your attempts to be the conduit for all things, but know indeed choices must be made and prioritized. For indeed the work at hand is of much importance so we thank thee for the focus and following the suggestions of Source. Be aware that the thoughts of those who have followed Source have not always been pure, so we applaud your efforts, Sweet One. Know indeed the love of God for mankind is of this very nature— for in truth its focus is of the same nature, for indeed its focus is the total and absolute saving of the souls of mankind. For indeed mankind has lost its way and the source or life of God's sole focus is to control the rudder of the ship, to turn it around and thus avoid disaster least the ship should smash into the rocks and sink.

Thus, Little One, we see and know that the love of God is that great calming force, which allows man to take the time to look at all options before deciding where to go. The love of God knows all, yet in its truest form, still allows the laws of the Universe to come into being for humankind, and to allow man to be the captain of his own ship.

Why allow mankind to be the captain, when in effect, he is bound to take the ship into the storms of life, and into shallow water, and even steer into the rocks?[46] Simple! O Sons of Men, to allow him to experience the very thing he most craves: the ability to be the decision-maker, and the decision-maker of his fate. For indeed, Mother Father God has given mankind the ultimate gift: that of free choice. The freedom to determine his own fate, and to determine whither[47] he should go. It is this very special gift that allows mankind to take himself headlong into disaster and despair. For, even as Mother Father God is working to keep man safe, even so his free will allows him to continue to make choices of whither he should go.

Thus is the greatest dilemma facing the Sons of Men born, for man was given this choice by God, and thus it sets him apart from all others. Even so is the difficulty of man borne, for in his heart, he has the burning desire to be his own captain, and to find his way and to continue to determine whither he should go.

Know, Dear Ones, that the task of helping the Sons of Men is thus made much more difficult. For even so, the Angel Band cannot make decisions for man, but must find glorious ways to try to point him in the right direction. In the end, know, Dear Ones that the choice must be made by man, and the Angel Band must stand aside at times and see man follow his own guidance, and destroy himself upon the great rocks of life. For indeed, he can run over a great precipice, if such is his desire, and naught can be done, if such is his final desire. Thus, the love of God must likewise be therefore offered to mankind, and

---

46   Problems :disaster

47   To what place: where

man can be reminded of this great gift he possesses. But if he chooses to ignore the help, and the knowledge, and the guidance, he can and is able to ignore all the signs and the pointers in life, which scream to him to move in other directions, and to follow different paths.

Know, Dear Ones, this wonderful gift given to mankind, has been part of his own undoing and destruction, but yet, a gift once given by God, will never be removed. For it is this special ability which sets mankind apart and allows him to make decisions, whether to choose the path of destiny, or to let the storms and distractions of life lead him astray.

All humans enter this life with the equivalent of a guidance system, implanted—if we may use this term—within their heart. It is the knowledge and love of God, which if remembered and followed, will lead him safely through the storms of life, and allow him to gain the very experience to let him flourish and grow in this incarnation. That the storms of life, and the distractions of the physical, should distract and pull man from the path, is the one thing that sets man apart. For even though he can shift from his original direction, and move instead to paths anew, he is still allowed— if such we may say— to continue. For it is his adventure, and likewise, his choice whither he should go. He can make decisions, and choose the path in life that these choices may provide, and any additional growth opportunities for the soul that are evident. But, know Dear Ones, that these same opportunities will likewise provide opportunities for his destruction of self, or others.

Thus, we see and know that the path of free-will will help man to grow. But at the same time, can lead him to self-destruction, and the complete loss of memory of his reason for being upon the Earth:

his majesty, and his gifts as a child of the Most High God, and his right as heir to the kingdom. Thus, the plight of man is born, and he can lead himself to places unknown, and choose to remain in pain and misery even though he is being guided by Spirit. Thus, we can see the answer to that question, "If there is a God, why is there so much misery in the world of man?" Simple, Dear Ones, because man has free will to choose whither he will go, and what he will do, and thus, the trials and tribulations of mankind are born. Why then not save man from himself, is the question? Since in his ignorance, he has forgotten who and what he is. He has no purpose, and is self-destructive. The answer, Dear Ones, is simply this: Man has free will, and as such, can choose his direction in life, and his path in the world. Thus, he is the most valued of all God's children, and has this special ability given to him by God.

Thus Dear Ones, you see the special nature of each incarnation upon the Earth. For only in his incarnation on the Earth, is the soul of man given this opportunity, to experience this great and most glorious temptation in order to grow, and to expand his horizons. For the ability to experience free will, is a most magnificent and wonderful gift. Thus, man has battled within himself for eons, with this wonderful, yet most dangerous of gifts.

Like a protective parent, Mother Father God could shield his children from the pain and suffering of life, by removing this gift. But yet, if that were done, he would lose so much of what makes mankind unique within the Universe. Know, Dear Ones, we say with much exaltation, that mankind has progressed with great and wonderful speed to reach the current levels of development. Looking back, at the development and the great advancement of his soul over eons,[48] we see that indeed, he is learning how to manage the gift of free will, without wishing to slaughter all around him, and to trample upon the weaker brethren.

Know, Dear Ones, the advancement of mankind upon the Earth has been a most glorious and exciting development. For indeed, with this most powerful and wonderful ability, he has moved to higher and higher levels of advancement of soul development; so that he can use his powers for good, if such we can refer to it. For indeed, man can make choices, and choose whither to go with greater insight, and thus, is the advancement possible. For his soul development has increased, and has allowed him to become that which he most desires: A co-creator[49] making his way in the world, and in the light of God.

Thus, we see and know that while man has free choice, if he chooses to remain in the depths of despair, and to be lost in the world in spite of all the Angel Band's efforts to help and guide him, during a particular incarnation, know that even so must it be. For while we weep at the loss of a soul, we must nevertheless allow man to make his choices, and do that which he was programmed to do: MAKE CHOICES, and know the joys of free will. He must know the ability to choose his own way in the world, and if the results of those choices are negative, despite the attempts made to help and guide him and return him to the path. Even so must it be, for man is a co-creator of his own destiny, and must be allowed to choose his own way, and his very experiences upon the Earth.

---

[48]   Existing throughout eternity

[49]   Partnering with God to create what is desired

Know, Dear Ones, that the heart of God, if such we may describe it, bleeds for man: When in choosing, he leaves the path and brings more pain upon himself or his brother. For these are the times that try men's souls, and indeed, the soul of God. For, like a loving parent watching helplessly as the child runs into danger, even so is the heart of God in much pain, when the Sons and Daughters of man are drifting into the darkness and wandering in the desert of despair: Unable to find their way back to Mother Father God, and unable to remember who they are.

Know, Dear Ones, that the free will of man can and is able to lead him to destruction; in spite of the desire of the Mother Father God, to protect him from harm at all times. Be strong, and know, Dear Ones, that this ability, though difficult to control when in the physical body, is what makes man so special upon the Earth. For in having this ability, and being able to choose his path in life, man is still able to find his way back to God, and to choose the path of life and love, instead of negativity, fear, and disillusion. We say, praise be to God, and indeed blessed be the Sons and Daughters of Zion, who make choices to find their way back to God, instead of to be distracted and to remain in the undergrowth[50], and wither, and suffocate, and die. Know, that in spite of the choices made, Mother Father God never abandons his children, and will always welcome them back to the fold; like the 'Prodigal Son,' with thanksgiving and praising. For indeed, he has weathered the storms of life, and returned to spirit, and can once more return to the Earth, if such is his choice to gain more experiences upon the Earth.

---

[50]   Remain ignorant of the truth of God's love and light

Know, Dear Ones, we watch you lovingly, and we hail your attempts to follow the path and to find your way back to Source. Know indeed, we are ever with thee, and God is ever with thee, so be not afraid, but know you are never alone, even in your darkest hour; for the love of God is always available to protect and shield thee, and to be that cloak that will protect thee always. For it is thine to hold, and to keep always, without condition and without cost. Let your light shine therefore, and know that with your gifts, you are able to choose your path. No one makes you choose; you determine whither you go, and what you do, and thus is the life of man special upon the Earth. For you are the Sons and Daughters of God

Let your light shine and know that you walk always in the love and light of God and all is well, if such is your choice. For you indeed are the creators of your life and your experience upon the Earth.

Be the magnificent co-creators you were meant to be! Let your lights shine, and know your magnificence. For you are light, you are spirit, you are love, and you can choose the path you follow in life.

Be at peace, and know that all is well with thee, for you are children of the Most High God, on the path of learning upon the Earth. Open your eyes, and hands, and see the gifts you have been given, and live, live, live, and be joyful. Be at peace with one another, and know all can be well, if such is your desire.

Adieu

Know indeed, that the great and all-encompassing love of God, is such that wise men seek it, and those with power and might deny its existence, in order to keep the masses of people bound in chains. For to be sure, the knowledge of the power of the love of God can cause much changes upon the hearts and minds of the people of the nations of Earth. Know, Sweet Ones, that the knowledge of the love of God has been a closely guarded secret for eons. For in truth, in order to keep the Sons of Men in order, and in line, the love of God has been told to the Children of Men as a prize to be won, and something given only in, and under, special circumstances to the select few: Who, by their piety, and goodness, have earned this most precious of all gifts. Thus, if you, Dear Ones did not follow the rules and the letter of expected behaviors, under no circumstances, could you ever hope to win and/or even ever secure this great prize. Thus, was the beginning of the downfall for the Sons of Men, who now believe that the love of God has to be gained as a favor, and not as an innate right, given to all the Children of Men, by Mother Father God.

Know indeed, that the love of God does not get to the Children of Men only through special favors, but is given to all equally by Mother Father God. Even as the Sons of Men take in oxygen at birth in order to survive. Even so is the love of God given at birth, and in fact is given prior to birth. For all souls are given the love of God in the creative process. For, as they are created, even so is the love of God made, and coded into the very DNA of the soul, if such we can describe it. For in truth, in coming into being, the love of God is an integral part of the fabric of the soul.

Be you happy to know there is no favor to be earned that is selective in nature, which says who will, or will not, receive the love of God. For in truth, it is given in equal measure, to all the Sons of Men and there is no charge exacted, and no price to be paid, in order to receive it. God's love, Dear Ones, is not contingent[51] upon anything. It is given to the Children of Men unconditionally, in equal portions, so that all souls equally gain the same amount, if such we can describe it. For the thought that some souls are more favored above others, or are valued more than others, shows in great abundance the vastness of the misinformation and the failure of the Sons of Men to know and to understand the true nature of God. For in God, all are ONE. All are loved equally, and all are given equal access to God.

There are no differences between the souls of black or white, or among nations. For God sees not nations. God sees not race or color. All are children of God, loved with equal vigor, and loved with equal intensity. For how can God choose one above the other, when all his creations are of equal, and special value to him? All the

---

51   Dependent upon the happening of something else

Sons of Men are loved, and valued, and protected by God. All are made of the same fabric of God. All are **one**, so all are loved in the same way. Know, Sweet Ones, that God knows only that he loves all his children equally. The Sons of Men have made the work, and the heart of God, into a business and have put measures, and limits, and conditions, upon all aspects of God for eons. Thus the common belief that God's love and favor must be won. Know indeed, Dear Ones, that God's love, once given, is never revoked, never denied, never taken away. It is freely given to all, and is part of man, even when he is not in the physical body.

Thus, to say that God will lead me to triumph over my enemies, is a fallacy. For even your enemies are also children of Mother Father God, loved equally by him. There is no favoritism; no special relationship with one nation above another. All that would separate man from the love of God, are those very behaviors he adopts when upon the Earth. But even those behaviors cannot cause man to ever lose the love of God. For it is an integral part of each soul, and thus can never be removed. Man and God are one, and man is ever loved by God, for he is a part of God, so how can he ever be cast away, and left to die in the wilderness of despair?

Know, Dear Ones, that this cannot happen, for it is the thought and belief of the Sons of Men, that when I am favored by God I receive his love. When, and if I am not favored, I lose the love of God. Know, Dear Ones, that you have the love of God, always within you even until the end of time. Know, therefore, that you are chosen of God, ALL are chosen of God, all are special in the heart and love of God. All are valued in the same special way by God. Thus, there is never a need to separate thyself from God for fear of rejection, for there can be no rejection of thee by Mother Father God. For, since all souls are loved equally by God, know Dear Ones, that even so, you are favored by God.

The only way you might consider that you are separate from God is in your forgetfulness; when you remember not who or what you truly are. For indeed, you are the Sons and Daughters of the Most High God, loved and adored by God always, until the end of time. Fret not, and neither consider that you are not special in the eyes of God. For indeed, you are all children of God, loved equally, and given all the gifts and the love of God equally. Be not fearful, Dear Ones, that you can ever lose the love of God, for it is thine forever, without payment or the earning: For you are given it at birth, and it is part of who and what you are always. Even when you doubt that God can love you, know Dear Ones, he can, and does love you all equally. Rich or poor, high or low, in the thoughts of who or what you are; know that in the sharing of the love of God, all are given equal portions, if such we may describe it.

No one group, or race or religion, is given more, or shown more favor with God. For in the eyes of God, if such we may describe it, there are no differences seen among you. For all are the same. Only you, Dear Children, choose to see yourselves as different. For this is part of the human condition, to view self as separate and different, and better or worse, than those around you. Only you, Dear Ones, imagine walls which separate you from your brethren. Only you, Dear Ones, erect barriers to separate you from your brethren. For God sees you all as equal, and God knows you all are equally loved, and adored by him. Open your hearts, O Sons of Men, and see and know the wonderful power of the love of God for mankind. For in loving man, you are all loved. You are all loved and adored with equal fervor, and loved with equal intensity, if such we may describe it. For you are the children of God, and how can he ever select one above the other? Open your hearts, and begin to see there are no differences between you. Why see the things which exist only in your thoughts, and yet are not able to see, and to know the truth of your very beingness; for you are given the true, and most powerful gifts at creation: That being the love of God. When the veil of forgetfulness descends upon you when in human form, you see only the separateness of self, and the thoughts of special selection, one above the other. Thus are the walls of separation erected, and thus, are you kept separate from the family of God, only by your thoughts.

For in truth, these thoughts of separation are the most divisive[52] of all things. For they lead you to believe that you are separate from God, and that you are not in favor with God, and that the only way to redemption is to earn the favor of God. Know, Dear Ones, this is not the truth of God, for God's love is given in equal measure to all upon the Earth, and thus, all are seen as one, regardless of the teachings or beliefs that lead you to believe that only you are chosen, or that you are separated from God.

Know, Dear Ones, try as you might, you can never be separated from the love of God, and try as you might, you can never lose the love of God. You are the children of God and thus can never lose the love of God. How would your Mother Father God ever remove his most precious gift from you? How could he ever deny his children, and

---

[52]   Creating division: tending to divide

remove his love from them? Know, Dear Ones, he cannot remove his love and never would he want to remove it from you: For you are his children, the very heart and soul of God. Know, Dear Ones, that the love of God is that prize that is seen by man as a special thing to be attained, but know indeed, you need not strive to attain it for it is already thine, freely given by God. Know now and forever, that you are loved and adored by God. Regardless of race or religion, regardless of creed or color, you are equally loved. For your Mother Father God sees you all as ONE, and loves you all with equal fervor. You are the children of God, given the most precious gift that God can bestow: his love.

Know therefore, Dear Ones, you are loved by God, from birth to death, and beyond the physical throughout time forever. You are adored by God, even in your darkest hours of forgetfulness, when you would try to separate yourself, or see yourself as not worthy of the love of God. Know, Dear Ones, you are indeed worthy, for you have the love of God, even though you have forgotten this truth. Know that it is thine always, and can never be taken away from you. Hear not thoughts or words, that say that you must win the love of God, for indeed, it is always thine; already a part of you, even though you may not remember it. Know, Dear Ones, it is yours until the end of time.

Let not the words of those who themselves have forgotten that they indeed possess that most valued and precious of all gifts, lead you to believe that you can ever lose the love of God. For indeed, this is an impossible feat, for once given this gift it is thine forever. You are all given the same gift, and thus your charge, Dear Ones, is simply to remember who you are, and to know that you are loved and adored by God: Never shunned[53] or rejected by God, but always loved unconditionally by God. You are the heirs to the throne of God, if such we can describe all the blessings given to you by God. So, step up, remember who you are, and return once more to the fold of God's love. Open your hearts, remember your nature, and know that the love of God is thine eternally, and that none can remove it from thee. No behaviors can cause God ever to remove his love from thee; for you are his children ever loved, ever adored, ever in the arms of God. Remember your nature, remember your heritage, and live the lives of love, peace, happiness, and joy you were meant to live. Know abundance, peace, love, and joy and be the wonderful children of God that you are, deep within you. Put away anger, fear, and ideas of separation from God. For in truth, nothing can ever separate you from the love of God.

Know this, and know true peace. Know this and know true peace within you, for you have already been given the love of God, and you are ever loved; regardless of your thoughts of lack, or unworthiness.

Know you are LOVED, NOW AND FOREVER, by your Mother Father God. This is the truth of your beingness; this is the truth of your essence. This is who you are, for you are spirit, you are light, you are love, and as such, you are ALWAYS loved and adored by God. Remember this, and live. Remember this, and know true peace, true joy, true happiness, true bliss. Fear not that the love is ever taken from you, for it was given to you freely, and will be thine always until the end of time.

---

[53]   To avoid deliberately: to keep away from

For, you yourselves are spirit, you are light, you are LOVE. And love is at the very core of who and what you are; so show love, be love, and know love. This is your only charge upon the Earth, Dear Ones. To BE LOVE, BE PEACE, BE JOY. In this way, and only in this way, you will know the true peace of God within your souls. Let go of thoughts of separation and separateness, and LIVE, LOVE, and be joyful upon the Earth. For you are all ONE, in the love and beingness of God.

Adieu Dear Ones, we will here again with thee.

Adieu

16TH October 2011

Know, indeed, that the love of God for mankind is like a gardener taking care of the flowers in his garden. For as he plants them, there are seeds or tiny seedlings and he watches them grow to become the beautiful flowers or trees they are destined to be. Even so does Mother Father God plant the seeds of love in the hearts and souls of all men, and then watches them grow into the most beautiful of all plants. Let not your hearts grow weary, but know that the plants and flowers will grow into the beautiful expressions of love that they are destined to be. For even as they are tended and nourished by the sun, and the rain, which helps them to grow and flourish, even so does the love of God provide the nourishment and very food for the Sons of Men; so that they can grow and flourish and show their beauty to the world.

Know, Dear Ones, that as the gardener tends his plants and flowers, even so does the God of your being tend you lovingly. For in truth, the gardener would never leave thee unattended with no access to sun or rain, for he knows you would truly wither and die. Even so does the God of your being never leave thee unattended, for in his great and wonderful love for mankind, he would never leave you, for he knows that without his love, you will wither and die. Know, Dear Ones, that even though you may forget that you have the love of God, it is nevertheless there made available to you, so that you may get that which will give you life and allow you to thrive. Know, indeed, that you are thriving and surviving even though you forget your Mother Father God's great love for you… and like the flowers and the plants who know there is something to keep them alive, they lean towards the light: Even so do the Children of Men lean towards the love of God even though in their forgetfulness, they may forget its true value.

Somewhere buried deep within the heart of man is that knowledge that the love of God is that thing that can bring him life. The flowers and the plants know the sun and the rain will give them life, and willingly accept this; but the Children of Men are not so, for in truth they believe they must earn the gift of life. Be like the flowers and the plants, Dear Ones, and accept the love of God and know that it will give you all you need to survive; for it is the very source of life you need in order to survive upon the Earth in happiness, peace, and joy, for this is the way of God. Accept the gift of the love of God as the most natural of all blessings, and know that it would give you life, and allow you to grow to become the most beautiful and strong flower in the garden of God.

Know, Dear Ones, that you need not ask God for the rain and sun, and it is not paid for: Its blessings and gifts are freely given to all without cost. Thus we say, Dear Ones, know that the love of God will be the very lifeline you seek in order to be the flower, and to live and grow in beauty and happiness. Accept the love of God, even as the trees and flowers willingly accept the love and blessings of the gardener; and grow to be the strong, healthy, and beautiful plants that they are. They ask not why the rain or the sun is made available to them. They look not for reasons, but instead accept the blessings and rewards of the rain and sun, and grow. They know innately to lean towards the light in order to gain that which they need to survive.

O Sons of Men! Lean towards the light of God's love, and remember, it is that thing that gives you the very life source you need to survive. A plant never turns away from the light, for it would indeed die. Live not in darkness, and wither and die, Dear Ones, but stretch up into the sunshine of God's love, and know life, know peace, know happiness, know love.

Become the blessings of God that you are. Know the peace, love, happiness, and joy that you are. Watch yourselves shine and glow. See your magnificence and know that you need this love, and above all know that it is given to you freely: And like the rain which falls on all the flowers and trees without unequal intensity for any one flower, even so is the love of God made available to all the Sons of Men with equal shares.

All are given the same water in the garden. All can thrive, as they are all loved and tended by the gardener; for he has planted them, and will be there to tend them and rejoice at their blooming and blossoming, with great joy. Even so is Mother Father God always there to tend to the Sons of Men, for he will never leave thee alone, for he knows that without him, you will wither and die. The gardener knows the needs of the flowers. He asks them not if they need the sun and rain, but instead makes it available to them: for it is their very source of life. Accept the love of God given to you freely, O Sons and Daughters of Man, and live. Grow into the beautiful flowers and trees you are destined to be. For with this love, you will thrive, and grow, and bloom, and can be envied by all who look upon you. For even so are the Sons of Men known in the Universe as the favored of God. For indeed you are, O Children! Look on and know that the garden of God was created and nourished for you; made available to give you all you need to flourish. For when in the physical, you have the love of God to keep you, and to guide you to the sun and rain.

Forget not that you need this to live. Forget not your very nature and needs to survive and turn away from the sun, for indeed when you try to do this, you turn into something other than what you were meant to be. Turn to the light and grow.

Come out of the shade and shy not away from the sun, for even as the plant must accept the rain as it falls on all in the garden in equal amounts, even so is the love of God made available to all that is there in his garden. Your only need should be to bloom and grow. For even as the plant knows of itself that it needs the light and leans innately to it, even so do the Sons of Men search for the love of God: For it is part of the plants' very DNA to lean towards the light. Even so does the heart of the Children of Men lean towards the love of God, even though they know not why. Open your hearts, O Children of Men! And see and know the sunshine and rain of God's love in your lives. Know the peace, happiness, joy, and love of God.

Let not the storms of life turn you away, for they will cause you to wither and die. Be like the flowers that rise up after the storm, and continue to search for the light when the storm has passed. Know always that the Sun and rain will give you life and reach ever for them. Know that you can live, you can thrive. You will grow and flourish. When you accept that the love of God is made available to you and is there freely given to you. Let not thoughts of worthiness come upon you.

The plants never ask if they are worthy to receive the sun or rain. They simply lean towards the light, and take in the benefits of the water and live. Be as accepting as the flowers in the garden. Take on the love of God and live, for this is the very source of life for you. For thus it is given to thee free of cost: For like the gardener, Mother Father God knows what you need and gives it to you without the asking. He knows you need his love to survive and grow, and thus it is there made available for you. Know that you will wither and die if you do not accept this gift of sun and rain. Accept the blessings and the love of God, and grow and thrive, Dear Ones, for even so will you be able to live upon the Earth. This is your only charge: to be successful and happy in the garden of life. Know that the rain and sun will always be there. Accept the benefit of their very blessings, and live and grow. Know that you are beloved of God, and that you will always have this love given to you to nourish and keep thee alive. For as the rain and the sunshine are the very source of life, even so is the love of God that very thing which strengthens and gives thee life.

Plants and flowers do not ask, "What must I give to God in order to get the rain and sun?" They simply take the benefits, and grow and bloom, and blossom and live. They are nurtured, and even so are the children of the Most High God provided for by Mother Father God. Be you like flowers, Dear Ones, and know that God will give you all you need to survive. For the gardener loves his garden, and would never let it wither and die. Thus, he tends it every day and it is nourished. Know therefore, that even so are you loved and nourished by the love of God.

Stretch your roots deep into the ground, and continue to grow and flourish; for even as you do, the sun and rain will continue to be there in abundance to strengthen you and give you all you need to survive upon the Earth. It is this that will keep thee alive and allow you to thrive. You are the chosen of God, the heart of God, O Children: Given all you need to keep you alive. Know therefore that you are not left unattended; for the Angels here on Earth water you daily, and are here to keep and to uphold thee, even when the storms of life would blow you over, and cause you to lean away from the sun. Know that the sun is always there to give you life-giving energy and food, to keep you alive. When the storms of life toss you hither[54], and cause you to bend to the Earth, know that the sunshine will always be there to continue to uphold and to build you up... to strengthen you and to give you all you need. For you are the Sons and Daughters of the Most High God and will ever be protected and cared for. Remember the teachings of our Dear Jesus: "Consider the lilies of the field who toil not, neither do they spin; yet their heavenly father feeds them."[55] Know, even so are you provided for by God, and even

---

[54]   In this or that direction

[55]   Matthew 6:25

so are you provided with all you need. Know that the blessings of God are available to all, free of cost. Know that it is yours, given to you since the dawn of time. Know, like the lilies of the field, it is yours, given free of cost. Accept it and live, O Sons and Daughters of Mankind: For this is your only charge upon the Earth.

Know that God has given you all you need to survive upon the Earth. Accept the love of God and live, for it is the very source of life for you. Know it is thine. Take it into your hearts and live, grow, and thrive. Flowers never question why the rain falls or why they need the sun. They know that it is the source of life for them, so they lean into the sun. Even so, Dear Ones, lean into the sunlight and thrive.

You are precious in the heart of God for you are his children, so take the gifts of life and live, live, live.Take the gift and grow, and be the most magnificent that you can be. For you are the children of God. Be like the flowers and plants, and accept the rain and the sun, and know the love, peace, and joy of God in your hearts: for this will give you the life you seek.

To turn from God is as unnatural as the plant seeking not the rain, and refusing to let its roots take in the very thing that will give it life. Know that you have the need for the love of God in your DNA, and thus you search night and day for it, even though you know not that you seek this. Know, O Children! That you need not search any longer, for it is given to you, and you have it. All you need is already provided by Mother Father God, and even so will you be able to thrive when you partake of this life-giving source.

For you are the flowers in the garden of God, and he has tended, and nurtured, and provided for thee all that you need to survive, and flourish, and grow.

You are loved, O Sons and Daughters of Mankind! Never left unattended, never deserted, and never alone. For Mother Father God knows what you need and is ever there to provide it for you: Without the asking, it is given. Open your hands and hearts and receive the gift of life willingly, for if you refuse it, you will wither and die. Accept the rain and sunshine of God's love and live. Know that you are adored by God, and can never be left alone and unattended... for you are his to protect, his to love, and his to nurture. You are the joy of his heart; you are his children. Be the flowers, be the joy, and live, and bloom, and grow. For you are the chosen of God. You are the love of God. You are the heart of God. Remember the sunshine and live! Remember the nourishment of the rain and live!

Turn not away! Accept who you are! Remember your heritage and live. For you are loved, you are cared for with all the love and caring of the most loving of gardeners. Be like the flowers in the garden and know that Mother Father God will always be there, and is always there providing for you. Remember your abundance! Know that you are given all you need to live and grow in happiness, peace, and joy. Accept it and live: for you are the flowers in the garden of God.

Breathe in the sunshine and the rain, and live, live, live. Accept it, for it will give you life. It is within your nature to accept it, so take it willingly and live. You cannot go against your nature, for to do so is to cause your destruction: For you will wither and die. Drink in the sun and rain, and live, live, live, O children! Know happiness! Know love! Know abundance, strength, peace, and joy. This is your destiny, this is your joy, this is your truth. Accept it and live!

Adieu

Know indeed, that the love of God for mankind is like the wind blowing through the trees; for it gives them the ability to show off their leaves. Know, Dear Ones, that the wind allows the trees to show off their beauty, and as they bend in the wind, it causes them to move and to flow with great ease. Know indeed, the love of God is the sweetest breeze that gently strokes the leaves. It gives them the ability to move to and fro, and to take on wings as though in flight. Lo, indeed the breeze becomes the wind beneath the branches of each and every tree. For, indeed, it is the very source of the strength and happiness for the tree; for it allows it to move, and be as graceful as the very birds that fly through the air.

Know indeed, that the love is so potent, that it becomes the source of life to each leaf; for it can suspend them or indeed cause them to fall from the great branches. Know, Dear Ones, that this love can cause the tree to move fast or slow, to bend this way or that. For indeed, it controls the very life of the tree. Know, Dear Ones that so powerful and strong is the wind in the life of the tree, yet many think not of its power or affect upon the functioning of the tree. Know indeed, that the love of God even so is silently at work in the hearts of men, for it is there, buried deep, so none may know that it is there... but yet, even so it becomes an integral part of the movement and beingness of man. For it can take him this way and that, and cause him to do those unexpected things. For indeed, it is not controlled by man, but has always been buried there. Even so is the love of God buried within the hearts and souls of men... but yet becomes a part of his very beingness, which can allow him to shine, and to be the most beautiful of souls. For, when the storms of life come upon the hearts and souls of mankind, and would move him this way and that, know that the love of God is that great force that causes you to bend even to the floor, but yet lifts thee back to the sky once more.

Know, Dear Ones, that the love of God indeed can give thee wings. For it is that ever powerful force behind thee, that causes thee to do that which is innate to thee. For the tree asks not whither it should go or why it should bend, it simply bends as dictated by the winds that blow. Thus, Dear Ones, we say the love of God is that very driving force which dictates where we go, and what we will do... if the Sons of Men would simply allow it to take them in its current. See the beautiful way that the winds cause the trees to blow and to move with grace and ease; even so does the love of God allow man the freedom to move at will. For it blows, but if the tree struggles, then all would be lost. O ye Children of Men! Struggle not against your very nature, but instead allow the love of God to wash gently over you, and take you with it. Allow it to move you gently, and to take you on its path of beauty and grace; for such is the strength of the wind. For, though it is ever there, it is ever careful to keep thee strong, and to allow thee to shine and to show your true nature.

Let not fear of the storms come upon thee, but know indeed, that the wind will not harm thee. See the love and feel the gentle breeze of the love of God, and know sweet bliss. For like the power of the wind on a hot summer day, it can bring thee relief and cause thee to know great happiness. For such is the power of the wind to cool the soul. For, indeed, it rests in the branches of the tree and causes thee to know sweet bliss.

Thus, even so is the love of God to mankind, for it is that source of bliss and happiness when the storms of life come upon thee, for it can give thee peace. Be not foolish to say that it will destroy me, for indeed the love of God will keep the smallest of leaves and the most delicate of flowers in their place, causing them no harm, for they will not fall unless they are ready to be blown away. For though the tree may bend in the breeze, all the leaves do not fall but holds fast, and goes with the force of the wind and lives. Even so we say live, Dear Ones, live... for the love of God can sustain thee, and keep thee whole. It can allow thee to show your true colors. Think ye of the peacock in the wind opening its feathers, and see how the breeze causes it to become even more beautiful in the eyes of those who behold it. Let your light shine, and let your beautiful plume be seen. Open up your hearts and glow and shine! Show your true colors and be your magnificent selves, for this is your heritage, this is your beingness: to shine and be the wonderful stars you are.

For with the wind beneath your wings, you can fly with ease. Be like the bird that uses the wind to travel the miles it needs to go, using the currents to take it effortlessly on its journey. Use the source of the love of God to help you navigate the storms of life. Flap not your wings all the time, but remember when to allow the wind to take you effortlessly onward. For such is the power of the love of God, that it can take thee ever higher into the skies, ever higher into the beingness of God. For it is the very source of help when you grow weary, if you will but remember that it can help you on your journey: For with it comes relief. For with it come the effortless being, and the effortless journey of man upon the Earth.

Birds and leaves ask not why the winds blow but accept and know that it is there available for them; for they use its strength to survive in the world. Know indeed, Dear Ones, even so can the Sons of Men use the love of God to navigate effortlessly through the valleys and peaks of life.[56] For it is constant, and it is always there available for thee. Know indeed, all that the birds need to fly is given to them. All that they need to take flight is provided, and the wind allows them to move and to travel with ease upon their backs. For it is within the nature of man to take on the mantle,[57] and to accept the love and grace of God; and know that all will be provided for mankind. Let not your heart be troubled, but know like the wind that is always there, even so is the love of God always made available for the Sons of Men.

No price is exacted, and nothing is paid; for it is there made available to one and all. Remember your nature, and soar into the heavens on the winds of the morning; for even so will the love of God allow thee to travel to places beyond your wildest dreams, Dear One. Let the wind take you where it will, and know that no harm will come to

---

[56] Ups and downs of life

[57] Figurative cloak symbolizing preeminence or authority <accepted the *mantle* of leadership

you, for you are loved and protected by the love of God: For you are the children of Mother Father God, and all your needs are supplied, and everything you need is made available, Dear Ones. Look not to say God does not give equal access to the wind to all the leaves; or causes only some of the birds to fly upon the wind. For, indeed, all can fly and all can take the joys of the wind beneath their wings and soar into the heavens.

No one child of God is given more than another. All have access to the same love, and all have the same gifts given before birth: For ye are all the children of God given the same love, the same nurturing, and the same blessings by Mother Father God. This indeed is your strength. This is your gift, to know that you possess all these gifts in equal portions, as the children of the Most High God. For, ye are indeed the most beloved of God.

All men are the beloved of God! No clan, or race, or creed, is given more than another, or is loved more than another! Since God does not differentiate among the birds, or among the leaves on the trees which may come in different shapes, sizes, and colors, know even so the Mother Father God provides for all with equity. For the blessings, and the love of God, are there made available for all men. It is thine to take and to be strong: To take and to know happiness, love, and peace, if such is your desire. Your only charge, Dear Ones, is to take that which is freely given and come to know true happiness. For like the birds of the air, you can soar into the heavens on the wings of the morning, with the warm breezes of God's love to carry you onwards... and to lift thee up when tiredness would overcome thee. Let the Mother Father God be the winds beneath you, Dear

Ones, and come to know the true happiness of God. For with little effort, you can soar into the heavens and be the master of all you survey. For such is the love of God for mankind, that you have all you need freely given by God. Take it, O Sons and Daughters of Mankind, and live! Move upon the face of the Earth and have your beingness in God. For this is your destiny. This is your life. This is your rescue. For you are spirit, you are light, you are love. You are the children of God, loved and adored by your Mother Father God.

Be not afraid to soar! Know that the wind is ever there to take thee higher into the heavens, if such is your desire. Take that which is freely given, and know true peace and happiness, Dear Ones; for this is your nature. This is your destiny. This is your path, for ye are the children of God. Soar, soar, soar into the heavens at will and know true peace, true bliss, and true happiness. This is your charge, this is your destiny; this is your path to know true happiness, Dear Ones. Accept the blessings and the gifts of your Mother Father God, and live, live, live. For you are the chosen: The beloved Sons and Daughters of God. Know the true happiness and peace of God and live, Dear Ones.

Adieu

14ᵀᴴ NOVEMBER 2011

Know indeed, that the love of God is like the very flower that brings happiness to the sight of men in the viewing of it. For indeed, it produces a wonderful bud, and indeed even so is the essence, which is given by the flower. For behold, it pleases the senses of man and in giving so much pleasure, allows man to see and taste new and wonderful things. Thus, even so is the love of God, for indeed it is the essence of the very sight and smell of everything wonderful for the Sons of Men. For it gives much pleasure to the sense of man, and allows him to see and know all that is truly best upon the Earth. For it is provided to mankind through the same senses of the eyes and the smell; yet it comes in so many different hues and colors. It comes in different sizes and varying intensity, yet it still manages to touch the same senses.

Look on and know, Dear Ones, that the love of God is all that is beautiful upon the Earth, for it provides the best to the Sons of Men... for indeed, it comes to him in different forms, yet it reaches the senses of all the Children of Men. For indeed, no two flowers are exactly alike when created by Mother Father God, but yet they affect the senses of man in the same way. For visually, the eyes are stunned by them and then in the smelling they are likewise such powerful delights for mankind; yet even so are the Sons of Men upon the Earth affected by the love of God. For indeed, we know that all men see and know each flower and each smell, but is affected not in the same way. Look on and know that the love of God is that awe-inspiring thing which is given to mankind but is appreciated in very different ways by each child upon the Earth. For in the seeing and the appreciation of the love of God, each man is affected by it in such different ways. Know indeed, that the love of God is not seen and appreciated by all men in the same way, for each man does not notice the great beauty of a flower, and stop to marvel at its wonder and the glorious and stunning qualities it contains.

Know indeed, Dear Ones, that the love of God is that very thing which some men see and know by sight, and stop in awe to sing and to say of the bountiful love of God for mankind; while others move along from day to day, oblivious of its great and wonderful beauty. Know indeed, Dear Ones, even so daily we see and know most men are blind to the powers of the love of God in their lives, for indeed they know not that it exists in the kingdom of men. Thus, they wander upon the Earth, oblivious of the fact that their Heavenly Father has given them all the blessings they will ever need to survive upon the Earth.

Know indeed, Dear Ones, your eyes are blinded, for even though they are open you see not, neither do you taste the beauty of all that is there, made available to you through the bounty, and gracious love, and gifts of Mother Father God. Know, Dear Ones, that this most beautiful gift, though given to all is only truly recognized, and admired, and appreciated by some. Why then, O Children, do not all of the Sons and Daughters of Mankind openly see and know the true bounty of God? Know, Dear Ones, it is the veil of forgetfulness which is cast upon mankind when they are upon the Earth which causes them to forget what the love of God is, or how beautiful and wonderful it can be. For thus, it is made available to all but mankind looks on and sees it not. For they wander daily upon the Earth, taking in all the sights and sounds, yet manage to miss all these beautiful ways in which Mother Father God is making wonderful provision for them.

For in truth, they see it not, and think they are in solitude: For they see not the handiwork of God in their lives. They know not of the great blessings daily heaped upon them since the dawn of time; and they take not the time to smell the roses or to fully appreciate all the bountiful harvest of precious gifts, given to mankind in so many different shapes and sizes. For in truth, even as the flowers are presented in so many glorious colors, and hues, and fragrances, even so is the love of mankind shown to man by Mother Father God. For it is there made available, free of cost to all, and is provided in so many different ways; yet it goes unnoticed by man for indeed, the distractions of the Earth cause him to forget his way, and he is blinded to all that truly exists within his environment. For his eyes are open, yet he sees not the many gifts of God given to him. His only task is to take the time to stop and drink it in. For in all the myriad of ways that God provides for men, even so are there different kinds of flowers upon the Earth, and each one provides something so special to those who take the time to stop and drink in the glory and wonder of the love of God: For it is that most powerful and intoxicating of all things, which is there made available for the Sons of Men. For indeed, it is the very life of God given to mankind in the shape and form of all the gifts mankind is given by his parent, Mother Father God.

Know, Dear Ones, that the love of God is there. It is indescribably wonderful when seen and appreciated in all its glory, but yet so many of the Children of Men see and know it not. For it can be as intoxicating as the flower of the poppy, which man has utilized to cause himself such experiences. Look on and know, Dear Ones, that the love of God can cause man to reach the same heights, when he is aware of how much he is loved and adored by God. For in truth, the full knowledge of the vastness and the great intensity of the love of God for mankind, ever causes man to enter into that very state of euphoria[58]; as though he is subjected to the introduction of foreign substances into his body. Thus can be the effect of the love of God on the hearts and souls of mankind, for it is the only drug that would be needed. For indeed it would awaken the senses, and bring such euphoric dreams and visions that no drug known to man can ever allow man to reach and experience those feelings. For in truth, it is the highest of highs, and the most magnificent of all feelings. For the great and most powerful love of God will and can allow mankind to fill the very void that lives within his soul; for it is that which can cause him to know no wants or desires. For it is indeed the ultimate in all satisfaction for mankind, for it will be the joy that reaches the depths of the very heart and soul of man.

---

[58]   A feeling of great happiness or well-being

Open your eyes, O Sons of Men! And see and taste the blessings of God, given to you in so many different forms upon the Earth; for indeed it is a feast for the eyes and the nostril of man: For not only can you take it in with one sense but with much more. Think, Dear Ones, of the healing nature of the flowers upon the Earth, for indeed they are not only to be viewed as beautiful gifts from God, but know indeed that they can even so heal the physical body of man when ingested. Know, Dear Ones, the love of God is the very food for the soul of man, for it can relieve all wants and needs, and cause the heart and soul of man to know true peace: That peace which cannot be achieved by the accumulation of wealth, or the material things found upon the Earth, for naught can provide the Sons of Men with that which he can acquire only from Mother Father God: For indeed, God is the only one able to provide that gift to mankind.

Indeed, even though it has been provided, yet still the Sons of Men fail to recognize its brilliance, and its great works; for his eyes are not open and his senses are not yet alerted to the beauty and majesty of all that he truly is, or the wonder of the gifts given to him by his Mother Father God.

Know, Dear Ones, that the love of God is thine to have and to hold... to appreciate and to drink in by opening up your eyes, and taking in the beauty that is evident all around you. Know indeed, all is given freely; all is there made available to you, free of cost, so know that it is yours this day and always. Open your eyes, and see and taste the beauty and the healing qualities of the gifts of God; given freely to all men upon the Earth. For the Sons of Men walk daily in the garden of God's love, yet see not the great variety of gifts given to him to bring him peace, happiness, love, and joy: For he walks with eyes closed.

Open your eyes, O Children of Men! And see all the beauty that is around you, given freely by God. Drink in the visual beauty, and smell the blossoms. For therein lays your salvation; therein lays your rescue. For it can set you free from the pains you feel, and the loneliness you experience; for you think you are alone. Know ye not that you are never alone, and never forgotten? For such is your importance to God, that you can never be forgotten: Never ever left alone, never forsaken, for you are loved by God, your Father and Mother. Be you ever alert, Dear Ones, and take off the veil of forgetfulness, and see and appreciate all that is truly around you; for you are the most beloved children of God, given all you need.

Like the flowers given to you, even so do you come in many shapes, sizes, and colors upon the Earth, but know that all are loved and adored by God, for you are the flowers in his garden, and he loves and cares for you. Daily tending to your needs, so that you can continue to grow and to bloom, and be the most beautiful of all things.

For, indeed, you are his children, and he has loved you since the dawn of time. Remove the veil, and see and know your perfection. See and know your true magnificence. See and know your special blessings; for you are fed and watered in the garden of God, and given all you will ever need to thrive and grow. For even so is the love of God the very food and the fertilizer, that will cause mankind to grow even sturdier, and allow him to reach to greater heights. For this is the strength of the power of the love of God for mankind.

Know, Dear Ones, that you are the blessed, the Sons and Daughters of the Mother Father God. Be your magnificent selves, and bloom and grow in the garden. Be the flowers, and let all see and know your true fragrance, for it will enrapture the soul, and cause you to enrapture the hearts of all who come upon you: For such will be the power you have upon those who come into your viewing, that they will experience your joy, your happiness, your peace, and your tranquility. For such is the magnificent power of the effect of the love of God, upon all those who are able to truly appreciate, and to become aware of all the bounty of God, given freely to all mankind. Open your eyes and your hearts, O Children of Men! And see and know the true and most beloved peace and joy of God. For therein lies your rescue, therein lies your peace, and the eternal joy of God.

Know that all will indeed be well with thee, when you can see and know that you are truly a flower in the garden of God: Loved, and tended, and nurtured by your Mother Father God, so that all may come to see and know the true and wonderful beauty that you are. Not just by sight, but also deep within you, for a flower has so many different qualities that makes it special, and even so are all the special aspects of all the Children of Men, nurtured and adored by God.

Open up yourselves! Open your hands like petals in the morning sun, and taste the true blessings of God, and know true happiness, true peace, and the true joys of God. For such is the bounty of God given to you, O Sons and Daughters of Mankind that it is the life-sustaining source; that is the very heart and soul of God. For you are the children of God given all you need. You are the joy, the hope, and the love of God. Shine like the stars you are, and open your petals to the rays of God's love; and become your magnificent selves for you are the peace, the hope, the joy, and the love of God. Open your petals to the sun, and bloom and become that which you were meant to be; for you are a flower in the garden of God, and you can no longer live as though you are a weed to be trodden under foot. You are a flower to be nurtured and adored; to show your true beauty, and to be that most beloved of God that you have been since the dawn of time. For this is your nature, this is your charge; so live and be who you are meant to be. For you are the children of God, so live, live, live, and bloom in all your splendor; and be adored by all. For you are truly magnificent, and will always be the favored of God.

For even as God attends to your every need, even so does the gardener attend to all the flowers in his garden; providing them with the food, and the nourishing rain and sunshine that is needed.

No flower pays for the water or the food, or the sunshine, and even so does God provide for the Sons of Men: For it is his joy to nourish you, and to give you all that you ever need, so that you might become the beautiful and most magnificent flowers in the garden of God. Open your leaves to the morning sun, and know the happiness and the true bliss of God. Remember your nature, and know once more the true peace of God; for you are the Sons and Daughters, of God, loved and adored by Mother Father God for all eternity. Open your petals and bloom and grow! Open your petals and live, for you are the chosen, the nurtured, the loved of God. Open your petals and be your magnificent selves; for you provide the perfume for the joys of God. Open your petals, and feel the warmth of the love of God fall gently upon you every day of your lives; for you are the love of his heart, the joy of the heart and soul of God.

Adieu

24TH JANUARY 2012

Arise, O Daughter of Zion, and face the morn! For this is the day that the Lord has made, so let us truly rejoice in it and be glad, and give thanks for the love of God for humanity. Know indeed, Dear Ones, that the love of God for man is eternal in scope, and everlasting in its intensity. Know also, Dear Ones, that nothing can remove it, for it is given in love and is eternally there made available for the Sons of Men. Know also that naught that is done by man can ever cause this love to be lost or removed, for it is thine forever. Know indeed, that the Lord, the giver of all things since the dawn of time, cannot and will not ever remove his love and devotion from the Sons of Men. Know indeed, Dear Ones, that you are all that exists in the mind of God when in his heart if such we can describe it, he thinks of those who are most in his thoughts and in his heart.

For truly, the Sons of Men are the pride and joy of God. For in his wisdom, he knows only joy and gladness; for in truth the Children of Men are the heart and soul of God: For your pains are his pains and your joys are his joys. Your suffering is his pain, for the love is so intense and unabated[59]that he feels the pain of your heart. Know therefore, that this love, so awe-inspiring, causes your Mother Father God to be there unceasing, and to be with thee forever; ever beside thee to guide and to protect thee. Know, Dear Ones, that this love causes him never to harm thee or to be the cause of any harm or punishment to come upon thee. For in truth, this God who is your Mother Father God cannot harm thee, for he sees thee only as children playing in the rain, who lose sight of all else and themselves, and cannot go home when it is time. For they are overjoyed with happiness, and then find they are wet, so they fear the return home for they wonder what their parent will say.

Know, Dear Ones, that the love God holds for man, is such that he cannot scold thee and will not punish thee, because in his heart, he knows that as a child you were swept up in the moment and have lost yourselves. Like a child, you thought only of the moment, and the great desire to dance and sing and frolic. Now when the time draws near and it is time to return home, you fret and worry, for you feel you have done wrong, and fear the retribution of your parents. For indeed, you feel that you must be punished, for you have not listened to the warnings of old, and the tales of those who have danced in the rain;[60] so you fear the wrath of your parent.

Know, Dear Ones, that naught that you do can cause the love of God to be removed from thee. Naught that you do, or say, or think, can cause the love of God to be removed, and cause you to be punished or deserted by Mother Father God. For you are indeed the heart of

---

[59] Being at full strength or force: not diminished in strength

[60] Gone against the wishes of their parents

God, the love of God, and as such he will never leave thee or forsake thee. Never turn his back upon thee, if such we can describe it, for indeed, God has no back or front or side, for he is SPIRIT and only Spirit.

Know indeed, that while the human mind ascribes these physical attributes to God—for this is how the mind can see or imagine God, only in human terms with human attributes— know indeed, they do not describe God or indeed say anything of who or what God is.

For God is spirit, he is light; he is LOVE, as is man: For man is made by God, but the essence of man is spirit. The spirit is the eternal beingness of man which is eternal. It cannot die, cannot be killed, and lives ever with God. For man only knows of the physical being he sees in the mirror, but know, Dear Ones, this is only the shell or the outer covering of man, which comes in different shapes and sizes, different colors, different hues, and yet below the surface, are all ONE.

Like the apples on a tree, which are all the same, even so are the Sons of Men; for you are made of the same fabric of God. You are all SPIRIT, so God sees and knows only this spiritual being, and not that vestige[61] that is seen when you look upon the mirror: For while man sees the exterior when he sees himself, know indeed that God sees only the spirit that is man. Thus, you are all the same in the eyes of God.

Know, Dear Ones, that the great love of God allows man to be upon

---

[61]   A visible trace, evidence, or sign of something that once existed but exists or appears no more

the Earth, and allows him to come into each incarnation to see and know the joys of life in a physical body, and to taste and enjoy those things that can only be tasted and enjoyed in the physical body. For being spirit in all your beingness, you long to know what other experiences are possible in the Universe.

Know, Dear Ones, that you are here upon the Earth to learn and to grow in a multitude of ways…to learn and know the joy and the sadness of the human condition, to know the joy and the sadness of love and loss, and the joys and the sadness of the human condition and the very heart of man. For in his wisdom, man, when in physical form, has the gift of free will which allows him to determine whither he will go and what he will do. This greatest of all gifts is that thing which has served to separate mankind from all others, for indeed it allows you to choose what you will do. This gift so precious, has also been the very cause of much of man's pain when in physical form; for it is this very thing which allows him to wander the Earth like a headstrong child and take what he will. He can choose his way and do what pleases him, for he is ever able to make choices.

Know, Dear Ones that the choices made by man has caused great wars and famine…has caused great destruction and hatred upon the Earth, for in being in the physical, he forgets that he is spirit—as he must— and like someone stripped of all true memory of who and what he is, he wanders the Earth in search of himself, trying to remember his identity and his purpose here upon the Earth.

He has forgotten his true nature, for the distractions of the earthly life would take away all memory of the things he knew when in spirit, where like the nature of God, he is love and only love. Thus, with the cloak of the human condition upon him, all else is forgotten and he is lost to his spiritual existence, and all that he was. For now, his only desires are to find and to know pleasures and things of the flesh that would, indeed, give him the experiences he sought when in spirit.

Know, Dear Ones, that when in the physical, you lose your way and forget the things of God, which were second nature to you when in spirit. For now, you hurt and kill your brethren. You take from the weak, and look not to those in need, and you think only of self and the things that bring you pleasure.

Know, Dear Ones, that these distractions are only temporary, and cannot ever fill the great void within your heart, for you find that there is something missing from your life, your beingness, and your heart. For it is unknown to you, yet deep within, you know there is something that can give you peace, so you search tirelessly for this thing. Know, Dear Ones, that the very thing you search for, you already have; for it is the love of God which fills thee up, and causes you to be satisfied so that you search no more. You need search no more for trinkets and toys to fill your heart and give you joy, for they cannot. For indeed, what you search for is something so wonderful and awe-inspiring, that it cannot be described in words.

It cannot be seen or touched or tasted or felt by any of the senses of man, for it is the love that created thee. It is the eternal and everlasting love of God which gives thee the joys, the peace, and the contentment, deep within the soul. It is this love of God which indeed makes thee whole; the realization of which brings man to the place of knowing within himself that says, "I am home. I am home in the love and peace of God."

Know, Dear Ones, that search as you might upon the Earth, nothing tangible can ever be found that can give thee this peace and inner joy that is found in the love of God. Nothing can give you the happiness that is experienced, when you come once more to know the love and peace of God. For in truth, there is nothing that is comparable, that you can experience upon the Earth that is greater than the peace and love of God. Know, Dear Ones, the spirit which is who and what you truly are, knows the magnitude of this love and it is part of the beingness of each of you. For you are love, you are light, and you are spirit. Yet, the darkness[62] that is entered when in the physical body, removes all these memories from your mind, and you would forget your true nature as a love being, and turn upon your brethren.

Your mission upon the Earth, when in physical form, is to learn, Dear Ones, and to come to know the true peace, love, and joy once more. This same peace, love, and joy that you knew in spirit, is lost to you when upon the Earth, you think…but know always, that it is possible to attain this great peace, love, and happiness—this same bliss and joy you knew before— the faint traces of which remain with you when in the physical. And so you search and search, looking for yourself, looking for your former self, your former joy, and know not what you have lost: For in truth, you think you are alone. You think you are forgotten, and you live in a place of forgetfulness and pain, trying to find your way back to the love, peace, and joy you knew in spirit. You know not these things when in spirit, for you have forgotten all you knew, but now you search for meaning; you search for happiness, peace, love, and joy, and wander upon the Earth. You find it not and know not why. For no amount of fame or fortune can

---

[62] Loss of memory of the things of God

give you these things, Dear Ones, for your heart cries out for one thing only, and that is the love and peace of God you knew when you were cradled in the arms of God, when in spirit.

Your longing cannot be satisfied. Like a man lost in the desert, you thirst forever. Forever in search of the water that will give you life. You remember not that you have the very thing you need within your heart and soul, and so you die (spiritually) without finding it. Listen! O Sons of Men! And know once more your true identity, for you are all children of a loving God. You are searching for that which you think is lost, but know, Dear Ones, naught is lost, for it has always been and will always be thine.

Know that this love will ease your pain, and quench your thirst, for it is all you need to fill your soul with joy. It is all you need to bring you the joys you knew once more into your lives. See and know, Dear Ones, that only you bring pain and suffering upon yourself, for you forget your destiny and your heritage. You forget your true nature, and you forget the nature of God. For now on Earth you would attribute war and famine and pestilence[63] to God. Know, Dear Ones, these are not the things of God, for God cannot harm his children... only man can do that. For in truth, you have taken it upon yourselves to be divisive and to cause hurt and pain upon your brethren. To see only the differences between you, instead of the similarities that exist: To see want, and insufficiency, and lack, instead of abundance and plenty upon the Earth.

---

[63] Any contagious and malignant disease that is epidemic and mortal: morally evil or destructive

You have killed your brethren, abandoned those in need, and cared only for self when all about you suffer... and still claimed that you were creatures of love! Know, Dear Ones, that men can say this whilst they cause others to know pain and lack and suffering. Whilst you live in splendor, others beg at the table of plenty, like dogs waiting for scraps of food. Open your hearts, Dear Ones, and know that you are brothers and sisters, all children of the same one and only God; all loved and given the same blessings by God. All endowed with the same gift of love, even before you were born. For this great love is your heritage, your birthright, and your gift from God.

Look you not outside yourself and think that the answer lies there, for indeed it lives only within your heart and soul. Search within you, Dear Ones, and let go of the pain, and fear, and hopelessness, and you will find the true peace, blessings, and love of God. Know, Dear Ones, this is your salvation, this is your hope, this is your purpose in life; for you come into this life to be love, to teach love, and to know love.

That you forget this when you come upon the Earth is the most difficult part of being in human form, for now you must endeavor to find your way home, even though the storms of life would toss you this way and that. You cannot be at peace and know true happiness, until you return once more to find that place of knowing, deep within you, and can come once more to rest in the love and peace of God. For you are spirit, you are light, you are love, thus you search for all those things that will help you to remember and give you the peace, happiness, love, and joy you want to experience once more. Know, Dear Ones, that you must remember your true selves and live; for without this memory, you strive always and will know no peace, no true joy, and you will ever search for that which you know is lost... even though you know not for what you search.

Know, Dear Ones, that your Mother Father God is ever beside thee, ever with thee, holding you up; for every soul is precious, and every soul is loved unconditionally by God. And nothing you can do can ever take away the love of God from you, for you are loved and adored by God. Even though you may forget God, and forget that you are loved, know indeed, Dear Ones, that his love for you is eternal and he will ever be beside thee as you travel upon the road of life.

Be at peace and know that the love of God can and will lead you back to God; for you need no intercession between you and God, for you are his children. So you can always turn to him and know that he will ever be there to guide you, to love you, and to uphold thee. These truths are given to you this day, that you might remember your true selves, and live in happiness, peace, love, and harmony upon the Earth.

Adieu, Dear Ones! Know that your Mother Father God is ever with thee, and show love and mercy to those around you, and know once more the love of God, which is thine. May the light and love, which is your Mother Father God, ever continue to live in your heart as you walk the roads of life. May you continue to know his peace, and remember his great love for you!

Adieu

The Brotherhood

Know indeed, that the love of God for mankind is daily seen in all the blessings heaped upon the Sons of Men. Know indeed, Dear Ones, that this great and most blessed gift is seen in all the magnificence and splendor of the joys of nature. For indeed this is one of the greatest of all blessings heaped upon the Sons of Men. Know indeed, Dear Ones, that the Children of Men are the chosen of God, thus how fitting is it that this most treasured of all blessing is heaped upon the Sons of Men. Know indeed, that the Children of Men see and know not all the many blessings which are daily provided for them by Mother Father God; for in truth, they see not with the eyes of the "Ancient Ones," who knew and daily recognized that the blessings seen upon Mother Earth were indeed gifts from God. Know indeed, Dear Ones, that the Children of Men take these things in stride, and see them not, for they look not to the beauty around them; for the blindness and the fog would keep them blinded. Thus, they see not the beauty of the rose or the trees, which provides food for the Children of Men. They look not up, or see not the golden boughs of the trees, which stand in stately honor and blow gently in the breeze.

Know, Dear Ones, that the Children of Men are blinded to the beauty that surrounds them, and thus they destroy and pillage the land; for indeed their only thoughts are of the acquisition of the material things of life that are available upon the Earth. They see not the beauty of the skies or the oceans, or even the wonderful colors that are painted each day in nature. All thoughts center only on the distractions of the Earth and they see not, neither do they recognize the true bounty of Mother Father God. For in truth, all eyes are cast down.

Open your eyes, we say! O Sons and Daughters of Mankind, and see and taste the beauty that is Mother Earth! Open your eyes, which are the windows to your very soul, and see and know the blessings and riches of God! Know indeed, Dear Ones, that the things of God that are there made available for thee upon the Earth, are put there for you to enjoy. Know, Dear Ones, that the things of God are all gifts from your Mother Father given to show you the great depths to which you are loved. Given to show you the greatness of the Earth, and the true abundance that is her treasure and her prize, given to the Sons of Men. Know indeed, Dear Ones, that the Sons of Men, who see and know not the blessings of Mother Father God, are indeed blinded to all the glory and goodness, which is indeed the blessing of Mother Father God.

Know Dear Ones, until you open your eyes and see and know how greatly you are loved, you cannot fully appreciate the love that is given to you daily from Mother Father God; for indeed you cannot value these gifts, for you see them not.

All that is of worth in the eyes of men are the things of the physical world, to which a price has been affixed, and there is naught that is more valuable in the eyes of men, than the earthly value placed on these gifts. Know, Dear Ones, that the gifts of nature are without price, and are amongst the most valuable of all gifts placed upon the Earth for the Sons of Men to enjoy. For in truth, where naught exists but the things of men, there can no true joys exist. For the gifts of the Mother Father God are without equal, and are the rarest of all gems. For in truth, they cannot be duplicated or perfected by man, for they come directly from the love source, which is Mother Father God, and as such are without equal.

Know, Dear Ones, that these special and most wonderful gifts are given from the heart of God to the Sons of Men, and naught can be equaled; for they are truly the most valuable gifts given by Mother Father God.

Know, Dear Ones, they are truly without equal, for they are unique, rare, and wonderful gifts which light up the morning sky, and bring happiness and love into the hearts of men when they are ever seen and appreciated. Know indeed, Dear Ones, that the Children of Men must open their eyes and hold up their heads to feel the glow and warmth of the sun, and to see and know the beauty that is a snowflake, and the gentleness of the rain falling softly upon the lips and hearts of men. Know indeed, Dear Ones, that the Children of Men daily pass these treasures, but see them not, neither do they marvel at the wonder, which is nature. For in truth, the bond of man to the Earth has been established since the dawn of time, and until man remembers this connection to Mother Earth, and can drink in the beauty of a blade of grass, and taste the nectar of the flowers, he cannot come to truly know and understand the nature and love of God. For in truth, only a loving and benevolent parent would provide such gifts for his children. Only a loving parent would create such blessings and such beauty, and place them in plain sight for his ungrateful children.

Know, Dear Ones, that the love of God for man is such that all these gifts are daily provided, but no recognition is there seen in the eyes or the hearts of men. For indeed, they are like children blinded at birth, who can see and know not those things of beauty that are scattered around about them.

For how in truth can you describe the beauty to one whose eyes are blind, and whose senses are dulled? How can you show and share the beauty that is Mother Earth, to those who are blind and deaf to all around them? For they see and hear not. They taste not, and they feel not; for all the senses are dulled and they rush to and fro, looking for that which will bring them happiness, peace, and joy.

Open your eyes, O Sons of Men! And see and know the truth that is Mother Father God! See and know the love that is daily presented to thee! See and know the glorious gifts strewn at your feet! Open your eyes, and remove the fog from your face, and see and know the beauty that is here made available for thee! For in truth you are blind to all that is given to thee! You search for beauty, but lo, it is in front of thee, yet you see it not. For this is your curse, O Sons of Men, to walk the Earth and live with this beauty but to see and know it not! For indeed, your eyes are cast down, and your pain is so great, you cannot come to know the light and beauty that is everywhere around thee.

For if you could but see and drink in this beauty, you would stand in awe and amazement, and sing the praises of Mother Nature each and every day. Know indeed, Dear Ones, that your eyes are chained shut, and your hearts are hardened so that naught stirs thee. For you are focused on the things of the flesh, and so you see not the gifts of Mother Father God, given to thee from the bosom of Mother Earth. Know, Dear Ones, that the love that is here expressed for thee is beyond measure, for it cannot be compared to naught upon the Earth. For indeed, the treasure which is Mother Earth is seen not, and is destroyed by the Sons of Men. For they see and know not, that in destroying Mother Earth, they destroy themselves. They take away the life source that is the very gift of God from themselves; they destroy all around them, and have naught left.

They cut down and burrow into the ground, robbing all the treasures found within. Let go of the greed, Dear Ones! We say, release your hold on the ways of destruction and return once more to reverence and the celebration of Mother Earth, for therein lies your refuge and your peace. Therein lays your hope, and the happiness that is mankind. Be at peace, Dear Ones, and know that the life you save will be your own, and the love you gain will indeed bring you great peace; for these are indeed the gifts of God given to you in abundance.

Stop, Dear Ones, and smell the glorious fragrances that are Mother Earth! The glorious colors and the array of all that is daily presented for thee: For even so, all is given to thee from Mother Father God to allow you to taste, and to enjoy, and bask in the blessings and love, which is God. Know indeed, Dear Ones, that these things are given to thee daily, free of cost but you see or accept them not.

Leave the Earth as you find it, Dear Ones, and replenish that which is old and withered. Plant and reap and sow in due season, Dear Ones, and thank the Earth with reverence and gratitude; for even so will she continue to be abundant, and to provide thee with more blessings each day.

Be you alert and aware, and stare and look up at the night sky and see the wonders which are God… the gifts that are God, and the bounty that is God. For to live without love and the joys of Mother Earth, is not to live at all, Dear Ones! For the nature and beingness of God can be seen in the stars, the ocean, the flowers, the trees, the birds, and all the gifts of nature. To live without these joys is not to live at all! For when you are bereft[64] of eyesight and love and appreciation, you live not, Dear Ones. Know indeed that you are children of the Most High God, provided with a life in this garden, which is Mother Earth… so take, enjoy, and be glad, for this is your hope. This is your joy, your peace, and your happiness.

Be ye aware of all that is round about thee, and come to know the beauty, love, peace, and joy which can be thine. For these are the gifts of Mother Father God, given for thee so that you might know of the depths of the love of God for his children here upon the Earth. Be at peace and know that the Sons of Men can and must come to know the many blessings of Mother Father God! For, until man can come to know these gifts, he cannot yet comprehend the magnitude of the love of God for the Children of Men.

Adieu, Dear Ones! Rest always in the love and peace, which is Mother Father God.

Adieu

---

[64] Deprived : Loss: refuge lacking something needed or desirable, wanted, or expected

13ᵀᴴ March 2012

Know indeed, that the love of God for the Children of Men is one from the ages, crafted and cemented in all that is most holy, for the Sons of Men. Know indeed, Dear Ones, that the love of God carries for mankind that great and awe-inspiring love that is Mother Father God. For in truth, it allows the Sons of Men to come closely into the bosom of Mother Father God and to taste first-hand all that is most blessed in the ways of God. Know indeed, Dear Ones, the Sons of Men are in need of nothing; for all their wants are supplied, and they are always held and cradled in the arms of God. Know, Dear Ones that the love of God is the very glue that cements and bonds the Universe. For it is this most sacred of all things which allows mankind a glimpse into the very heart and soul of God. For in expressing and providing all that is needed for mankind, God shows the depths of his love, devotion, and support for his children. For indeed, he is the provider and the one who holds, supports, and protects his children.

God is all that is needed by the Children of Men, for in truth, with God naught else is necessary. Know indeed, Dear Ones, that the Children of Men have no need to ever fear lack or separation, for in truth whether he is aware of it or not, all his needs are ever met by his Mother Father God. Know indeed, Dear Ones, that the love of God can take mankind to the heights of the tallest pinnacles, or to the very crest of the Golden Moons: For indeed, it is the very source of life for mankind. Know indeed, that man is ever held and supported in the loving arms of God, and he is ever protected and cared for by his most beloved parent.

Know indeed, Dear Ones, that the love which is God, comes from the wellspring[65]of creation and was given to mankind, never to be removed. Know indeed, Dear Ones, that the Children of Men cannot escape from the love of God, even when they would deny his very existence. Know, Dear Ones, that this love is the most powerful of all known desires and emotions: For in truth, it is all there is, and will always be made available to the Sons of Men. Know indeed, Dear Ones, that the Sons of Men are naught without God's love, but with it, he is all there is! He is the very source of love and light upon the Earth, and he is the joy of all that is sacred. Know indeed, that the love of God for mankind is daily shown in so many different ways. Be not dismayed to know, Dear Ones, that it is the very essence of life. It is the all-powerful, the all-encompassing thing, which daily causes man to awaken to his potential… and to see those things which will bring him peace, love, and joy whilst here upon the Earth.

Know indeed, that this love will never fade and will never diminish. For in truth, it grows, rather than fades, with the passage of time. For when man looks in the mirror, and can see the reflection is indeed the face of God staring back at him, he is indeed at the

---

[65]   Fountain: source of continual supply

most sacred of all places in his life. For in recognizing that the face staring back at him is indeed the face of God, he is indeed charged to take on new and exciting adventures. For in recognizing it, he sees, knows, and begins once more to know that the reflection in the mirror is indeed the face of God. Thus, he comes to know his own path in life.

For when he recognizes what has been accomplished, he is destined to greatness, and is ready to take his rightful place. For in recognition of the self, he can now look to ways to see and know the gifts of God, given to mankind.

Know indeed, Dear Ones, that the love of God can become your shelter whenever needed, and your compass. For all he needs has been supplied, and all his nature craves is likewise presented there for his pleasure. Know indeed, that the love of God is all that is needed if man is to survive upon the Earth. Know indeed, it is the wind beneath your wings, and the very sails of the boat. It is the anchor in the storm, and the rudder on the boat. For this and only this can help the sailor (man) to navigate through the storms of life, and to find his way safely home, back to the arms of God. Be you on guard, and know that it is the candle in the wind that can never be extinguished, and the everlasting loving arms of God.

Be not afraid and say, "God has deserted me," or that "I am bereft of all those who care for me!" Know indeed, that your refuge will ever be beside thee, and the sails of your boat will ever take thee home! Let none fill your heart with fear, but know indeed, that all your needs will be met, and your Heavenly Father will ever guide and uphold thee.

Know indeed, Dear Ones, that the eternal love of God is thine, now and always, and will ever be with thee for all the ages. Know that the love and beingness which is God is an integral part of the essence of man. For indeed, it is that thing which allows man to be man; and to function throughout the days of pain and sorrow, until he is once more united with spirit. He is never forgotten, lost, and alone! For such is the way of God; the peace, love, joy, and hope of God.

Never be afraid that you are bereft of love, but know indeed, it is thine... given since the dawn of time! Be at peace, and know you are loved, cared for, nurtured, and held always in the arms of God; for such is the nature of all, so be mindful and remember your heritage and your name. Be at peace, and know that all is indeed well for and with thee, each and every day of your lives. For this is the true essence and beingness of God!

May God's peace continue to enfold thee, and may you walk always in the joy, peace, love, and happiness which is the love of God!

Adieu

26TH MARCH 2012

Know indeed, Dear Ones, that the love of God for mankind is like a flower in the wind, for the wind tosses it this way and that, but try as it might, the rose —for indeed that is its name— remains constant. For although it is blown this way and that, until its blossom touches the ground, know indeed, that still it remains intact and will not break. Know, Dear Ones, even so is the great and powerful love of God for mankind, as it is given by Mother Father God. For even as the Children of Men are tossed to and fro from one place to another, even so, Dear Ones, does the rose continue to flourish. For although it would bow down and touch the ground as the fierce winds blow, even so it does not yet give in to the storms of life, but continues to live through the trials… ever swinging and moving with the breeze instead of trying to escape it. Thus, Dear Ones, is the love of God for mankind, for it will not allow the Children of Men to fail and fall down when the storms of life howl around your doors.

For indeed, the Children of Men find the strength to continue to roll with the wind, and not to struggle, but to move and sway gently in the breeze… even so becoming part of the wind. Thus, the Children of Men can survive, even as a rose on a bush, in its gentlest and yet most beautiful state, does not get torn from the branch, but instead remains even though the strength of the storms would intensify.

Know indeed, Dear Ones, that the Children of Men, with the ability to bend with the wind like a willow tree, will even so be able to survive where others have failed for lack of this knowledge and skill. Know indeed, Dear Ones, that the Children of Men must find the ability whilst here upon the Earth, to 'go with the flow' and to know who they are meant to be: For to become a conformist and to sit and watch the world go by is not a part of the great love of man for God, or God for man. Thus, man must learn to take all opportunities to become their true selves.

The peace of God which surrounds thee daily can truly bring thee the peace and joy of God but in truth, there is much to be discussed if that is the wish of those around him. For indeed, the Children of Men are bereft of the joys of love and peace, and thus they would select only those, who in their hour of need, would call upon the Lord of Hosts to seek reassurance, and to come to know that all is indeed well.

Be you happy to know, Dear Ones, that the Lord of Hosts will be your refuge and shield, and will be there to deliver thee when times are indeed difficult within us and also outside of us. Be at peace and know that the love of God can and will comfort thee, for like that beautiful rose, it brings such intense pleasure for the simplest intent. For indeed, now man will prefer to do that which will remain unseen, instead of focus on self or on things that would cause them to bend needlessly this way or that way. For such is the very path and nature of God to allow the Sons of Men to bend this way and that way, and to wander away from, and return to Mother Father God. For lo! Even as they bend and touch the ground, yet even so do they lift their heads to the skies, so that they may, once more, see the beautiful sky and the glorious sun… and once more come to know the loving source and power, which is the love of God.

Know indeed, Dear Ones, that this way of being in the world, will in every way cause man to come to know, once more, how precious he remains in the heart and love of God. Know indeed that the bush bounces this way and that, and constantly moves, yet loses nothing along its way; for indeed it remains intact and all its beauty is constant and true. Know, Dear Ones, that the love of God for mankind is steadfast, even as this flower swings and sways. Know, even so is the love of God for mankind; for in truth all is one and so it is. Be you ever happy to know, Dear Ones, that the love that is felt for even a wildflower bobbing in the breeze, epitomizes the fact that there is much love between mankind and all else in the Universe.

For in truth, even though the stars would appear and disappear as signs of the changing from night to day, even so is the love of God for mankind ever so carefully delivered? For man must, of self, come to know the myriad of opportunities for daily growth in his life. Thus, he would help to give robes to the poor and to take not from the millions of people who would come forth, to toast and to sing the praises of Mother Father God. For even so, Dear Ones, must the Sons of Men come to know and to understand the things of God. For indeed it has been thus. For in truth, we are one and are ever here with thee during this incarnation… and from these things will come all the perfection, and love, and caring, that is possible within the

Universe. Know indeed, Dear Ones, that this must come into being, yet they can be changed, for it is their course and that which men must do to give them peace of mind. Be not sad, but know indeed that the love of God will continue to carry thee always in good. Be kind and know he will always call upon man so that he might rise. Be not afraid, Dear Ones, but know that all will indeed be well... for and with thee.

Adieu

9THJUNE 2012

Know indeed, that the love of God for humanity is like the golden flower of the morning, which opens in its entirety at the beginning of the day, and closes likewise at the end of each day. Know indeed, Dear One, that the flower when viewed seems in no way special or remarkable... but yet know, Dear One, that in truth, special is a very good descriptor of her for in all her splendor, she is the most beautiful of all the flowers. For indeed, her task is to rise and greet the morning, and then to likewise bid goodnight to the sun and hello to the moon. Know indeed, Dear One, that this love is springing from the wellspring of God, and is, above all else, the most special of all the glorious blooms found upon the Earth. For indeed, in being she who rises in the morning and smiles and greets the sun, all is special in the life of this great story; for it is indeed owned by Mother Father God. For these things are of God, and the great beauty that is seen is there to be enjoyed by all who look upon her.

Know indeed, Dear One, that the glorious love of God is there to be seen at the dawn of each day, and then again at the end of the day.

For, indeed, that is when the great celebrations should best be made available to all, to see and know her great worth and her great joy. For the task which is performed each day is at the core of all that is being awakened.

Know indeed, Dear One, that the love of God for humanity is however known in all the world, for this is truly the task of God. Know indeed, Dear One, that those who rise to salute each day with love, peace, joy, and wonder are celebrated, for this is the way of God in celebrating all that has been provided with the knowledge and love of God. Know that on opening, the flower—for such she is seen— is opening into her magnificence and is there made to sing the praises of Mother Father God, and to know that all is indeed well in the nature and beingness of God.

Know, Dear Ones, that the flower, once opened, remains to smile at the passers-by with great beauty and intensity. All who gaze upon her sing of her praise to each child during each and every day. Thus, Dear Ones, the love of God is seen evidenced in this format and is there to be experienced and to come into communion for the time upon the clocks of man. For indeed, since the flowers have no clocks, one is in much amazement to ask how the flowers know that the end of the day has come into being, and thus know it is time to retire and to glow and bloom no more.

Know indeed that the love of God, which is the flower, is ever constant and is ever sure. For indeed it changes not, but yet in form is seen in different ways by those who look on. Know, Dear One, that the opening and the closing of the day is of great importance in the lives of all who daily see this miracle of the night. For indeed the flower will, of self, determine when it will put itself to sleep and thus is seen no more this night by those who would come to gaze upon her great beauty. Know indeed, Dear One, that the love of God is that thing which allows the flower to be displayed and seen by all in the golden sunlight, but yet to be hidden at the end of the day. Know indeed, that the love of God opens the door to the true light and love of God, and allows the eyes of man to be opened to the truth of the beauty of the night by also allowing the flowers to show and shine their great beauty to the world. For indeed, although the sun is no more in sight, yet still we know that its great influence can still be found.

For indeed, the love and light of God is all that is, there made available to all, and is that great and marvelous thing which brings joy and happiness to the eyes of the beholder… of even such a process as this blessed adoration of the Earth by a simple flower.

Know indeed, that the love of God is that joyous occasion for the Sons of Men, for it allows the great celebration to begin in earnest. Know indeed, Dear One, that the love of God is seen in its entirety, but is not always fully appreciated… for indeed, it was the great igniter of all the works of man. For in truth, it delivers the very signal that the shift has begun and it is time to change and move to the next level. Know indeed, Dear One, that even so will the Sons of Men come to know that all will be well.

Let your hearts sing with victory songs of praise and glory, and let all who gaze upon this flower do so no more. For great, indeed, is that which has happened in far off distant lands. Know that as the sun sets, even so does the moon rise. For in truth, her warmth and glow can be seen by all, for it lights up the night as though with a great candle. Know indeed, Dear One, they can truly enjoy the love and devotion of the Sons of Men. This gift will allow the Sons of Men to truly see and dance with delight at this great unveiling, which is a part of each day's celebrations. Know indeed, Dear One, that the love and light is that very thing which opens each day, and yet remains to sing the praises, and to revel in the glory and love and light of God daily. Let your light so shine, Dear Ones, that you may see the great handiworks of God and come to once more know that the day and night of God is part of this great and glorious plan, Dear Ones. Be at peace and know always how deeply you are loved, held, and cradled. For this is your truth, your joy, and your hope, Dear Ones. Let the blessed of the Lord say, and so it is.

Amen

22ND JUNE 2012

Know indeed, Dear Ones, we say that the love of God for the Children of Men indeed has been a long and arduous[66] journey. For indeed, that God would allow his dear children to be separated from him for a long period of time is truly a measure of the love of God for man. For indeed, the truth of the tale that God, indeed, loves his children beyond measure is clearly seen, Dear Ones. Know indeed, that the love of God for man has been there etched upon the heart for eons... for in truth, God truly loves the Sons of Men as is evidenced in the sonnets and the beautiful psalms of long ago. Know indeed, Dear Ones, that this love is unable to be measured, and in this immeasurable state, we find that the very love and the relationship between the Sons of Men and Mother Father God has been in place, and will ever be in place. For truly, how can the very ways in which man is loved by God be truly counted? Indeed, we say that it cannot be counted, for indeed even as a number is sought, circumstances would turn to produce more opportunities for the great depth and intensity of the affection to be even so demonstrated.

---

[66] Difficult: strenuous

Know indeed, Dear Ones, that God and the Children of Men are part of each other; thus one without the other cannot fully be imagined. For in truth, man has ever been with God since time began; for in truth he—man—could not exist without the evidence of the love of God in his life. Know, Dear Ones, that the wonderful relationship has been and will always be; for indeed, man cannot come into being and be in peace without the relationship of the two being called into play. Know, Dear Ones, that God loves man and indeed, man loves God... and thus it has always been. That one is dependent upon the other is apparent; for man, in his very lineage, must search for the source of meaning in his life until it is found.

For without this, man is ever in turmoil; for it is part of the very nature of man to ask the question of his parentage and his lineage and to make sense of his world. Without this opportunity to make sense of his world, man is yet in turmoil: for indeed, his life is lived without purpose, and he is bereft of a reason for being upon the Earth. For in truth, man must know, at the core of his beingness, why he is here upon the Earth and the very reason for his sojourn here upon the Earth. Thus, he uses this knowledge to bring focus and meaning into his life, and comes to understand the reason for his pain and loss at times when, deep within him, he understands not why he is here upon the Earth.

Know indeed, Dear Ones, that man and God have been the focus for eons, and indeed, the relationship between the two has been that most treasured of secrets. For indeed, man has always asked the questions, "Why am I here, and what is the purpose?" Not only are these burning questions for the Sons of Men, but indeed, they ask "Who and what is God?"

For indeed, these most basic questions are daily upon the lips of men as they travel the highways and byways of life. Finding struggle and strife, they seek to know always the reason for the great struggle upon the Earth. For in truth, he wants to know his place in the Universe and his reason for being: the thought and the questions that pertain to the place of man in the hierarchy of God, and the thoughts of his place as a child of the beingness known as God. For, indeed, always the question has been asked "Why God would love man at all?"

For in his lowliest of states, when man, in total forgetfulness, would cause great pain and suffering upon his brother, and commit the most heinous[67] of all crimes against his brethren. The question begets itself, how can a God ever love those who would bring such pain and suffering to his fellow man?

That man is built to love is lost in this question, for indeed, no focus is seen on love or the thoughts of caring and sharing for anyone, except the self. Know indeed, Dear Ones, that the bond between man and God, being an eternal one, has never been grasped by men… for in their wickedness and in their demonstrations of cruelty to his brethren, man shows no thoughts of God. All is bent and focused on the selfish needs of gain and the will to inflict the desires of one, upon weaker brethren.

Know, Dear Ones, that the love of God for man is deeply entrenched in the very beingness of man… but in truth, he spends much time trying to determine whether indeed God does exist at all. That man in his infancy, believes that he is superior to all else upon the Earth and indeed in the heavens, is a testament to the belief that he is all supreme and none else can surpass him

---

[67] Abominable: hatefully or shockingly evil

in might or wonderment,[68] for indeed he believes he is a mighty powerful being. Know indeed, that in no way does he feel that he is simply a child learning the most rudimentary of all lessons, and thus is yet to know and fully grasp the reason for his existence and his time upon the Earth.

Know indeed that man judges himself and others, and finds that he is not that which he should be. Thus, he judges and finds himself in need of punishment when he falls short of his own expectations. Thus, in the mind of man, doctrines are born and established which call for the establishment of structures and penalties for those who fail to do what is required. Know that man contrives various kinds of torture to punish his brethren for non-compliance with the rules he has established. Even so, there are rules he believes that describe the pain and torture for his failure to follow the rules he has imagined are given by God.

Thus, Dear Ones, we see that man judges and punishes, and then turns to do these things in the name of God in order to legitimize the behavior. For in saying it is the will of God, no blame is exacted for inhumane punishments conceived in the mind of man. Thus begins the pain of man, and the great belief that he must win favor with God… and the thoughts of his great unworthiness are placed in the hearts of men. Know indeed, Dear Ones, that they know not the true nature of God and would thus ascribe all manner of things to the nature of God, which indeed are in no way things of God. Know, Dear Ones, that the love, which is God, was frequently not known or recognized in those days; for in truth, God was established only

---

[68]   Wonder: surprise :astonishment

as the vengeful and punishing God who would destroy his children when they erred from the path. For in truth, they saw God as quick to judge and to punish his children.

Know, Dear Ones, that this view of God has been— and was never— the true picture of God. For indeed, we say that God is only pure love, and at his core if such we may say is only LOVE. No thoughts ever of exacting pain and suffering upon his beloved children, has ever been in the mind of God. For all that he would do is to provide for and love his children unconditionally, even though man would conceive of him as bringing wrath, destruction, floods, and pestilence when he was not happy with the Sons of Men.

Know indeed, Dear Ones, that this God existed nowhere except in the imagination of man; for in his infancy he could conceive of naught else, and thus the pain of man upon the Earth was continued. Listen, O ye Sons of Men and know the truth of your being, for you are the children of a loving and forgiving God, whose joy is to give you all the keys to his kingdom and his abundance. Know that you are, and will always be loved beyond measure, and your task upon the Earth is to love and be love upon the Earth. For ye are the golden stars of God: Ye are the heart and soul of a loving God, and you are never punished of God.

Only within the heart of man is there ever punishment, for the human mind cannot conceive of a loving and forgiving father who would not chastise his sons and daughters. Know indeed, Dear Ones, you must cast off this belief of lack, limitation, pain and punishment and come to know the love, peace, joy, and true happiness which is truly the love of God. Release the fear from your hearts, and come to know the light and love of God that lives within you and is a part of God itself.

Be not alarmed, but know that God is spirit first, last, and always, and you cannot ascribe human emotions to God... for God is Spirit, and in no way feels anger or pain, and the need to punish his children. For indeed, he is a God of love, whose only purpose is to love, guide, and protect his children. Be you happy to know that the only pain in the lives of men comes from the pain of man, and his own agony and failure to understand the ways of God, and not from God.

For in truth, the two are not in any way descriptions of a loving God. Be at peace, Dear Ones, and know that God is only love... and pain, hurt, and anger are parts of the human condition, and are not the things of God. Be you happy to know that the Sons of Men can live in peace, love, and harmony, instead of warring and bringing pain upon his brethren. Know, Dear Ones, that the time is upon you for you to open your mind and your heart, and know the truth of God and finally know peace within your hearts. For God is indeed a God of love and a forgiving God, caring for his children. Be at peace, Dear Ones, and know that you are loved beyond measure by God, and all those who believe that God would punish his children know naught of the true nature and beingness of God.

Know that all is as it should be in the heart and soul of God, for naught lives there but love. Likewise, Dear Ones, the heart and soul of man is also built on love and only love. Let the blessed of the Lord say, and so it is.

Amen & Amen

Adieu

23ᴿᴰJUNE 2012

Know indeed, that the prayers of the Sons of Men are daily given up to Mother Father God; for in truth the Sons of Men constantly seek the love and guidance of Mother Father God. Know indeed, Dear Ones, that the questions asked of God are those which ask for the completion of tasks and for the aid and assistance to do that which will bring peace into the hearts of men. Know indeed, Dear Ones, that the great love of God for humanity would indeed help the Sons of Men to come into their own beingness and to aid the leaders of the world of man. Know, Dear Ones, that this great love and the questions that would be asked are the very things which would bring naught but pain and anguish into the hearts of the Sons of Men. For lo, they seek help and guidance with the questions which plague mankind daily.

Know, Dear Ones, that the love and peace of God are the things which would not hold man in fear, doubt, or worry for indeed, that man, of self, lives there in the land of fear, doubt, and worry is most apparent. Know, Dear Ones, that the love of God for humanity is such that they are ever shielded and protected from those things that would bring them pain and suffering. But it is clear however, that man does experience the very things of which we speak, for only through the learning of these things do most men ever come to fully understand and know the depth and intensity of the love of God for mankind. For in truth, God cares deeply for the Sons of Men and thus would go through all manner of trials in order to protect man from the effects of the hurt and pains of life.

Know indeed, Dear Ones, that the task of God is to daily provide for and protect the Sons of Men from all those things that would bring him grief. Know, Dear Ones, that in most instances man and God's wishes are not separate; for in truth, it is apparent that God and man are one and the same. For in allowing man the choice of free will, God allows man the experiences that he seeks for soul advancement. Thus, if man has expressly asked for certain things, then man will get to experience the things asked for in order to advance the soul. Know indeed, that the needs of man are different in different places upon the Earth, for indeed the farmers of one region will ask for rain to water crops, while others ask for sunshine to allow them to understand different ways… to see the magnitude of all that is truly desired to be experienced while incarnated upon the Earth.

For in truth, the love and beingness of God is ever at work, helping the Sons of Men to realize their own dreams, wishes and aspirations, if they are indeed all part of the plans of men which will help to determine how man progresses. Know indeed, that the Sons of Men know not that all that is being requested of God must, in some day and time, come to fruition.

Thus we say that the love, which is God, is ever-present in the lives of men; for in truth, man will request things of God which they know cannot in truth come to fruition. For when the very nature of the task at hand goes against the very fabric of God, then those prayers are not fulfilled by God but only by man. For instance, in asking for the retribution between the Children of Men, we see that the love of God would gladly cause all the blessings to be poured out upon the Sons of Men… but when the things requested would cause man to be hurt or harmed, then God cannot of self, do what must be done.

For in reality, man and God are ever in communion, and man knows the things of God which are within the heart of God to give to him. Know, Dear Ones, that the desire of man to bring pain and suffering is not a request that God would fulfill.

The might of men would, however, cause this to be fulfilled, and man would thus look on to see and know what was being done, and assign the credit or blame as is necessary to the God beingness. For in truth, man can call upon God and look to see all that is coming into the very dreams and schemes of men, and tell him of its limited nature or of its potential impact on the provision of these gifts to the Sons of Men.

For indeed, man may see only a small part of that which is being requested, but God would indeed see all things. For thus it is written, that the love of God for man is everlasting and will ne'er be taken away. Thus, man can come to expect to hear those words come forth, which echo the will and blessings of God upon the Sons of Men.

Know indeed, Dear Ones, that man truly becomes his own creator, for indeed he allows or disallows the answers to all the questions of men to be ever answered, so that man might always feel that he is in closer union with God. Thus we say, be ye always careful about the things which are requested from God. For even as it is indeed requested of God, even so is it on its way to thee, if the giving and receiving of it would not bring pain and anguish upon the Sons of Men. Know indeed, that the love of God is so very close to the heart and soul of God. Know Dear Ones, that man can always make himself available to his children, that they might come to know the true peace, love, and guidance, which is the love of God.

Know that when man requests those things of God which would bring him peace, love, and harmony, know indeed that the answers are always available to the Children of Men in quick succession, even though man in his entirety cannot see and know the things of God without coming into view with the thoughts and aspirations of man. Know, Dear Ones that this great love which exists between the two, causes the beingness of man to expand to that place where he is able to be fulfilled. For since God will not kill or punish an enemy or indeed cause any harm upon another, know indeed that technically these prayers would indeed never be granted. For it is in not allowing them to come into being, that man might come into his own beingness and live once more in the wisdom and grace of God the Father.

For in the offering up of the prayers of man to God, they must be released that they might come to fruition in the light of day, in the experience and happiness within the awakened soul of God. For never will God kill an enemy for man, and never will he cause harm to another based upon the physical incantations, for the Children of Men are a warring breed and this would lead to pain always upon the Earth. Know indeed, Dear Ones, the might of men would be released and the problem or question then is followed by war. Know, Dear Ones, that mankind will ever learn and know of the great goodness of God in the lives of men on a daily basis, so that man will daily know of his great connection with God.

Be not disheartened or downhearted, Dear Ones, but know that prayers for peace, joy, love, and happiness can be seen in all their intensity being answered daily, while those which seek wrath, vengeance, death, and pain upon another soul, would be slow in coming, if at all; since man would have to take on this great request and determine its practical need to the Sons of Men. Thus we say, that the love of God for men is ever available to the Sons of Men, so that indeed he will grow and flourish upon the Earth, for such is the nature of God, to bring health and happiness to all the Children of Men.

Know always that your Mother Father God will never leave thee, and will ever be with thee to select that given day, and the need to make all things available for men upon the Earth. Know indeed that man is the beloved child of God, and God's plan is that the Children of Men must ever know that they are loved and held in the bosom of God. But in no way will God be held responsible for the killing and maiming of enemies. For indeed, God is a God of LOVE only, first, and foremost: So know indeed, that no harm comes to man except through his own neglect and failure to take care of Mother Earth, and to protect all the things of the Earth.

Know, Dear Ones, that no harm comes to another from God, but that the free will of man is there to impact the happiness of the Children of Men. Every blessing is ever being poured out upon the Sons of Men, and God is ever present in the lives of men; even during the darkest of times to the Children of Men. Be ye alert, and know always that your Mother Father God is ever in view to remove some of the pain of life in the soul of men. For God cannot kill for thee, and cannot maim for thee, but instead will and can always be there to join with thee to live in the peace, love, joy, and prosperity, which is God. Know always, Dear Ones, that you are loved beyond measure, and it is the pleasure of God to give thee all within his kingdom.

That God cannot kill or harm any of his children to appease another child must be known and understood; for being a loving God, he cannot harm his own children.

Any hurt and pain brought upon the children, are done by the Sons of Men, who with might and force use weapons to destroy his brethren. Let not your heart be troubled, but know that the peace and love of God is thine always, Dear Ones. Love your brethren and know peace. Love your brethren and know joy, for these are the ways of God. Bring no pain or hurt upon your brother, and come to know the true peace, love, and joy of God. Let the Blessed of the Lord say and so it is.

Adieu in the peace, love, and blessings of Mother Father God.

Adieu

1ˢᵗ July 2012

Know indeed, Dear One, that the love of God for man has been evidenced for eons upon the Earth... but in truth, that man was not able to see or know and appreciate all that has been given to him upon the Earth, has been evident. For in truth, the love of God is the great equalizer; for in truth, it allows mankind to know that all are seen with the same love and passion as the other. For it is evident that the nature of man, when in the physical, is such that he is convinced that there are inequities in all things related to Mother Father God. For nowhere in the mind of man does he see or know of God as a God who loves all his children with the same intensity. For in truth, the mind of man would lead you to believe that God, like man, thinks and behaves with human emotions and attributes. Thus, God would love one group more than the other, and would cause harm to come upon one group in retribution against another group. Know indeed, Dear One, that the love of God knows no such thoughts or actions. For indeed, all the Sons of Men are children of God, so God cannot turn against one child in favor of another; so there is no way in which God would show more love to one group than another, and would help to destroy one group in favor of another. That man attributes victories in war to the will of God, to defeat one group in favor of another, are therefore beliefs that are not, in truth, the things of God.

For in truth, man and his might would be the things which hold sway in a conflict, not the mighty hand of God: For since mankind is in lesson when upon the Earth, Mother Father God would not, in his love for one against another, interfere. Know indeed, Dear Ones, that the love of God for man is only that of a loving parent, and not the love of one who would intervene in the quarrels of children. For indeed, since man has free will to choose whither he will go and what he will do, it is difficult for God to step into the mêlée and take sides: For this would not be akin to allowing the Sons of Men to make their own way upon the Earth. Thus, as in any classroom upon the Earth, the children are allowed to make choices and then to see the results of these actions. For in truth, man cannot, of self, be taught how and what to do upon the Earth, since these are choices that must be made from the mind of man. Know indeed, Dear Ones, that the love of God for man will take him to great heights of learning, and will cause him to search within himself to look at all things, and to determine whither he will go and what he will conclude... but God will not go against one of his children. For this is not the way of God. For the way of God is love, peace, and joy, and the way of man is not always like that of God. For indeed, the physical world would cause man to see with different eyes the very Sons of God, and to look upon his brother and see him as a stranger. Know indeed, Dear One, the ways of God and the ways of man upon the Earth must be as one. For in truth, since man is made from the essence of God, his inner being is that of love.

Know indeed, Dear One, that the heart of man must change if he (man) is to advance upon the Earth: for in truth, he must let go of the need for war and the great desire to acquire wealth and weapons whilst upon the Earth. He must open his eyes, and see and know that he and his brethren are one. For until this can come to pass, he can never truly know the peace of God, which he has searched for throughout time. That the "great shift" is upon us is evident, Dear Ones, and in truth, the nature of man is changing; for in truth, it is evident that the warring ways of men are coming to an end in many lands. For it is known that the ways of hate and separation go against the things of God.

Know indeed, Dear One, that the love of God is glowing in the hearts of men, and as such, he can see and know that he and his brethren are one, and that there are other ways of being upon the Earth. Know indeed, Dear One, that the love, which is Mother Father God, will always show mankind that there are other ways of being upon the Earth, and then man must make his decision about how to be, think, and behave to his brethren. For in allowing man to know the truth of his nature and his beingness, he can make the choices that show he is truly a child of God: For when in the darkness of ignorance, man knows not who he is, and knows not of his true magnificence. Thus he can make choices only based on this limited knowledge, which says he lives in a world of lack and limitation instead of one of plenty. He knows not that all is provided for him by Mother Father God, so he would hoard and take from the weak. Know indeed, that when given the true knowledge of who and what is the joy of God to provide for man, mankind is able to make those choices that reflect the God within him. For in truth, he is able to allow the light and love of God to shine through him as he greets his brethren. For now with the dawning of this new age and time, when man can see and know that he is not alone in the world, but that his brothers and sisters have the same basic needs and wants as he does, he is able to see him and to know that indeed, the Children of Men, at the core of their being, are one.

Know indeed, that the love, which is God, is evident in regions of the world where man would conceive that it exists not. For in truth, the love of God and the peace of God is evidenced in all places upon the Earth, Dear Ones. Know indeed that the Children of Men are all that the beingness of God would show upon the Earth as the evidence of God in action. For in coming to know that man, at the core of his beingness is love, can change the very nature of man. For when man can see his brethren as Sons and Daughters of God, then he can begin to know all the true joy of God that can be his.

Know, Dear One, that the love of God for man is ever evident in the nature of those who strive for peace and equality for all; for in truth, that man cannot demonstrate God upon the Earth without seeing his brethren in love, is evident. For the greatest of all emotions is love; for the love for one another can soften the heart of those who would only see division and separateness. Know indeed, Dear Ones, that the nature of God and the nature of man are one, but the fog of forgetfulness would allow man not to know of his true magnificence, or to know not of his true nature. For thus, in this ignorance, he can cause great harm to come upon his brethren when he sees them as separate instead of as united upon the Earth.

Know indeed, Dear Ones, that the love and light of God, when it shines in the love, light, and compassion of man for his brethren, knows no bounds. For indeed, since man is a being of love, at the core of his being, he is ever able to live in peace: Where once only pain, and anger, and separation existed, he can relinquish this in favor of a way of love. For to love, is to be in harmony... not only with your brethren, Dear Ones, but also with Mother Earth. For in truth, when your heart glows with the very knowledge of love, then you can see and be love, in all your daily actions. For in truth, when your heart is open to the things of God, your world can change so that you come to know all the beauty that is around you, and you can take the time to see all the wonder that is the love of God, in expression upon the Earth.

Know, Dear Ones, that the love of God is ever thine, and is ever in your heart, so that when you allow it to express through you so that it is seen by those around you, you come to know the true peace and love which is God, in evidence upon the Earth. Know, Dear Ones, that you are loved with the greatest of intensity by your Mother Father God, and you have that same capacity to show that love to your brethren. Know indeed, Dear Ones, that you are the very heart and soul of God, and the delight of God, for you are the evidence of God upon the Earth. Let your light shine therefore, Dear One, that you may always show this evidence to those you meet upon the Earth. When you show love you receive love in return. For this is the nature of man, and the very way of God upon the Earth. When you give of your gifts, your heart and soul receives the same in return. Know that you are vessels of love, and you can share your blessings with everyone you meet... that you might multiply the evidence of the love of God for man upon the Earth.

Be not afraid to show your true nature, Dear Ones, but know indeed that the love of God will always shine through you, if you open your heart and soul, and allow that which is truly within you to pour out: for this is truly your nature to love and to be loved. So, be not afraid but know that the victory will be thine when you open your heart in love to those around you, even when you cannot see evidence of love where you are. Know, that indeed the seed is planted in everyone you meet, so when you allow it to shine forth from within you like a beacon on a hill, it calls forth to the love within others and activates that very thing which may be dormant within them. Let your light shine always, Dear Ones, that you may help others to see and to know of their own light, and their own magnificence. For indeed, the life you illuminate is that of your brother.

Know always that you are part of a great whole—the brotherhood of man—and thus what you do upon the Earth affects your brethren. Live therefore in love, peace, and harmony, and come to know the true peace, love, and joys of God upon the Earth. Know always that you are the children of God, one united family regardless of race, color, or creed. All are one for whether you live in light or know only darkness; you are all still Sons and Daughters of God: So be you the evidence of that love in all your daily works, and come to know the true peace, love, and light of God always in your hearts. For this is your charge, this is your hope, this is your joy, Dear Ones; for in doing this, you show God upon the Earth. Be at peace, Dear Ones, and know always that the love, peace, and joy of God are ever thine. Shine! Shine! Dear Ones, and come to your full expression of God upon the Earth. This is your only charge, Dear Ones, to show LOVE, that you might show God in expression upon the Earth.

Adieu, Dear Ones. We send you God's love, peace and joys. May you continue to glow with the light and love of God always, and share the love which is God with everyone you meet. Let the blessed of the Lord say, and so it is!

Amen

2ND JULY 2012

For indeed, Dear Ones, the love of God for man is such that it is the air that is daily breathed in by the nostrils of the Children of Men. For, it is indeed a part of everything that is found upon the Earth, or that is a part of the nature and beingness of man. For without the love of God, the Sons of Men would surely die. For since the love of God is like the very oxygen to man, we know that without it, man dies. Thus, even so must the Children of Men consider the importance of the love of God in the lives of man; for without it, no provisions would be made and man would, in his bid to stay alive, do all that he could to survive.

Thus, we say, that when man realizes that the love of God is like the very air he breathes, he comes to know that he and God are joined, and that without God, he is not able to survive upon the Earth. For in truth, it is this very love of God that provides all the elements that man needs in order to survive upon the Earth. Thus, man becomes aware that God is the life-giving source for him. For in truth, it is God who provides the air, food, and water that keeps man alive: That it was God who created this magnificent home for the Sons of

Men is known, so truly that man should know that without God he is naught. Thus, Dear Ones, we say that the love and beingness of God courses through the veins of man and gives him life.

That this love is the life-giving source for man, is evident, when man sees and knows that without God, he is naught... and without the love of God, he is bereft of all that makes him whole. Thus, man can begin to understand that the relationship of man and God are the very core of the reason for the existence of man upon the Earth. For indeed, without God, man could and would not ever be able to exist. It would be like putting a newborn baby out into the world alone, and expecting it to survive without the aid of a parent. For in truth, the child would soon die, for he is incapable of taking care of self, and must rely on those around him for help, and assistance, and security.

Thus, Dear Ones, we see and know that the love of God is the very life source of man, for it is this which provides the basic necessities of life, which will allow man to grow and mature, so that he can truly grasp the magnitude of all that he truly is. For indeed, that man is alone and desolate without the love of God is evident, when man is seen wandering all over the Earth, searching for his parent, that he might help to feed and clothe him and keep him safe. Even so is the magnitude of the love of God for man, for it is that thing which allows man to be who he is destined to be, and to allow him to take his place as heirs to the kingdom of God: For without the knowledge, the children cannot be protected. For in truth, he would wither and die (spiritually) in the desert of despair; as he searches for that thing which would give him life and allow him to come to know the true reason for his sojourn upon the Earth.

Know indeed, Dear One, that without God, man has no purpose and would spend all his days pursuing all the distractions of life; for this would give him relief and serve to be his imagined reason for being upon the Earth. For even as man sees and knows not the reason for the things of the Earth, even so would man not be able to see and know of all that is necessary.

Be you aware, Dear Ones, that the joys which are the things of God are all linked to the places of God and the things of God. Know indeed, Dear Ones that the many varied and wonderful ways that man can live upon the Earth would pale in comparison, if and when man discovers that he possesses not the keys to the kingdom. For in such times, he would truly be turned out of the garden and a new and glorious search would begin for that which would bring peace to the Sons of Earth. For here would now emerge a problem to be resolved; for in truth, the Sons of Men would ne'er consider themselves to be among the Children of Men.

Know indeed, Dear Ones, that the love, which is Mother Father God allows the Sons of Men to come to this garden called Earth, and to experience this great learning which will allow him, in turn, to know other things which are related to prosperity. Know indeed, that the path to God will wind this way and that, for in truth, it is based on the experience and learning of man to share what can or cannot be made available to the Sons of Men. Know, Dear Ones, that the Children of Men would be able to share the wealth of the day so that there is adequate supply to meet the needs of all the Sons of Men.

Know indeed, Dear One, that the love which is God does not ridicule. It does not envy. It does not hate. It is not greedy but shares with his brethren. Know indeed, that this love can be found anytime, as it is within. For with or without this knowledge of all the things of God —that God never closes any doors and his mission is perfect—in- that it will allow man to be and to do those things which will make the Sons of Men more aware of their heritage as brothers and sisters in God. For to love God is to love self, and to love God is to know self; for man and God are one, in that man is made from the spark and beingness of God.

Know therefore, Dear Ones, that the love and light of God, which is evident in the heart of man, is ever shining. Thus, man can and will come to know all of that which is truly God; for if he opens his heart, the love of God will pour into it and man will then see and know that he, of self, has changed. For the nature and beingness of God can and will allow man to change and to come to know who and what he truly is; for in this way, all the parts of God will and must shine forth. For the ways of God are evident in the hearts of men, even though man may not recognize it as such; for since God is at the core of the beingness of man, then man must come to acknowledge and know that which is God.

That man may not be able to give it a name and call it God is not important, Dear One, for what is truly of importance is that the heart and soul of man should be changed by the very experience of God. For in truth, man may know God in his heart and express God in all his ways, and still not know that he is expressing that which is God: For the human mind conceives of God as a powerful, vengeful God, who destroys and kills enemies or anyone that would go against them in battle, or in life. Thus, they fail to know and fully comprehend that which is the true nature and beingness of God. For since there is no place where God is not, and there is nothing that is not known by God, man cannot yet comprehend the vastness or the complexity of such a being.

For in truth, since God is spirit, all these things are possible except in the mind of man, where God is imagined to be a human with super powers. Know, Dear One, that that which is God is all SPIRIT and in no way looks like that image of God held by the Sons of Men. For in truth, the love and light which is God is spirit and must be understood as such; for how else could God be but spirit, Dear One?

Know that this benevolent loving and most wonderful creator is there made available to all the Sons of Men and as such is able to be in all places at once. For he is spirit, he is light, he is love, and thus is not constrained by time or space, Dear One. Know indeed, Dear One, that God, in all its essence, is only LOVE, for at the core of God is LOVE now, and always. It governs how and what is perceived by the Sons of Men, and makes provision for all the Sons of Men, so that there is an abundant supply of food and water for all the Sons of Men upon the Earth. There is an adequate supply of air and all the basic tenets of life for mankind upon the Earth.

Look not to find a vengeful and punishing God as of old, but know instead, Dear One, that you will never find him, for he exists not. He was brought into being only in the minds of those who would blame God for all occurrences upon the Earth when no other explanation was at hand. Thus, when those who would seek to subdue the Sons of Men looked to find a way to control them, they looked no further than to find a God of their own making, who would punish those who failed to do what was considered right.

Thus, the Children of Men came to know and believe that God was there, and could be blamed for all occurrences, whether they were or were not attributable to him. Thus Dear One, we say look you no longer for God outside of thee, for the God you seek lives within your heart in a place of love. It is this great love that guides and protects thee daily, and sends Angels to watch and be beside you all the days of your lives. Know, Dear Ones, that you are loved by this most benevolent God and he will always be beside thee, for you are children of this God and as such, you are loved and forgiven every day as you come to learn and know the things of God; as you come to know the beingness of God. For to learn this truth is to come to realize the place of man in the Universe, and to come to know how deeply mankind—all the children upon the Earth – are loved beyond measure. Be you ever happy to know that you are Children of God, loved and adored since the dawn of time by your loving parent, Mother Father God

Know indeed that you are known by God, and loved, and shielded, and provided for by God in every area of your life: For you are his beloved, the very heart of God. God is LOVE. God is PEACE. God is JOY, so be you comforted to know that God will never destroy you, and will never kill any of his children upon the Earth for another; for all are precious in the sight of God and all are beloved by God. Know indeed, Dear Ones, that you are the heart and soul of God; the light of the eyes of God, ever loved, ever shielded, ever guided by God. But even so, does man have the ability to choose which way he will go upon the Earth, for he is given "free will" to make all decisions about his life and his way upon the Earth, without fear of condemnation or retribution: For his Mother Father God is a loving God who will love his children always, even when they make decisions which would hurt his brethren.

Be at peace, Dear Ones, and know that the God of Love is your parent, and as such you are always held and cradled in the arms of Mother Father God, even when in your forgetfulness you know not who or what you are. Know that you are guided by Angels, and that life goes on, Dear Ones, for such is the nature and beingness of man. Know that you are LOVED! Oh, how you are loved: For you are the Sons and Daughters of Mother Father God, for this is the ONLY way and beingness of God.

Adieu, Dear Ones! May you come to know the truth and love that is God, and know always the peace, love, and joy of God in your hearts. Let the blessed of the Lord say, and so it is!

Amen & Amen

CHAPTER 2

MAN AND HIS FORGETFULNESS

The veil of forgetfulness has descended upon thee Dear Ones, and caused you to forget your nature and to know not the things you always knew when in spirit. Now, you see your brethren and would know them not, and thus would turn to kill, maim, and disown them for they cannot be seen as your brethren; for you are so different now in the physical that all is erased, and all is forgotten and you hurt and kill your brethren as though they were animals in the wild.

The soul of man is destined to move forward in his quest for God. For from this quest, his search will take him ever higher into the realm of beingness. Truly it is here that the un-flowering begins to take shape, and it is here that man truly begins to awaken into his manhood, so that he can then begin to move towards his true nature in the arms and love of the Most High God.

The nature and love of God for man causes him to move ever forward, if he is able, for this pursuit of the love of God is the all-encompassing task of man's soul. For deep within him, he must strive ever onwards to achieve this perfection and union with the oneness and beingness of the infinite. Without it, he— man— must ever be in search of who he truly is.

The connection with God is the true source of what man seeks as he continues in his journey through life, even though in reality he is unaware of the real reason or source of his quest. He continues to seek that which he knows is lost, even though he has no idea what is lost to him.

The nature and love of God is the driving force behind all of man's thoughts and his pursuits. Therefore, life, the true power, is ever evident as man continues to move on in search of the one thing that will make him whole. What it is he knows not, for his memory is erased by the pressures of the mortal life, but deep within him lurks the distant memory of something he knows he once had but now has lost. Like a child in search of a beloved toy, he seeks for it day and night, knowing it will provide him with love and comfort, but yet he cannot remember or know the thing he seeks most. For even so is the love of God a very distant memory. He searches in all manner of ways... ever looking, ever knowing it is there, but yet not knowing from whence it came or even its nature, but yet still knowing it is a desired toy, like gold in the eyes of man. And so, the search goes on and on. He stays on his quest, ever looking, and, in some cases, never knowing that the toy is already his to claim.

Like the blind man in his fog, he is not able to sense that his precious toy is already in his possession and all he needs to do is to claim it and know that it is his. For the love of the Most High God is always there for man. It is that gift which he is given from the dawn of time, when the soul, in its infancy, is first brought into beingness. Only the drudgery of life on Earth and the toil and sweat of man has left him blind to all, so that he forgets his Godness[69] and is lost, wandering in the desert of despair, looking for that which he knows he desperately needs, not remembering he already has it from ancient times.

---

[69]   God nature

Look on, Oh Children of Men, and remember your Godhead.[70]Know thyself and the true power of God within thyself. Look not outside thyself for God, but know that he lives within thee. See the God within thyself and then know that it lives in all. For when we can glimpse the God without —outside— ourselves, we can begin to see it in others outside of us...not that any other being is truly outside ourselves, since we are all a part of God and so are joined. Since in being part of God, sparks must come together as in the way atoms will gravitate to each other, since they are all particles of the same origin.

Even so, when man can begin to see and know that he is part of every man, because of the God likeness that is the source of every other man, he will come to know that in hurting another, he is truly harming or hurting God and himself.

Only then can man ever begin to see and fully understand his true nature, and know the magnitude of his power, and why he cannot continue to do what he has always done upon the Earth. The nature of man must change if he is ever to find the peace that he seeks. He cannot continue on the same path of self-destruction or he will destroy all within this world. He will never be able to move forward in his evolution until he can find his way back to the memory of God, and the knowing that he is his brother's keeper, because his brother is God. His brother has the God-beingness and spark and that must be preserved if he is to move forward to closer union with God.

Closer union with God is not a solitary action. It doesn't center only on the single soul, but is a migration and merging of all souls

[70]   deity; divinity; divine nature or essence

collectively. In this migration of souls, we find the collection of God's or God-beingness; so where they are gathered is more power and love of God found.

Look not to the hills for your help, O Children of Men, but look within thyself for the help you seek. Know that your help is coming from God, but that it is within thyself. Look not outside, but go within to that most sacred of places and commune with the Godhead deep within your heart. Know no other truly can help thee find the way to God, for he truly is already y here in the heart and soul of man. Seek ye not for God in the hills, the mountains, or the plains, but know that God is living in your heart, oh Children of the Most High Father. Know that you search for that which is already freely given. Worship not the powers of others, but look within to know that you truly already possess much love, and that it is freely given, and is and always will be available here for thee.

Man is God's beloved child, put upon the Earth to continue his development as a soul, so that in perfection and perfected form, he may return in his knowledge to the source of all— God. Each spark is part of God and will always be attracted to find its way back. Like a magnet must attract all forms of metal to its nature, even so is God. The soul must return to God, for without the knowledge and love of God, he perishes, as the soul continues to look for the reason for being. It can never be fulfilled. It can never know true peace. It can never know true happiness, for the loss of the happiness that the soul memory knows is possible, is akin to the tearing apart of that most loved child from a parent. He is alone and desolate. He cannot go on and is inconsolable. He must perish without the ability to find the only source of comfort he truly knows and seeks. All other things or people presented can never fill the void, for the soul seeks the fulfillment that can only be found in the love of God. He— man— can never be truly contented. No riches or power can ever fill the void of the loss of the knowledge of the spirit and love of God.

Man cannot be consoled, for he knows the greatest desire of his heart has been removed. He must continue to search until he can reconnect with the source that will give him the peace he seeks. This peace is the love of God, which he thinks he has lost.

Communion with God can help man to reconnect with the soul source. Communion with self is the true goal, but man cannot see and know this. Peace within himself is peace with God; the God that lives and is ever present within the soul of man. The blinders must be removed so that man can see that which is present within himself. When this happens, only then can the magnet and the filaments become one once again. Only then can man begin to find that peace that he so desperately seeks. For it is the peace within his soul that will bring him joy, and allow him to move in closer union to the true nature of God.

Think of God as the "big God" and man as the small sparks of God. The one ever seeks the other, for in coming together they form the whole and complete. When man finds the "big God," his 'Godness' comes forth and the two become one in true harmony and peace. When this happens, man is at peace because he is home. He is now one with the source, the love, and power. Like a child nestled in the arms of a loving mother, he is at peace. He is blissfully happy and all is well. He is home, he is with God. He is contentment. He is love. He is one. He has returned to the source of his former self, and the soul is at peace within, for it is no longer splintered, and scattered, and lost. It is whole. It is one. It is love. It is with God and all is well. The cares of the world are lost to him, for now he can be cradled in the arms of God and be at peace forever. All desires are met. There are no desires, and no needs, for all are provided. He is at peace in the oneness and love of God, and all is well. He can finally be at peace, since he has returned, like the splinter to the magnet. They are one!

Adieu

12TH APRIL 2010

For many are they who seek the love of God, thinking that it is something that they cannot secure, when the reality is that they already have it as a precious gift, buried deep within the soul. For even so, as they seek far and wide, they never stop to think that the gift may already be a part of their very essence and soul. For they do not remember the simple truth of their bond with God, or their connection to the Most Holy of Holies; the eternal being, Mother Father God.

The search is on and they wander to and fro, all the time, looking for that which they already possess. So even now, Children of Men, we see you continue to search for that which you already have. The answer to the most burning questions of "Why am I here, and what is my purpose upon the Earth? Why am I here at this particular time in the history of the creation of the Earth? What is so different about this time that makes it such a wonderful time to be upon the Earth?"

Children Dear, remember the former things of old and know the reason for your sojourn here. Know that the time is ripe for the shift to happen in the consciousness of man, and for great changes to come into the beingness of man. For without these changes, man will be destined to continue along the same self-destructive path that he has always travelled. He will continue to do what he has always done, and the world's consciousness will diminish, and the wars will continue, and man will go deeper into the dark depths from which escape will become more and more difficult.

This, then, is the time of liberation for the Earth. The time, when man can help to lift its collective consciousness out of the mire of stagnation and despair, and lift the consciousness of the Earth to higher levels. This, then, is the reason why so many souls have required and requested that they exit the planet in large numbers. Look, you children! It is the start of the great consciousness shift, and look to see what things are happening to large numbers of souls across the world. Look you and see as the changes begin to come about, even so does the loss of life increase as thousands of souls decide to return to the "love source."

Know that these choices are made so that they can feel secure in God's love. For they fear this great unknown state that they cannot fully comprehend. To remain is to face the uncertainty, and so for fear of this great unknown, they choose to return to the safe and loving arms of God.

Hear, O Children of Men, and understand the changes that will be evident upon the Earth in the years to come. See and know that these changes are for the betterment of human kind and the planet. Know that they must happen if man and the Earth will survive. Without them, man and the Earth cannot survive as things have been known. There must be a shift in consciousness for man to save the Earth and himself. Hear, O Children of Men, and see and know all the wondrous things that await thee. There must be less wars and the world must know peace within its varied borders. There can no longer be this vast separation that currently exists between the Sons of Men considered to be different creeds. For as you all know, you are one brotherhood of souls belonging to God the Father.

All are ONE, emanating from the heart of God, whose creative source brought you into being. Know that the changes must come or the Earth will not be able to survive. Know that without the shift in consciousness there can be no change in man, which will be significant enough to bring him into a chapter of the history of God's love for mankind.

Man must be able to see and learn and grow, at a faster rate spiritually. If he continues on the same path he has been on for eons, then the shadows will creep in and fear will drive man into the shadows… and he will totally forget who he is, and his divinity. If this happens, disaster will ensue and man will be lost to God. Know, O children, that the 'shift in consciousness' has already begun, as is evidenced by those who have already been able to touch so many millions with the 'Word.' Even so, Little Ones, know that this must continue if the whole planet is also to hear the word of God, and to fully understand that the changes are a most necessary and important part of the consciousness development of the people of the Earth. For they begin to remember that, without this shift, they will wither and die, like souls on a hot summer day without water in the desert.

Know that the Angel Band is working tirelessly to assist man at this time, in all and in any way possible to remind him of his divinity, and to help him find his way back to the God-source, from which he emanates. For without this, he is lost. The Angel Band is still trying to unite man to the God-self and to remind man of his sacred nature and his connection to God. For they know, that this time in the development and advancement of man is crucial, if the necessary changes will come into being upon the Earth. Know, O children, that the days of change are upon you and you MUST take action to remember your purpose upon the Earth, and to pick up your mantle, and regain your charge, and to continue to fight for that which you know is right.

Help the poor and the oppressed. Help the lame and the blind. Help all your brethren who live in darkness—spiritual— to see and remember the greatest light of God, which is the love of God for man. Your task is to help one another, and to love one another, and to remember who you are, so that your joys may increase.

Know that the love of all must change how man sees and acts upon the face of the Earth. For without this, they cannot hope to shift the consciousness of all, and to truly make that great difference that is necessary. Listen, O Children of Men! Find your course, and remember your divinity. Know your true reason for being upon the Earth and take action. Do what must be done to help those in need, so that all can make the changes necessary to help the souls of man to evolve to the next level, and to grow as they fully comprehend that God is all there is, and that the love of God is the most blessed, precious, and wonderful of all gifts which has been given to humankind.

All must begin to see and know that to change; we must all remember and do our part to help our brother on his soul journey, for we cannot complete this journey alone. We must all collectively travel the road together, so that we can get to the other side of the desired path together. We must learn and remember who we truly are: Light Beings who are here on Earth to learn and to experience those things that can only be experienced here, Dear Ones. Know that you are wonderful Beings of Light, who have traveled for eons to be here at this time, and in this era, to be a part of the Army of God, who will help to bring about this great shift in consciousness. Know that the change must come or there will be no Earth for the generations to see and to love as you have experienced it. For the dark night of the soul will increase and the darkness will envelop man and all will be lost. Arise, O Children of Men, and know your power, and see what must be done.

This is the time for action. Take charge and do what must be done, for without your actions, you will all perish spiritually. The time is here and the action must be taken. We must move forward in love, peace, and harmony, if you are to enjoy the fruits of the Earth, and come to know the true abundance of the love of God. Know that man is a child of God, and is the source of so much plenty upon the Earth. Look to no future kingdom, but know that the kingdom of God is here right now, for you are workers in the garden of God's love, planting seeds, and watching them grow. Allow yourselves to shine like the blessed souls you are, for it is time for you to know that God is truly here with each of you. For you are each a part of the creative source, carrying within your being that part of God from which your soul was developed, so many eons ago.

Look you no further, outside yourself, but know that he is ever-present within you, every minute, hour, and second of every day, since he is here within you, and as a part of you, blessed ones. Know your true selves and remember your path back to God. Look to love to find the answer to your beingness, and in order to understand your nature and your reason for being upon the Earth.

Amen

For even as Angels walk the Earth, they are here as messengers of God's love and grace. Their charge is to protect and to guide the Sons of Men on their path back to God. Daily, they fly between Earth and other regions making sure that all is well and keeping man on his path. Winged messengers such as they are here to do those tasks, which must be done if man is to return to the bosom and love of God. For, they know how and what must be done to keep man on his path.

The Diadem Band of Angels are here on Earth, and remains here all the time. But, there are other groups who travel to and fro to other realms, and it is these beings who are the spiritual messengers of God; for their task is to oversee, and to make sure all is well. They are the Super Messengers, if such we may describe them, for they can commune with the spirit and essence of other beings in many distant places, and planets, and can bring news to them of what is taking place here on Earth.

(Note that these are descriptions, in your terms, to give you the information in terms you may easily understand. For in no way, Children, do they physically fly to and fro. For, as Beings of Light you would not see them flying. Note, O Children, the passage and text here is to bring you understanding at the level of man, so that you might begin to grasp, however microscopic, a portion of the vastness of the essence of God, and the task of those who sojourn here to protect and guide the Children of Men.)

Know, O Precious Ones, how much you are loved and valued by the Source essence called God. For even as a father tends and protects his children, so does God protect, love, and care for thee. For the Children of Men are precious in the eyes of God, and as such he is mindful of your needs and wants. Know you not that his joy is to give you the kingdom? Surely, O Sons of Men, you know your true worth in the eyes of God? Know you not the depth of the love of God for the Sons of Men? Know you not how dearly and closely you are held to God's bosom? For only when you can begin to see and know this within your very soul-essence, can you ever hope to fully understand the vastness of the very nature of God's love for you. Only then can you see and know that you are truly Sons and Daughters of God, whose value is beyond the most precious of gems, and rarest of objects known upon the Earth.

All the Angel Hosts are here for thee, to guide and to teach you how to perform your tasks so that you may return to the bosom of God's love. Know you not how long you have tarried[71] here, like lost sheep unable to find your way home to God? Know you not how long you have lived here in these incarnations upon the Earth, forgetful of your true selves, unable to find your way like a blind man in a desert? Know you not that your soul essence demands and needs to find its

---

[71]   Lingered; remain behind

way back to the Creator, from whom it originated? Know you not your true identity as Sons and Daughters of the Most High God? Listen, O Children, and understand all that is yours to know, for the times they are a-changing, and must change if man is to progress. The Angel Band is here to assist you. The Diadem Band is here to guide and protect you as you daily go on your way. Look to your soul, and the spiritual development, which will allow you to return to the bosom of God with ease. Know of your true essence, power, and source, and help your brethren to find their way upon the Earth.

Look you, O Sons of Men, and know your true magnificence for the God-beings that you truly are, for even so are you able, if you choose, to do the very miracles you read of about the man Jesus. For even so, can you perform great miracles, if you can begin to see the Christ-spirit[72] within yourselves. Know your God essence, and accept the gifts you have been given by God, so that you may advance your soul development as you find your way back to God. Know, Dear Ones, all that is promised to the Sons of Men, and all the goodness, and the love that awaits you on your return to the bosom of God. Understand, O Children, the magnitude of the power and strength of God; the love that is there for you when you return. For all the pain and anguish you pour out upon yourselves are done only by you. For only man can punish the way he does.

Only man can harm his fellow man in the creative ways you have found to harm your brethren. Only man can do these things, while calling upon the name of God, the love source of all. Only man can forget his essence and the true knowledge of his soul essence and

---

[72] The divine light of love and peace that dwells within man.

identity, and hurt his fellow man as he does. For in ignorance, he acts in these ways like lost sheep. Like lost children, they forget all they have been taught and return to the days of savagery from whence no light flows, and there is no rescue. Lost upon the Earth, they wander like children in search of a parent... looking for their identity and trying to find their way home; looking for their way back to God.

O hail you, O Sons of Men. Open your eyes, for the road is set before you, and you are already on the path. Remove the mist from your eyes and see that the path is there. You can find your way back to God if you will only open your eyes and see all that is to be seen. Open your heart and know that you can return to God, for the road is clear, and all you need to do is to take the first step. Open your hearts and your eyes, and see all that is yours to do. Open your heart and remember the love of God, for you know that you are so precious in the love and sight of God...That you are his children, the spark of his beingness, and that you will remain lost if you cannot turn back to him and remember who you are. For your task is simply to remember who you are and all will begin to fall into place.

Show your God-selves[73] to your brothers here upon the Earth, and act in loving ways to them. Know that your heart and your soul and theirs are one. Know thyself, children, so that you may know others. Like children of the Most High God, you must open your eyes. For how can you ever hope to see and understand your task here, if you refuse to open your eyes? – Instead keeping them tightly shut, like one who is afraid to open them for fear of the unknown— Know there is nothing to fear, for God is in charge and all is well. Know that you

---

[73] That part of man which is God-like which is the soul or essence of man.

may open your eyes safely, for no danger awaits you. All that awaits you is love, Dear Ones. All that awaits you is the dawn of a new day. All that awaits you is heaven here on Earth. For the loss of fear brings you God's peace and love. For the loss of fear brings you all the joy your soul can hold. For with the opening of your eyes, comes the opening of your hands to receive the gifts of God's love, peace, and grace.

O wonderful Children of God, know your magnificence and worth, and see the love of God. Let go of the pain of separation, and return to the essence of who you are.

Remember your reason for being upon the Earth, and return to the love of God. Demonstrate that which is yours to do. Open your eyes and see and know the love of God. For this, and only this, is your charge. The time is now and the task is at hand, for only when this is done will you find peace. Only when this is done will you find your true purpose as children of God...to protect the weak, to help the sick, and to minister to those in need; giving of yourself to others. This is the true charge of man. To move outside his own selfishness, to his selflessness where he takes care of his brethren, and is able to guide and protect all forms of life on the Earth. For all life is sacred, and all things upon the Earth were placed here to beautify it, and to make this God's own garden and paradise.

Stop the destruction of this home, for you will have no home, O Sons of Men. Remember your divinity and the precious gifts of life that are here and keep them safe. Stop the wars and famine, and share the wealth of this planet with those in need. Save your souls! Be at peace! Leave the selfishness behind, and put on the mantle of selflessness and know true peace and harmony in your lives, O Sons and Daughters of the Most High God.

Put away the petty squabbles and hurts and pains, that for centuries have kept you bound in the chains of anguish and pain, and learn to see your magnificence and power. Learn to know your grace, love, and wonder. Learn to see the love in others, and to see the God-light in all. Only then can you find the peace you seek. Only then can you find the love you deserve and have searched for, for millennia. Only then can you truly find the God you seek, for only then can you truly find yourself: Know your power, and find your true source and essence. Only then can you know your true divinity and find your reason for being upon the Earth. Remember your mission upon the Earth, and be who you are: the Sons and Daughters of God, bearers of the love and power of God, children who contain that same spark of God that makes you all brothers and sisters.

Love your brethren, for you are one. For only in this way can you find peace, and advance in the light and love of God. Only then can man make the transition into his real self, and hope to find his purpose… and live his true destiny as Sons and Daughters of the Most High God.

Amen & Amen

30ᵀᴴ April 2010

For surely the Children of Men cannot ever hope to meet the challenges of the human experience, and move onwards without the knowledge of God. For truly without the knowledge of God, man is bereft of his true faculty, and cannot hope to do all that must be done to advance into the spiritual realms of the elite. For without this knowledge, all that is left available to man is the most basic and banal[74] existence... in which he barely exists and is doomed to a life of mediocrity and pain, instead of living out his life as that true and mighty human potential that is possible for man to attain.

The Sons of Men can never advance to the true levels of his potential without God, for he is ever alone... and in this state of aloneness, he cannot reach his true most glorious and wonderful potential. All that is left available to man is the simple yet unaffected position, of existing in a state without God, light, love, or awareness of any kind. For he cannot hear, see, or understand the true nature of all that is around or upon him, and to that end is lost with no hope of rescue.

---

[74] Commonplace: dull: boring

To give man the sight he so desperately needs, man must increase his awareness of his God-source, and with this comes the opening of the eyes. The shadow of ignorance, like a veil, is lifted, and man is able to see and know all those marvelous truths that hitherto[75] had been a mystery to him. Thus, as his eyes are opened, all the knowledge of God allows him to become his true self and he is reborn to the new levels as a man of sight, and with knowledge of his divine potential.

Man cannot, of himself, move to this place, for he must get there only through experience and knowledge of the love of God. For without this knowledge, his eyes remain closed, and he is even more lost and alone, unable to find the reason for his being. He must remain alone and disconnected in his thoughts of God… only in thoughts, one might add, for man is never disconnected from God, since by his creative source, he is part of God. Thus, only his thoughts are disconnected from God, and he is lost without a life compass. The knowledge of God is the life compass for the sons of men. Without this compass, man is lost like a sailor on the vast ocean of life, unable to find or to see the shore, which is only a short distance away on the horizon.

Thus, man on his search for meaning, and his nature, cannot advance in learning without increasing his knowledge of the love of God. He cannot ever hope to move to those places where his soul can gain true satisfaction and joy, without knowing those most basic and simplest of truths; that with the love of God, all is possible and everything is achievable.

---

[75]   To this time: until now

Man cannot see his true spiritual potential, without the knowledge of God. Thus, the sailor is tossed on the boat in the ocean of life. His sails need attention, but he knows not this simple fact, and the winds, like hurricanes, toss him to and fro and he is calling for God... calling for rescue, when by pulling down his sails he can adjust his life and move safely on his journey.

O Sons of Men, we ask your eyes to open, so that you can see and know instinctively what to do when the storms of life prevail upon you. When the winds toss you to and fro, you will be able to weather any storm, and reach safely to the calm of the bosom of God's love.

Know, Sweet Sons and Daughters, all the guidance you need on how to live and to be true children of the light can be found in the knowledge of the love of God. For this knowledge brings oh such joy, oh such peace, and oh such love, to the lives of men. The boat will not fail and the water will not lap into the boat, and man can be saved, and can move closer into the bosom of God's love.

All that man needs to do to gain this great prize, is to learn and to know of the power of the love of God. Once this is accomplished, he will be able to advance, and move towards his true spiritual potential. To live without God is to live alone and disconnected from the true life source of God. It is not to live at all. For the existence is banal and of no worth, and there is no direction, and no soul development... for the spirit is subdued and cannot thrive and flourish as it should, like a shoot pushing its way up out of the ground and opening up in order to grow into the tallest of oak trees.

Thus is man alone, without the knowledge of the love of God. And even so, is he unable to take advantage of the beauty of the light that gives it energy and strength. Thus we can say, the love and knowledge of God is like the power given to the seed by its knowledge of the sun. It reaches for the sun and continues to grow— ever in search, ever-growing upward, looking for more sun and strength, into the heavens. This is the parable of the mustard seed as told by Jesus, for even so the small seed begins its life in the darkness, without the knowledge of the love of God, or the knowledge of its own value and power as a God-being: Once he finds the light, he begins the process of growth and continues to reach for the life source until he is free of the darkness of the soil, and his stem takes root and is anchored in the soil of God's love. He can now advance and continue his search upwards, ever upwards, using the light as a source of energy to help it grow, so that he can reach his true potential, and become that tall oak tree and the spiritual wonder that he truly is.

All of this is only predicated on the fact that the seed begins to grow in the dark earth, but when the bud pushes forth, and is warmed by the sun, his true growth can begin. Thus, the seed knows from within its DNA what it is destined to be, but none of this can be attained without first breaking forth from the dark earth into the light. Thus is man bound! For sometimes the seed opens below the ground, but never manages to reach the light, and withers and dies.

Without the knowledge of God, the life-giving source is not found and man cannot grow. The plant is like one left in a dark place, endlessly in search of the light. He waits and tries to grow but he cannot reach his true potential and may die.

Sometimes, he learns how to adapt to the darkness and grows into something quite unintended. Thus he is lost and cannot remember who he is supposed to be. He becomes something very different and is lost to the source and nature of his God-self. His roots grow deep but he cannot flourish. Instead of growing up into the light and expanding his branches, he grows in other directions, twisted and bent.

He finds other distractions, and forgets that buried deep inside him is the knowledge that the light and the sun calls him to reach upward. Instead, he remains in the lower depths of the forest, underneath the brush. Unable to get into the light, he is strangled by the undergrowth and may eventually perish. For he knows that the light will save him, but he cannot remember how, or what it is.

He knows not of the value of something he doesn't remember, so he lives his meager experience and never gets to enjoy the warmth, joy, and strength experienced in the light. He cannot see it or describe it for he knows it not, not having ever fully, really known it, or its power. He is ignorant of the powers hidden within him to be that mighty oak, so he exists for a time as something other than his true identity, in a form not resembling anything of his true magnificence, and thus he never finds his purpose—that of being the magnificent oak—and settles for something else and withers and dies.

The soul is not expanded and developed to its true potential, but is choked in the underbrush by other plants in a similar existence. They struggle daily to survive in the underbrush, forgetful of the knowledge that there is light that can help it to grow upwards, strong, healthy, and magnificent into a mighty tree.

If we see the knowledge of the love of God as the sun, with its power to transform and grow all things, you may begin to understand and comprehend what the power of the knowledge of the love of God can do for man, as he searches for his purpose upon the Earth.

It is to look upwards, and to push toward the light so that you can bloom and blossom, O Sons of Men. It is to push up to the light and to continue to move towards the light, so that you might gain the life-giving energy from the sun and grow to reach your true potential as the spiritual giants that you are. Like the oak beginning as the seed, but growing into the most beautiful and strongest of trees, even so can man find his way out of the darkness into the light, and grow with the knowledge of the love and power of God.

The tree can become a sapling and remain there in the shadows, choked and strangled by the distractions of life... or can continue to reach up to the light in search of his true potential, in search of that which he is programmed to be: an Oak. Without the knowledge of the love of God, the tree forgets his true maturity, forgets his mission to grow into an Oak and is strangled and dies (spiritually). He knows he is missing something, but his identity is lost. He cannot remember, and has lost the DNA marker to tell him who he is, or his destiny, so he wanders aimlessly among the saplings on the forest floor, sending out branches which never reach upwards but instead spreads sideways but never upwards.

Man is lost. He faintly remembers his mission but he doesn't know how or what the light can do for him. He cannot remember his purpose, and so he settles for so much less than he truly is meant to be. Withered and strangled by the undergrowth— others in the same predicament—he remains in this place, believing this is who or what he is destined to be, and so adapts to this and is lost to the love and wonder of God's love and light.

Open your eyes, oh Sons of Men, and remember your true source as Sons and Daughters of light. Remember your nature, and move towards the light so that you can grow into the spiritual giants you were born to be.

Why settle for being a weak and gangly sapling, when it is in your nature to be the tallest oak or the grandest redwood? Remember your nature. Know thyself and grow to be the proud Sons and Daughters of Spirit that you are.

Man is naught if he forgets his spiritual identity and fails to grow into his true spiritual self as that most magnificent of all beings, the Sons and Daughters of light. For without the knowledge and memory of your spiritual nature and source, you will perish from the Earth, unable to fulfill your destiny and find your way to God, your source of strength and life. Become your magnificent selves, O Sons and Daughters of Light. Remember who you are. Reach for the light of God's love so that you can grow into the magnificent spiritual beings you are meant to be.

Amen & Amen

23RD APRIL 2011

ALL MEN ARE BROTHERS

Welcome, Little One; indeed, we say welcome. Know, indeed,
much good words and news for thee this day. For from afar
comes news of talks of peace, and the harming of those who
struggle for life with each passing day.[76] Let all see and know
that the blessed of the Lord must find relief from those who
seek to destroy the very fabric of life. Look on and know the
days and times of man, will see peace upon this land once more.
For the struggle cannot be contained and the captives will be
set free. Look on and know that the Children of Men must be
free to make their own decisions; for in truth, they were given
the essence of free will and allowed to make decisions upon the
Earth. They must, therefore, be set free from those who would
sublimate[77]and chastise[78] them. Let all know that the Children
of Men must be made free, so that he can make decisions of his

---

[76]   Libyan people fighting in Western Mountains region against Kaddafi forces.

[77]   to divert the expression of (an instinctual desire or impulse) from its
unacceptable form to one that is considered more socially or culturally acceptable.

[78]   To inflict pain on for the purpose of punishing; to correct; to restrain

own, and come to know God and his true power all by himself, if he so chooses. Look on and know that man is not to be held as captive, but allowed to roam free, in thought and action upon the Earth. Let all those who would cause man pain be put aside and cast down, for the Children of Men must be free.

Know ye that all men will be free, for these are the days and the awareness is upon us. Let all come to know that God is in his heaven and all is right with the world. Let the blessed of the Lord say aye, and rejoice, indeed, for great is the name of the Lord. Let all know of the true majesty and power of God, for great is he and worthy, indeed, is he to be praised. We hail thee, Little One, and say blessed, indeed, is the name of the Lord. For man must come to know sweet peace upon the Earth, if he is to dwell in the land of peace and freedom. Blessed, indeed, is the name of the Lord.

Much are the changes that will continue upon the Earth, and great are the blessings that will be heaped upon the world of men; for, indeed, God the wonderful father will provide for his children each and every day, so be ye full of praise and take on the mantle of freedom, justice, and love for the sons of God. Let all come to know that God is truly worthy to be praised. Hail, oh Sons and Daughters of men; know ye that the Lord is God and reigns in the heavens, and upon the Earth. Let the blessed of the Earth say aye! Let all the Children of Men come forth, and sing a new and wonderful song of praise. For the Lord will be praised. For the Children of Men are like sheep who scatter in the heat of the noonday sun, only to run to find the shade of God's love. Let all see and know that the love of God will guide and protect, and keep man safe from harm in all his ways, and will protect him from those who would bring harm upon him. Let all know that the love of God will be the very source of protection, for man will cause him to become special upon the Earth. For in truth, he must be that which he is upon the face of the Earth. Let all see and know that God is in his heaven, and all is right with the world. Be ye full of peace and know that all is indeed well, Little One. For the blessed of the Earth will come forward with jubilation and song, and will cause peace to reign upon the land. Be at peace and know that all will indeed be well, for the Lord God of Hosts will guide and protect his children. Let the blessed of the Earth rejoice and be glad upon the Earth, for great is the rejoicing that will come to pass this day.

1ST MAY 2011

Welcome indeed, Sister, welcome… for we are much happy to be here with thee on this happy of happy days. Let all the blessed of the Earth say welcome, indeed, for the eye of the Lord looks upon thee and brings forth the joy of all, like the rush of a great wind that calls all to be reverent and to pray. For the love of God can and will bring changes upon all who experience it. For it cannot help but do this to all with whom it is in contact. For lo, all who come into contact must be affected, even if only for an instant. For such is the very nature of the love of God that all must be affected by it, even though in some instances, it lasts but for a very short time.

For, indeed, some are so unaffected that the impulse does not last for any extended time. We know, however, that these are the very souls who will have the greatest need to remember, and to know the true value of the love of God. For so is the nature, Dear Ones, that all must in effect be affected by it, but when they are so clouded by the distractions of the world, they are unable to see or to remember how much love and power is available in this for them. So, they put it aside and continue with the morbid distractions of the world, and are never able to receive the true value of that most precious of all gifts. Hail, Sweet One, know that all is indeed well and there is no need for concern at this time; for, indeed, the great love is not affected by man, because in his great fog, he has forgotten how to access it and its true value to him. Thus O Children of Men, we see man lost like a stumbling infant in the dark, unable to find his way, not knowing to turn on the light switch to illuminate his life with this most magnificent of all gifts: Unable to remember his way or his purpose upon the Earth, for all memory is erased and he is alone in his plight, as far as he is concerned... all the time forgetting that he is and can never be alone, for the great God of love can never leave his children alone to suffer in ignorance.

Hail, O Sons and Daughters of Mankind, open your eyes and remember your heritage so that you can come out of the darkness, for such is your plight that you feel you are so alone that despair creeps into your heart. Open your heart and know that all is well with thee and thine, for the love of God will be your very rudder in a stormy sea, and your lifeline when you are lost at sea. Hold on, O Sons and Daughters of Mankind; cast not your eyes down in despair, but look on and know that you are the light of God, and you are never abandoned and never alone. For the light can never be cast down or put aside. It must be in the place of great pride, so that all can see its glow and become also full of light.

Hold up your head and cast not your gaze downwards, but know that you are the favored of God. All are favored of God. For mankind is the favorite child of the Most High God. Look on and know that like the 'Prodigal Son,'[79] you will always be seated at the head of the table, and given the best of all that exists in the beautiful city of God. For thus, man is favored of God and given the keys to the kingdom. ALL men are favored. No special group stands out, for you are all Sons and Daughters of the Most High God, loved and adored by God, with the same strength and passion, in exactly the same way.

Behold, O Sons and Daughters of Mankind, know that all your needs will be met and all the gifts that God possesses can be laid at your feet, if you but remember your heritage and return to your former selves, and your former state, as the most beloved of God. For God's love never waivers or changes, it is ever constant, ever sure, ever precious, and always bountiful... Oh so full and completely available for all those who would come to grasp it, Dear Ones.

Be you always full of love, full of hope, for those who are your brethren. For, indeed, all men are your brethren, and should be one with thee. Behold, Dear Ones, the love of God is there for all to savor, with equal access and vigor, to see the true joys that are available for all to partake from this cup of love and brotherhood. For all are welcome at the table of love and brotherhood. Come along and take the best seat at the table of brotherhood and love, and enjoy all the wonderful gifts given by God the Father, to all his children, with equal shares, in all areas of their daily lives. Know there are none more favored among the Sons and Daughters of mankind, for all are one and are of equal value to the Most High God.

---

[79]   Luke 15:11-32

Behold, you are welcomed at the table of love, if you will but remember that you are the guest of honor, the special one, the only one that the Father Mother God can truly bring into his presence at the table and bestow all the great wonders of the world upon. Wait not, for the invitation was extended since the dawn of time, and you can turn to God at any moment to receive your gift. There is no expiration date and the invitation has never been withheld. All are welcomed, all are special, and all are desired of God as the most special of guests at this great table and feast.

Behold, I stand at the door and knock; who will hear my voice and open the door unto me? Open your heart, for this is the great door, at which the Great God stands knocking; who will hear his voice and open unto me? For, the door will remain closed, and the gift cannot be given if the door is never opened, and the love of God cannot be made available to his children.

Harken, O Children, hear the words of God's love and open the doors to your very heart and soul, and see what marvelous treasures await thee in the beautiful City of God. For only love can open the door to the throne room, and the great storehouse of God's grace. Remember, O Sons and Daughters of mankind, that there is no cost for this great and wonderful gift. All that is required is an open heart full of willingness to be the truly wonderful creatures you were meant to be.

Adieu

6TH June 2011

Know, Little One, that the path of love and kindness continues to draw the Sons of Men; for even so, we see that the flock of sheep grows weary, yet indeed, they turn not away from that which would bring them no peace. Know, indeed, the love and protection of God even so allows man the joy of knowing that the peace and joy of God's kingdom are his without pay and without recompense.[80]

For the Sons of Men do not need to pay for the pleasure, all is freely given. Know, Little One, that the pain of the separation from the memory of the love of God, is payment enough, and even so, does man accept the charge to return to Earth, knowing full well that he may forget his lineage, and forget his birthright. Yet, even as he continues to choose this path of enlightenment, even so, does he know that he will one day return to the fold of God's love; so therefore he has lost nothing, save his memory for a while. Yet, in this time of loss, is the greatest pain that man can suffer –the pain of alienation and loss—for lo, he has no memory and no thoughts of God, or of the full nature and beingness of the Most High God.

[80] Repay: reward: compensation

Thus is the pain heightened, for the soul, indeed, longs to return to the Source and reconnect whenever possible. So, in this alien land he is lost and alone, with no memory of the great love that he carries within his breast. Even so, Little One, we see that still he continues to come into this incarnation, looking to learn those things that can only be learned when in the incarnation of man upon the Earth. Look on and know, Little One, that the great and mighty love of God, which is forgotten by man, then becomes the biggest burden, for he knows he has lost something, yet cannot, of himself, determine that which is lost. Thus, he seeks night and day, looking for that which he had. (But cannot yet remember what it is that is lost.)

The great longing is built, established deep within his soul, and he wanders the Earth, looking and searching for that which will bring him peace and happiness. It is this very thing that creates the distant longing, and the pain within the heart of man. Know, indeed, that the quest becomes the sole focus; for even though he cannot identify the most magical thing that was lost, even so, he knows that a great jewel has been taken from him. Know indeed, Little Ones, that the days and nights of loneliness and pain, are part of the legacy of the forgetfulness, and so begins the travails[81] of man. Lost like a small child in the market remembering he has been there before, he strives to find his way home; only to discover he is indeed lost. For all memory has been removed from his heart, and thus he is alone, he thinks; going from place to place, seeking that which was taken from him: The very memory of the Most High God the Father, Creator of all things.

---

[81] Work especially of a painful or laborious nature : toil: agony: torment

Thus is man seemingly lost, seemingly alone, waiting for someone with good news to find him and to tell him all is well, and to give him directions on how to return to God. Poor child, he is lost and alone in his despair, not knowing that **he has all he needs** to find his own way, already given to him by Mother Father God. Yes, indeed he has the love of God buried inside his very soul, and it is this that he mostly seeks, but yet never fully realizes he already has.

Look on and know, Little Ones, that these are the joys of God that are already deep within you. These are the things that bind you to the eternal, and so you are never lost, never alone, never without guidance, hope, or the warmth of the arms of God. For all these blessings are yours every day. All these wonderful blessings are possessed by you. Only the memory of them is lost. The gift, once given, cannot be taken away. It is yours for eternity.

Your thoughts of your worthiness for this magnificent love may keep you bound in chains, or indeed, may help to keep you lost of memory (forgetful). For if the heart feels worthless and broken, then it is indeed difficult to bring it back or to remind the self of any great thing that can happen. Thus is the great pain of man, for he knows not that there is no need for pain, for he has all he needs.

The mind says you are unworthy and unlovable, and with no redemption possible, the soul sinks further into despair, until he cannot lift his head to see what lies in his very eye-sight… or to see and to acknowledge that there is hope for himself.

Thus we see those lost in despair, who turn away, and become the very opposite of the God-being that they are. For in truth, they turn only from themselves, because you cannot turn from God. You can forget, but you cannot turn away; for God is who you are, so how can you turn away from yourself? Thus, the turn from God is only in memory, for truly the beingness of man is always fixed on God, whether man is aware of this great truth of his self or not. To turn back to God, and to the memory of the God within, is the very nature of man, and is the happiness of his heart. Like a duck to water, even so, is the return to God the most natural of all things. For it is in the very nature of the beingness of man, that he returns to commune with his own beingness. Know that this is the very source of the deepest happiness of man, when he remembers his true nature, and remembers his true purpose, and is ready to reclaim that which he didn't know he had.

Thus is the great and overarching happiness of man found, for he is all he can be at this moment, when in communion with the nature and beingness of himself. He finds that he is back in alignment with his very purpose and now he can be who he has always been: the child of the Most High God, loved and adored by God. Loved and adored until the end of time; for such is the vastness of the great love and caring of God. For he is ever with the Sons and Daughters of mankind; ever present, ever ready, ever willing to do what is needed for mankind to remember their path and destiny upon the Earth.

Even so, these are the times when prophets are sent to remind mankind of the great loss, and to help to spur him on his way. Know, Little One, that the vast and all-encompassing love of God is the greatest of all desires of man. It is that which calls him home, and that which beckons him back to his source.

The feeling of loss is gone, and man can return to the comfort and feelings of home. He can be at peace. He can be who he meant to be. He can be the "God" that he always has been. Turn again, O Sons and Daughters of mankind, and remember your nature, and know the joy, happiness, and peace that is you. Know that this joy is available at all times, when the reconnection or the remembrance of all that could be happens, and man is once again united in his memory with God.

Thus we say these are the most glorious and wonderful moments, when all connections are made, and man can rest comfortably in the arms of God. These are the moments; these are the times when all will be well for mankind. For in finding his memory, he has found the great love he has for the world. Thus, can the great peace descend upon him, and his heart can grow in pride... for this is his moment in the sun: His moment in the starlight, when all is possible and, indeed, all can be made to come to pass.

Adieu

16ᵗʰ July 2011

Know, Dear Ones, that the time of the great change upon the Earth is indeed upon us, for such is the vibration that fills the Universe. For the peoples of the Earth are in revolt, and will no longer suffer in silence. Know that those who oppress and would crush the will of the people will be deposed, and new leaders will be brought forth, who will lead with dignity, and respect, for the brotherhood of man. Know, Dear Ones, that this change must come, for only in this way can peace truly ever reign upon the Earth. For without this recognition that all are one in dignity, and peace, and brotherhood, there can be no peace upon the Earth.

Know, Dear Ones, that the pain of the great separation from Mother Father God has taught man to live selfish and pain-filled lives. Without thought for his brothers, he seeks only to bring himself the satisfaction of life, and thus the pain and cruelty is imposed on others, for he sees not the light and love of the Mother Father God in his eyes. He sees, instead, only the desires of his own heart, and thus he is lost; unable to find the true peace and love of God in himself, or in his brethren.

Know, Dear Ones, that the peace of God will guide thee home, for it is this great peace that will bring you the joys so richly deserved. Know, Dear Ones, that the nature of God will echo in the hearts of men, if he is to be changed, and to seek the peace and love of God that lives within him. Know, Sweet Ones, that the pain and the suffering imposed on those who do not see the light of God's love cannot be continued. For we must love our brethren, and do all that is right and acceptable for him: Caring for those who cannot care for themselves, and following the teachings of our dear Brother, Jesus, which explains so fully that ye must indeed be your brother's keeper: These are the ways of the Mother Father God.

This is the heart and love of God, that all who serve and love the Lord should do, even the least of these things. For in loving your brother, you show your love for God. This great love, which lives deep in the hearts of men, can and will bring him from the depths of despair, to the light of God's love here, Dear One. Know, indeed, that the table is set with the blessings and gifts from God the Father, and all may partake of this great feast.

Let not the hurt or the pains of life lead thee to believe that there is no seat for thee. For, indeed, all may sit at the table and partake of this great and glorious feast, Dear One. All may eat their fill of the bountiful gifts provided by Mother Father God. Know, Dear One, that all are welcome and all may partake. For the bounty is freely given by God, and is there for all. Be ye not one of those who would choose to separate the hungry and cause them not to come to the table. Open the gates! Open your hearts, and allow all to come to the great feast. Know that God is calling all his Sons and Daughters to share in the feast.

There is no call for one above the other. All may partake and gain the grace and love of God so freely given since the dawn of time. Open your hearts, Dear Ones, and know that ye are the children of God with an invitation to dine. Pull up your chairs and feast on the bounty of God's love. Know there is no cost, for the meal is free, and the value will feed the soul; for such is the desire of God to feed his children, and to watch over them in love and peace.

Know, Dear Ones, that all may eat freely and fully till they can eat no more, for there is ample supply in the storehouse of God. There is an ample supply to feed all his children; so do not separate them and say, "Oh, ye are not worthy," and move them to the farthest corners and give them less than others.

Know that all are seen in the same way by God. All are of equal value; all are valued and loved by God. All are special; all are, indeed, the favored children of the Most High God.

Stray as you might, but know the Mother Father God will always love and keep thee in his bosom, for this is the way and will of God. There is no special group or country. All are brothers and sisters in the light and love of God. All are made in the light and love of God, and are the children of God. Look ye upon each other with this blessed light of love and know that you are one. You are indeed one, for you come from the same parentage; from the one source; you are all children of God. Look on and know, that you are your brother, and you are your neighbor, and your neighbor and your brother are you.

When you kill your brother, you kill your Father God. When you starve your brother, you starve God; for this is the nature, this is the task of man upon the Earth: to remember his true identity, and to return to the love of God and the bosom of God. For such is your task, such is your calling upon the Earth, to love one another, and to share in the gifts and bounty of God. Be full of the love and joy of God, and know that you are the joy, the love, and the peace of God, for this knowledge lives and burns deep within your soul. Know, Dear Ones, that you are all the chosen of God, and now you are the peace and love of God. Be who you were meant to be upon the Earth; the great bringers of peace, love, and joy upon the very foundations of the Earth. Be the passion, the love, and the light of God upon the Earth, for this is your calling, this is your destiny, this is your way. You are the children of God, given all you need; already programmed, knowing all you will ever need to know deep within you.

Open your hearts, and remember your heritage, for you are the chosen of God and you are the divine seekers of God. Remember! Remember and live! Cast not your eyes to the dust and say we are full of lack, for this is but an illusion. Open your eyes and see that you have all your needs met, for you are a child of the Most High God, given everything in his kingdom. You are the beloved of God, given all that you need to be happy and fulfilled. There is only lack and limitation in your mind, so release these thoughts, and see once more the bountiful table set before you. For you are light, you are love; you are the chosen of God, the children of God: All equal, and all special in the eyes of God. Like a parent, Mother Father God will watch over you, and even so will he bless and keep thee, for you are the chosen of God.

No race or creed is special, all are one, all are chosen, and all are Sons and Daughters of the Most High. Lift up your hearts and remember who you are, for you are light, you are love; you are the peace of God. Let not the darkness make you forgetful. Walk out into the light of God's love, and breathe the sweet fragrance of love that is there waiting for thee. Walk out into the light and feel the great peace of God. Feel the warmth of the radiance of God's love shining down upon you. Open your hearts. Remove the veil of forgetfulness that would tell thee, you are lost and alone. Step into the light and know that you are one with God. You are light, you are peace, you are joy, and you are LOVE. Forget not these truths; for this forgetfulness will lead you into despair.

Remember your birthright, and all the gifts you already possess. Know you are the Sons and Daughters of the Most High God. Know, Dear Ones, that you are loved and cherished by God... for you are the very beingness of God. Be your true selves, and see and know sweet peace, love, and happiness, for it is your birthright to know and to possess these gifts given to you by God. You are light, you are love, you are the chosen of God. Be the light in the world, and see and know the truth of your beingness: For you are the children of God, Sons and Daughters of the Most High.

Let not your minds tell you that you are separated from God, for indeed you are one with God; made from God, and ever a part of God. Like a child is ever connected to the parents, even so are you ever a part of God. For this is the truth of your being, this is who you are, Dear Ones. Return to the table, and eat and drink from the spiritual storehouse of God's bounty, for you are light, you are love, you are spirit, you are joy, you are peace. Return once more to the knowledge and love of who you truly are, and know the sweet peace, happiness, love, and joy, given to you at birth by God. Open your hearts, Dear Ones, and know once more the sweet bliss of God's love; for it is thine, if you will claim it and live. Be at peace, Dear Ones, and know that all your needs will be met, and all your wants supplied, for God has given you all that you need. You are light, you are love, you are joy, and you are the Sons and Daughters of God. Why would you be created to suffer and to know lack? It is only in your minds: for in truth the table is set, so pull up your chairs, and eat and drink and know sweet peace, for this is your heritage: this is your right, this is your gift.

Adieu

17ᵗʰ July 2011

Know, Dear Ones, that the love of God is the great leveler and the great teacher of mankind, for, indeed, it serves to take mankind out of his comfort and into new and unknown paths to test and to show his faith. For, indeed, man would not need to be tested, but of himself, he constantly worries and frets that he, of self, is not adequate and is not able to receive the richest blessings and the love that is daily poured out upon mankind. Thus, he feels he must be tested and tried and found eligible to receive the favor of God. O, know ye not, ye Sons and Daughters of Mankind, that ye are the chosen of God, and therefore there is no test or eligibility that you must prove? All is given freely without payment, so there is no measure to say this one is more worthy than the next. For in truth, each one is given equal measures of the boundless and eternal love of God.

Why think ye that the Mother Father God would need to measure or find thee worthy? Simply by being a child of the Most High God, each one is found eligible to receive the gifts from the Father. Know that no additional price is levied, no additional recompense is necessary. Each one, as a precious and loving child of God, is given all that he needs in order to be happy upon the Earth. Each one is given every blessing, and each one is given every joy that he can hold. For ye are the chosen of God, and so there are no reasons why you would not receive the blessings and the joys of God. Know, Dear Ones, that the Mother Father God will never not be there in your hour of need; never not love thee, and never not be there to love and to hold thee. For you are the beloved of God, the chosen of God, the Sons and Daughters of God. Know, Dear Ones, all gifts are freely given and all have everything that is needed. Only the physical mind keeps thee bound in chains and takes away the very memory of all that has been given by God. Know that it is this very forgetfulness that causes the pain of mankind. For in this forgetfulness, all the misery of mankind is found. For all believe that what they see with the physical eyes are all that exists.

O children, awaken from the dream, and remember that this is but a dream, and that you have all you need, already provided by Mother Father God. For this, indeed, is the nature and being of your Father, to give you all that you need. Know, Dear Ones, that the bountiful gifts are provided for all, but you fail to see and to remember these truths. Know, Dear Ones, that the very nature of your beingness cries out for help and for all that you already possess. Know, Dear Ones, that you are the Blessed; the chosen of God, and all is given to thee already.

Know, Dear Ones, that the love and blessings of God, flow without ceasing to you each and every day, but the blindness of the Earth causes you to forget, and to see not, all that is there prepared and given to thee. Open your hearts and remember your true nature, and return to the source of your strength, for it is God. Return once more to the very nature that created thee, and gave you life. For your Mother Father God is an abundant God, who is and has always, provided for thee from the beginning of time. Know, Dear Ones, that you are blinded by the distractions of the physical world, and so forget your own truths. You have forgotten your own light, and your love: For the distractions of the world would pull thee away from what is real, into the land of that which is true illusion. Know in truth, all that exists upon the Earth is true illusion. It is not of true value, for daily we see those who amass great physical wealth, but yet find no abiding peace: For the physical things which are not of God do not, and cannot, bring peace.

Thus, the soul continues in pain, searching… ever searching, for the elusive thing that will bring peace, love, joy and contentment. Know, Dear Ones, you search in vain, when you consider that what you seek can be found upon the face of the Earth. For truly, what you seek is within you, and no amount of searching can help you to find it. For unless you look deep within, you will wander upon the face of the Earth for many lifetimes in search of that most valued, and precious of all gifts: only to find that it exists not. For it cannot be found on the tallest of peaks, or in the deepest oceans of the world. Only in one place does it exist, and that is deep within the soul of man. Turn inwards, Dear Ones, and return to the peace found only inside your heart, and learn once more of the great peace, love, and joy of God which is possible: For it exists in you.

Know, Dear Ones, you cannot find the happiness you seek outside of yourself, for it is an elusive thing. It exists not. That is why so many have strived in vain, looking for the greatest treasures upon the Earth. Know, Dear Ones, that nothing in the physical world can give you the joys you seek; for you are doomed to wander the Earth, if this is your quest. For you will never find it there, for it lives only within you. So seek it not in outer trappings[82] and objects. Know that it lives only in your heart. There it lives indeed, the great love and peace of God, given to you eons ago. Know, Dear Ones, we are much in service to thee, for we see your plight and are anxious, if such we may say, to help thee to return to the peace that you seek. Know that this great peace can be yours, and you can attain that which you so desperately seek, Dear Ones. For, you are the ones that carry the joy of God within you. Remember your true nature, and begin to find this joy within your heart, for you are the vessels of joy: You house it in your very souls. So look not to the four corners of the Earth to find the joy of God, but know that this peace resides in you already.

Pull off the mask of forgetfulness, and return to your former state. Turn within, and see and find the eternal peace of God: For there, lurks and lives all that you need to survive and be happy. Turn within, and find the simple, yet beautiful and most wonderful of all gifts, given to you by God. Remember your true nature, and find once more the simple joys, and see and taste the happiness you seek. For it is within your nature, to see and know that these are the true joys and beauty of God. Turn within and understand your true self. This is the gift that is free. It is the joy that is free. It is the eternal peace of God. For you cannot find that which you seek in the outer trappings of life, for it lives only within you. Know the simple joys, and the true peace of God. Look within, for the simple, yet most beautiful of gifts. Look at the rose, and see the beauty; see the love that created this treasure… and see and taste the blessings of God.

---

[82]   Material things

Look upon your brethren with the same eyes that see the beauty of a rose, and see that same beauty, love, and grace within your brothers and sisters: For when you can see the beauty within yourselves, you can see it clearly everywhere. Remember your nature, and begin to see the beauty that is around you. For you are love, you are the children of God. Forget not all that was given to you, placed in your DNA coding since the dawn of time. Forget not who you are for you are joy, you are peace, you are love. Put away thoughts of lack, fear, and war. Put away thoughts of lack, and the inability to be satisfied, for you have all you need each and every day. Open your hearts and remember.

Look at life with the simplicity of a child and know all your needs will be met. Look at all those who strive daily for creature comforts, but find no peace and can never truly enjoy all they have amassed. For without the memory of the love of God, they are like lost sheep searching for that which will give them hope. They continue to toil and to wander aimlessly, never fully enjoying what they have gained. For they do not yet remember that they have all they need already. Know, Dear Ones, that indeed; you are the blessed of God, for you have all that you need within your soul. Search no longer outside yourself but go deep within, and recapture the peace and joy that is your birthright; for only then will you know the true happiness, peace, and joy of God.

For naught that you will find in the world, can give you the inner peace, and love, and joy of God. Know, Dear Ones, you carry this knowledge within you, and you can find the peace, happiness, and love you seek. Search no more in the world for that which will give you joy, but stop and go within, and find the treasure that lives within your heart. For the physical world cannot bring you that which you seek, when your soul yearns for God. As the soul yearns for the peace, love, and joy of the Father, it cannot be satisfied with trinkets and toys, for all these things are naught to the hungry soul. So take not the time and the energy to think that you can be fulfilled with the trappings of life. For only the love and peace of God can give you the true happiness you seek.

Once you find the joys of God, then all your needs can be met, and you can live in the true peace and love of God upon the Earth. Know that you have all you need within you, and all that you need to do is turn within. Let your hearts soar, and learn once more the true way to happiness. For you can never be fully at peace, until you return to the nature and love of your beingness. No thing or things can bring you peace, for your soul yearns for that one elusive thing it knows exists, which will bring joy, peace, and contentment; this is the love of God.

Open your minds, and return to the Father, by going within and shaking off the cobwebs that surround your memory. Sweep, as with a large broom, and remove all the trappings that would dull the senses, and cause thee not to remember the true mission here upon the Earth. Look for the love of your brethren, and give your love to your brethren, for you are one; made from the same "stuff," and being all a part of the family of God. For you are all indeed brothers and sisters.

You are all the children of God, and until you remember these truths and stop the killing, and the maiming, and the torture of your kin, you can never return to the true peace and love you seek. For it is against your nature to hurt those you love, so shake off the veil of forgetfulness, and see your brethren as though for the first time, and see and know that you are one; all brothers and sisters of the same family of God, not separated, not separate but one in God: One in love, one in peace, one in joy. When this is seen, then you can know true peace, true joy, true happiness; for then once more you will be reunited with your source energy, and can see and know you truly are the children of God, the Sons and Daughters of the Most High God. Then and only then, can you shine like the wonderful stars you are in the heavens. Be at peace, Dear Ones, and know that you will be well, and your hearts will be filled to the brim with the love, peace, and joy of God once more. Remember your heritage, and remember your joys, and shine like the stars you are, for you are joy, you are light, you are peace, and you are love.

Adieu

18TH JULY 2011

For the love of God, is that great peace which covers the Earth, and brings sweet peace to the hearts and minds of men. It is the very blanket that covers thee on a cold night, keeping out the frost and cold. It warms the body and keeps the soul in perfect happiness and peace. Know, Dear Ones, that this love that can keep thee warm, is that which the body craves. For like the blanket that covers and keeps thee warm, even so does the love of God cover thee, protect thee, and keep thee safe.

Know, Dear Ones that it allows you to know the sweet peace and bliss of repose [83] without cares or worry. For deep within the soul of man, lives the knowledge of the power of the love of God. Know, Dear Ones, that with this blanket comes the security that all is well and that the soul of man is protected; just as the blanket protects the body from the cold. Know, Dear Ones, that though the storms of life may come, naught can penetrate the blanket, for it keeps thee secure and it keeps thee dry and warm. Even so, does the love of God keep the Children of Men safe and secure in the arms of God. For

---

[83]   Resting the mind: tranquility

in truth, it keeps them safe and allows them to rest in sweet repose, without fear or worry, for it can quiet the troubled mind and keep thee safe in all storms that persist in life. This is the way of survival upon the Earth, for it allows the heart of man to fly while tethered to the ground. For indeed, the soul of man, whilst here on Earth, forgets how to fly into the heavens once more and so, like a man clothed in armor, he is unable to fly. With the love of God, he finds the wings of the morning once more, and can soar into the heavens; for such is the nature of the love of God: For it calls upon the souls to fly like the Angels they are, and to cast off the weight and chains of the Earth in favor of the golden wings of the soul. Know, Dear Ones, that it allows the soul of man to fly and to soar into the heavens once more; for without chains, he can now soar towards the heavens and be at peace, like the Spirit-Being he truly is.

Know, Dear Ones, that it is the nature of man to want to soar into the heavens, but he forgets how to get there without the love of God. His feet become like lead, and he is tethered to the ground, unable to move, and bound as though in the heaviest of chains. He is lost and alone, but weighted down and unable to move to the right or left, he remains in the vast emptiness of the regions of the Earth… unable to move upwards or to soar into that which he sees as the heavens.

Know, Dear Ones, that the love of God will cause man to soar into the heavens, for he feels like a bird in flight, free and unencumbered. He is light as a feather, and free to move through the air with the greatest of ease. This powerful love is that very thing which calls to him so that he knows that something is missing from his life, even though he cannot quite explain or imagine what it is. He searches, therefore, for this elusive thing, which will bring him the peace and joy he seeks. Know, Dear Ones that you will be safe and secure, when the wings of God's love are given to thee once more. In truth, we know that the wings, and the ability to fly, are always within the grasp of man... even though he has forgotten that he has this innate ability to fly.

Know that you may spread your wings and soar into the heavens at any time, Dear Ones, for you have the gift of flight, given to you eons ago. For this great love that is already thine, is there to be utilized and to enjoy. It gives thee sweet peace, love, and joy, and allows thee to soar and to grow. For this is the will of God to keep his children happy and to give them all the richest blessings available in his kingdom.

Look on and know, Dear Ones, that the love of God will, indeed, give thee the wings of life and allow thee to soar into the heavens; for this is the strength and the power of the love of God that has been given to humankind. Only the memory which is now buried in the soul can come once more to remind mankind, that all that he needs is already available to him. Know, Dear Ones, that the memory of all the joys, the peace, and the true happiness that is available to mankind can and will allow man once more to reach the stars, and to know the true and everlasting peace, love, and happiness that his soul yearns for, each and every day.

Know, Dear Ones, that the ability to fly and to soar into the heavens is thine. The ability, to be at eternal peace whilst here upon the Earth is already thine. Only the memory, the forgotten memory, keeps thee bound in chains and anchored as though with a great weight upon the Earth. Know indeed, that shackles exist only in your physical minds, and keeps thee ever bound in chains in the ignorance of the physical body, with the implied limitations of the physical body. Know that all is indeed possible for thee; and all is indeed available for thee, for these are the gifts of love of the Mother Father God, given freely to all the Children of Men.

These are the treasures of man, given by God to every one of his Sons and Daughters upon the Earth regardless of creed or color, race or ethnicity, for such is the beingness of man that he was created to reflect the many faces of God—if such we may say—for indeed we know that God has no face; for indeed he is Spirit, but in terms of the physical, we say the face. For the Spirit created man in the image of God, but that of course, entails the physical, and all the beingness that encompasses the very nature of God which is love. This then, is the likeness of God, to be love, to know love, and to show love to others. This, then, is the image and likeness of God... to be like God upon the Earth, doing and being the example of God upon the Earth... showing love, mercy, joy, peace, and happiness to all: Caring for your brethren and being the peace, happiness, and joy of God in human form. For without this man is naught, but with the spirit of God within him, he is all: the total joy of God; man in the physical flesh, with the love, peace, joy, and knowledge of God within the shell of man.

For such, man was placed upon the Earth to learn, and to experience the things of the physical world, and to grow and to become that most special of all God's children. Yet the memory fades, and man forgets all his gifts, and all his true innate ability, and becomes tied to the physical world, and is bound in chains by the forgetfulness, and forgets his nature. For he believes that he is a physical being, and has forgotten that he is a child of spirit, and is the spirit of God upon the Earth. He walks and carries himself like one bound in chains, instead of as an exalted Son and Daughter of the Most High God.

Know, Dear Ones, you keep yourself in chains. Cut them, and soar into the heavens. Release yourself from that which would hold thee to the ground, and keep thee tethered and in chains; for you are like an eagle whose wings are broken. You have forgotten how to fly. You know not who you are. You forget your joy, your history, your ability to fly and soar into the heavens, and all that you have ever known. Wipe away the things that keep thee in forgetfulness, and remember once more, you are the king of birds; the master of the skies, and return to your Mother Father God. For this is your true heritage. You are an eagle, walking along on the Earth, when you have the ability to fly, and to soar into the heavens, like the king of the skies.

Soar once more, my sisters and brothers, let your wings soar into the skies, and feel once more your true magnificence. For you are the mighty eagle. Be the boldest heart, and the proudest of all the birds of the air. Know you can soar at will into the heavens, so remember who you are and fly, fly, fly, with the knowledge of the love of God once more as your anchor.

You can do anything you wish in the skies, for you are not bound to the Earth. You have wings, so soar, soar, soar, and know once more the love, happiness, grace, joy, and peace of God. For you are the Sons and Daughters, given all you need. Soar, my dear brothers and sisters, soar, soar, soar into the heavens, and know sweet peace. This is your joy, this is your life, this is your destiny. Claim once more your heritage as Sons and Daughters of the Most High God, and fly, fly,

fly, for you were born to fly. It is your nature. It is in your heart. It is your gift. It is who you are. Fly, and return once more to the fold of God's love. For you are spirit, you are joy, and you are love.

Adieu

25THJULY 2011

THE GREAT RELEASE[84]

For, indeed, the time of man is limited upon the Earth. He spends a short time only upon the face of the Earth, and then he is gone. Gone from sight for certain, but not necessarily gone from the Earth. For indeed, we know that when the soul leaves the body, and the last breath is taken, the body dies but the soul returns to its former state and joins with the larger oversoul,[85]if such we may call it. For indeed, when a child is born, the soul spark that enters the human frame is but a tiny spark of the vast expanse which is the entire soul. For indeed, the entire soul cannot ever enter the physical body of man, for, indeed, the frail body cannot contain the vastness which is the soul.

Thus, only a portion of the soul enters the physical body of man while the remainder continues to exist in the very VORTEX as mentioned

---

[84]   This knowledge was given on the morning of July 25th 2011, prior to the transition to spirit of my dear friend and brother, Bob Jackson. I was later instructed to share these words with those who are grieving.

[85]   The absolute reality and basis of all existences conceived as a spiritual being in which the ideal nature imperfectly manifested in human beings is perfectly realized

by Brother Abraham.[86] For indeed, it exists simultaneously in both places at the same time. Thus, when the physical body dies, and is no more; the spark that was within the physical shell of man is once more joined with the greater or larger oversoul, and is once more One.

Thus, the leaving at the point of death is a glorious return for the soul. For it truly becomes One once more, and basks in the true freedom of spirit in its totality.

Know, Dear Ones, that death and the return to spirit, is indeed a glorious event for the soul of man; for indeed, it is returning to its natural state. For you, Dear Ones, are spirit, forced if you like, to exist within a physical frame, with all of the difficulties and the limitations of the physical body. Thus, the release of death is a joyous return to become that which it is, (all spirit) once more. The leaving of the physical body, is akin to one being in a deep, dark dungeon, then being released to the light once more. For it takes a while for the soul to fully release all the attributes it had acquired whilst in the physical body, (in order to allow man the freedom to be at peace and to exist within the frame) if such we may call it. With the release of death, comes the great awakening, and the freedom, as if given wings. For indeed, the soul soars, and as with the wings of the fastest birds or even of Angels, if such we may describe it: It has left the body, and is seeking to return once more to its natural state, and to become one with that part of itself which was always already living, if such you can call it, in spirit.

---

86   Getting Into the Vortex…Esther and Jerry Hicks: The Teachings of Abraham

For this is the reason for the great peace seen on the face of man as he leaves the physical body. For it is a releasing of all that was cumbersome, to the light and happy un-bounding happiness of spirit. Here once more, it can soar through the heavens, if such is the desire, and move unfettered without the need to return to the prison, if such we may call it, of the physical body. Know, Sweet Ones, that as spiritual beings within a physical body, there is much adaptation that takes place at birth.

But indeed, all of that is forgotten when at the moment of death or 'The Great Release' the spirit can leave the body and soar back to its very nature.

Know also, Dear Ones, that in truth, all souls do not depart the Earth with quick and unencumbered speed. For in truth, when the grief is strong, and the attachment to other souls within the incarnation are emotionally intense, the spirit will remain upon the Earth to comfort those who grieve its departure. For such is the nature of death and loss, that man will sometimes feel that he cannot continue to live without the presence of the departed one. In such cases, the spirit will remain until the pain of the loss is not as strong, and it is able to leave the Earth and return to the Mother Father God. For indeed, the pull of the spirit to return to its source is strong; but yet, even so is the need to comfort those who grieve the loss of the physical contact of the soul who has left the physical body. Know, Dear Ones, that this is indeed one of the most difficult tasks for man to bear, and it is indeed complicated by the fact that man has forgotten that he is a spiritual being, and is only able to grasp that he is a physical being: And believes that the soul that has departed is no more.

Know, Dear Ones, that this is not so, for indeed the soul lives on and is indeed returned to spirit that it always was, and always will be; for it is eternal, and thus, will never die. For in truth, the connection of all souls will continue. For the death has simply removed the body from view, but the soul lives on.

The soul of man will thus be able to return to the Earth for many eons, if it so chooses; but know, Dear Ones, that death is simply the end of the current life-cycle and the rebirth of a new and greater opportunity to return once more to spirit, and to the joys of that state: unencumbered by the needs of the physical body, and all that is associated with living in a physical body.

Thus, the departure from the view of man at death is but the turning of the page of a great book, and the ending of a chapter. For with the beginning of the next chapter, upon the next page, comes new opportunities, and new knowledge which will help the soul of man to progress upon its journey through the vast experiences possible within the universe of experiences.

Know, Dear Ones, that death is nothing to fear, and that man fears it simply because he forgets that he is Spirit, and that he is returning to his natural state. Thus, the return is a joyful and happy experience which frees him from the Earth, and returns him once more to the joys of the spirit... which is who and what he is.

There is no sorrow in spirit, for all is well. There is sadness when the connection with man and the physical body is involved, but without this, there is only peace, love, and the light of God; which is all that the soul needs. For in truth it is blissfully at peace, basking in the love, peace, and joy of God from whom it does not like to be separated for too long. When the soul can be released from the physical body, and return once more to its Mother Father God, there is indeed great rejoicing in spirit, but pain on the physical side where there is experienced a great loss. For the belief is that the departing soul/spirit will never be seen again. Know, Dear Ones, that all are one in spirit and so the departing one will be experienced once more when all are returned to spirit.

Be not fearful of death or the 'Great Release,' if such we may refer to it, for it is a joyful state, not a fearful one. For there is but peace, love, and joy which awaits the departing soul in the uniting, once more in its natural state of bliss and great happiness.

Know, Dear Ones, we are always there in some state, when souls return to the Mother Father God. For this is indeed a great celebration: For a great return to the fold has happened and the return is celebrated in spirit, whilst on Earth the pain is experienced and seen as loss. There is no loss in God, for we are One. We are simply separated then reunited. That is in its simplest form, the explanation of what has occurred. For such is the nature of Spirit, and such is the nature of the release, and the joining of man, at the moment of death.

Be at peace, Dear Ones, and know that there is and can be no loss; for all are One in God, and all return to God at the time of death. For this is the way of Spirit, this is the way of God. Thus you may come to understand why when in the physical, the Angels are here upon the Earth, to support man when in the physical form upon the Earth. For as a beloved and most cherished part of the Most High God, it is necessary to protect, defend, support, love, and uphold man, so that he can experience all the things that were put in motion to be experienced in that incarnation. Know there are no coincidences, and nothing happens by accident: For all happens as it should in God. Know that the great love of God will not cause him to leave his children alone in physical form, without the love, comfort, and guidance, of his parent.

That man has forgotten his parentage, and knows not who he is when in the physical, is the difficult part of the experience. For he must forget his link to God, but must then learn once more how to return to the Father. The distractions of the physical world remove most of the memory of who he truly is, and thus we find the problem. For the true task is for man, whilst in the physical body, to remember who he is…and to find his way back to God. For this is the greatest of lessons for man. (How to be a spiritual being in a physical body, and yet keep the connection with God at the forefront of this life; throughout the experience.)This, then, is the great challenge of man. For in truth, he forgets his link to the Divine, and is lost upon the Earth.

Like a sailor lost at sea with no compass to guide him, he is alone in a sea of despair, tossed by the storms of life night and day. He can find no solace, no comfort, and no peace; for he is alone, he thinks, and is forsaken by God: So he wanders the seas, unable to find his way home.

Remember your heritage, O Sons and Daughters of the Most High God, and know you are never alone; for you are never forsaken of God. You are always guided. Even though you may not recognize it, you are being helped and guided by Angels, if you would pay attention to the still, small voice within you, telling you that all is well: For this is indeed the voice of God calling you, and trying to remind you that you are never alone, for he is ever with and within thee. Be at peace, and know that all is indeed well with thee, for your Mother Father God will never leave thee; and you can never leave him. For you are one with God, and thus can never be separated from the love of God. You may forget your heritage, and forget your link, but it is always there, and you are always loved and cherished; for this is the nature and beingness of God.

You are ever loved, ever cared for, and ever in the grace and loving arms of God. Know this, Dear Ones, and know true peace, joy, and happiness, for this is the very nature of God, and this also is your very nature as a Son and Daughter of the Most High God. Be at peace, and know that all is well for thee, and with thee, for you are ever in the loving arms of God.

While your physical memory may fail you, and you think you are alone, know that you are ever in the arms of God and enfolded with his love. Be at peace and know that all is indeed well.

Adieu

30ᵀᴴ OCTOBER 2011

Know indeed, that the love of God is like the flower of the sweetest and most beautiful of flowers, for lo, it gives fragrance and great beauty to all around it. For indeed, it has the power to bring joy to all who would look upon it: Even so, is the great happiness and joy that is evident in the hearts of men, who when in doubt and fear, call upon the name of the Lord. Know indeed, that the knowledge of the love of God brings even so the greatest joy and happiness to all within its viewing. Let not your hearts be troubled, Dear Ones, but know indeed that the love of God is that most beautiful of flowers, for to be sure, it brings that same happiness and joy into the hearts of men. For indeed, without it they wander to and fro, unable to find their way home.

Like lost sheep, they go this way and that, not knowing why they wander aimlessly; but yet fully aware, that some great prize is lost. Look up, ye Children of Men, and know that the prize you seek even now sits in plain sight: For it is indeed within your heart, and is not gone from view. Open your hearts and remember your heritage, and know that the Lord of your beingness continues to live within you. Let not the fear of forgetfulness confuse thee and cause you to think that you are alone, for you are never alone; for your Mother Father God is always with you, always there beside you, when you would walk through the storms of life. Know indeed, Dear Ones that this love is all that you need. For with it comes the knowledge that you have all that you desire, already available to you in your palms at this very moment.

Open your hearts and look not to the hills for your help, for your help comes, indeed, from within for there, indeed, is the knowledge of the love of God, and the true knowledge that all that you need is indeed always made available to thee. Know indeed, Dear Ones that this great love is the source of life for mankind; for from it has been provided all that you will ever need. Know indeed, that the very foundations of the Earth will quake with the knowledge that the love of God is that great treasure that man has craved and hunted for, for eons.

Know indeed, Dear Ones, that the knowledge of the absence of nothing, in the lives and hearts of men, will cause you to say, "Surely this is not so, for we have hunted and search for this thing for so long. How can it be that we have had it all along?" Know indeed, that the darkness and the great clouding of your minds to protect thee when in physical form, allow the Sons of Men to forget all things. Thus, they know that something of great value is missing in their lives, but in fear, and doubt, and worry, cannot yet identify what is lost or where it could be.

Open your hearts and shake off the veil of forgetfulness and know, Dear Ones that your loving Mother Father God, would never leave thee alone: And indeed, has given you all you ever need to survive upon the Earth. For the love of God is thine, given freely since the dawn of time; given so that all may know it and live: So that all indeed may know it and come to know the true love, and light, and happiness, that is there made available to the Sons and Daughters of man.

Know indeed, that the fear of loss or the longing and wishing for more, which has always been a part of the nature of man, comes from this very thing. For to be sure, Dear Ones, the great knowledge of the power of the love of God is indeed the treasure that man has sought for eons.

Know indeed, it is that most powerful of all gifts, for it has the power to bring peace, joy, and happiness to those in turmoil, and to calm those who, in peril, know no peace.

Let not your heart be troubled, but know indeed that the Sons of Men have this most precious gift given freely. Open your hearts and remember your heritage, and know how precious you are to the very heart of God. For indeed, you are the Sons and Daughters of the Most High God, given all you will ever need. All you need to do to access it is to remember that you have it. Once this has come to be, you will know once more how precious you are, and will then be able to flow like the mightiest of rivers into the sea of God's love. For indeed, it is there within you, but the memory of it has faded from your minds; so now with the veil of forgetfulness lifted, you can be the most blessed and mighty beings you are. For indeed, with this knowledge, man feels he is whole. He is invincible, and needs nothing else in life. For he truly has everything a man can ever need or want already within him.

Let not your hearts be troubled, Dear Ones, but know indeed that your Heavenly Father has given you all you will ever need, and you have indeed been carrying it around with you, totally unaware of the precious gift already available to you. You have spent so much time searching for that which you already have been given. Open your hearts, O Children of Men, and see and know that the peace, love, joy, and happiness you have been seeking is already yours.

You can now stop the aimless searching, and the wandering upon the face of the Earth: For the treasure has been found. Look you no longer outside you, for the bounty of God was already given to thee so many eons ago. Now is your charge, to use this knowledge to change your way of being in the world. For indeed, the knowledge of the power of the love of God will cause you to change your ways; for indeed, you now know that with the knowledge of the love of God, you can no longer continue to kill or maim your brethren. You can no longer do these things to cause hurt and pain to your brother and say, "We do it in the name of God." For indeed, you know that God is the God of love, so to say you kill or maim in his name is to go against all that is God. For God is the God of love, not a God of hate, or fear, or anger, or wrath. He does not love one child more than another. He has no favorite nation or clan, for all are indeed one in the eyes of God if such we may use these words, for indeed, God has no eyes.

Know indeed that God, like you, Dear Ones, is spirit, and light, and love. God does not exist in physical form, and you cannot see him in the physical, for he is spirit. Know, Dear Ones, that indeed you see representatives of God—if such we may describe it— when you see evidence of love, joy, peace, and happiness. When you see or show evidence of caring and sharing the bounty of the Earth with your brethren, you see God. For God is love, and when you show acts of love and benevolence to anyone, you see and show God in you; for God is indeed within each of you, Dear Ones, and you can show this. When you show love and kindness to others, you show God. When you kill your brethren, you show not God, for God does not condone the killing of anyone regardless of the cause: For indeed, this is not the way or beingness of God. For a God of love cannot kill and cannot starve his brethren. A God of love cannot condone the bringing of pain against your brethren, for this is not the way of God. For the way of God is love. The knowledge of God is love. The path of God is love. GOD IS LOVE! God is not hate, fear, wrath, or anger. GOD IS LOVE!

You are a part of God, so likewise, Dear Ones; know that you are also LOVE. Know indeed, you must know and remember this truth, for this will set you free and cause you to turn away from the path that would cause you to bring pain and hurt to others. For this has never been the way of God. The understanding of man for eons, has led him to believe that God was a punishing and unforgiving God. Know indeed that this knowledge or belief of God was not given. For indeed, the teachings of our Dear Jesus taught that God is love. Look ye also to the other prophets and messengers who taught the message of love and peace upon the Earth. Know indeed, that the message of peace and love and the joys of God, when distasteful to the will and desires of man, were changed so that they echoed the will of man and not the will of God.

Know indeed, Dear Ones, that this is indeed the time for the great knowing, and a great reminder to open your hearts, and see, and know, that most ancient of truths as spoken so many moons ago: that

God is love. God is and can only be love; for he is an abundant and loving God. It is only the will and desires of man who would take from the weak, and gather up wealth in storehouses and banks, that say God is not a God of love.

Look on and know that the Sons of Men have taken the teachings, and removed the truth of God from within them, in order to satisfy the will of men...and to justify the will of men and the greed of men upon the Earth. For in truth, look back in your history, O Children of Men, and see and know the truth. For in order to justify the killing of your brethren and pillaging of the goods or wealth of others, man has taken it and claimed it as the will of God, in the name of God. Know indeed, that Mother Father God has no need for possessions of land or wealth, for he has given all these things in abundance to the Sons of Men. Take ye not, therefore, the name of the Lord in vain any longer, Dear Ones, and no longer say we kill or maim in the name of God, for this is not the way of God! When you kill, your do so not in the name of God, but from the forgetfulness of the true way of God! For a God of love does not kill! It is the way of mankind—when they forget that God is the God of love— to kill and to starve his brother. For in so doing, he is using his power to harm, not to help his brethren.

Look on and know that a God of love does not cause man to kill, or maim, or starve his brethren. Take not from the weak and store up the wealth of the world in storehouses for yourselves, but instead come to a new knowing that when you show love, you show joy, happiness, and the true ways of God. For it is the nature of God to love, and to love his children unconditionally. Know that his love was, and is, given to all without condition, and thus, man is to share the wealth of the world with his neighbor. For you are ONE, from the same parent, Mother Father God. Look into the eyes of your brethren, and see that God lives there. Look upon the face of a stranger, and know, even so, that God lives there: For this is the truth of God, the joy of God, the blessings of God.

FOR GOD IS LOVE, and that is, and always has been, the true nature and beingness of God. For the love of God is there for all. Know, Dear Ones, each and every soul upon the Earth is a child of God. Tear down the walls that would serve only to divide you, and to show you what you believe to be differences among the Sons of Men, and look instead to the brotherhood of all mankind.

For this is the true nature and beingness of God. This, then, is the nature of God. God is a God only of love. He is not a God of hate, or envy, or war. He is a God of LOVE!

No longer can you say, "Our cause is just, for we kill in the name of God." When you kill, you kill not in the name of God, but for the cause of man. For to say you kill in the name of God, is to go against the very heart of God. For how can God condone the killing of his own Sons and Daughters? Know indeed, Dear Ones, that when you remember who you are—that you are the Sons and Daughters of God— you cannot continue to kill and maim others, and forget that they also are children of God. All are one in the eyes of God, and all are given the same gifts for eternity. To kill or to maim is to go against the very heart of God, and to forget the true nature of God. For a God of love cannot be a God of war or hate…and a God of love cannot support one group against another, for all are his children. Remember, Dear Ones, that a house divided against itself cannot stand, and only a house united can face the storms of life and live. Know, Dear Ones, you have the memory and love of God buried deep within your heart. Use this knowledge to help each other and to be the shining lights you were meant to be upon the Earth. Let not fear and greed cause you to forget your true selves or your true nature, for you are love, you are peace, you are joy upon the Earth. For you are the children of God upon the Earth.

Look ye no longer for the differences that you see with the eyes of man, but look ye at your brethren and see them with your heart instead, and know these truths. For when you see your brethren with your heart, you see them as they truly are: your brothers and sisters in God. When you see them with the human eye, you see them as strangers and enemies, and you see them as different.

Close your human eyes, and use your heart to look upon your brethren, and know that what you see are only the things of God. Leave behind the fear that would make you believe you are different. Know instead that you are all one. When you are cut, do you not all bleed? When the outer trappings of men are removed, do not all men look the same under the skin? Are not all men the same? If and when you turn out the lights how do you know that your brethren are different? The answer, Dear Ones, is that you are misled, by that which you see, into believing that this outer trapping is that which defines man; for indeed, you are not defined by what you see. The heart of man is that which defines him. Look on, and know, and remember, that you are all one even though you come in different packaging— if such we may describe it— for indeed, you may look different but you all have the same needs, wants, and desires. You have the same parentage: Mother Father God, and thus you cannot continue to kill your own brothers and sisters, and justify it to say we do this in the name of God. For this is not so, for none can kill in the name of God: For God cannot justify the taking of one human life in his name. Only the veil of forgetfulness and the desires of man cause you to kill or starve your brethren. Forget not that you are ONE. See the similarities and grow. See the love, see the heart of God in all you meet, and know that you can know true peace, love, and happiness upon the Earth. Know that these are the ways of God: Love, peace, joy, and compassion…these are the ways of God.

Hate, killing, starvation, envy, and negative actions are not the ways of God. Choose therefore to remember who you are and to follow the ways of God, for this is your hope, this is your joy; this is your destiny, Dear Ones. All else is folly, for they would lead you astray and cause you to say there is no God.

Know indeed God exists, even though you fail to see it; for it is more advantageous to think that God exists not. Open your hearts, and see and know that God exists in all men, so forget not this truth. Try as you may, know that at the center of the being of all men upon the Earth, regardless of creed or color, race or religion, lives the heart of God. For though you may call God by different names, you all search for the one same elusive thing that already lives within you: The LOVE of God.

Call not God by name, and say he serves our cause but look to God in your heart and know that there are no favorites, for all are one in God. For this is your true hope, this is your joy; this is your way to true happiness upon the Earth. Remove the veil of forgetfulness, and live, Dear Ones. Open your eyes and see your brethren with new vision, for the old vision was indeed clouded by the fear, hate, envy, and jealousy, and the things that would divide the Sons of Men.

Open your hearts, Dear Ones, and see only that all are one, united in the love of God... and begin to know the true joys that can be found upon the Earth. For to kill is to go against the heart and soul of God, if such we may describe it, for God is the God of love, and thus he cannot condone the killing of his own Sons and Daughters. Open your eyes and see, and know the true peace, joy, and love of God. This is your only charge, Dear Ones, to see the truth of God and then you can taste all the riches and the blessings of God; for this is your true nature, this is your true joy. This is your birthright. This is the truth of your beingness, for you are the Sons and Daughters of the Most High God, and to love is the very heart of your beingness. Open your hearts and close your eyes, and see the love of God come upon the Earth: for therein lie your happiness, peace, and prosperity upon the Earth.

Adieu

19TH JANUARY 2012

YOU ARE LIGHT, YOU ARE LOVE, YOU ARE PEACE YOU ARE JOY.

Know, indeed, that the loving power of the Most High God is given to the Children of Men to allow them to prosper upon the Earth, and to come into the fullness of the realization of the love of God. Know indeed, Dear Ones, that the love of God is such a wonderful and beautiful aspect of the nature of man, that the two cannot be separated. Know indeed, Dear One, we say that the love of God is truly all that man needs in order to come into his glory upon the Earth: For he is the very source of all that is most noble, and all that is most blessed in the name and nature of God. Know, Dear One, that the love of God for man is shown each day in the very nature and way that the Earth provides all that man needs in order to survive, and to be able to live and grow upon the Earth.

Know indeed, Dear One, that the love of God for man is the all-encompassing truth and blessing that will take mankind to the very source and blessing that is God; for indeed God is love, and has always been love. Yet the nature of man has not been able to conceptualize that God is such, and instead he was seen as a punitive, willful, and vengeful God.

Know indeed, Dear Ones, that this has never been the nature of God, but only the mind of man who has seen God in this way, and has helped to bring this thought of God into fruition. Know, indeed, that the love of God for mankind has, and will always be, the most blessed of all things upon the Earth and indeed, throughout the Universe. For in no way does the Mother Father God need to bring vengeance upon the Sons of Men, for indeed he (man) is able to do this of his own self. For indeed, when you look back upon your history, you see only too clearly the evidence of man's forgetfulness and his willful, wanton, destructive behaviors, which have caused great pain to come upon the Sons of Men... not of God's doing, but of man's doing.

For indeed, the nature and beingness of God is that of pure unconditional love, and thus we say, Dear Ones, that God could and would never be a vengeful God; for He is the essence of only love, so acts of vengeance are not within the thought or actions of God. For indeed, that would be as if God were to turn upon himself, if such we were to describe it, for in truth, God cannot turn upon himself and go against his nature, for his nature is only of love. Thus, Dear Ones, He cannot harm or turn wrath upon the Sons of Men, because God has no wrath. He is love ALWAYS and forever, and can only give love and be love. Ever loving, ever protective, of his children; ever wanting to give man all that his heart craves.

Only man's forgetfulness keeps those gifts at bay, for indeed when in the forgetfulness of the human frame, man knows not himself and turns to all the self-destructive vices that are made available upon the Earth. He is destructive to self and all those around him, and thus he is not able to show those very acts of love and compassion to his brethren. For his thoughts are of self, and the gratification of the immediate needs of the self. Thus, all his focus is upon attaining the things of his heart, and he would take from the weak and condemn them for their failure to do and be strong.

Know, Dear Ones, such has been the nature of man for eons, and such has been the behaviors of man upon the Earth; for indeed he has been the source of the pain and suffering of his brethren and indeed of himself. For he, and not God, has caused the wars, the famine, and the very plagues attributed to the vengeance of God. Know, indeed, that God would not harm his children, for he is a loving and forgiving God. God would not destroy his children or bring pain and suffering upon them, for this is against the very nature of God. For God is LOVE, and only LOVE. There is no negative side to God. These things are attributed to God, but know indeed they are human characteristics, and the human mind can only see God with human traits; thus he characterizes God in his heart as all powerful, all knowing, all destructive, all vengeful.

Know, Dear Ones, that God is ALL LOVE and only LOVE. His thoughts— if such we can describe them— are only of love and protection for his children. Thus, his Angels here on Earth are charged to save man from himself, and to help him to become his true God-self: For indeed, since man is made from the essence of God, he is also love at his core. Only the forgetfulness, when in human form, brings the pain of separation, for he knows not who he is and he turns to the ways of pain and suffering not only for self but for all in his path. He sees no love but only pain in his life, and thinks he is alone. He sees not life, but death. For indeed, man lives with the thoughts of death as the final and only way that he will go; for indeed he has forgotten that he is a spiritual being having an earthly experience, and thus all is temporary; all is not eternal. The pain and suffering he finds in his life are not eternal, but indeed are lessons he would learn while here upon the Earth in physical form.

Know indeed. Dear Ones, that this love of God of which we speak, is truly all there is; for with it, man is able to do and be all things that he craves. He has the love of God given to him freely, yet he sees and knows it not, for in his forgetfulness, he sees only lack and he is separated from the great field and force that is the love of God. Thus he turns to ways of greed, and anger, and destruction, and hurts those around him. He is lost. He is separated, he believes, and so he acts alone, and is not able to see all the wonders and the beauty that is the love of God made manifest in his life. He is alone in his heart, as one walking in the desert. In this desolation and loneliness, he loses himself, and he knows only pain; thus he can now inflict pain upon his brethren. The wars and the destruction brought upon the Earth by the Sons of Men, for eons, have been because of his great pain, but yet in his infancy, he has attributed all these things to the name and nature of God.

Know, Dear Ones, that this is not the nature of God, but the nature of man when in physical form, that is here seen in evidence. For God cannot ever leave his children. He cannot desert them; he cannot punish them; for it is not within the nature of God, for he is all LOVE, all COMPASSION, all PEACE, and all JOY. This is the beingness and nature of God, and nothing that man can do could ever cause God to turn away from him, for this would be like the mother deserting her infant child. For indeed, when in physical form upon the Earth, man is once more an infant learning about his world by touch and sight, until he has the words to give it more deeper meaning. Know, Dear Ones that the LOVE of God is ever present, never absent, if you would but come to know this truth; for it is and has ever been thine.

Turn, O Sons and Daughters! And remember your truth, and know once more your true nature; for you also are LOVE! You also are SPIRIT! You also are PEACE and JOY! Turn away from the thoughts that say you are neglected by God, or forgotten of God; for such a thing cannot be, for you are ever loved, ever cradled in the arms of God. You are the children of God, loved and adored by God. You are the joy of God, unconditionally loved by God, and provided for by God, if you would but open your hands and your heart to receive all your blessings: For you are the peace, the love, and the very joy of God.

Be you not torn and separated in your thinking, but know you are the Sons and Daughters of God, given all you need to survive upon the Earth. Let not the veil of forgetfulness cause you to think you are alone and without LOVE, for you are loved beyond measure, and you are the heart of God. You are the peace, and the love, and the joy of God.

Be you happy to know, that God has loved you since the dawn of time, and will continue to love you now and forever; for that is his nature and you are his children. Be not afraid and say, "God cannot love me for I am without worth or favor," but know indeed that you are of immense value in the eyes of God, if such we may describe it, for you are his joy, his heart, his love, and his peace. You are the jewel of God, and the most precious of all gems imaginable. Know indeed, Dear Ones that the love of God created you, and remains a part of who and what you are. You are spirit, you are light, you are love, you are peace, you are joy.

Turn away from thoughts and acts of negativity, and know that you are so much more than you can ever imagine, for you are supreme in the eyes of God. You are magnificent beings, given all you need to be happy and contented upon the Earth. Turn away from greed, selfishness, and pain, Dear Ones, and come to know the true peace, happiness, joy, and love that is God.

Turn inwards, and know your true selves, for that which you see reflected back at you in the mirror is not your true self. It is merely the shell that houses the true selves. Go within, and find once more the essence of who you are, and then you will come to know the true peace, love, and joy that is you: And then you can come to realize that this also is the truth of God. For God will not judge thee or condemn thee, for he is unconditional love, and as such, cannot judge. All that he can do is love, and support, and provide for thee. Look within, Dear Ones, and find the truth of your being, and know once more that you are the Children of the Most High God, given all you will ever need to survive upon the Earth, given all the gifts of God, the greatest of which is LOVE.

Adieu, Dear Ones! May the peace and blessings of God continue to reign in your hearts, now and forever.

Adieu

25ᵀᴴ FEBRUARY 2012

For indeed, the love of God for mankind is daily evidenced in the very stars and the joyous sounds of nature; for indeed, you are shown the wonders of the power and majesty of the great and glorious Mother Father God, who in all his blessings and love, provides all that is needed by the Sons of Men. Know indeed, Dear Ones, that the Children of Men are daily given all they need to survive upon the Earth, but in their forgetfulness and the great fog that blinds their eyes, they see not all the marvelous works of God: For indeed, they are aware only of themselves and their needs. They know not of all that is possible in the heavens and upon the Earth, as it is shared by Mother Father God with the Sons of Men.

Know indeed, Dear Ones, the Children of Men are daily loved and provided for. Daily watched and loved by a loving parent who provides all that is needed by his children. Know indeed, Dear Ones, that this love which allows man to stumble and fall, and yet rise and learn, are parts of the very heart and soul of the teachings of Mother Father God for the Sons of Men. For indeed without this knowledge, the Children of Men would falter and die upon the Earth. For in truth, they are like fledgling birds who, if removed from the nest before they are able to fly, will indeed fall prey to the things around them and will be lost. Know, Dear Ones that even as each fledgling is protected and provided for by Mother Father God, even so are the Children of Men carefully watched and protected, and fed by Mother Father God. For like any parent; he is ever protective, ever loving, ever caring, and always there and available to watch over his children.

Know, Dear Ones, that the Children of Men, like the birds, are still learning how to fly, and thus like a fledgling, although they flap their wings, they are as yet not fully versed in the art of flying. So with tenderness and love, Mother Father God continues to teach his children how to master the art of flying.

Know, Dear Ones, that once the knowledge is gained, the lesson is learned, and the child has no more need of the parent. For in growing and gaining independence, he is now able to survive in the world.

Know, Dear Ones, that the love of God is and will always be thine. For although you have gained the knowledge of flight, know there are many dangers still to be faced, and much to be learned about survival upon the Earth. Know indeed, Dear Ones, that the Sons of Men will ever be in need of the love and guidance of Mother Father God; for in truth, they cannot survive without continued lessons in survival. For the children, though able to fly, must learn and understand the dangers of the material world. For indeed, the distractions of the physical life averts the gaze of the children, and thus as one temporarily blinded by the rays of the sun, they lose their way along the path and are lost.

Know indeed, Dear Ones that the Sons of Men are ever in the learning and growing phases of life; for in truth, this is a constantly changing and emerging field. For each day, as new distractions arise, the Children of Men are pulled this way and that, and they lose their way in the world. For they know not how to be in the world but yet not of it. For lo, they leave and forget all they have ever known, when distracted by the things of the world. They forget their divinity and their nature as children of Mother Father God, and so would spend their time in play.

Know, Dear Ones, that the reason for your time here upon the Earth is to grow, and to learn, and to remember once more who you are. For you are the Children of the Most High God, loved and cherished since the dawn of time. Your path is to grow and to remember once more your true nature, for you are the Sons and Daughters of God.

Know indeed, Dear Ones, that you are ever loved, ever cherished, and ever held in the bosom of Mother Father God. Know that the days and nights of pain upon the Earth are due to your forgetfulness, Dear Ones. For as you forget your path and your nature, you suffer the great pain of separation from your Mother Father God; for only in your mind do you feel you are separated from God. For in truth, you are ever enfolded in the loving arms of God. Only your forgetfulness would make you think you are alone.

Know Dear Ones, that you are ever guided, ever loved, ever protected; for your loving parent would never desert thee, never allow you to be alone and bereft of the love and support of your Father. Be not alarmed and say, "I am thrown from the nest and forgotten with none to care for me," for in truth you are never alone, never forsaken, but always loved and adored. Know indeed, Dear Ones, you are precious in the eyes of God, and are ever guided, if you would only awaken from the fog and the path of forgetfulness, and come once more into the realization of your true nature. For your nature is one of love, peace, and happiness; yet whilst in your state of forgetfulness, you would remember not these truths.

Know, Dear Ones, you are the blessed of God, the children of God, the beloved of God. Be not afraid to know and to believe these truths, for this is truly your heritage, your joy, your heart, and your beingness as children of the Most High God. Know indeed, Dear Ones, you are the love and light of God. Be you ever at peace and know indeed that the peace and blessings of God are ever yours. Know that the love of God is ever thine Dear Ones.

Adieu

4TH March 2012

Know, indeed, that the love of God is likened to a man walking along the shores of a great lake. For in truth, he stands at one bank and looks in the distance at the other bank. He wonders how he will ever cross this lake to see what is on the other shore, and is bereft of all thoughts of how he will get to the other side. Know, Dear Ones that the love of God is the very boat that lies tethered to the pier in front of him, for it is the very thing which will take him across the water to the other side... so that he may indeed see all that is there made available. Know indeed, when he looked at first, he was alone and naught was in sight. But now on looking again, his eyes are opened and he sees the very means of his travel made available to him.

Know indeed, Dear Ones, that the boat was always there, but he could not see it until he had the need; likewise is the love of God made available to the Sons of Men. For it has been thine since the dawn of time, but yet in your ignorance and forgetfulness, you could not see or know of its existence. Yet when you are ready, Dear Ones, and your eyes are opened, even so can you suddenly begin to see that which you need, provided for thee by Mother Father God.

Know indeed, the love of God is the boat, and it will take thee wherever you would go on calm or on troubled waters; for indeed, it will allow thee safe passage. It will allow thee to travel to places yet unknown and undiscovered, and will give thee the peace, love, and joy that you seek. Know indeed, Dear Ones, that the love of God is the boat that can carry thee safely to the shores of God's love. It will protect thee from the storms of life, and keep thee warm and dry. Know, Dear Ones, it is the life giving stream that flows for thee; the essence of happiness, peace, and joy. For with it all your needs are met, and all your desires are provided without thought of payment.

No life or sacrifice is exacted, for it is given freely. All you need to do is open your eyes and your arms, and see and receive this most wonderful of all gifts. Get into the boat, Dear Ones, and see and know it will protect thee. Know that the waves cannot come into the boat, for the love of God is the great protector of all things for thee: For it is the source of your true life, and it is that thing which gives thee life and wisdom. For it allows you to see and know how much you are loved and adored by Mother Father God: For in truth, it is all that you need, and with this knowledge made available for thee, you are in need of naught else, for your every want and needs are supplied.

Know, Dear Ones, the boat of life is welcoming you, and is made available to take you wherever you may wish to go. You simply need to remember that it is there and climb in. There is no need to worry or fret, for the oars and the rudder are set and are ready to steer you safely to the other side of the vast lake that hitherto you thought was too far and wide to cross.

Know, Dear Ones, you have the ability to go wherever you would travel, and to see all that is upon the lake and along the shores; for indeed it is a wonderful lake, and has many hidden wonders.

Know indeed that your former thoughts that this lake is large and wide, and you were unable to see or know of its beauty, are now lost thoughts. For indeed, you see you can step into the boat, and see and know all that was formerly out of your reach.

Know indeed, Dear Ones, that even so can the love of God ferry you across the oceans and the storms of life; for it will keep thee safe, and warm, and dry. Even when the waters of life would lap around you, and you would think and believe that all is lost, know that the love of God can and will protect thee, for it will give you life. It will give you the knowledge and the skills to keep you safe, and to help you to be that which you were meant to be upon the Earth. Wander no more like lost sheep, O Sons and Daughters of Mankind, upon the land, trying to think of a way to get to the other side! Open your heart and your eyes, and see this means of travel! Recognize it for what it is. It is your means of safe travel upon the waters and the very storms of life which daily press round about thee. Think not that you are destined to forever be lost, and to find no way to cross the storms and the great barriers of life; for the love of God will forever be your means of travel and the way for you to get to the peace you desire most.

Know indeed that if your eyes are open, you can see the boat. But if you close your eyes, you are indeed like a blind man walking along the shore, for indeed he cannot see and know that the boat is there made available for him to use to cross this great divide.

Thus, he wanders night and day when all the time, the very means of his rescue and his liberation lies there beside him, well within his reach.

Know indeed, Dear Ones, that you can cross the lake and leave this desolate bank if such is your desire. Open your eyes, remove the veil, and shake off the forgetfulness that would keep thee a prisoner here on the banks of the lake. See the boat, and know it is there made available for your safe passage, and get into it. No harm will come to thee, for you are guided and protected by Mother Father God; for he is the captain of this boat and will ever protect, guide, and love thee. He will steer this boat, safely avoiding all rocks, and any other danger that might present itself; for he is the one who loves and guides thee if you will but allow him to take charge of your life.

Open your heart, and remember who you are. Know indeed that you are guided, loved, and protected at all times, if you would but hear the voice and the guidance given to thee each and every day. Open your ears, O Sons and Daughters of Man, and know that you are, indeed, loved and guided in all your actions if you would but listen to the voice within you, which is the love of God! For it will always take thee to safety on the shores of God's love, where you can live in happiness, peace, and love.

Know, Dear Ones, this is your hope, your joy, and your happiness if you will but accept it by getting into the boat. Sit gently, Dear Ones, and let it gently glide upon the water, for no storms can cause you harm in this boat; for you are in the gentle arms of your Mother Father God. Be at peace and know that the love of God will always be and is always available for you, for it has been yours since the dawn of time.

Open your hearts, Dear Ones, and take the boat. Step in and know true peace, love, happiness, joy, and the hope of God, for all these things are thine. For when you step into the boat, they encircle thee and protect thee; so that you might live and know true peace, happiness, joy, and love.

Know that all is ready for thee. Wander no more along the shores looking for a way to cross. Know, indeed, that the boat is ready and waiting for you to access it to cross this great lake that was once so wide and inaccessible. Now it is easy for you to cross, Dear Ones, for you are led by the love and the presence of Mother Father God. Be at peace and know that all your needs will be met, and happiness can once more be thine.

Let none tell thee that the lake is too wide, and that no one has ever been able to cross it safely. Know, indeed, that the God of your beingness will help you to cross all the lakes, and all the barriers that a life upon the Earth would present; for with the love of God as your boat, you can cross all waters and come safely to the shores of God's love: For God is the captain of your ship, and in this boat no harm can befall thee, for you are safely held in the arms of God. Let all who would say, "There is no boat, and none is needed, for we can remain here for all our days," know that the time is upon you to decide whither you will go, and what you will do, for for so long you have wandered along this shore, wondering how to cross. Let those who would remain in darkness not stand in your way, Dear Ones. Open your hearts! Open your eyes! And see and know that the way exists for you to know happiness, peace, and joy upon the Earth when you climb into this boat, and remember your nature and your heritage as Sons and Daughters of Mother Father God. For this is indeed your rescue, your hope, and your joy. This is your peace.

Be at peace, Dear Ones, and know that the boat is ready and you are ready to climb aboard and sail away in peace, love, and happiness. Know that the day is here, and you can go across this great divide if such is your desire. All is in readiness, for you have always had this boat available to you, Dear Ones. Only your blindness, caused by the distractions of life, would keep thee ever on the shore and never able to cross to the other side. Know indeed you can do as you will, for no obstacles exist to keep thee bound to this shore; for you have the means to cross this water and to be safely ferried to the other side. Open your eyes, Dear Ones, and see that your true peace, happiness, and joy awaits thee; for all is indeed there made available for thee. May the peace, love, and blessings of Mother Father God continue to reign in your hearts, Dear Ones, as you come to remember once more your oneness with the Divine.

Adieu

7ᵀᴴ MARCH 2012

Know indeed that the love of God for mankind stirs the heart of man and causes him to awaken to the truth of his being, on those rare instances when he is stirred by nature and the things of God. For in this remembrance, he holds up his head and sees glimpses of the glory, the beauty, and the majesty that is Mother Father God; and in so doing returns to the truth of his nature as a child of the Most High God. Know indeed, Dear Ones that the love of God when awakened in the heart of man, causes him to see and to appreciate all those things which hitherto had been hidden to the eyes of the Sons of Men. Know, Dear Ones, that the Children of Men are like lost sheep roaming to and fro, but with the recognition of the love of God in their life, there is come upon them a great shift which allows them to see, taste, and appreciate all the love that is made available to them since the dawn of time. For in truth, when the Sons of Men are awakened to the true wonders of the love of God for mankind, they are changed throughout their beingness and can finally come to appreciate the wonder and awe that is the love of God.

For lo, this vast and most wonderful of gifts when recognized by the Sons of Men, takes on new meaning in the life of man; and he can finally begin to taste and to appreciate all that is there made available to him, as a child of the Most High God. For in truth, it is as though a great door has been opened, and the secrets kept hidden within were finally revealed, so that all might see them. Know, Dear Ones, such is the great and glorious excitement experienced by the Sons of Men when they first come to know of the love of God for mankind. For in truth, man will never fully know of the vastness of the expanse of the love that is held and nurtured for the Sons of Men. For in truth there is nothing with which it can be compared upon the Earth, and thus the Sons of Men cannot grasp the vastness and the intensity of the power of this great and unconditional love, which Mother Father God has for the Sons of Men.

Know, Dear Ones, that the love of God is that warm blanket that covers the naked on a cold winter's night. It is the first morsel of food for one who is hungry, and the first taste of water to someone who has wandered in the desert for days searching for food and water. Know indeed, Dear Ones, it is all! It is everything! For it is indeed life to the needs of man. It is the air, the oxygen, and the very life-giving substance that will preserve the life of man. It is the way of survival, the way of love, the way of peace, joy, and happiness for the Sons of Men. Know, Dear Ones, the love of God is life itself; for indeed without the knowledge of it, the Sons of Men suffer, and are doomed to wander night and day searching for that which they know is lost, even though they cannot name it or call it into being: For they realize not their innate power, and their ability to call upon Mother Father God, and get an immediate answer.

Know, Dear Ones, that the child who thinks he is bereft of the love of God, is full of anguish and pain, and knows not why; for he knows that something is missing from his life, yet he can in no way identify the missing element.

Know, Dear Ones, we say awaken from the dream! And open your eyes, for indeed there are great treasures to see and gifts to receive, so that you may fulfill your destiny as Sons and Daughters of the Most High God. Open your eyes and be who you were born to be! Open your hearts and become that which you already are, Dear Ones, the Sons and Daughters of Mother Father God!

Be not alarmed and say, "I am bereft of all that is given to others," for indeed you carry all that you need to survive, etched within your heart, Dear Ones. Know indeed that the light and love of God will shine through you, if you would but allow it to come forth.

Look in the mirror, Dear Ones, and see your true selves; for you are truly magnificent beings, for you carry the seed of God within you. You are Daughters and Sons of the Most High God, so remember your true identity once more, and come into the fullness of who and what you are.

Know, Dear Ones, first and foremost how much you are loved and adored by Mother Father God, for such is your identity. This is your course, this is your path. You are children of God, and you carry the spark of God within you; so be your true selves and know once more the true happiness, peace, love, and joy of God whilst still upon the Earth: For this is your plan, this is your calling. Do that which must be done, Dear Ones, and know that all will truly be well: For you are the children of God, the chosen of God.

ALL are chosen of God! None are singled out and removed. ALL are loved, and guided, and protected, if you would remember these truths: But know, indeed, that changes will abound for thee when you recognize your true magnificence as the Light Beings you truly are. For you forget your majesty and your lineage, and think you are that physical being you see staring back at thee in the mirror. Know, Dear Ones, you are so much more than what you can see, know, or even imagine, for you are eternal beings. You are Beings of Light, living within a physical frame, so awaken and remember once more your true selves. Open your eyes, and see and remember your name, and know once more that you are the evidence of the love of God upon the Earth. You are the joy, the heart, and the soul of God! You are the beingness of God manifested upon the Earth! You are the proof of God upon the Earth; the light and love of God, for such is your nature, your joy, and your peace.

Be not ashamed to shine and to glow like the eternal beings you are, but shine, Dear Ones! Shine! Shine! For this is your destiny. Speak not of loss of hope or despair, for you are loved eternally of God, and guided by God, if you would but open your eyes and your ears to know the words of God, and become that which you truly are.

Be not afraid to present yourself to the world and say, "Here I am; for I am a child of the Most High God, for this is my path upon the Earth. This is my destiny, my hope… and all is given to me to keep me whole by Mother Father God." Remember always your name and your lineage, Dear Ones, and know that you are guided, loved, and ever present in the bosom and heart of God. For this is the very promise of God! Know, Dear Ones, that the light of God surrounds thee at all times, and all is well with thee forever!

This is your nature; this is your path, Dear Ones! Shine like the stars that you are, upon the roads and the harshness of the physical life! Know you are loved always, and be at peace, Dear Ones; for in truth this is but the dawning of a new age, a new era; if you will open your eyes to see and know what lies ahead for thee! Be confident and open your arms! Extend them and hold on to the love of God! Caress it and claim it, for this is your heritage! Take the wondrous gifts that have been offered to thee! Know that all will be well with thee! Adieu Little One we are much happy indeed to be here with thee.

Adieu

8ᵀᴴ March 2012

Welcome indeed Little One, for we are indeed much happy to be here united with thee. Know indeed the process of joining quickens even as you have become aware, and will continue to be so as the practice continues. Know indeed Little One we are indeed much happy with the progress that is being made in this area, and with happy hearts we say welcome indeed.

Know indeed, Dear Ones, that the love of God for mankind cannot be measured or equated, for indeed there are no known measures upon the Earth that could be used to quantify the depth and the breadth of the love of God for mankind. Know indeed that the thoughts of God, and the depths of the love of God for man, knows no bounds; for indeed there is no place where man is that God is not, and there is nothing that man can do that can ever serve to separate him from the love of God. For in truth, the love once given is not, and cannot be removed. For indeed, the nature of this love is such that it is without guilt, or blame, or shame; for there is no judgment found in the heart of God. Thus, no tithe is paid, nothing is owed, and there is no blame placed on the Children of Men... even though in the logical mind and heart of man, he is being punished by God for wrongdoing. Know, Dear Ones, this is attributed to God, but in no way are these the things of God; for Mother Father God does not judge his children: For you are loved unconditionally, and as such there is no blame and no punishment exacted by Mother Father God.

Know, indeed, that like children learning on the playground how to be in the world, even so are the Sons of Men when incarnated upon the Earth. For in truth, they are learning how to utilize the joys of 'free will' and to live with their brethren upon the Earth. That they kill and destroy is part of the learning, Dear Ones, but know indeed that this behavior causes great pain to Mother Father God...but in no way does he remove his love from the Sons of Men. For in truth, as children of the Most High God, you are ever learning and growing. Ever learning how to live upon the Earth, and to be that God-light, shining brightly upon the Earth.

Know, Dear Ones, as such, the love of God remains with thee throughout all generations, and is ever thine. For you are the children— and as such you are seen by Mother Father God— who in his love and benevolence are held and secured in the arms of God when you would stumble and fall. For your loving Father asks not perfection, but simply that you learn during each incarnation. That is your charge, Dear Ones, to learn and to grow upon the Earth. Thus, your loving Father, the God of Love, would never punish thee, for in truth, the Sons of Men punish themselves enough.

Know, Dear Ones, that the love of God for man is thine forever, and can and will never be removed from thee. Know, Dear Ones that this great and awe-inspiring love, is a love of and for the ages; for it never wanes, but is always there when needed, and is always given in abundance to the Sons of Men. Know, Dear Ones, that the love of God for man is ever present, as is God ever present in the life experience of man: For while man searches in vain for the treasure he thinks he has lost, know indeed, Dear Ones, that even so the love of God remains constant, and is always deep within your heart.

That the fog and the forgetfulness of the human condition keep thee ever lost is part of the great difficulty in the search of man for God. For in truth, man searches everywhere upon the Earth looking for that thing which he most desires, knowing not that he already possesses that very thing.

For in truth, it is within each child of God, and you, Dear Ones, are all children of a loving and benevolent God. You are all cherished and adored by your Mother Father God, so know indeed that this truth is indeed the truth of life, and the way of all ways in the world.

Know, Dear Ones that the Sons of Men who search in vain come never to know that the very nature of man is also that part of God. Thus, in abject fear, man travels and travels, ever searching for that which he thinks has been lost. Know indeed that all your gifts are given at birth, etched into the very fabric of your DNA. How then, Dear Ones, can you imagine that you are not loved and adored by Mother Father God? For this is indeed the essence of who and what your nature would suggest. Know, Dear Ones, that the love of God for mankind never wanes, never decreases, but remains constant throughout your days upon the Earth and beyond: for you cannot lose the love of God like a toy or a trinket. It cannot be misplaced, for it is given and remains with thee always throughout time.

Know, Dear Ones, that the wonder which is man is special in the very eyes of God, and none can take his place in the heart and love of God, for he is special in the eyes and love of God!

Be at peace, Dear Ones, and know always that God's love is thine since the dawn of time, and will remain with thee throughout all ages. Be not discouraged and say, "I am cast down for I have sinned." For in truth, the love of God knows not the word 'sin,' for God is a loving God and thus no punishment is exacted, as is conceived by the Children of Men to punish the Sons of Men. Only the mind of man would conjure up such notions, Dear Ones, and would envision thee in damnation and hellfire…for this is not the way of God. This is not the way of a loving, caring, and benevolent God, who daily provides for his Sons and Daughters.

Know, Dear Ones, you are guided, loved, and adored, all the days of your lives; for you are the beloved Sons and Daughters of God. You are ever present in the heart of God, and never absent from his love.

Even though your forgetfulness would make you believe you are alone and lost without hope, know indeed, Dear Ones, that you are always held and loved in the bosom of God: For you are his children, loved unconditionally since the dawn of time. Be at peace and know you daily rest in the shade of God's love, and are cradled in the arms of love. Pure love: A love that is of the deepest and most unfathomable[87] kind which has no limits. Be you happy to know, Dear Ones, that your Mother Father God is the one and only God, the ruler of the Universe, God of all that exists. Such is the nature of your Mother Father God, Dear Ones, so know that even as you are the children, you possess the heart and love of God.

---

[87] Impossible to comprehend: limitless: immeasurable: endless

Be not afraid to celebrate, and to bask in the glow of the love of God, for this is your right. This is your charge; this is your heritage, Dear Ones, so accept your gift and live, live, live. Accept the joy, and the grace, and the love which is God, and behave in a fashion that demonstrates the God within you! Know that you possess these attributes, Dear Ones. Know that like your Brother Jesus reminded thee, "Greater things than these will you also accomplish."

Know, Dear Ones, you are powerful beings for you possess the love of God, and you are birthed with the loving source and nature which is God. Be never ashamed to claim your birthright as heirs to the throne, and as children of God. For indeed this is who you are, O Sons and Daughters of Mankind! Release the fear and come once more into your true nature, and become your true selves. For you are the children of the Most High God: given all the gifts and the blessings at birth. Open your hands and see you are Royal Beings! For behold, you wear the garments of the Mother Father God, and as such you are held in high esteem in the heavens. Hold up your heads, O Children, and claim your heritage with pride and honor! Step proudly into the sun, and stand with your body erect; for you are Royal Beings, the Children of God! Be not afraid to claim your heritage, and to be the children of God in all ways, and at all times; for you are held in high honor and are chosen of God. All are chosen! All God's Children are exalted!

No race is relegated to the farthest reaches and left in shame! All are invited to sit at the table and to make merry, for such is the nature of your parent that no favorite exists, for all are favored. All are exalted! All are special in the eyes and love of God! No race or clan or creed is exalted above the other, for all are children of God. All are loved with the same intensity and fervor! All are valued and all are chosen! Such is the way of God, for you are all made from the spark and fabric of God, and thus are viewed equally in the eyes of God.

Know, Dear Ones, you are the joy and love of the heart of God, and you are ever his children. Be not afraid to acknowledge your parentage, and to love your brethren, for they are indeed your brothers and sisters; always loved in the same way as you are: Always provided for by God, and ever in the arms of God, as are you all, Dear Ones. Be you happy to know that as children of God, you are always in the mind and heart of God; for he mourns thee when you are in pain, and he holds thee when the storms of life would toss thee to and fro. Know, Dear Ones, there is no place in the heavens or upon the Earth where God is not! Be at peace and know you are loved eternally, and are never rejected or abandoned, for you are loved. Oh, how you are loved, Dear Ones! Turn not away and say, "I am not chosen and am unloved by God," for this is not the way of God. Be you happy to know your Mother Father loves and supports thee; upholds and cradles thee in his arms each day. For you can never be where God is not, so you can never be alone.

Adieu, Dear Ones! Rest always, in the knowledge of the unfaltering[88] love of God for thee, his Sons and Daughters. Doubt no more the depth or intensity of the love of God for thee; for like a parent you are loved unconditionally for all time. Be proud of your heritage, and know these truths: for you are the children of God, the love of God, the heart of God. Know these truths always in the core of

---

[88]   Not wavering or weakening

your being, and live in joy, happiness, peace, and love, Dear Ones, for this is the essence of who and what you truly are: Children of the Most High God. Remember always that you are loved and adored, and you will want for nothing upon the Earth. For you will know that your Father will supply all that you need, and be with thee at all times, throughout all trials and fears: For he is your Father, your hope, your friend! Know this always, and you will always know the true peace, love, and joy of God.

Adieu in the love and beingness of God,
for you are loved ETERNALLY

Welcome indeed we say welcome for it is good to come together. Know indeed, Dear One, that the love of God for mankind is shown in many different ways each and every day throughout the lifespan of man. For, indeed, it is that man knows not of his own connection to Mother Father God; yet even in this state of abject forgetfulness, he still feels deep within himself that there must be more to the physical life than can be daily seen or imagined. Thus, he searches for that which will give him purpose for being upon the Earth, and allow him to know that his presence upon the shores of this great planet has made a difference. Know indeed, Dear Ones, that in truth, man searches in an effort to understand his world, and to find meaning for why things are the way that they are.

Know indeed, Dear One, man knows not why or how he knows that— for it must be understood— but for some innate yet unknown reason, he searches throughout his lifetime for that thing that will give him reason for being, and help him to understand why he is here upon the Earth. Know indeed, Dear One, he is bereft of reasoning or understanding, yet he continues this prolonged search for that which he somehow knows will help to bring him peace.

Know indeed, Dear One, that this search, though long and tiring for some, is shorter for others; for it seems that some find that inner light and truth, that helps them to understand and know the very reason for their sojourn here upon the Earth. For lo, like a thief that cometh even in the night, even so comes this knowledge from whence he knows not... but it is able to fill him with that great, inner peace that tells his soul that the prize for which he has searched so diligently is even now at hand. Know, Dear One, that even so does the knowledge of the love of God present itself to the Sons of Men; for in truth, it creeps into the heart and mind of man, and he knows not from whence it cometh. For indeed it appears one day in his wisdom and knowledge, even though man cannot, of self, trace back to that date and time when he knew he had found the greatest of all possible prizes upon the Earth: For in truth, he knows that it is more precious than gold or any precious metal, and will be with him for the remainder of his days.

Know, Dear One, that the magical insight which is the love of God, descends upon the Sons of Men and they find that wonderful peace they have searched for as they come to know the love of God. Know, Dear Ones, that the love and peace of God is yours to treasure and to store however you choose, for it is your personal gift, given to thee by your Mother Father God. Thus, it is only fitting that you would choose how you should protect this wonderful gift. Know indeed, Dear Ones, that the love of God for mankind is the greatest gift given to the Sons of Men, and naught upon the Earth can equal its value, for it is of such worth that nothing can be compared with it. Know indeed, Dear Ones, that the loving power of the love of God is thine forever, so be always proud of the blessing you have been given and know indeed that naught can remove it from thee: For it is given by your parent, and thus cannot be removed, even by death. For in truth, the love of God is thine eternally, traveling with thee always throughout time, so that you are always in possession of it regardless of where you are. For being spirit, light, and love, you are eternal beings and carry this gift with thee always.

Know indeed, Dear One, your Mother Father God is that wonderful benevolent parent who is ever beside thee. He is the still, small voice you hear in times of danger or in times of anguish. He is the consoling and loving voice you hear when you need reassurance, and that most blessed and beloved friend who is beside thee when you need a friend to caress thee and to hold your hand. Thus, Dear One, is the magic, which is the true and most powerful love of God for mankind, made available to the Sons of Men. For in truth, that you are loved by Mother Father God is no accident. For every day, every minute, and every second of your life, you are loved with the deepest love imagined, or conceptualized, in the mind of man: For such is the love of God for mankind. Know, Dear One, that you are eternally blessed and loved, if you would but listen to the gentle voice which speaks to thee, and provides the loving guidance that is needed by the Children of Men. Know indeed, Dear One, that you are eternally blessed, and eternally adored by your Mother Father God; for such is the nature and beingness of God that you are never alone. Even when in your hours of pain you would feel separated and alone, know, Dear Ones, that you are ever surrounded by the love of God.

Only your forgetfulness, when in human form, would make you think that you are alone. Know indeed, Dear One, that you are surrounded at all times by the love and light of God, and you are ever cradled in the arms of your Mother Father God. Know, Dear One, that the love never leaves thee, even though you would forget it is there, made available to thee, and believe yourself alone and deserted. In this time, when you feel lost and separated, for you have none to call upon thee, and hold and support thee, know, Dear Ones, that you can forever call upon the name of God, and know that he is ever with thee: For he is your Father and would never leave or desert thee.

Be you ever mindful and remember these truths, Dear One, for they will set you free from the pain and bondage of the separation of your heart from the love of God. Know indeed, Dear One, that your human mind will tell you that you are alone and separated from your Father; yet in truth, this is not so: For you are ever held and caressed in the bosom of Mother Father God. Be you ever anxious to be in good health, and to know you are loved eternally by the Divine. For this is your hope, this is your rescue, this is your peace and this is your joy.

You are loved! You are adored! You are the chosen of God! And when you remember these truths, you can live a life of plenty and of happiness; for therein will live your peace, your heart, and your joy. Be you ever full of love, and share the blessings with your brethren that you daily meet. Know them even in their hidden splendor, and know that you are a child of Mother Father God, who is loved and adored since the dawn of time. You are the favored of God and the children of God; for such is your true heritage. Think not of earthly bonds, but know, indeed, that you are ever loved and guided to reach your true potential... and to learn those things which can only be learned on the Earth. Know indeed, Dear Ones, you are mighty beings whose task, whilst upon the Earth, is simply to be and to learn.

Let not the distractions carry you to your doom, so that you would know not of all that is thine to enjoy from the bounty of God. Be you ever fulfilled and know the peace, love, and joy which is of God. Be you happy, for it costs nothing to smile! Be joyful, be radiant, be you full of the joys of God on all occasions, and allow your beautiful light to shine: for this is your mission, your peace, your joy and your hope.

Let it all be taken away from thee, if you would let go of this gift and return home in pain and bereft of all that is good upon the Earth.

Know, Dear Ones, that you are light; you are love, now and ALWAYS. Be you kind to one another and see the peace of God descend upon thee, that you might learn of the true and glorious parent that you possess. Let all see and know that the love and light of God will be ever for thee, for this is the gift of God, given to thee. Never feel alone and keep you ever satisfied, for this is your task; this is your reason for living upon the Earth: to know always that you are ever loved. Live at peace with self, and all that is provided for thee by Mother Father God. Let all who would say you have no faith come forward, for such is your hope, your love, and your light, Dear One.

Be happy always and know that your parent loves and supports thee always. Let your light shine and be your magnificent selves, for you are creators in the Universe of God, so go forth and create a world of love, peace, harmony, joy, and hope: For this is your mission. This is your hope. Be you ever happy to know that all is well. And so it is!

Adieu

21ˢᵗ March 2012

Know, indeed, that the soul of man and the soul of God are one. For indeed, man emanates from that same wellspring from whose source the Children of Men are also born as spirit, if such we may use that term. For indeed, being spirit, man is only born when coming into the physical. For, when in spirit, he is not born but created as a spark of God. Know indeed, Dear One, that the soul of man and that of God are one, emanating from the same eternal source as Mother Father God. For lo, he is a piece of God, and thus, like any piece of a larger whole, he spends his whole life trying to return to that place from which he was created. Thus, Dear One, is the trial of man, for indeed, while he searches upon the Earth, desperately searching for that great love and that piece of him which is missing, he is, in effect, searching for God... even though he may never realize that he is actually searching for God. For indeed, the great fog of forgetfulness, which is cast upon mankind when he enters the incarnation at birth, renders him lost and forgotten of all that he knew formerly when in spirit.

Know, Dear One, like a baby entering the world, he is bereft of all knowledge of his Mother Father God, and his link to the Divine. Thus, he is wandering the highways and byways of life, searching for that which he knows not; for indeed he is in reality searching for that part of him which lives still with the Divine. Know, Dear One, that when you enter the physical, you are bereft of all knowledge of your past or your present, or anything other than that NOW moment, in which you are surviving. Thus, you feel lost and alone, and without a memory of who or what you are. You are without purpose, wandering upon the Earth. You seek daily for that thing which will fill the hole within your heart, and once more make you whole.

Without knowledge or history, you wander night and day looking for the vestige of who and what you could be. Know indeed your memory keeps you isolated and desolate, for you seek the love and companionship that was so familiar to thee when in spirit. Now here upon the Earth, you are isolated and alone, for there is none to comfort thee and to provide that love that you so desperately seek, or the reassurance that all will indeed be well. Know indeed, Dear One, that the sojourn upon the Earth can be a very lonely and isolating experience, for once more you are left isolated and alone. For indeed, that is the thought of men, but know, Dear One, there is no truth in this; for you are never alone, for your Mother Father God would never desert thee— for you are always loved, guided, and protected... but your forgetfulness makes you think you are alone. Know, Dear One, this is not so, for you are always held and loved by God. Know that while you search faithfully for that which you think is lost, know that there is nothing that God would not do or provide for thee, for you are Sons and Daughters of God. Know indeed, Dear One, that the love, peace, and grace of God are thine forever, and that you possess these gifts, even though your awareness of these truths are dimmed. Know indeed that the love, peace, joy, and happiness you seek are always made available and are always thine; for you are the Lamb of God[89]. The innocent, yet wonderful lamb, which is carried and gently caressed by Mother Father God in his arms at all times. You are cradled, loved, and carried all the days of your life, even though you would forget these truths.

Know indeed, Dear Ones, that the love which is God is thine and is ever thine. For this is the way of God. Know, Dear Ones, that all your needs are met, and your desires are fulfilled, for you are the Sons and Daughters of God; so know you are ever loved and fed by God. For as the parent, it is the peace, love, and joy of God to make these things available for thee at all times.

Know indeed, Dear Ones, that the fear that would blind thee to the joys of life can so easily be brought down, and then you will remember once more your heritage and your true joy. For in truth, this is the very essence of who and what you are meant to be upon the Earth. Know that if you follow this path, all will be well for thee, but without the memory, you wander aimlessly to find that which was in plain sight all the time. Know, Dear Ones, that you are the children of God, and thus you are protected by Rome no more, for in truth, these are no longer the days of Nero or any of the great rulers whose task was to bring to bear pain and harm upon thee. Know that in those ancient times, you were guided and protected by groups of

---

[89] That valuable and precious child carried and loved by God forever, even as a shepherd carries and cares for each lamb lovingly in his arms.

the sacred, and the precious and mighty warriors, whereas now there are no groups to keep thee enlightened. For indeed, all your focus is bent on keeping the tenets of the laws sacred, while in truth, man dies and all is lost, and thus is the pain and fear of God, for you are loved with such vigor and valor. Know indeed that the joy, peace, and love, which is God, are for thee only. Be not afraid, but know the message and the fear that is come upon thee, saying that you are not the chosen of God, is naught.

Know, Dear Ones, you are desired of God and loved of God, and all rewards will find their way to thee. Know indeed you will meet your fate, and all will be well with thee. Be at peace, Dear Ones, and know indeed you will have all the joy and peace, and come to know that you are loved and adored of God. Be you ever faithful, Dear Ones, and know that all will be well for thee.

Adieu

Know, Dear Ones, that the love of God for mankind holds no mysteries; for indeed, it has been written in the stars throughout time. For indeed, the Ancient Ones knew of the love of God for humanity, and prophesied its news to all and sundry, who would understand the messages given. Know, Dear Ones, that now the message that once was heralded and heard by so few is now made available to all the Sons of Men, in all the corners of the Earth. Know, Dear Ones, that indeed this love is the purest and gentlest of forms, and indeed it is that most divine of all things: For it describes the love that exists between God and man, and will forever be.

Know, Dear Ones, that this love is as deep as the deepest oceans and without measure, for indeed it is there made available to all the Sons of Men. That this love is given to man is but a small token of the eternal blessings of man given by the Mother Father God. That man, of self, cannot survive without the love of God has never been tested, for indeed all humans were gifted with this love when they were in spirit. Thus, even before man was formed in the womb upon the Earth, he had already been gifted with the love of God by his parent God. Know, indeed, that this love is with man throughout all his days upon the Earth, even though he may not even be aware of this truth. Thus, man is upon the Earth laboring night and day to find the peace, love, joy, and contentment which he desires from the deepest depths of his soul, yet he is unaware that he already possesses this great and most marvelous of all gifts. Know, Dear Ones, that man has searched for millennia but never knew that the thing he most desires is already his to control.

Know, Dear Ones, this magical love which allows man into the inner sanctum of God, is given to each and every human prior to his sojourn upon the Earth, when the soul is first created from the divine spark of Mother Father God. Thus as Jesus said, "The Father and I are one," even so are you and the Father one, because you are made from God. Thus, as you and your earthly parent or offspring are made from the same fabric or DNA, even so are all souls made from the same spark as your parent God: Thus, you have the divine within you, Dear Children.

That when you are incarnated upon the Earth, you forget your divinity, is the great tragedy of man. For indeed, as a spirit you take on this charge to be upon the Earth, knowing full well that in accepting this task to be 'in lesson upon the Earth,' you also accept the biggest challenge of all: that of being in total forgetfulness of your divinity and your connection with Mother Father God. In truth, all that remains in the distant memory of man is the knowing that you have lost a precious treasure. Thus, the search of man upon the Earth begins, and you start to search for that which is lost without knowing its nature, its name, or its source. All that is known is that it is a great prize, and must be found at all costs. Know, Dear Ones, this is the great struggle of man upon the Earth, to find his treasure.

Know, Dear Ones, this great treasure is naught but the love of God. For in finding it, the soul knows that it will be once more at peace. Thus, the journey of man upon the Earth is a long and winding road, as man searches for his treasure or his prize. He amasses great wealth, but still his soul cries out for more. Like a thirsty man in the desert he cannot taste the water, and thinks it's a mirage; for his mind is lost to him and he struggles past the thing he has longed for, continuing the search. He walks over hills and through valleys while the storms of life rage at his door, and still he struggles on, looking for what he knows not.

He calls for help, and even though the help is at hand, he sees it not; for he is indeed blinded by all around him. For years, the Children of Men search for the prize without knowing its name or its source. For indeed, they are driven by an urge from deep within them, with a fire which will not be put out, and a thirst which will not be quenched. They amass more things, and trinkets, gold and silver, and yet their hearts remain empty, for the one and only thing which will bring them peace has still not been identified or found.

Man is now a desperate creature upon the Earth, for he has searched for millennia looking for the treasure of his life, and has found naught but pain. He tries to end the search, but the emptiness within him will not let him be. He must find his way back to God, but he knows not that this is the true reason for his great search. Try as he may, he cannot hear the words or see the signs telling him who he is, and the reason for his sojourn upon the Earth. He thinks he is here to rear children and to gain worldly treasures, but never does he realize that the great search is a search for his parentage, Mother Father God.

He is a being of light. He came from love, but all these things are forgotten, for when he looks into the mirror; all that he sees is the face of a human staring back at him. He knows not that he is a Light Being. He knows not that he is a child of the Most High God. He believes that he is the face in the mirror. He knows not that he is an eternal being, and that he is eternal. Therefore, when in human form, he is clothed in a physical body but for a short time.

Open your eyes, O Sons and Daughters of Earth! And see once more your true divinity. Know once more your eternal nature, for you are children of the Most High God, and are eternal beings. Open your eyes and remember once more your true divinity! For you are the Sons and Daughters of Mother Father God, made from God; eternal beings living here on Earth in this physical body. Know indeed, Dear Ones, that the lessons of the Earth are many, and the biggest one of all is that in order to be upon the Earth, you must willingly forget your parents, and be orphaned upon the land. For you search for that which is elusive, and that is because you search for the meaning of your life, and the origin of your very nature and source.

Know, Dear Ones, this search will take thee back once more only to your Mother Father God, for this is the only answer to that which you seek. Your search will end when you find yourself once more cradled in the arms of your loving parent, Mother Father God. Know, Dear Ones, that when you make the magnificent discovery that it is God that you have searched for, only then can and will you realize the true reason for your journey upon the Earth.

Learning and growing in lesson upon the Earth is a task of man. When undertaken, it can be a most dangerous mission, for indeed the forgetfulness is so complete that man knows not who he is or the reason for his stay upon the Earth. He looks for reasons, and is lost amid the distractions of the physical world. Thus he forgets his journey and spends his time in the pursuit of worldly pleasures. He is lost and alone... and desolate, he believes. He cries out in despair, and believes there is none to hear his cry or to answer his plea for help.

Know, Dear Ones, there are Angels all around thee, willing and wanting to help thee to find the way through the darkness and despair, if you will but remember your heritage, and your origin, and call upon the name of your parents for help. Help will come to thee when you call, Dear Ones. Know that you are never alone, and are always guided, if you would but listen to the voice of God, which speaks to thee from within your soul. Know, Dear Ones, that you are the joy, and hope of God and you are eternally loved and adored. Remember these words, and return once more to the knowing of your true selves, for in this way will you find once more the peace, joy, hope, and love of God which was thine at your inception[90] and will be forever available to thee.

Be not alarmed, Dear Ones, to know that you are never alone, but relish the thought that God is ever with thee, and that you are eternal beings made from God. And, like your Dear Brother Jesus who transcended the physical life, even so can you, Dear Ones, return to your Father. For in truth, you are forever joined to God. Forever held, nourished, and cradled by your loving parent. Forever in the arms of

---

[90]   In the beginning when the soul was first created

God, and you will forever be with your parent. Even while upon the Earth in physical form, you can commune with your parent and learn once more the nature of your true beingness. For you are Sons and Daughters of God; ever loved, ever protected and guided by Mother Father God… if you will but listen to the voices within your heart, and know that this is but the guiding hand of your beloved parent.

Be at peace, Dear Ones, and know that you are guided, loved, and cradled, by God every moment of each day, and you are loved beyond measure forever. And so it is!

Adieu

Know, indeed, that the love of God for mankind is like the flowering of a beautiful rose, for indeed when first she appears, she is enfolded and her great beauty cannot be seen. Thus, all those who know not of the beauty that lies beneath in the bud, would look to say it is just a flower. Those who know of the true and lasting beauty that lies within the bud will wait in glorious anticipation to see what will emerge. Know, Dear Ones, even so is the love of God for humanity, for indeed those who remember and know not of the magnificence of the power of the love of God, will look upon the gift and yet not be able to see and appreciate its great beauty and depth. Then, as the flowering and the magnificence of the love of God in the life of the Sons of Men become evident, truly the ones who look on will marvel at the great works and sing the praises of Mother Father God.

For in truth, they see the magnificence which is God, and know the magnitude which is the love of God, and will and can then hold up their heads and sing and shout with joy, at the wonder and magnificence which springs forth. Know, Dear Ones, that the love of God, when completely apparent to the Sons of Men, is a world full of wonder, for indeed they begin to see with small glimpses the first taste of all that is truly available to man in and through the love of God.

Open your arms, Dear Ones, look upon the gifts you have been given and see the flower within the bud within your heart. Look not with the outer eye but use the inner light to shine, and to see, and to know that you are looking into the divinity which is man, and seeing the magnificent gifts given freely by Mother Father God. Be not ashamed to claim this great prize but know, indeed, that you have been bequeathed this precious gift free of cost.

You are the heirs to the throne, and as such you have been given this gift. Look at the flower, and remember what lies beneath the bud. Dismiss it not and say it is only a flower, for in truth it is O, so much more; for the potential of all that lies buried deep within it, cannot be seen or valued by those without memory or imagination. You, who see only the exterior things of life, will see and know not of the beauty which is the love of God, for when your memory fails you and you know not what you see, you will discard it and throw it away as meaningless waste. For in truth, those who can see not, or appreciate not the beauty of the rose, will look at the thorns and see not the beauty which is waiting to be unfurled. Let your eyes be the windows to your soul indeed, Dear Ones, and like any window, open it. Clean it inside and outside, so that all that is beautiful can be truly seen and appreciated. Let not the exterior things of life be your guide, but look deep within to find the real beauty that is waiting to be recognized and appreciated. Let your voice tell you not that beauty exists not in this place, but look closer, Dear Ones, and see and taste the true magnificence which is God, as it is seen in the flower when she opens and shows her face and her beauty to the Sun: For indeed what the sun sees, and indeed the breeze sees, is beauty in its fullest and most wonderful form. For in truth, the bud opens and the rose, in all her splendor, is shown to the world. Be not full of derision[91] and dismiss such beauty, but know indeed that the love which is God, like the rose, lasts for more than a day.

For indeed, she is warmed by the sun, and fed by the rain, and thus she continues to shine and radiate; bellowing and showing her brilliance to those who would look upon her...for she calls to them to be noticed, and to be seen in all her radiance. Look upon her, Dear Ones, and know that she is perfection. She is beauty. She is love. She is joy. She is brilliance, and thus she must be given all her powers so that she can truly shine and come into her powers. Know, Dear Ones that the love which is this flower, is all that is given by God. For in truth, the days of her existence may be short, but the memory of her fragrance and her beauty will remain long after she has faded and is no more. Thus, we know, Dear Ones, that this is the reason why the Sons of Men would seek night and day, trying to find that which is lost. For like the memory of the rose, they know of her magnificence and search tirelessly to find this beauty once more.

Look no further, Dear Ones, but remember that the love you seek is already thine, for it lives deep within your very heart, buried there. Let the bud open once more. Be the sunshine and the rain, and allow the rose to open and show her beauty to the world, so that all may see her and know her radiance and her beauty. Let not the night come upon thee so that the day closes and will hide her beauty, but be the sun, be the rain, and let the love of God shine within your heart.

---

[91]   Contemptuous ridicule or mockery

Water your garden and watch the love of God multiply in your life. Let your glow be seen. Be the rose, be the love of God in the world and let all see and know who you are, for as you open up your bud, all may see and know your magnificence and come to know that you are children of the Most High God. So be you ever in the grace of God and ever enfolded in his loving presence. Open your petals, Dear Ones, and smile at your Mother Father God who gives thee the gift of life. Be well within yourselves, and know that all will be well for and with thee always, as children of your Mother Father God. Let the blessed of the Lord say and so it is.

Amen & Amen

Know that the love of God for man is akin to a great and wonderful wheel, which when first discovered by the Sons of Men, is outside of their comprehension, for indeed since it is the first of its kind, holds much fascination for all who look upon it. For indeed, Dear One, we see that the Sons of Men cannot determine its function or its purpose. Thus, they set out to determine how and what this thing might be.

Know, indeed, that they roll it here and there but without thought; it is seen simply as an amusement and naught else. For indeed, it doesn't allow them to do anything but to play. Know, Dear One, that this is the state of being for some time as the Children of Men look upon the toy and try to figure out how it might be utilized in the life of men. Know that time passes and indeed, the great excitement about the new toy wanes, and it is now become part of the daily routine to spend some time playing and amusing self with the toy. Know indeed that this does continue until one day, one of the children becomes inventive and suggests other pursuits that this great wheel might be able to help with. Thus, Dear One, we see the beginning of the inventiveness of man; for what was given as a toy has now taken on new meaning, and will now have multiple functions... and may indeed no longer ever be seen simply as a means of amusement. For indeed now, that which was simply for amusement now has multiple purposes and functions within the mind of men. Know indeed, Dear One, we say stay within the confines of the game, and know that the hardships of life will not encroach upon thee, for indeed as a child, only the things which are thine for amusement will ever be thine, and thus will cause thee no pain or anguish.

For indeed you will never be troubled by the things of life, when they are seen only as toys to amuse. Thus, when the game is no longer a game— because there are now other functions and purposes built into the same framework, that once housed only amusement and pleasure for the children— we see now the pain of man. For the fun and laughter is no more, since the game that was life is now looked upon with serious intent and thus there is associated pain, pressure, and anguish. For all is now serious, and the element of excitement, and fun, and amusement, has left. Be not stifled by the changes you have brought upon yourselves, Dear Ones, but know indeed that because of the love of God for humanity, he brings thee no pain but only pleasure: For he has given thee all the gifts in the kingdom, so that you have taken a great gift and will now use it in many different ways, and cause yourself grief and pain over this thing that once was only a toy.

Now, instead of the glorious toy, the mind sees only problems and turmoil surrounding this toy. For indeed it can be utilized as a weapon, which would bring pain and fear into the heart of his brethren, and indeed it can cause a great divide between the children, because those who wish to use it as a toy for their amusement can no longer do so, for it is seen as a weapon by so many. Know indeed, Dear Ones that this gift that was given by Mother Father God, is now a tool which divides. For indeed, one group sees it as something to be used to conquer, while another wishes to continue simply to play and to be amused.

Thus, the toy that was, has now in the mind of man taken on new purposes and functions, and now divides that which once was a united group.

Know indeed, that the love of God produced the toy, but now it is used as a weapon against your brethren, which it was never designed or intended to be. It is used to say that you are wrong and will be punished, for I will use this weapon against you.

You, O Children, have forgotten your brethren! For once upon a time, you played in the garden of love which was the arms of God… but now you would find fault with your brethren, for they do not do that which you do. They, who do not think as you think, are ostracized and put aside as strangers on the path. For you no longer claim them as your own, for you see their minds and their hearts as separate. For, indeed, they do see things differently. Know, indeed, you would now make plans to use that which was a toy to make war upon them and to destroy them, for they are not seen like you, for they are different. You put great emphasis on all the ways in which you differ, and see only the things that separate, not the elements that unite you. For, indeed, you were once of one mind, but now you are divided.

For indeed, we say that a house divided cannot stand. Only a house united will prosper. For the fighting and the warring between you who are brothers must end, Dear Ones… and a new time of peace, love, and harmony upon the Earth must reign. For indeed, you war against your brethren, and you see the differences between you but in no way do you look to remember you were once ONE, united in the joy and happiness of love, playing in the mid-day sun. Now you see only separation and differences, for you see religion, and race, and creed, and color, and no more do you look upon your brethren and recognize them as your brothers. For the things that divide you are many, and the things that would serve to unite thee are few.

Look to yourselves, O Children of Men! And return to days of play, and remember the joys you felt as children playing. For indeed, there were no thoughts except of fun, and peace, and love. For you were ONE, united in a single cause to enjoy the gifts and the pleasures of life. Know indeed, Dear Ones, that the Children of Men are united in all things, for you are indeed all children of the same parent, playing at the game of life. For indeed it is the thing on which you all focus, but yet you would steal and rob your brethren, and begrudge them the very life force; for you would selfishly say that all is mine and you would have none to share. Know indeed, there is plenty to share, for your Father has provided enough for all his Sons and Daughters, that you might all enjoy the playful times. Only you would bring rules to bear that would separate and divide the players. For all are one in God, but between the Sons of Men all is seen as separate, for we see not our brothers as brothers and sisters, but instead we see them as foreigners and we see them as those to be excluded, for they think differently.

Remember O Sons of Men! The days, when you played together and ran and played as one. Now we say put away the thoughts that would divide, and know that indeed, the toy has myriad functions but yet it doesn't mean that any one function is wrong. Know, indeed, all can be appropriate based on the needs of those who would utilize it. Know indeed, Dear Ones, we say that the love of God sees no differences between you and your brethren, for you are all ONE in the heart of God. You are all loved equally and your parent sees no differences between you, for you each are loved.

Oh, how you are loved by your parent! Thus, we say, Dear Ones, put away thoughts of warring[92] and division, and look for the ways that would unite you with your brethren. For in uniting, you are a mighty force! In uniting, you can be so much more!

For now, instead of using the wheel only as a toy, you will find myriad[93] ways to use it to aid you all. For, indeed, your differences in thoughts, and actions, can indeed be your greatest strength. For indeed, if you all thought and acted in the same way, from whence would come the great soup which is humanity? From whence would come the great dance of life which is humanity? For in all doing the same thing in the same way, no room is left for those who think or see things differently. Know, Dear Ones, that the glorious soup which is humanity, is the heart of God, for your very differences are what cause you to be so wonderful. Remember, O Children! How much joy would you receive from a garden of flowers where all looked the same? For the variety is what gives life exuberant color, and flair, the joy, and the love of all.

That the Sons of Men should turn once more and return to the knowledge that you and your brethren are ONE, regardless of the

---

[92]   Hostile :antagonistic

[93]   Countless: infinite: innumerable

exterior covering you bear, is imperative. Look upon your brethren, Dear Ones, and know that within your shell, you are all the same. For, indeed, if the skin is removed, you are all one. Return to the knowledge of your beingness, and know that there is no color, or race, or creed that is not loved by God. For God, indeed, has no eyes! For God is spirit and love; therefore like a blind man who cannot see the external trappings of the person in front of him, he is led to know that person by that which he does, and not by the categories and the things that would serve to separate.

Know, Dear Ones, that once upon a time when you were all in spirit, you loved all your brethren as one, for you are love and naught else. Allow not the labels and the things that have caused division and separateness to divide thee, to continue to do so, for your hearts and your kinship[94] are one.

You have the mind of God in your DNA, and you are all children of God. Therefore, we say, remember this truth and see your brethren everywhere...for each one you meet is your brethren. Each is your brother and sister, for you are all united in God. For you all serve the same God regardless of name, for you are no longer pagans who serve and worship different deities. Indeed, Dear Ones, you all serve only one God and he sees not color, creed, and religion. He sees only his children whom he loves. He sees only the heart of his heart, and he weeps for thee when you forget your parentage, and would kill or maim your brethren.

Remember who you are, Dear Ones, and know once more that without the covering you wear when in the physical, you are one

---

[94]   A group of persons of common ancestry

when in spirit. Remember the love and joy which is you, and see only these things that would unite you, instead of looking at those things which divide you from your brothers and sisters. Show love and be love to all, for that is your only charge, Dear Ones, that you will live lives filled with happiness, peace, and joy. For indeed, the blessings of Mother Father God are poured out and made available to all.

Say not that ye are separate or are different from your brother, for indeed you are ONE. All are one in the eyes of God—if such we may use this term since indeed, God has no eyes— know indeed that all are ONE in the consciousness of God, for you are all created from the same love source which is God, and you possess the same spark of God within you. Turn not away from your brethren, Dear Ones, and say that, "You are not known," for indeed you know them in love, and light, and peace. For you are indeed a part of each one you meet, for you are all children of God and therefore are all brothers and sisters. Be you always living in the love and peace of God, and know, Dear Ones, that the love of God is thine always.

Remember your nature and return to the truth; that is who and what you are, for O, how you are loved! Be love! See love! Know love! And see these things in your brethren for therein lays your peace, your joy, and your hope, Dear Ones. Play once more with the great wheel, and see how many ways you can utilize this gift, for it will set you free. Know that there are indeed many ways to look upon your brethren and know that variety can be, and indeed is, the very spice of life.

The rainbow that is humanity is the very heart and soul of God.

Know indeed that the love of God is thine always, and all the Sons and Daughters of Humanity are children of God.

Be at peace, Dear Ones, and know that the love that is God resides within you all. And so it is! Amen and Amen!

Adieu

Know, indeed, that the love of God for humanity is the wonder of the Universe, for indeed many would ask why does the God of Love spend so much time—if such we may say—trying always to rescue the Sons of Men and to bring them back from the brink of despair and destruction that is self-imposed? For indeed, the Children of Men have been a warring breed since the dawn of time, and have caused great destruction and devastation upon this planet, their home. Know indeed, Dear Ones, that the reason is crystal clear and is simply and easily explained: for like any loving and forgiving parent, Mother Father God knows that, at the heart and soul of his children, lives and beats a heart of love. That man knows not that he is a being of love and is easily distracted by the outer trappings of the world is easily known. Thus, Dear Ones, we see that man knows not who he is but yet even so, his Mother Father God sees into his inner most soul, and knows all that truly lurks within the shell you would call a physical body. For, indeed, the body is naught but the temporary home for the magnificent soul which is part of Mother Father God.

Know indeed, Dear Ones, that the truth of man is that he is very special to the mind of God; for like any favored child he holds a special place in the heart of God. Thus, he is always at the forefront of the concerns—if such we may say of God—for indeed, as it is known, God has no concerns for being spirit and being eternal: he is focused on love and only aspects of love. Thus, Dear Ones, he is the protector of the Sons of Men, for in truth, he knows their weaknesses of the flesh and the things that would cause them to be distracted and to turn away from the things of God. For the love of humans, for those things that would provide mankind with great wealth and power are amongst those very things which will bring mankind to his knees. For from ancient times, these things have been able to bring man to his knees, so that in all his might and splendor, he has been able to be beaten and taken captive by the lusting for great wealth, power, and the desire to acquire all that is before him.

Know, Dear Ones, that the plight of man has been the pain in the heart of God—if such we can describe it—for indeed it is known that God, being spirit, has no heart. Know we use these terms to explain concepts in their simplest form, that you might grasp the essence of that which is being described. Know therefore, Dear Ones, that the love of God for mankind is that thing which allows him to ever be there to hold, love, and protect the Sons of Men. For indeed, there are moments when the Sons of Men need to be protected from self. For without this protection, he would gladly destroy himself.

Know, Dear Ones, that the Earth offers for mankind that ever-blooming garden of free will. For this is what allows for much of the pain of man to become evident in the world. For indeed, we know that man has been given the opportunity to make choices and to determine his own destiny. Thus, Dear Ones, it is seen when man makes choices to harm self or others and naught can be done to save him from himself. For in truth, the essence of man upon the Earth is likened to a great classroom into which all the Children of Men are found. Here in this classroom, many lessons are learned for this is indeed the classroom of life, and it is indeed to this place that all souls who choose to dwell upon the Earth must enter and be schooled.

Know, Dear Ones, that like children, the Sons of Men learn their lessons in a myriad of ways—some quicker than others—for the nature and reasons for each lesson are determined by the children. Know therefore, Dear Ones, that like any classroom upon the Earth, even so the Sons of Men are given opportunities to try new and varied experiences and to see how they fare. Each lesson is selected by the soul on entry into the physical experience, and thus it is controlled by that soul experience. Know, Dear Ones, that the love which is Mother Father God is never one of condemnation, of retribution, or punishment; for like all children, man must be allowed to learn from different experiences so that he can progress as a soul. Know, Dear Ones, that indeed the heart and soul of man is built on a foundation of love, peace, and harmony, so that it emulates those parts of God from which his very beingness originates.

Know, Dear Ones, that at the heart and soul of man beats this wonderful loving spirit, which is the love of God. That man knows not that he possesses this great gift, is one of the many facets of the classroom of life; for indeed, man enters the arena with no memory or knowledge of his true parentage, which is Mother Father God or of himself. For he is as a blank slate, void of knowledge and whilst in this great classroom, his task is to remember who he is and to find his way back to God. Know, Dear Ones, this is no easy task, for whilst in this great school of life, man is plagued by the temptations of the world which promise all that is good and all that is beneficial… but yet is empty of meaning. For in truth, man is easily fooled into thinking that all that glitters will bring him happiness, peace, joy, and contentment.

Thus, he adopts these things only to find they are naught but empty vessels, for indeed they do not bring joy for more than a moment, and the soul continues to yearn for more fulfillment. Thus, man may turn to external stimulants with which to numb the body and bring temporary relief. But in truth, this leads to addictive behaviors and naught else, for the effects are fleeting and the soul continues to yearn for that which it knows not. For in truth, it is searching for fulfillment, love, peace, and joy that come not from external forces or objects, but that which comes from deep within the soul of man. Thus we say, turn not to the distractions to find your hope and your rescue, Dear Ones, but look within you to find that peace that will calm the soul and bring you joy.

Know that no external stimulants can give you the peace, love, and joy you seek, for in truth, what you seek is the love of God: a love that is eternal and unchanging, a love that reaches deep within the heart and soul of man, and causes you to know happiness and peace beyond compare. This is the love of God, the love force which is within you, Dear Ones, and allows you to know the love, peace, joy, and happiness beyond measure. For this is the love of God buried within the soul of man. That man can activate this great force within himself is a true gift, and that some men can go deep within and find this great peace of God is a miracle of the age. For in truth, this allows man to see himself as a child of God, and to know that he is much more than the physical shell walking the Earth. Man can go within and find himself and find the love of God he has housed within his heart. Know, Dear Ones, that the lessons of life which man would learn will help to advance him into the spiritual realm of understanding, so that he can begin to appreciate his power and might as a child of God, given all the blessings of the kingdom... for indeed it is this great treasure that leads man ever onwards to discover new and more verdant pastures— if such we may say—for indeed, that man continues to seek God and to try to discover his identity as a child of God, is indeed a testament to the beingness of man.

For indeed, he comes into a world and must find his way back to God and learn the lessons of the physical world, while resisting the temptations and the urges to forsake it all for the pleasures of the physical body.

Know indeed, Dear Ones, that the love of God for man is ever available, for it is given to man and is always made available to him. Know indeed, Dear Ones, that the light and love of God will shine always on the Sons of Men, for indeed they are the favored of God. All the children in the great classroom of God are favored, for indeed Spirit washes the feet of man, who in his ignorance of his own divinity and his greatness, would believe himself to be so much less than he is, and to think himself weak and fearful. Know, Dear Ones, that you are mighty beings, for you are the Children of God and your eyes and your heart should ever be turned on God… for therein lives your rescue and your hope.

For naught else can save thee but the love of God. Naught can carry thee to the shores of God's love, save Mother Father God and the love that is borne for thee. For you are never alone and never deserted. You are loved with the greatest intensity and you can overcome the pain of the physical body and graduate to greater heights. For like any classroom, the Sons of Men can graduate to new heights and newer lessons, which will assist with growth.

Know that the love and beingness of God is thine ever, for you are wonderfully loved…oh, so much more than you may ever imagine. Be not alarmed, but know that you possess the God spark within thee, and you may do those things which will bring you peace all the days of your life. Know that all is well, Dear Ones, and know that the lessons in the great classroom of life are many and the opportunity for advancement is built into the plan.

Know that your dreams and aspirations are seen and heard in prayer, Dear Ones, so know that you have the power to create this reality of which you speak. Be at peace, and know that your loving parent, Mother Father God, encircles thee, and holds and protects thee, for you are a child of the Most High God, with a soul older than time which is here upon the Earth, to learn and to experience the joy and the emotions of the physical life. This is your classroom, so learn all the lessons that you can, that you might advance to advanced lessons and come into your own. Remember your heritage and your name!

Know once more that you are a child of the Most High God, and be at peace. Know that you are loved and cradled each day in the loving arms of God, and all will be well for thee, for you are children of a loving and benevolent parent who wants nothing more than to give you all the desires of your heart, and the keys to the kingdom of love, joy, peace, and happiness eternally.

Let the blessed of the Lord say and so it is!

Amen & Amen

20ᵀᴴJᴜɴᴇ 2012

Good morrow Sweet One. Know indeed that it is good to come together. Know indeed Dear One that the Angels in heaven sing the praises of Mother Father God and salute thee Dear One for indeed the task progresses as it should and happy are we to know of your success and the things that bring joy to your heart.

Know indeed, Dear Ones, that the love of God for mankind is ever present in the lives of the Sons of Men, even though in truth, the children know not of the many blessings that are daily heaped upon them. For in truth, they are like lost sheep wandering in the wilderness, knowing not where they go or why, and with no idea how to find their way back to the loving guidance of the shepherd. For indeed, they think they are alone and would go whither the wind would dictate. For indeed, being without purpose, they know not where they should go. Thus, Dear Ones, they are seen running and wandering alone and lost. For now their only thoughts are of ways to meet the most basic desires and instincts, so that they might survive upon the Earth. For their thoughts rest only on these needs, and they are driven by the survival instincts buried deep within them to try to find food and water.

Thus, they wander night and day, searching for food and water, lest they die. Know, Dear Ones, that even so are the Sons of Men seen upon the Earth, for in their turmoil and their forgetfulness, they wander night and day upon the Earth, searching for the means to fulfill their most basic needs. They forget all else and would focus only on survival, for they believe they will die without these basic necessities. Know, Dear Ones, that the children can see naught around them and they taste not the fresh air, see not the flowers, and continue to wander upon the Earth, looking for those things that will allow them to survive. Thus, Dear Ones, the Sons of Men are ever in search of those things that they think will bring them peace, happiness, and joy, for in their hearts they fear that death will come upon them, for they have no knowledge that they have all they need to survive already given to them.

Thus, Dear Ones, they continue to roam from place to place, searching for the life-giving sustenance they believe will give them life and allow them to survive upon the Earth. Know, Dear Ones, that they halt not for the drive for survival is strong within their hearts, and they will not stop to acknowledge anything around them which is not recognized as food they would desire or expect. Thus, Dear Ones, the Children of Men are seen wandering aimlessly upon the Earth, for they think they will perish if they do not continue this search. Thus they roam all over the land, searching and searching for that thing which will give them peace. For in truth, they know not the way to cease from wandering, since they have wandered for eons upon the Earth and now would know no other way to survive upon the Earth. Thus, Dear Ones, the Children of Men are now distracted by new and exciting things they see whilst upon the road.

For in truth, there are very many distractions which would cause them to temporarily forget their pain and hunger, and instead turn to see and to drink in the new things which come into view. For at such times, Dear Ones, they are without memory of the journey or the purpose of this journey, and so they spend much time focusing on the distractions round about them, to the detriment of all else. Know, Dear Ones, that man can now cease to wander the Earth, for in his heart he feels fulfilled and free. Thus, there is much rejoicing and happiness, for the hunger has been satisfied and the bellies of the Sons of Men are full.

Thus, Dear Ones, they can now focus on the distractions and turn away from God. For indeed, the urges to do the things of God are seen as problems to be solved. Thus, man has no impact upon the situation at hand, for they would indeed be held in the lowliest of places, where all is lost and no peace reigns within the hearts of men. For in truth, the children come to know that those who would willingly join them in pastimes are now also swept up in the moment, and are lost to rational thought.

Thus, Dear Ones, we say that the path to God is paved with smooth stones, for indeed it is a rocky path full of the pitfalls of life which need to be conquered, so that man might move to a place of happiness and peace in this new environment. Thus, Dear Ones, we find that the Sons of Men have not only lost their way, but in essence, have forgotten their reason for the journey or adventure. Thus they continue to wander, searching for the elusive thing that will give them life. For now they are growing weary, and would refuse to move along the path lest they get nothing and wither and die.

Know, Dear Ones, that the food is forgotten and all else falls by the wayside, and none can help or point them in the right way, for all are lost together with none to save them, and thus they all wander with haste... lest the measures of food would be consumed before everyone has had their fill.

Know that the children are indeed trying to hold fast and be strong, for even they are aware that the answer to the dilemma is a simple one. Be not disheartened, Dear Ones, but know that your Heavenly Father will search for thee, find thee, and determine whither you would go: For thus is the way of the Lord, that the needs of all the Sons of Men will be satisfied and the children will want for nothing. For to walk justly in the ways of God is indeed the only food and nourishment that is needed by man. For there is, indeed, an abundant supply of these things found upon the Earth, and indeed the Sons of Men can be seen running to and fro, picking up the very food items strewn about, for it will indeed give them peace, and love, and liberty. Thus is the surprise of man, for indeed they have travelled these paths day and night but were oblivious of the wealth of food which lay hidden. Now, Dear Ones, the doors to the harvest of God can be found in evidence upon the Earth, and the children can now move as they should; for the brave ones who stopped to see, smell, and in fact, taste the very love, joy, and peace of God unceasing are rewarded. For in truth, all is as it should be and now the children can be fed.

Know indeed, Dear Ones, that the love of God is that thing which is the life force for man. Know, however, there was a great tumult and much singing and dancing, for this is the way of God and the way of love to always make provision for the Sons of Men, even though no way was known. Thus, like sheep whose innate system will help them find their way home, there are many different measures that can measure that which is seen as successful upon the Earth.

For unlike the flowers, which are not able to stand erect in the midday sun, they can now make great changes in their lives and can see and taste the many different forms of the blessings of man given upon the Earth. For in truth, that man can count out the very stars at night— even so that this blessing is seen by many millions—but yet cannot find his way home, for such is his confusion. For this is not the way to communicate all the needs of those around him.

Be at peace and know that all will be well for the Sons of Men, for no more is there a need for pain and hunger when baskets of food are gladly placed in front of thee at no cost. Know indeed that the love of God is racing away to meet him and to give him comfort, peace, and joy; for this is indeed the basic tenet of life. Be not afraid, Dear Ones, that your search for God is useless, for indeed God is within your very soul. Know you are children of God, the heart and soul of God, so all should be well. Be you well and say all is well, for Mother Father God is my shield and strength, for such are the ways of God. Be at peace and know that all is as it should be.

May the God of your love and life surround thee with his many blessings, and show how the Children of Men will be fed. Be at peace and know that the love of God will always cause you to be clothed and fed, so fret not, Dear Ones, for Mother Father God will remember your names and always provide food for thee so that you will want for nothing. For like the sheep, they have found them wandering upon the Earth in search of a place of safety.

He will provide food, water, and clothing for you, Dear Ones, that you might indeed never hunger or thirst. Wander no more, Dear Ones, in search of that which you think you need, for in truth, it is laid out before thee but your blindness causes you not to see or to know of its presence in your life. For you are always provided for by Mother Father God, so know that all your desires are met by your Heavenly Father. So wander no more upon the land in desperation, but know that you have all you need, already made available to you by your Mother Father God.

Be you alert and look around and see all the bounty of God given to you and laid at your feet. Open your eyes and be fed by the love and grace of God. For you are always provided for by your loving parent, so be at peace, Dear Ones, and come into your own beingness, that you might see, and know, and taste the true bounty of God. For this is your birthright; this is your gift, so take, eat, and be satisfied, Dear Ones, that you may rest in the loving arms of Mother Father God forever.

Be at peace and know that all is well for thee, and you hunger and thirst not; for all your needs are supplied and you are at peace. This is the promise and the blessings of God given to all the Children of Men, so wander no more like lost sheep, Dear Ones... but rest in the loving arms of God, always in comfort, peace, happiness, and joy. Let the blessed of the Lord say and so it is!

Amen

21ˢᵗJuly 2012

Know Dear One, we are much happy to be here with thee and to continue with the text at this time. Know indeed, Dear One, the love of God is like a great book, on whose pages are written the truth of all things that man might truly come to know his nature and his beingness. Thus, this great book is given to the children of a great family, that they might gain this great knowledge and come to know all that exists for them in their lives. The book is given as a gift to the parents, and they then pass the book to their children, that they might learn and be well-acquainted with all the truths of their heritage. Know, Dear Ones, the book is not given to one but shared equally with all the children, that they might all come to know that great truth which lies within its pages. Know, Dear Ones, that the children of the parents are anxious to see within the pages and to also become learned with the pages of the book, for they have been told that this is the way to seek and to gain all the riches of the world— by reading this great book and coming to know all that is truly available upon the Earth.

Thus, Dear Ones, the children of this parent try to decipher[95] the great book, but when each one reads the book, they find within its pages different stories. Thus, soon they begin to feel that the book is indeed special, for it contains a special magic, which allows each one to see and to know different truths from within its pages. Thus the children come to love this magic book, for indeed they each read it daily but come away with different stories, and thus they are happy, for they feel special because they each receive different stories when they read the pages of the great book. As time goes by, the children grow and it is time to leave their home and to come to their own beingness. Thus, they gain homes of their own but still return to the home of the parents to read the great book and to come to know once more the content that lies within its pages.

When the parents die, the children are much saddened and would each wish to own the great book, that they might always possess the great truths found within. Thus begins the quarrels and the fighting for who will gain possession of the book, for indeed it is seen as a magical text, which can allow them to amass great wealth and to bring each fame and fortune. For indeed, each one comes to believe that the truths contained within their stories are the only truths, and those stories mentioned by their brothers and sisters are not as wonderful as the ones they receive.

Thus, the great quarrels continue, and there is unrest and turmoil within the family of brothers and sisters, and there is no happiness… for indeed they would now look upon each other with disdain[96], and

---

[95] To discover or explain the meaning of

[96] Feeling of contempt: regarded as worthless: to consider to be unworthy of notice

say that the stories related by their brothers and sisters are not true, and only their tales are the truth. This is the pain of man, Dear Ones, for indeed, the love of God was given to all the Sons of Men in equal portions and given to all in the same way that it might give them pleasure…but the Sons of Men have taken the words and changed them in their hearts, so that they are all different. For each in their turn see only their version as the truth of the love of God. Know indeed, Dear Ones, we say that there is only one truth within the great book, but each child, on reading, would see the story in a different way and thus came to believe that it was a different tale.

Know, Dear Ones, that this is the cause of the division among the Children of Men, for indeed each of the sons says their truth is all that exists and all other truths are false truths; for only their truth can lead you to happiness. Know, Dear Ones, that the love, which is God, is the same for all the Sons of Men, for indeed it is given to all the Sons of Men in the same way. It is the same for all. Even though the Prophets upon the Earth were given the same knowledge, it was given to them in their own tongue and custom; thus, so that those who heard it would all understand it in the context of their lives. Let not the fear and hatred continue among you, Dear Ones, and let not the segregation by region keep thee separate from your brother; for in truth, you all worship the same God and the truths are universal truths.

That you have read the story and have interpreted it in your own way, and would now come to believe that it is a different truth is inaccurate, Dear Ones, for indeed there is only one truth of the great love of God for mankind. For indeed, that truth tells of the great and eternal love of God for the Sons of Men. It is the truth of the deep and unending love of God for his children, and the teachings that God is, indeed, a God of love and not a God of separation, divisiveness, and anger. It is not a God of separation or one that discriminates between the children upon the Earth; for indeed, all are one, and all are seen in the same way by Mother Father God. That the children have not been able to see that there is only one great truth in all their interpretations of the stories from the great book is, indeed, the greatest of all tragedies; for indeed they read the same pages yet saw differences within their own hearts, which were attributed to the magic of the book.

Know indeed, Dear Ones, there is no magic within the pages of the book, for only your heart would interpret it in this way. Only your hearts would see differences where none exists. Open your eyes, Dear Ones, and come to know that there is only one great truth, and that is of the love of God for all his children; for each is loved in the same way, even though the mind of man would turn this to say God loves me and not thee.

For the mind of man cannot consider that there is an abundance of love for all mankind, and each is loved with the same fervor and intensity by God; for there are no differences seen between the Sons of Men by God, for you are all the same in the eyes of God, for you are his children. Let not the eyes of man and the will to be different cause you any more pain, Dear Ones, but come to realize you all speak of the same truths when you speak of God, for indeed, you are all reading the same page.

For all the information given came from the one source, and all tell that love and peace are the ways of being in the world; loving your brethren and showing kindness to the weak are the ways of God. That you have taken these truths and changed them in your hearts, so that you no longer know the truth of God, is the pain of mankind. For now you see each other as different, and would even forget that you are related, for you are all brothers and sisters of the same parent, Mother Father God. So why do you war against your brethren, and discriminate against your brother, and see not the similarities about you instead of looking to see ways in which you are different?

That you remember not to love your brothers and sisters and to show love and mercy to those in need, is the pain of God; for when you hate your brethren, you do not the things of God. When you rob the poor and look not to those who are in pain and who suffer upon the Earth, you do not the things of God.

For these are not the teachings of God, given to the Sons of Men. For they say love your enemies— but indeed, you have no enemies— for this is the belief of men: that there is insufficiency and lack upon the Earth, thus the only way to survive is to take all for self and leave none for your brethren. Know, Dear Ones, that when you show this great disregard for your brothers, you do not the things of God, for indeed you are making your own rules and ascribing them to God; for it is not the way of God to hate and to divide. It is not the way of God to make no provision for his children upon the Earth, for indeed all are one and there is an abundance of all the bounty of God upon the Earth: Put there and given to all the children that you might all live in happiness, peace, and joy upon the Earth.

That you see not the abundance but live in the belief of lack is not the way or the teaching of God. For all is made available to the Sons of Men that you might know peace, love, and joy upon the Earth; for all has been made available to you, O Sons of Men!

That you hoard while your brothers starve, is not the way of God. That you kill your brethren who do not believe as you do, is not the way of God, for you are all the children of the same God, and you have forgotten the truth of your beingness, and thus you are separated within your heart. For there is no separation in God, for you are all seen in the same way by God. For God sees not color, creed, or religion, for there exists no such things in the eyes of God— for indeed God, being spirit, has no eyes— and all are known only for the love, which is who and what you are, Dear Ones. Let go of the thoughts and belief of lack and separation, and return once more to the great book, Dear Ones, and realize that the story within tells the same tale of love, peace, and joy, and naught else. For though your mind would tell you that you see things differently, know indeed, Dear Ones, that there is only one way of being in the world and that is the way of love, harmony, and peace, Dear Ones. For in living in the world in this way, you come to know all the true joys of God, and you can be that wonderfully cherished being which you are.

For you are all the Sons and Daughters of God, all loved with the same vigor and intensity, Dear Ones; for there are no differences between you, for your loving parent, Mother Father God, gives you the keys to the kingdom, which is delivered and made available to each of you, free of cost. That you see this not and would believe you are alone and separated in the world, is part of the pain of God, for he weeps for thee, Dear Ones, when you would kill and maim your brethren, believing them to be separate from thee, when in effect you are all one: All part of God, with the same chemical make-up, with the same DNA, and the same abundance of the love of God given to thee at birth.

Know, Dear Ones, none is loved more than the other, for you are all loved the same way, and all are cradled in the arms of your loving parent each day. Let go of the thoughts of separation and come to know of the truth of the beingness of God, Dear Ones, for this is truly who and what you are. For you are the Sons and Daughters of God, given this great gift which you have manipulated and changed in your minds, until you know not who or what you are. For indeed, Dear Ones, you would change the words to make them more palatable for your taste, and to bring them more fire and to make them yours alone, when they were given to all.

That the love of God is only made available to one religion is false, Dear Ones, for it is given to all, even though you would change it so that it resembles not the same teachings. Know indeed it is one, and thus when you turn to this, you all turn to God. You all turn to the same loving and benevolent parent, and you are all given the same blessings from God. Be you of one heart and mind, Dear Ones, and come to know once more that you are brothers and sisters, and that the stories from the great book are all the same. For there is no magic in the pages, even though your mind would have you believe that there are differences between you.

Know indeed, Dear Ones, that all are one in the love and beingness of God and all are children of God. You need not fight for the book, Dear Ones, for it belongs to all, and you can share in the beauty of this great gift, if such is your desire: For indeed you are all endowed with the great wisdom at birth. For this is the nature of your Mother Father God, to give you all within the kingdom. So live in peace, love, and harmony, Dear Ones, for this is your true heritage and your hope. For it is the will of God to make all upon the Earth available to the Sons of Men, that you might live in truth, love, peace, and harmony.

See the world with one heart and one mind, Dear Ones, and you will come to know the true light and love of God, which is possible upon the Earth. See no more the differences, but see instead those things that can serve to unify thee. For this is your rescue, your peace, and your joy. Know the true happiness that can be thine, when you see and know once more all the true gifts of God that were given to all the Sons of Men eons ago, when you were created in the mind of God.

Be love, show love, and love, Dear Ones, and remember your true nature, for these are the ways of God, which will bring you joy, peace, and abundance always. Return to the book and once more know that there is only one story, and that is the story of the love of God for humanity. Be at peace, Dear Ones, and know that the love of God is thine always, so let not the human mind lead thee astray and lead thee to forget who you are, for you are the Sons and Daughters of God, regardless of what your human mind will tell you. Open your hearts to your brethren, and know you are one, united in the peace, love, and joy of God always. Let the blessed of the Lord say and so it is!

Amen & Amen.

Adieu Dear Ones

The Brotherhood

22ND July 2012

Know, indeed, that the love of God for humanity is like an ever growing and expanding circle, for indeed it has no beginning and no end. It does grow, however, and fills the vast expanse which is the universe of God's love. For indeed, it is all that there truly is throughout the Universe, for naught else continues to exist except the great love of God. For try as man might, naught else can echo through the vast expanse, which is the love of God, and remain untouched and unknown: For the great love of God is all that there is, from the rising of the sun until the setting of the same. For though all creation may crumble and naught else would remain, know indeed that the love of God would ever remain constant, for it is that ever-expanding and ever-growing part of God— if such it can be described— for the love which is given to mankind knows no bounds and is endless. It is eternal and everlasting, Dear Ones, and once given, can never be removed.

For the God of Love, which is your parent, would never remove any gift once it is given. For all the blessings of Mother Father God are given in love, and thus can and would never be removed, for this is not the way of God. For the God of Love is not a God who gives gifts which are contingent upon good behavior or the ability of the recipient to earn favor. All gifts are given in love, and all gifts, once given, will never be removed, for it is impossible that God would ever take his blessings from the Children of Men: for this is not the way of God.

That the Children of Men feel they must be worthy in order to receive the blessings of God is part of the very nature of man; but know, Dear Ones, that this is in no way part of the way of God, for God's goodness is not contingent upon the good behavior of man.

Thus, Dear Ones, you see that there is nowhere where God is not, and there is nothing that man can do which would ever serve to separate him from the love of God. That the Sons of Men measure God with earthly measures, and see God with human qualities which would cause him to desert his children when they go astray, is naught but the mind and imagination of man at work. For God is not bound by the measures of mankind, and cannot be comprehended by the human mind; for man knows not the complex nature of that which is God. For indeed, he can never hope to fully comprehend that which is God, for God in his very complexity is simplicity at its best.

For, lo, the nature of God is one of love, and at the core of the beingness of God is the seat or table of love. From this great table— if such we can describe it— comes the great abundance of God, for indeed all the blessings and the goodness that is God is available to be given in totality to the Children of Men. For indeed, they are so loved by God, that naught within the realm of man or God is not available to the Sons of Men. For thus is the might and true power of the Sons of Men, found and made available to all the Children of

Men. For indeed, they are loved with such intensity and fervor that their loving parent, Mother Father God, is ever able and ready to give all within the kingdom to his children.

That the God of love sees thee only as children is the nature of the beingness of God; for indeed, since man is learning the very ways of God, you are like children likened to those in a great classroom. For you enter this classroom that you might learn all that is available to thee, so that you might grow to become that which you were destined to be.

Thus, Dear Ones, you enter the great classroom, which is the earth-plane, and take on physical form that you might truly come to know the many pains and joys of the human condition and from these great experiences grow as spiritual beings. Thus, Dear Ones, when you falter along the way, your parent will not scold thee, for you are learning the ways of life, and thus no scolding is necessary: For in order to grow, you must experience many things over many lifetimes. Thus, now in the great classroom which is life, it is now time to turn the page of a great book and see where you will go with the next stage of your learning. Know that for eons, Dear Ones, you have toiled and struggled in ignorance, killing and maiming your brethren, for you knew not that you were one in God; even though many prophets have been sent to remind you of these truths. Yet still, you continue to rob the weak and to harm your brothers and sisters, for you remember not who they are. You have forgotten the kinship and the love you have shared and would kill them willingly upon the Earth.

Now is the time, Dear Ones, to stand and look to the future and determine whither you will go and what you will do, for indeed, your choices abound. Will you turn and cease, or will you continue along this path that can lead to naught but destruction? For, indeed, the time is upon you all, Dear Ones, to determine your truths. For the love, which is Mother Father God, will continue to be with thee whither you would go: For you are children in the classroom of life and you must choose your path. For you have seen much, Dear Ones, across the centuries of your history, and you have seen wars, and famine, and destruction, and death, that you have brought upon your brethren; so know that, indeed, you are free to choose whither you will go and what you will do, for you have the free will, Dear Ones, to determine your path and your fate.

For indeed, you are the Children of Men, given the right to choose and determine your fate. For thus it is written that the Children of Men can choose where to lay his head. For indeed, he has been given all the bounty of God and can go wherever he would choose upon the Earth. Know indeed, that the love of God is planted within you even as a seed is planted deep into the earth, and is watered, and fed, and nourished so that it might indeed grow to become that which it was meant to be. Now even so, Dear Ones, even so are you programmed with the love of God to come to know yourself and to recognize your brethren, even when they come disguised so that you do not know them. For in truth, they come to you in different skin color, and wearing different garb of religions, so that you recognize them not. For when you knew them last, they were all a part of you in spirit and you were one.

Now, when you see them, they are disguised as strangers with different garments, and they are no longer familiar to thee. For you recognize them not and they know you not also. Thus you meet like strangers on the road of life, and know not that you are one. Once you loved and laughed and played in the garden of God; now you turn your backs upon them and would harm them lest they steal your wealth and bring you to destitution.[97] Know, Dear Ones, you separate yourself from them and you would turn your backs upon them in their hour of need for you know them not, and they are, O so different from anything or anyone you have ever known. Know, Dear Ones, that the love, which is God, is forgotten… for although the lessons are known to you, they are not applied, for the people you meet are strangers and naught else.

The veil of forgetfulness has descended upon thee, Dear Ones, and caused you to forget your nature and to know not the things you always knew when in spirit. Now you see your brethren and would know them not, and thus would turn to kill, maim, and disown them, for they cannot be seen as your brethren; for you are so different now in the physical, that all is erased, and all is forgotten, and you hurt and kill your brethren as though they were animals in the wild.

Turn, O Sons of Men! And remember your heritage and your joy. Return once more to the true knowledge of who and what you are, that you might once more come to know the love, peace, joy, and happiness that is you. Look to the circle and know that there is room for all within this expanding circle, for it can contain all you need. There is room for all in this great circle, and there is an abundant supply of all things, that all of the members within it might have all they need and much more. Turn not around and say there is room enough only for a few who look like you and all others must be removed from the circle, for this is not the way of God. Know that this circle is ever-expanding, and all is there made available within it.

All is given to the Sons of Men, that they might come to know the true blessings of Mother Father God. For you will all be provided

---

[97]   Poverty: deprivation: a state of utter want

with everything you need, Dear Ones, and you will never know lack unless you feel that there is not enough. Know this is your mind telling you that there is a limit to all things. Even though your Mother Father God would tell you that all your needs will be met, you accept not this truth, and would believe that you will be left without the basic tenets of life. Know, Dear Ones, that your life is the life of God and your Mother Father God has provided for thee in abundance. For you will never be left alone and desolate. You will never know lack, and you will always have the love of God within you, Dear Ones. Know, indeed, that you are the children of God, sent to learn in the great classroom of life, so that you may grow in the awareness of the great love of God for mankind, when in physical form.

Your task is to find your way back to your parent and to be kind to those you meet along the way; to be kind to those in need and to show love and mercy to your fellow classmates, for all are one. All are the same as you are. All placed upon the Earth to learn, and to grow, and to remember your nature as children of a loving and benevolent parent. You want for nothing, for everything you could ever need has been provided for thee so that you will want for nothing. That you feel you have nothing is part of the veil of forgetfulness and the human condition, but know that indeed you are the children of God, and thus have all you will ever want or need, for in your arms is the great and glorious bounty of God.

Only your forgetfulness would make you believe all is lost and you are alone, for your parent can never desert thee, for you are his children. Look to the love that is you, and know that your parent is ever by your side, for he would never send you away to a lonely, desolate place without his guidance, love, and support. For he fears that the storms of life will come upon thee, and you would have no defenses. Thus, he provides love and support for thee ever upon the Earth, that you would always know the love, peace, and joy which is God. Know always, Dear Ones, that you are guided, loved, held, and watched over by Angels, for it is their task to be with thee always, so that you might always know of the intensity of the love of God for thee. Know that the circle has no beginning and no end, thus there is no place where you can be within the circle where God is not.

For all within[98] and outside the circle are part of God, thus you are ever able to call upon the name of your parent, Mother Father God, and know that you will be answered. Be at peace, Dear One, and know you are ever held and cradled in the arms of God, from which you can never be removed: For you are children of God, loved and cherished every day until the end of time, that you may always know the love, peace, and joy of God within your heart for yourself and your brethren... for all are one, united in the love, peace, and joy which is God. Be at peace and rest easy within the circle, for you are always held, loved, and supported by God; ever in his care, and ever in receipt of his benevolence.

For you are children of God, sent to learn in the classroom of God called Earth. You must and will always return to God when the lesson is done, for this is your home, your peace, and your joy. Know this truth and know always the great peace, love, joy, and abundance of God. For the circle has no end, and the love of God for thee is limitless, so fear not that you will ever lose this great love, for this will never happen... for you are the joy, peace, and happiness of God. You are forever loved

---

[98]   Inside

and cradled by God, so know you are beings of light and not the physical reflection you see in the mirror. Know always the peace of God, and be you ever at peace, Dear Ones, for you are God walking upon the Earth. When you show love, joy, peace, and compassion upon the Earth, you show God, for this is who and what you are. You are emanations of God: You are light, peace, love, joy, and the hope of God.

Continue to show mercy, love, and caring for your brethren, that you may indeed show God upon the Earth: for this is the core of the lesson of life, Dear Ones, to show the things of God, when in the physical form upon the Earth, to those you meet each day. Be ever at peace, Dear Ones, and come to know all that is truly God within you, for you carry the spark of God within you, Dear Ones. Remember this always and glow and shine your light like the emanations of God that you truly are, for this is your course and this is your reason for being upon the Earth, Dear Ones.

Remember your nature and your reason for being in the great classroom is to learn and to grow. Be your brilliant selves, Dear Ones, and show all that is God within you, that everyone will see the evidence of God upon the Earth and grow into the full realization of who and what you are, and what you can become.

May the love, peace, and beingness of God ever continue to glow within you, and may you always radiate with the love of God that is within you. Let the blessed of the Lord say and so it is. Amen and Amen!

The Brotherhood

Adieu

CHAPTER 3

THE DIVINE WITHIN MAN

The beingness of man in the physical, is the essence of God's love shown upon the Earth; for though you are here in different shapes and colors, know indeed it is the very nature of your beingness which is the essence of God. For you are spirit, you are joy, you are light, you are love. You are all that is right and good. You are the peace and love of God incarnate.

IF I CAN HELP SOMEBODY

"If I can help somebody, then my living shall
not be in vain."- Androzzo A.B.

Indeed brethren, it is said that man's purpose for being on the Earth is
to find his way back to God, and to learn the power and source of love.
Man must learn these things before he can return to the Godhead,
and find the peace that he is inherently seeking. If he is not able to find
his true "raison d'être" or "reason for being," then he has not found
the source of his life and his power. Man must, therefore, spend his
time searching for the source of his love, life, and energy when he
may already know the answer to the burning question. Man must,
therefore, always learn how to find his source and to identify it when
it is found. Without this knowledge, it would be akin to finding a great
treasure but being unable to see or know its true value, and throwing it
away as useless pieces of colored glass, when they are in fact the most
precious gems available to man on this Earth.

The Daughters and Sons of Zion must learn the source of their
strength and power if they are to proceed upon the Earth. Man

cannot live by bread alone, but by all things. To identify the people who fall into this category, however, we find that we are alone but yet not so. Man must search to find those of like mind and then, together, they can create the magic, awe, and wonder from them.

Man's purpose for learning of the gap in time— truth— is to know how to respond and to know how to live with these super beings that truly exist within ourselves. Although man must go inside himself to find the true nature of his source himself, and his power, he must truly know all as it pertains to him because of the constant need for perfection, and the hope that he has already gotten God's favor. Because man fails to remember his own divinity whilst on the Earth, he must constantly be reminded of the power that he possesses. Man can do whatever he ought, but yet, he must make room for the love and growth of his friends and the grouping he calls family. If man is not able to do this, then perish he must, even though he is fully aware of the source of his own might and power. To gain entry to this place of power and to take full advantage of what is offered; man must become that shadow of himself that gazes back at him in the mirror. If he cannot do this, then he cannot become a shadow of his true self, and must remain in the shadow of his own beingness, and strength, and love. His focus cannot be on the development of his power, but on the power of those around him, for his power is gained at the price of the love of those other souls which rest and travel with him in this incarnation. He must become who he is truly meant to be if he is to advance.

Adieu

5ᵀᴴ MARCH 2010

The passions of man… they cause him to create wonderment and tribulations[99] upon the Earth. The depth and breadth of the passion will measure how the impact of the fate of men will rise or fall. For sure, it is seen that the measure of a man is but given in a day or a year in time, as it is measured upon the Earth. We say, of course, this is as it is meant to be, for the days and nights of man upon the Earth are measured in too small a span. For in reality, he is upon the Earth for longer than is known. The spirit of man leaves at the time of loss or death of the physical body, but in most instances, he is still found in Earth's layers and essence for much time beyond this. The magnetic pull of Earth will not allow man's soul to leave at the very time of exit, but will cause him to remain in the realm of man, clothed in many guises for some time.

The soul can see, sense, and be aware of much that is taking place, and can communicate with those selected ones to bring comfort to the grieving loved ones. Never fear for those who have travelled away, for the distance is very short and they are seated close by,

---

[99]   That which brings distress: trouble: severe affliction

watching and listening to much of what is said. Know, Dear Ones, that the path to heaven is paved with much of substance that man cannot fully understand. It is of interest to see man's interpretation in graphics of what is perceived of the road and path to God. Know, indeed, it is so much simpler than is envisioned by man, for in its simplest form, it is naught but a merging with the Cosmos within the length and breadth of the arms of God. Arms, we say, but know, indeed, that no such limb exists... for within the imagination of man, the presence and structure of God cannot be explained. The nature of God is such as to be unfathomable and indiscernible,[100] but know that exist He does, and real He is!

We use the term "He" loosely, but know, indeed, that God exists... not outside of man, but within him as well. For the realness of God is measured by the power of man to know and to understand his power and might. The Heavenly Hosts who dwell in the uppermost regions of the temple of God are the bringers of the light of man to Earth. Their task is to show the power and wonder of God, so know, Dear Souls, that the levels between God and man exist not to keep man separate, but to provide support for man upon the Earth. For it is from these very regions that the Light Bringers will help and assist the Children of Men as they develop and move toward the light of God.

Moving toward the light of God is the essence of the shift of man's soul from the concrete Earth to the heavens above: Moving from the mundane to the sublime. Man moves at the time of departure in mental stages, so that he can gradually join with the celestial band of souls and embark upon his journey home, back to the arms and love of God.

---

[100] Impossible to understand

Know, Dear Ones, this path is there for all, although some souls may choose to remain upon the Earth for limited times to continue unfinished work and be with the bereft in love and support.

Adieu

17ᵀᴴ July 2010

For behold, much has been said of the Son of Man[101] and his place with God the Father, but know, Dear Ones, that the Son of Man has no powers other than that which is given by the Father. For of himself, he is powerless to act or to do any miracles. By finding the strength and the will buried deep within himself, the man Jesus was able to perform all manner of miracles and to bring about untold wonders upon the face of the Earth. Know, Dear Ones, that nothing that is accomplished by man is done without the love and support of the love of God. For all creativity is given with the love and the blessings of the Father God. Man, of himself, is unable to create... but that very essence of God, which is part of the foundation of man, causes him to be able to reach to the stars and to elicit the creative spark and source buried so deep within himself. Man is the creative source of God, and as such, is also able to create. His powers of creativeness are limitless, if and when he turns within and pulls forth that which is there.

In letting his soul forth, the divine spark and creative essence is able to flow, and man is able to see into possibilities, and thus is able

---

[101]   Human being: man

to see and know the true source of most things. He is then able to ponder the secrets of all things, and the knowing of the true way of the formation of all things— or their unreal nature— they can see all possibilities and make all connections. Thus is the spark ignited and thus is the creative power ignited within man, and he is able to make the seeming impossible possible, and to solve great mysteries.

All man needs to do is to be able to go within to contact the God-being that lives within, and he is then able to bring into view that which, with the naked eye, is hidden from view. Man is the creative tool and spark of God, thus he himself possesses the power to be creative. All that is required is the ability to quiet the chattering mind and to see all that truly exists, or in some instances, does not exist. He is then able, by coming into contact with the truth of all things, to tell the story of how and what constitutes the possible and the impossible in the physical experience of man.

Man is nothing, of himself, but yet lurking deep within him is the power to harness the wonders of the world, and to share the knowledge of all. All that is required is the time and patience to quiet the mind and to allow the true knowledge to emerge. This is what man labels as creativity or genius. In reality, all it is, is the freeing of the innate knowledge of all that exists or fails to exist, and thus causes him to offer solutions to problems, questions, and mysteries.

The creative source is the part and essence of every man, which when set free, can show aspects of his true nature and demonstrate his true power and the magnitude of the connection with Source. Man must be able to link with Source if he is to survive upon the Earth. Living disconnected is to live without Source links, and to be a soul in isolation, unable to connect tentacles to the power source—thus they wave in the breeze—With the link to Source, they (tentacles of the soul) are grounded and can recharge with God-knowledge, remember who he is, and share the knowledge and power he possesses with all.

Adieu

4ᵀᴴ OCTOBER 2010

For the Grace of God is the most powerful— and wonderful— tool of all that the spirit of man can access. This grace is such that its tool is the very essence and love of God. Know ye not that without Grace, man perishes? So ye are like flowers caught in the height of the noonday sun without water, that withers and frails[102]. Its leaves wilt and it is seen limply laying, waiting for the water to bring it back to life. Even so is the love of God. The love and grace of God is like the refreshing rain that falls on the flower and brings it back to life, allowing the flower to stand erect and strong once again. Firm in the love and light of God, the flower is beaming, and shining, and looking straight up into the skies. Listen, O Children of Men, and know the mighty works of God. For the love of God will be the water that can nourish the soul of man, and bring him nourishment and the life-giving substance that can make you whole.

Know ye not that, without this life-giving source, you wither and die in the heat of the noonday sun?

---

[102] To be easily broken or destroyed :fragile: weak

Know ye not that, without this, you fail to rise to your potential and remain in the dust of the day?

Know ye not that, you fail to flourish and to reach and attain your potential?

Know ye not that you fail to mature into the great and wondrous beings that you are?

Know ye not that you wither and die, like the tiny sapling on the floor of the forest, without the light and love of God?

Wait O Sons and Daughters of man. Wait and learn of your magnificence. See the strength and love of God that is ever present and available for thee. Know that you are Sons and Daughters of the Most High God. Remember your magnificence and know who you are. Remember your birthright and claim that which is rightfully thine. Know your heritage and live. Live and grow with the nurturing of your spirit. Live and grow with the life-giving energy, which comes from the source, your Mother Father God.

Live and become your true essence. Live and be you, who you were meant to be. Listen, O Sons and Daughters of man. Listen and learn of your birthright. For of such you are crafted and made. Know your destiny and your truth as Sons and Daughters of Spirit, as Sons and Daughters of light. Be you magnificent. Be you full of the love, light, and power of the spirit. Show your magnificence, remember who you are, and know that you can live, if you but choose to remember your way back to light, your way back to love, your way back to your eternal source, your Mother Father God.

Let your light shine forth. Let your soul shine forth. Let your light shine forth; for in this way, you will be able to allow your magnificence. Let your magnificent being shine forth and become your true selves.

Allow yourselves to feel the effects of the love of God and to become the beautiful flowers you are. Stand firm in the noonday sun, knowing that you will not wither, but will gain strength and vitality from the life-giving rain that will flow upon you.

Know yourself and remember that you are able to reach these heights, O Sons and Daughters. Remember who you are. Let your light shine. Let your love shine. Let your peace be evident upon the Earth; for even so, will you be able to maintain your place upon the Earth and bring peace to those who cry for fear of warfare. Be your magnificent selves. Know your birthright and become who you were meant to be. Leave the toil and tribulations behind, and look deep inside for the peace and love that will set you free. Ye are the salt of the Earth indeed, but if the salt has lost its flavor, where liveth its value? It hath no value, but will be tossed as useless and of no value. Be ye full of life and vigor. Turn ye to one another and see your brother for who he is. Know that you see yourself when you see your brother... for you are not TWO but ONE: Like twins from the same parent. You are ever joined and can never be separated, for your souls were conceived together and will forever be part of the same source.

You cannot harm your brother or you harm yourself. You are Brothers and Sisters of Light. Sons and Daughters of the same God, yet you forget your divinity and seek to destroy each other. Remember that the same spirit is within you both and that you destroy a part of yourself when you destroy a part of God. You are all a part of God, and each time you destroy your brother, you are destroying a part of God and yourself. Listen and remember, O Children of Men, that the only way to return to the source— your source— is to remember that love is the powerful force that can heal all wounds, and can cause you to return to that which you were meant to be.

You are the salt and the flavor. If you forget your value and your worth, you are like lost sheep, wandering aimlessly in the desert… unable to find water and food, and eventually will die. Look you to the green meadows ahead, see them and know they are what you seek. Why tarry[103] in the parched desert, when the green grass and the rivers of life flow so closely beside you? Turn! Turn and live, for life and love awaits you if you but turn and see it. Open your eyes, my children, and see the green pastures. Taste the beautiful green grass and know that all you seek is available if you but turn and look.

Take what is offered. You need not tarry in the land of pain and suffering. Remember that the grass brings peace and contentment, but the desert brings pain and death. Pain of separation; and the death of or loss of your connection to God… loss of your connection to love. Be you at peace, O children; see your divinity shine forth. Do not let it wither and die, but allow it to shine forth and you will be the divine beings you are. Be not afraid of the meadow, for no harm will come to you there. Only love, peace, and contentment await you, Little Ones. No pain or anguish will befall you, for you are the Sons and Daughters of the Most High God, ever in the bosom of

---

[103]   To put off going or coming: to delay :to linger: to wait

his love, if you but choose to be. Remember your birthright and be who you are. For you are that most magnificent being, the Sons and Daughters of God.

Hold fast! Look up, and see the meadow; see the sweet grass and lush pastures that await you. Know that all your needs will be met and that all your true desires will be fulfilled. You can and will be supplied in the storehouse of God. There is no lack, for there is enough for all, O Sons of Men. Become your magnificent selves! Know your full power! Remember! Remember who you are!

Love and Light
The Brotherhood

23ᴿᴰ MARCH 2011

Arise, O Sons and Daughters of the Most High God. Arise and face the morn of a new and magnificent day. Know, indeed, that the Lord of Hosts is thy refuge and strength, and thy help in trouble. When pain and sorrow come nigh thee, know that all is well in the arms of God. For, indeed, there will always be health, strength, and refuge, in the knowledge of the love of God. Know this day that the Lord is God and continues to bring support to the Children of Men. Know, indeed, that all is well with thee and thine.

Know, Sweet One, we have seen thee and thy search to return to ways of old. Know ye not that a return to the past is impossible, for the past has been and gone, and the NOW is all that exists? Rest ye therefore in the knowledge of the NOW, for here sweet memories will be made. Look ye to the present and make new discoveries, but leave the past behind for so it needs to be abandoned like a tree that no longer bears fruit. Look instead to what IS, Sweet Child, and know that all will be made possible for thee. For the Son of Man and the Children of Men are one in spirit, and one in heart. Look ye on and see and know that all is as it should be, for this is the time of great change that is upon us.

This is a time of new beginnings that has dawned, and no more can we live in the land of things that were. We must move to the place of what IS. Let your heart sing and soar, for many are the new things that will come to pass, for a new day and dawn brings new things into being, and new levels of learning to be awakened and realized. For such is the nature of man, that things will forever change and grow in his experience. His task is to grow with them, or wither and die, as one left to perish by a well or stream of water that has dried up. Let the blessed of the Lord say, "Behold that which is new is now in my sight, and the old has been cast aside." For the new things must replace that which was. Know, Sweet One, we see and know your struggle, but know also that your heart is strong and the resolve is great to move to new paths and create new destinies. Let the beloved of the Lord God see and know that all is as it should be, and all will be well in the world. For the changes and upheaval mentioned has, indeed, come with much force and vengeance. But the love of God for mankind prevails, and will always be available to the Daughters and Sons of Zion. Arise, O Children, and see the new dawn which here awakens on the horizon. Arise and see that many will be the changes that will come upon the Earth, for the past is dead and gone, and cannot be re-lived. A new day is upon us, and will show man the way to a different future.

Know that the love and power of God will be seen in the hearts and actions of men, who in true brotherhood are beginning to see the connectivity between he and his brother, for what happens in Japan[104] happens to you. And what happens in Syria[105] or lands afar

---

[104] Japanese Earthquake and Tsunami which killed more than 15,000 people

[105] Syrian civil war

happen to you, for you are all Sons and Daughters of the family of God: linked by the bond of kinship, love, and grace, together forever. You are your brother's keeper and he is, indeed, your keeper. You cannot ignore his pain, his anguish, his suffering, or his joys, for you are a part of the same body. If one part be in pain, then the whole body is in pain and suffers for the loss of that part: For it weeps, indeed, and is in pain for the hurt that has come upon itself.

For even so must man come to know that he is one with himself, for he and all mankind are ONE... one in the same, of the same lineage and clan: Of the same Mother Father God. Never to be separated, but always linked by the bond of love; the love of God which can never be taken away or forgotten, for it is an integral part of the beingness of man that he is connected to something outside of himself, and is part of the whole known as God. All particles of an atom must return to its source, and even so must the Sons and Daughters of the Most High God return to their source, and find that which makes them whole: the unity and love of God for his children.

Know, Little One, that much is ahead for thee and thine, and as the seasons change, even so must the experiences that are brought forth. Know the pain and anguish will not come nigh thee with changes, yet will be the order of the day. Look to the west for much to happen that is unexpected. Look to see and learn new things and discoveries. Know that you cannot dwell in the shores of the past, but must live in the bliss of the now moment, with the new things which will here for thee. Put on the armor, brave Princess of Light, and go forward to meet the new challenges that will present themselves to thee, and know that all will be as they should… for such is the nature of the day and the new happenings that will be here for thee. Look to new ways of coping and new ways of being, for such are the changes that are needed, Sweet One. The time for change is upon you and, indeed, will bring you much growth as you move to higher levels of learning, so hold on tight, Little One, and grasp that which is placed before you, for many will be the opportunities for growth that will present themselves to you.

Behold, a new day and new dawn of love and happiness for mankind awaits on the horizon. Open your heart, O Sons and Daughters of mankind, and see all that will come to pass. Know that the days of anguish will be no more. Let your heart sing a new song for such is the day, and such is the moment for the Daughters and Sons of mankind. Awake! Arise and see what will be, children. Look up and see all that can be there for thee… for a new vibration awaits, and the new dawn beckons thee. Know that love must be the order of the day and must be rampant upon the Earth, for this is the time and this is the moment, Sweet Children. We hail thee and we see your heart, and we know your pain, but know there is no reason for living in pain. Joy is here, abundant joy and love, so reach out and grasp that joy, and know that all will be well, Little Ones.

Adieu

26TH MARCH 2011

Welcome, Sister Sweet. Indeed, the power and depth of love is a fascinating and wonderful thing indeed. We see, Sweet One, the nature and the power of love that has been evident upon the Earth for some time. Behold: I send my messenger to bring peace, love, and joy to the nations, even as this message is given; even so do we find that the love of God is not always evident to man.

Knowing all that has been foretold, we see that the nature of man does not always allow him to look and to see with eyes wide open. In truth, we see that the eyes are open, but there is no vision. Like a book without words or a story without an end, they are endless and without form. For the ignorance of man can cause him to forget all that he was and can be. For the blindness keeps him in the dark, far from the gaze of onlookers. He is lost and seemingly alone to those around him. Let not the eye deceive you, O Sons and Daughters of Mankind. Look and see that which is truly there to be seen. Look and see that all is indeed well, and is possible for thee. For surely, man must come to know that he is a treasured and precious relic of God... a wonderful and most precious heirloom of the Most

High God. How can man think that he is worthless in the eyes of God? Know you not that your value is without price? For you are the Children of God, chosen and guarded and held in the highest esteem. Look on and listen, O Children; look on and know that you are, indeed, the chosen ones of God, and can delight in the love and light of his love, if you but choose to do so. Look on and learn, and know that you are the jewel in the crown, and the laughter and light in the sunbeam.

Look on and know that you are the water in the tears. For you are the chosen of God, loved and cherished all the days of your life; for the days of change are upon us, and the laughter and tears of mankind must come to know that the love of God can carry you to new heights of awareness, and new ceilings of love. Open your eyes and know you are the beloved of God...the Sons and Daughters of the Most High God. Look on and know that you are the apple in the eyes of God. Travel on, O Children, travel in the light of the love of God, and see and know your value and your worth, for you are the ones who must be able to teach those around you the full lessons of life. Look on, O Children, and see and know that you are, indeed, the blessed of the Earth, the chosen of God. Let not fear encompass thee or danger come nigh thee, for the love of God can shield and protect thee, and will be your rescue in the time of storm. Let no one say that God is without love for mankind, or allows destruction to come upon his children, for these are but man-made occurrences, brought upon himself in some instances.

The God of love does not punish, but in a world of form, man manages to find his own punishment and to make his own destruction, and then name it as the wrath of God. There is no wrath of God, for God is a God of love. How can a father or mother truly hurt or bring pain and anguish on his most precious possession? For the nature of man is to seek and learn, and in so doing, he unleashes those things that can help him to grow, or cause him to perish. Look on and know that no destruction is wreaked upon mankind by God as punishment. For God is the God of love, and not the God of pain or punishment. Let your eyes and hearts be open, and see and know the true power of God is all about love.

GOD IS LOVE. GOD IS NOT PAIN or HATE, or FEAR or RETRIBUTION. God is LOVE… a love so profound that it burns to the very core and beingness of God. A love that causes him to suffer when a heart is broken, or pain is endured by his children. Look on and know, Sweet Children, that you are the heart of God, the very heart and soul in the bosom of God. If such a thing existed and could be touched by the hand, you would find it full of nothing but love. A love so strong it defies all-knowing and a love so fierce that it defies all understanding. For that love, which emanates[106] from God, is put there and has been there since the dawn of time… and will remain there until the end of time. A bond which cannot be broken exists, but the only thing that can separate man from the love of God is his own forgetfulness and his inability to remember who he is. Remember your identity and know your truth, O Sons and Daughters of the Most High God. Remember your birthright, and stand up proudly and claim that which was so freely given to you eons ago, and continues to be yours, free of charge. Do that which you were programmed to do, so many eons ago.

Remember your heritage and claim your rightful place as the heirs to that most precious and wonderful treasure, the dream of happiness and the dream of love. A dream that can be fully realized,

---

[106] Comes out from: come forth

if you will but remember who you are. Come forth, O Sons and Daughters, come forth from the caves of forgetfulness into the light of knowledge. Look up and see yourself as you truly are, magnificent in all your glory. Hail, O Sons and Daughters of mankind; hail, princes and princesses of peace. Know thyself!! Know thy truth, and become that which you already are. Live your destiny, and find that star for which you have searched for so many eons. Look up and remember your name, and see and know your magnificence, for you are the BELOVED OF GOD. YOU ARE THE BELOVED. YOU ARE LOVED OF GOD.YOU ARE BELOVED OF GOD.

Remember! Remember that all that you need has been provided, and there is no cost, no penalty, no great payment is being exacted. Just remember your name and you can walk in the light and the love of God, all the rest of your days upon the Earth, until you return to your true source and origin in the arms of God. For you are a part of God, made from God, endless and without flaw. You are spirit; you are not your body. You are not your flesh: you are SPIRIT made from SPIRIT, and must return to SPIRIT… for without this, you are nothing: You are without direction, lost in the storms of life. A life that is without course and of no direction, tossed upon a sea of storms, night and day without rest, until you lose hope and perish. Look up and remember your gifts. Remember your talents. Remember, you are gods made from God-source and precious in the eyes of God. Forget not your nature or your value. REMEMBER: you are given all that you need to survive. It is built into your very DNA; your very soul, your very beingness. You are magnificent, powerful, wonderful beings, the heirs to the kingdom… if you will but open your eyes and see.

Open your hearts and remember who you are. Let the things of the Earth fall away from you, for you are spirit; you are love, you are peace, you are joy. Look up and see yourself. Look in the mirror and gaze at the perfection that is you. Look in and see your soul, and know that you are love. Show that love! Become that love! Become your true selves, and shine like the stars that you are. Shine like diamonds in the night sky. Shine like the beaming, glistening stars you are in the universe of God's love.

Look up, O Children, remember, REMEMBER, and know your magnificence. Know your brilliance and live, live, live, live. Live and become that which you were meant to be.

For you are the BELOVED Sons and Daughters of God. Formed, loved, and nurtured in the womb of God. Remember who you are, for only so can you survive and achieve your destiny.

Adieu, Sweet One, we leave thee now.

May the Lord of Hosts continue to guide and keep thee. Peace, love, and light are yours.

Adieu

THE NATURE OF LOVE

For in truth, the love of God is that boundless gift, given to man since before the dawn of time. Given to him freely, so that he might be able to partake of the boundless gifts available at the table of God— if such we may describe it—For in truth, no table exists, but in metaphor, we say this to describe the great bounty of God, and then use this to describe it in terms man can comprehend.

Know, indeed, the love and acceptance that is available for man is boundless and is eternal in scope. No lamb is ever led to the slaughter, for all souls are precious. No child is ever lost, for everyone is so very precious in the eyes of God.

Regardless of the errors that man makes, know, indeed, that the forgiving arms of God knows no count, and keeps no record. For even as the loving parent forgives the child, even so does the Mother Father God forgive his children without punishment or penance. For this is the way of God. This is the way of love. This is the only way of God, and this is the only way of LOVE. For love is not love which challenges, punishes, or creates fear in the hearts of men.

Love is not love which ceases to be. For true love is everlasting, and continues throughout the ages, reaching across time and thoughts to bring man home to the Mother Father God. Know, Little Ones, that love is the redemption that the Sons and Daughters of mankind see throughout their lives here on Earth. (Love, the smallest of words, which yet has the power to subdue the mightiest of men and women upon the Earth.)

What, then, is this nature of love? What, then, is this thing called love that possesses such great power, and can bring the most haughty[107] to their knees? That is the question that needs to be asked and answered. What is it that causes people to leave all they possess and go in search of this most powerful of emotions? It is love. But what is the source and nature of love? Indeed, this question has baffled man for eons, for in truth; it is yet simple but is so very hard to define.

It is more than physical, yet is not all emotional. It is found not in the head but lives within the soul-essence of man. All men possess it, yet they search to find it. Why search and seek something that is already in existence within the heart of men? The answer, Dear Ones, is that the nature of man allows him to forget his connection with Source, and therein lays the problem. For the very way to remember, and to find that love which is already buried inside you, is to open to your deep and inner connection with Source. This act of connecting with Source opens the channels and allows those feelings, if such we might refer to them, to find release. For in truth, in truly loving another we begin to release some of that which lies buried inside of

---

[107]   Arrogant: Proud and disdainful: having a high opinion of one's self with some contempt for others

man: For those who have lost the connection to Source, have truly lost the key to the location of the love that lives within them.

When they can reconnect by remembering that they are more than the flesh and blood they see in the mirror, then the process of reconnection can begin.

Know when we say reconnection, we refer not to something that was ever not connected, but in truth, refer to the realization that something greater than self exists within the heart of man. This, then, is the beginning of the awakening of the lost. This, then, is the way back to the peace, love, and joy that is inherent in the spirit and heart of man.

Know that this love is that most coveted of all prizes: It is the joy, the love, and the happiness that all men seek. It is the connection with something on a deeper and more meaningful level, outside of the self. This, then, is the love all men seek. Men seek it, not knowing they have the power within them to give it life, to give it the prominence it needs in their lives.

O Children of Men, remember that God has given you all you will ever need to survive; all you will ever need in order to be at your happiest... yet in forgetfulness, we strive for something, searching for love. Why search? It is already in your heart, already in your soul, already in your hands. For it is that essence which makes you the wonderful beings you are. This is the essence of love, this is the core of love, this is who and what you are. Remember, it is so much more than what you know of the physical love expressed here on Earth. It is that most deep and abiding part of man that creates unselfishness, thoughtfulness, sacrifice, sharing, wisdom, patience, kindness, joy, peacefulness, willingness to sacrifice, and to do and become one with another without rhyme or reason.

The nature of love is that thing that has toppled kingdoms and caused man to give up all that he has acquired in his storehouses. It is that most powerful of emotions put into the heart of man by the Mother Father God. Know, indeed, it is that tiny seed that grows to be the mighty oak tree. It is seemingly so small at first, but the magnitude of its power is truly unknown to man. For if he were to know its true power, it would cause him much anguish. For it is yet so powerful, that it can cause man to fall into the deepest of despair or to climb the highest peaks of happiness. It takes man to the depths of despair or to the highest pinnacle of happiness. This, then, is the nature of love. This, then, is the nature of God. For God is love, God is happiness, God is peace. To know God is to know love, to know happiness, to know peace.

Not to know God is to know fear, loss, separation, pain, hurt, anguish, and despair. Why, then, do we forget that we possess this most wonderful of all emotions and have the ability to live such joy-filled, peaceful, and the happiest of existences, when in human form? The answer, Dear Ones, is the veil of consciousness which causes the forgetfulness. And it is this forgetfulness that leads to the severance and the disconnection from Source. In our reconnection with Source— we are never not connected; in reality, we just fail to recognize it— we find that the peace we seek is available. The love we want can come into our lives simply. This happens because we open ourselves up to that which we already have, and that which we already are, and allow our God-beingness to find itself again. This, then, is the reconnection, or the reawakening, that must happen in the hearts of men... so that he can find his way back to who he is, that most beloved of God. If he can find his way back, and remember that his true nature is one of love, he can become himself, and share the love within himself with all others. This, then, is the task of man. This, then, is the great journey of man to find what lives within himself... that love, unceasing and unending, that boundless love that can bring him peace and joy.

That love that man searches for in the outward trappings of the physical world; daily striving to amass all he can, only to discover that it is all of no value. For the only things that matters are those things he has for free: the love, peace, happiness, and joy of God that was already his for free. Open your heart, O Sons and Daughters of mankind, and see and know that your gifts are in your hearts, and in your pockets. Reach in and pull out what you are freely given and live. Live in happiness, peace, and contentment, for truly all you really need is love. For this allows you to open your eyes and your hearts, to see all the wonderful gifts around you, given to you by your Mother Father God. Know, Dear Ones, this is the nature of love. Know that you have it; know that you have searched for it, but cannot remember that you have the LOVE of God deep within you. Let it show, and share it and live. Live in peace, live in joy, live in hope, live in love, and be your most magnificent selves. Live in love, live in acceptance, live in joy, live in peace.

Adieu

7ᵀᴴ JUNE 2011

Arise, O Daughter of Zion, arise and face the morn, for lo, much is there to be added this day. Know, indeed, that the Sons and Daughters of Zion are like children playing in a field of wheat. Lo, they travel to and fro, and play, with much happiness, looking from east to west, and north to south, trying to find the great peace that dwells within their soul. For the travails of the day are not enough to keep them focused, so there is much laughter, and much playing; for this is the order of the day, doing much to cause amusement. Thus, Dear Ones, they spend their days in hapless toil[108] playing, for there is nothing else to do to keep themselves amused. Thus, even so are the Children of Men. They spend their days in total amusement, playing and running to and fro, looking for simple enjoyment and ways to keep themselves busy so that boredom does not ensue. So, therefore, are the Sons of Men as they daily spend the time looking for much to amuse... but put no real effort into the task of learning and living, for all is set and all is in readiness, simply to amuse the Sons of Men.

---

[108]   Unlucky/happy labor, that oppresses the body or mind

All is as it should be. All is in readiness to amuse the Sons and Daughters of humanity, for in truth, there is no great purpose in the lives of most of these souls. They toil not, neither do they spin, yet they are fed and clothed by their Father in heaven. Look on and know that the Sons of Men are never satisfied, and are never without pain. For much is the hurt, and anger, and anguish, which lives within their breasts.

All is bent on the amusement of man, and the simple joys of doing that which will give him relief. Relief, not happiness. For there is little known as happiness in the lives of men; for they spin or toil not, have no great purpose in life, and are not held to be responsible for any great truths. These, then, are the people of Earth who daily exist with the simplest of goals: to live and to breathe, but with no great purpose. For so the Sons of Men have no purpose, and so they cannot perform their functions with much ease, for all is set on pleasure. All is set on the immediate relief of the pain of separation... a relief of the pain of the loss of God in their lives. For as man searches for God and cannot find him, he concludes there is no God. How can God exist without living proof of his presence? For if God existed, why the pain? Why the horrors? Why the wars? If such pain exists, there can be no God... for if God were in existence, he would remove the pain, and cause all the wars to cease, and the hate and anger to go away.

Thus concludes man that there is no God, for he is lost to the Sons of Men. Lost and alone, they search and struggle in a Godless land: no hope in sight. No hope of rescue. No hope of changing any of the fear to hope and happiness. Thus, they say all is lost, let us continue to lose ourselves in this pain from which there is no rescue. And so they continue to live in a numb world without any hope of rescue;

for all is lost, all is hopeless, all is gone. All is without flavor, all is without hope. There is no hope. There is only desolation and pain, for there is no great reason for being. There is no noble cause and no noble meaning for life. The Children of Men are without hope. They are without life. They are lost to all that is round about them. They cannot find peace or solace anywhere; they can only find more pain.

Oh awake, ye Sons and Daughters of Man! Open your eyes and see the hope, the joy, the love that daily shows upon the Earth. Open your eyes and see and know that all is well, all is hope, all is love.

Love is available in boundless measure. Love is everywhere, if you can but recognize it. Love is daily showing among all men. Look on and know that love is in the hearts of men, and can be the great healer, the great equalizer, the great source of all things. It can heal where there was pain; can soothe where there are troubled hearts, and can heal all that is broken. Listen, O Sons and Daughters of Mankind! Listen and know that there is a cure for the pain in your heart. A cure for the anguish you feel; a cure for the love that you have forgotten: It is a cure for all that ails you. It is LOVE, that hapless joy which abounds in the Universe, that single thing which can release fears and bring things to a close. That single source which can heal all wounds and can mend the broken-hearted.

This, then, is available to all through the love of God. This great, selfless love which can give the peace that is sought by all; this great love which can heal all wounds, and give peace to those who travail daily, looking for the peace and solace of God. This is the gift that is available to all mankind. This is the path to peace that hides from man. This, then, is the way into a heaven on earth. This is the love of God.

Simple as a child, simple as a flower, complex as a puzzle, but yet magnificent in all its ways. This, then, is the great and wonderful love of God. This, then, is the peace that is available to all. This, then, is God. That great and most wonderful of all love. That great and most mighty of all things. This, then, is the source of all; the freeing of all from bondage. This, then, is the love of God, that most powerful of all tools. That simple, yet such succinct tool, that can do and be all things to all people: That simple thing that can be the comfort in a storm, the peace like a flowing river that calms after a storm. This, then, is the most special, wonderful, and magnificent love of God. This, then, is the way of God, the being of God, the nature of God. This, then, is the love of God: Complex in nature, as seen through the eyes of man, yet so simple in its nature. Simple, in its very beingness, beyond reason, beyond hope, beyond belief. Open your eyes and see, and taste the simple, yet oh so magnificent, love of God given to all, each and every day of your lives. Given freely without charge; given freely without thought of payment; given to one and all, that you might rejoice and live in peace and happiness upon the Earth.

This, then, is the nature and beingness of the true and magnificent love of God. This, then, is the peace of God, beyond the concept of man to understand (he thinks;) yet oh, so simple to see, know, and understand. This, then, is the nature and peace of God. This, then, is the road to happiness, peace, and joy. This is the way to find that eternal peace, sought for millennia by mankind. This, then, is the simplest truth of the nature and beingness of God. This, then, is the joy of God. The love of God, the peace of God, the heart of God. This, then, is the path to God.

There is one path only, and that is found through the link with the unconditional love of man for his brother and sister: the love for all mankind, the love for Sister Earth. This, then, is the road to change, to love, to happiness. This, then, is the way to LIVE. This, then, is the way to LOVE. This, then, is the peace and love of God. Open your eyes and hearts and see, taste, and experience the love of God, for even so, does mankind wander in the desert, looking for relief when he has it already.

This, then, is the banal existence of man: always in search of that most elusive of things to bring him peace. This, then, is that which has been sought for eons. This, then, is the peace and love of God, already buried in the hearts of men. This, then, is the way to happiness: The way to peace, the way to joy, the way to total peace. This, then, is the way to the eternal City of God. This is the door. This is the way; this is the way to find the peace and the love that has been sought for so long. This is it! This is the way to love, and happiness, and light, and love. This is it! Open the door! Open your heart. Open your lives, open your hearts. Let it in! NO! Let it out, for it is already within you, buried deep.

Open the door and release that which has been caged within you. Open your heart and let it out. Let it release itself to the four winds: To the morning rain, and to the sunshine after the rain. Release it to the orange sky and the magnificent mountains. Release it, and see all the beauty and magnificence that exists in your life.

Open the door and release the love that is imprisoned within you. Open the door and feel the sunshine and the peace of God. Open the door and see joy, love, and peace upon the Earth. Open the door and know perfect bliss. For this is the great gift that is locked within the hearts of men. This, then, is the power of the gift given to man by Mother Father God. Open your hearts and release it to the four winds. Release it to the sky. Release it and be filled with the eternal joy and peace of God. Release it and know true and eternal bliss here on Earth. Truly release it, and know heaven; for that is the true and most magnificent nature of the love that is buried deep within the hearts of men. Release it and know joy, peace, happiness, and the intensity of a love unimagined by man. Release it and know God. Release it and be joy; be peace, be happiness, be LOVE. Be the gods you are. Release it and know God: For this is the way to God, this is the path to God; this is the very nature of God. This is God.

Release it and be LOVE. Be peace, be joy. Release it and live! Release it and grow. Release it and excel! Release it and become the gods you are: chosen of God, loved of God, protected of God. Release it and be the Sons and Daughters of God. Release it and be the eternal Sons and Daughters you are. Release it and grow. Release it and become your true selves. Release it and be. Release it and live, love, and be. You are light, you are love, you are Angels on Earth. Become your destiny, your life, your hope, and your own joys. Release it and climb the highest mountains and be.

Release it and become your God-selves. Release it and be the shining stars you are.

Adieu

4TH JULY 2011

For lo, it is the need of the knowledge of the great and powerful love of God for mankind, that leads the thirsty soul to drink from the pools of life. Indeed, these pools are naught but the knowledge of God and his great love for mankind. Lo, it is clear, Dear Ones that the need is indeed great, for the soul of man is like a man in the desert, searching in vain for mankind: Searching for all that he knows is missing. He wanders east, and west, and north, and south, but in vain; for although he knows that there exists this great truth and knowledge which can free him from his torment, yet still, he is not able to be delivered, and to find the great peace which would give him rest.

Thus he wanders to and fro, and all to find that great truth, which would set him free from the torment and the pain of the great separation. For he knows that there is a great emptiness, but yet, he can find no relief. For the thoughts of the missing truths keeps him ever in search of God. For in truth, man searches for his great connection with the Divine, not knowing the key lies buried deep within himself. Open your heart, O Sons and Daughters of mankind! Open your hearts, and see the great truths that can set you free. Open your heart, and see and know that all you need is already available to you. Look into your soul and know that the God of love lives there buried, but yet available, to thee. Open your eyes, open your souls, and remember who you are: For you are the Sons and Daughters of the Most High God, who lovingly cares for his children. Lift up your hearts, O ye Children of Men, and see and know that God walks among you. Look into the mirror and see the face of God, for you, indeed, are the face of God. You, indeed, are the light of God. You, indeed, are the love of God. Open your eyes, and see your magnificence... and know that you have the love, the power, and the peace of God within you.

Open your heart, and see, and know once more the wonders of God. See and know once more the great joy and peace of God that lives within thee. Open your eyes, O Sons and Daughters of God, and see and remember your magnificence; for you are heirs to the throne of God, the children of the Most High God who dwell here upon the Earth. Lift the veil of forgetfulness, and see and know your true heritage: For you are the chosen of God, the beloved of God, the wonder of God.

Be your mortal selves, but yet show the veil that hides the spiritual magnificence that you are. For you are the love, the beauty, and the joy of God. Let your soul arise and walk into the light of God's love once more, O you most blessed of God. Let your souls arise and awaken to the very joy of God, for such is your heritage, such is your birthright, and such is your eternal joy.

Lift your hearts and let them soar with the wings of eagles, for the great treasure which you thought was lost has been revealed to you, Brothers and Sisters of Light. Lift your heart and know that the sojourn in the land of death has passed. The sojourn in the land of the living is upon you, for that which was lost is indeed found. That which was buried in the bowels of the Earth is now revealed and great is the jubilation. For the treasure has been restored and, indeed, it is found. It was not lost. Indeed, only the great memory was lost, for the great and magnificent treasure was in plain sight, throughout this time of pain and anguish.

Open your eyes, O Sons and Daughters, and see and know that your heart, your love, and your joys, are once more in view. Your soul can rejoice once more, for you are once more available. In the search to find that which you thought was lost, you find the key is in the palm of your hand. Open your hands, O Sons and Daughters, and see and remember your joys once more. Open your mind and see the great truth, the great light, and the wisdom of God that you already possess.

For you are magnificent beings, possessing the keys to the happiness you seek: the keys to the kingdom of God. Open your hearts and know that all is, indeed, well for thee. For the God of Hosts is your Mother Father God. You are the bringers of the divine spark upon the Earth. Know that you have the power to change all the pain that exists into joy, and to turn the night of weeping into a morning of song. Open your souls and see and know that the Mother Father God lives in you, and you are the power, the peace, and the love of God that you seek. You are the source of the peace, and the light, and the love upon the Earth. Unleash the power of love and see the full force, for only you can bring about this great change that you desire upon the Earth. You are the Sons and Daughters of God, the keepers of all of the great secrets. You are the wonder, the power, and the love of God. You are the Angels of God, the very messengers of peace.

Open your eyes and your hearts, and see and know the wisdom, the peace, and the love of God returned to you. (Yet not so, in truth, for it has been with you throughout the ages... but buried, and forgotten, in the channels of your mind.) Open your hearts and your minds, Dear Sisters and Brothers, and see and know that all is well with thee and the children of the Most High God... for you are the love, the beauty, and the joy of God. Open your eyes and your heart, and remember the peace, the love, and the joy of God once more. Be at peace, Dear Ones, and know that you are the beloved.

All the Children of Men, regardless of creed and color, race or religion, all are chosen of God: for all are the children of a loving God, ever caring for his sons and daughters.

You are the joy, the happiness, and the peace of God. Open your hands, and see the evidence of the love of God, which is etched[109] there, waiting to set you free. Open your minds, and see and feel the great peace descend upon you; for you are light, you are beauty, you are love. You are, indeed, the love of God, the grace, the power, and the wonder of God, walking upon the face of the Earth. Open your hearts, and see and remember who you are. Awaken from the dream of forgetfulness, and come once more into the beingness of God, and be at peace: for you are peace, you are light, you are wisdom, and you are LOVE. Let your light shine, and know that you are the children of God.

Adieu

---

[109] Cut marks with something sharp: to cut a design or mark into the surface of something

4ᵀᴴ DECEMBER 2011

Know, Dear Ones, that the love of God is like a man walking along the sand. For behold, he is barefooted, and he moves gently, with peace and enjoyment in the sand, feeling all of the delicate grains of sand between the toes. How magnificent is the feeling of total peace and happiness! For in this simple act, there is much love, and much grace. For in no way is he trying to do anything but to enjoy the simple act of feeling the sand between the toes, and to feel the water flowing upon his foot. He is living in the moment, with the complete simplicity of all that it encompasses. Know, Dear Ones, that of such is the love of God given to mankind. It is given in all its very simplistic nature to the Sons of Men. For in truth, it has no other purpose than to bring thee total peace, love, happiness, and joy.

There is no planning and no great analysis that is involved, yet in this simplest of all acts, is found some of the greatest moments of peace for the Children of Men. Know indeed, that no thought goes into the act, no judgment is involved; yet so much happiness can be elicited. Know, Dear Ones, that in this same way, is the love of God made available to the Sons of Men. For indeed, it is given in all its simplicity.

No judgment or cost is exacted, yet it can bring man the greatest of all peace. For behold, it allows mankind to feel and to know sweet peace, love, and joy beyond compare. For in so doing, man is able to come to the table of brotherhood, and know the true peace, love, and joy of Mother Father God. Know, Dear Ones, that the love of God can carry you in all its simplicity along the shores of life; for although the waves may lap around you, and break upon the shore; they are naught to concern thee, for you are walking steadily along the sand. No harm can come to thee, for the storms of life do not encroach upon thee there. For though the fury of the storms of life can toss thee to and fro upon the oceans of life, know that when you are safely upon the shore, your feet are planted in the sand and you have no more need to fear.

Know, Dear Ones, that the love of God will carry and support thee always, for even though your feet might sink into the sand, know that it poses no danger to thee, for there is no harm that can come to thee there. Know, Dear Ones, that the love of God is the safety of the beach; it is the peace and surrender of the beach: For you need not worry or fear what will become of thee, for you are safely held in the bosom of God's love. Know, Dear Ones, that there is no fear of life and limb, or want of anything, when you experience the walk upon the sand. For the only thoughts upon the soul is of the magnificence of the journey, and the feeling of love, peace, joy, and contentment that floods the body and the mind. Know, Dear Ones, that this same great peace is there made available each and every day to the Sons of Men, if and when you choose to take off your shoes... and allow the experience of the love of God to flow into your very beingness. For in allowing this to come into your beingness, you welcome O, so much, Dear Ones. Know that the love source which is Mother Father God, wants nothing more than for the Sons of Men to hold fast, and then be the gentle feet upon the beach; making the self-aware of the feel and touch of the sand. For in so doing, you commune with the very nature of God. Know, Dear Ones, that the love and peace of God is thine; made available with such ease, and free of cost.

Take the time, Dear Ones, to remove your shoes, and to walk upon the sands of your life. For therein, you will find your peace, joy, and contentment. For all your needs are met, and there is no thought of the pain and stress and worry of the earthly life. For the focus is placed solely on the peace, love, and joy that is possible. Know, Dear Ones, that the love of God will carry thee on always: For it brings the peace, love, joy, and contentment that is sought by the Sons of Men. Know, Dear Ones, you can find your peace when you rest in God. For in him, all things are found. Know that the love of God is the very rock on which your hope and your life is built, for in so doing, you let go of fear, doubt, and worry, and rest in the peace, love, and divine grace of God.

Know, Dear Ones, that the love of God which is available to thee each and every day, can allow thee to gain much insight into the true nature and peace of God. For all is made available to thee, and all is given in abundance; for there is no want and there is no pain. For, lo, the love of God is all that man needs to be happy upon the Earth. For it brings thee true peace, love, and joy without ceasing, and can help thee to be the shelter when the storms of life would lap around thee and try to bring fear and doubt into your heart. Know, Dear Ones, that the love of God is that great peace that will bring thee naught but joy, happiness, and contentment. For even as it is thine to attain without payment, but free of cost, even so is it there for all the Sons of Men equally.

No clan, race, or creed is not able to walk upon the shores of God's love and to feel the peace, love, and joy that is there made available. All are able to go to the place of peace and remain there if such is the desire. For the beach is open and available to all the Sons of Men, regardless of where they are upon the Earth. All are exposed to the same experience, and the same joy is there made available to all. Know, Dear Ones, that the love of God is the very thing that can heal the broken hearts of men; for in letting go, and noticing this most simple of all pleasures, and focusing on only this one act, mankind can find such peace and happiness beyond compare.

Know, Dear Ones, that the Mother Father God wants nothing more, than for the Sons of Men to know the depth of the love that is given abundantly to the Sons of Men each day. For it is a testament to the vastness of the love of God for mankind, that the oceans cover so much of the Earth. Remember, O Sons and Daughters of God, that you are the children of God, loved and protected each day, and given all that you need to survive if you would only take the time to walk upon the beach, and return once more to the shores of God's love: For therein, will you find your peace, happiness, love and joy. For with this walk, you come to remember and to know all the true joys of Mother Earth, given freely to the Sons of Men. Know, Dear Ones, that the Sons of Men can find true peace, love, and joy when you return to the love and peace of God.

Listen to the waves, for they lap only around your feet, and cannot harm thee. They break upon the shore but your peace remains, for you are on the shores of God's love, and you are cradled in the arms of God. Know that naught can harm thee there, for you are nestled in the bosom of God. Let not your heart be troubled, but look out at the great ocean; see its beauty, and feel its peace, and know that all will be well for thee. For you are a child of the Most High God, held and loved and protected by your Mother Father God. Be not afraid, but rest in the peace of God: For all is indeed well for thee.

Know, Dear Ones, that the bounty of God is available to thee each and every day, and you will be protected, and guided, and loved, all the days of your life, for you are a child of the Most High God; given all the keys to the vast storehouse of God. Know there is an endless supply of all that you will ever need, and know that you are denied nothing, for all that you desire is yours, Dear Ones.

Know indeed, that the love of God will be the very strength that you need, and the very foundation on which you stand. For it is your rock and it is your support; for with it, you have need of nothing else, for all your desires and needs are supplied. Open your hands and your hearts, O Sons and Daughters of the Most High God, and come once more to know your true worth upon the Earth. For you are the Sons and Daughters of God, loved and adored since the dawn of time. Loved and adored unceasingly, without thought of payment, for you are the children of God. Ever loved, ever protected, ever in the bosom of God. Remember your peace is available to you at all times. Walk with ease upon the shores of God's love, and feel the gentle breeze, and know that all is indeed well. For the storms of life cannot harm thee there, for you are gently loved, held, and protected always by Mother Father God. Be at peace, Dear Ones, and know that all will be well for thee, for this is the way of God, this is the peace of God that is thine always. Take off your shoes, and feel the blessings of God, and come to know true peace and happiness. For you are the peace of God, the love of God, and the joy of God upon the Earth.

Be at peace and know that all can indeed be well for thee, if such is your desire; for all that you need has been given to thee already. Walk upon the shores, and feel the gentle breezes. Look upon the horizon, and know that like the ocean, the love of God is endless, and is free for all to experience. Look into the sunrise or the sunset, and know the love, happiness, peace, and joy of God; for this is your heritage, this is your joy; this is your path to happiness upon the Earth. For you are the children of God, loved in all your ways, and ever supported and provided for by God. Be at peace, and know that all will be well for thee, when you open your heart to the love, peace, and joy of God. For your feet will always feel his presence, and your senses will know that you are ever in his presence. Let not the distractions take you away from the simple joy that is God. Know that they will bring you no lasting peace, for they are naught of substance, but are fleeting in their very nature. For they only last for a moment, but the love, peace, joy, and happiness of God is eternal.

Be at peace, Dear Ones, and know that you are the Sons and Daughters of Mother Father God, loved and cared for always. Be at peace, and know that all will be well for thee, when you walk upon the beach, which is the love of God. Be at peace, and know that all will indeed be well for thee; for to walk upon the shore is to walk with the love, peace, joy, and happiness of God ever in your heart. Be at peace, and know that all will be well indeed, for no harm can come to thee there, and no danger can befall thee: for you are the children of the Most High God. Be at peace and know that all is indeed well.

Adieu

WHO AM I AND WHY AM I HERE?

Arise, O Sons of Men, and know that the God of your being is ever present in the lives of men. Know, indeed, that the days of the children of the Most High God are limited upon the Earth, yet in truth, they are forever. For the soul of man is eternal, and while they are here upon the Earth, they will be in the physical, yet they are spiritual beings that are eternal. Know, Dear Ones, that the very nature of man is such that he is ever physical and in human form upon the Earth…but in truth, know that the nature of man is one of spirit. For, the Sons of Men are spirit first, and naught else, after this most basic of all facts.

Know, Dear Ones, that you forget your majesty and your splendor when in human form, and consider yourselves only to be that which is seen through a mirror. Know, Dear Ones that you are not your body, but O, so much more. Know indeed, Dear Ones, that your entire beingness is so vast that it cannot be fully contained in this your physical body, but must live also in parallel form outside the body when you are in the physical incarnation. Know, Dear Ones, your vastness is only equaled by your greatness, for such is your nature as spiritual beings. Know therefore, you are so much more than you can ever visualize or even conceptualize, for you are indeed the children of the Most High God: loved and adored in all your splendor by your Mother Father God. Know, Dear Ones, that the love of God is this most blessed of all gifts given to you by Mother Father God, since the dawn of time and made available to you always. For, you are the children who are loved and adored by God, because you are made from the very fabric of God. For even as God is spirit, even so is the very nature of man spirit. For, you are spiritual beings here on Earth, to learn the very lessons of life, which can only be learned here in this arena in the physical body.

Know, Dear Ones, your nature is such that it cannot be explained, for in truth, it defies explanation; for such is the vastness and the complexity of the nature of Spirit. But know, Dear Ones, that you are first and foremost, and yet always spiritual beings, having this glorious physical experience. Know, Dear Ones, that your body is simply the vehicle that allows the spirit to be here in the physical, and to experience the joys and pain of the mortal life.

Know, Dear Ones that you have always been, and will always be. For you are spirit, you are light, you are love. You are the very joy of God, the peace of God, the soul of God, for you are the children of God. Possessing all the attributes of God, you know not your magnificence when here upon the Earth. You struggle and toil, and feel you are forgotten of God, when in truth, you are ever in the forefront, ever in the mind of God— if such we can describe it— for indeed being spirit, God has no mind. Know, Dear Ones, you are the glory, the peace, and the very heart of God. For it is indeed your nature while here in the physical body, to be the very ones who think you are naught but the physical body you see reflected in a mirror. Know, Dear Ones that the love of God for you goes beyond that which is possible to imagine here, for indeed it cannot be easily explained; for there are no words to fully describe these things. Know indeed, that you are the very nature and love of God:

The beingness of man in the physical, is the essence of God's love shown upon the Earth. For though you are here in different shapes and colors, know indeed it is the very nature of your beingness, which is the essence of God. For you are spirit, you are joy, you are light, you are love. You are all that is right and good. You are the peace and love of God incarnate.

When in the physical, you forget your true nature, because the truth of your beingness and nature is shielded from you; for in truth, the physical body cannot accommodate all that is truly you and your magnificence. So in truth, when in the physical, you are out of your natural realm, and you are likened to a baby, for you know naught of who and what you are. Your only focus is to obtain the most basic of creature comforts, food and warmth, and to be nurtured. Know therefore, that those are the basic instincts of the Children of Men, when you are in the physical body. For thus you strive for happiness and contentment in this simple way, and in so doing you forget all else. For in truth, the desire of the spirit that is truly you, is lost and forgotten and thus comes the very struggles and hardships of men. For you forget that you are this most wonderful spiritual being and believe you are this limited being, without magnificence and wonder.

Know, Dear Ones, the being that is you may be limited in the physical, but the spirit that is you is eternal and is wonderfully and specially made. Know, Dear Ones that the love of God for the Sons of Men is therefore eternal, and nothing can ever separate the Sons of Men from the love of God. Know indeed, that the children of the Most High God are beloved and are ever in the grace of God. Even when, in physical form, you forget your origin and forget your greatness, and turn to the distractions of this physical world, and hurt your brethren; you come to know that the love of God is ever thine. For when the spirit leaves the physical body at the time of death, the spirit that is who and what you are, is in truth returned to the natural state, and you are once more re-acquainted with all that is truly who and what you are. Know, Dear Ones, that the love of God can carry you ever in the love, peace, and grace of the desired attributes, while here upon the Earth. For in your search while here in the physical body, you must forget your nature, and forget your greatness, and be humbled; for in so doing, you can come to experience all the varied and wonderful experiences that are available to you here upon the Earth.

Know, Dear Ones that you are the very nature of God, the very nature of love, and peace, and joy, and happiness, yet you forget these attributes and know not yourselves. You turn to the darkness, and you kill your brethren, for then you forget the light of love, and joy, and happiness that is you, and see only desires and unfulfilled dreams and aspirations. You kill your brethren in order to take that which is his, and you forget your very nature, which is love.

For those who get glimpses of this true nature as spiritual beings, they live in happiness, knowing the truth of their being, and being able to grasp that so much more exists than is visible with the human eye... or imaginable in the human experience. You relegate yourselves to only that which is seen in the mirror, and your total magnificence is forgotten. Arise, O Sons and Daughters, and know that the nature that is truly you is one of spirit, and that the Children of Men are sisters and brothers dressed in different garments, like the very flowers in the garden of God. For to see you and to behold you, is to see true love.

For when in the physical, you wander to and fro aimlessly, for you have no memory, and are lost, wandering like lost sheep with no direction, and no memory that you are the magnificent spiritual beings you are. For like the very children who are struck with an infirmity[110] which causes them to lose all memory of who or what they are, even so you are found here living in pain, and fear, and loss. Believing that you are what you see in the mirror, you live lives of separation, anxiety, and fear; for you know not your magnificence and your nature. Like one who has no memory, you strive to find your way, and thus is the pain of man experienced. For without your memory of your very beingness as spirit, you lose your memory of who and what you are, and you are thus feeling lost and alone... when in truth, you are never alone. Know, Dear Ones, thus are the struggles of man experienced, for you are limited in your thoughts and experiences, and you think and see only that which is seen in the mirror. Know, Dear Ones that the love of God is there for you always, and only your forgetfulness keeps you alienated. For, in truth, it is ever there, ever available to you. Reach out and grasp it, and know it is ever thine. Let your heart be at peace, and know that you are the Sons and Daughters of God; ever loved, ever cherished by God. Be not afraid to face the dawn, but know indeed that each day is a glorious dawn for thee, for you are the heirs to the very throne— if such we can describe it—of God. You are the love, the peace, and the joy of God, if only you could remember these truths. Open your hearts, and remember and know that you can be all that you desire, and you can be that which you aspire to be, for it is all within you, O Children.

---

[110]   Disease: sickness :unhealthy body

Let not your loss of memory cause you to think you are forgotten and are alone, for in truth, you are never alone but ever loved, guided, and protected, and cradled in the arms of God. Nothing that you can ever do can take away the love of God from you, Dear Ones, so know these truths and remember them daily; for in so doing, you can live that full and rich life that you desire. For when you know who you are, you can begin to enjoy all the fruits in the garden of God. All that exists is given to you to bring you happiness, and to remind you that you are loved. So be not afraid to step out into the light, and grasp all that is there presented to thee.

Be kind to those who forget their magnificence and see only lack and limitation. Help them when you can, for they are, in truth, your brethren, and you are indeed ONE. For you are brothers and sisters of the same parent, Mother Father God, so protect the weak, and help the ones who are in pain Take not from those who have so little, but instead give from your abundance, and remind them of the bounty of Mother Father God; for such is your charge, and such is your duty, to help those who sleep in forgetfulness and despair. For you must be their light in dark places, and help them to find their way back to the light and love which is Mother Father God. Be at peace, Dear Ones, and know that this is your charge. This is your journey and your very destination, to know the love, peace, and joy of God which you have always known, and will always know when you return to spirit.Be at peace, and know, Dear Ones, that you are the children of God, and are spirit. You are light you are love, first and foremost. You are love... first, last, and always

Adieu

30ᵀᴴ DECEMBER 2011

For indeed, the love of God for mankind is like the very flower that delights the sight and smell of man; for its intensity is such that it sheds the light of beauty into the lives of those who come upon it. Know, Dear Ones that the impact of the flower upon those who come under its spell is not to be ignored, for in truth, it allows the ones who come into its environment to see and to experience oh, so much more than they would normally be aware of. Know, Dear Ones, that the love of God for mankind, even so is likened to this very flower: For it allows all who come into view to see and to know the true worth and value of things outside their realm. Know, Dear Ones that the love of God can be that very thing which allows mankind to see and know the great possibilities of life. For in truth, it allows man to glimpse those very possibilities which would otherwise remain unknown in his realm.

Know, Dear Ones, that the love of God can and does allow mankind great glimpses of all that is possible in this earthly kingdom, for in truth, it shows the depth of love and devotion that the Mother Father God has, and will always make available, for the Sons of Men.

Know, Dear Ones, that all are called, and indeed all are chosen but yet, only some will remember their true heritage, and remember their truth and the calling of their being, and answer the call. Know indeed, Dear Ones that the great and most magnificent love of God, so wonderfully given to the Sons of Men, allow them to taste all the truths and to know the blessings of the kingdom.

For when man can see and understand how much he is loved, even so is he able to see and know that he is the very child of God, and the chosen of God. For indeed, all the Sons of Men are given this wonderfully precious gift, and yet only some ever get to remember that they are indeed the chosen of God, for they spend their days feeling unworthy and desperate. They forget their heritage, and know not who they are, for they are lost and feel alone and cut off, from the love that is indeed their lifeline. For all the Sons of Men are able to activate this gift, and to come to know and remember all the truths that are theirs. Know, Dear Ones, that the love and blessings of the Father given to mankind, knows no bounds. They are indeed boundless, and are always available to the Children of Men.

Know, Dear Ones, that this is likened to the very parable of Jesus, who taught of the 'Sower of Seeds.'[111] For even though he sowed the seeds, as a farmer does evenly upon the land, the seeds fell in different places, and each, dependent upon its environment, flourished or died. Likewise, O Sons and Daughters of Mankind, the love of God is given and spread out equally to all the Sons of Men, yet only some will remember and know that they are the recipients of this great treasure.

---

[111]   Matthew 13:1-23

For without the recognition of what has been given, the gift goes unappreciated, and is indeed lost to those who have it. For even as one holds a precious gem before it has been cut, and knows not its true value, and conceives of it simply as a rock, even so is the value of the love of God not seen by the Sons of Men. Know, Dear Ones, that the great and wonderful love of God, which has been made available to all, even so remains unclaimed and unrecognized by the Sons of Men. For in truth, they see and know it not.

Know, Dear Ones, that the love of God allows all (everyone) equal access to all that is available in the kingdom. Yet, with clouded eyes, the Sons of Men know not the value of what they have been given, and would cast it aside like a worthless rock. Know, Dear Ones, that the precious gift is thine to be held and adored like the flower, for it will indeed bring you great beauty and happiness. Know, Dear Ones that this is the most precious of all gifts, and yet you see it not: For like one who is colorblind, you see not all the delicate shades and hues, and notice not the intensity of the very thing that is in front of thee.

Know, indeed, that the love of God supplies all these needs. It brings you to the shores of God's love, and allows you to see and taste the blessings of all that is there, made available to thee. Know, Dear Ones that the love of God is the single most blessed gift given to the Sons of Men, for with it all other gifts are able to truly come into view. Know, Dear Ones, that the love of God for mankind is the guiding light in dark places, and the beacon on the hill. It is the wonderful blessings, and the most wonderful of all things available to man. Know, Dear Ones, that without this gift, your eyes and your senses are indeed dimmed, and you see not all the great beauty that lives around you: For you are not able to see, and taste, and appreciate, the blessings heaped upon you by Mother Father God.

Know, Dear Ones, that the love of God is all that is needed in the lives of men, for it opens the door to all the possibilities, and allows mankind to see and taste the very wonderful bounty of God…and to see and know all that is available to the Sons of Men. Know, Dear Ones, it is the eyesight to those who are blinded, and cannot see or imagine the beauty that surrounds them.

Knowing not what they have available, they trample upon it, and it falls away unappreciated and not recognized. Even so, Dear Ones, is the love of God lost to the Sons of Men who know it not, even though it is there, made available to them every day. Know, Dear Ones, that the love of God for mankind is such that these gifts, and all that is given to him, goes unrecognized and is tossed aside and left for waste; for without the recognition of the true worth of all that is available, the gift is lost to all.

Let not your hearts be troubled, Dear Ones, but know, indeed, that you have the treasures you daily seek, already made available to each of you; for only your blindness keeps you separated and lost. Only your failure to recognize your true bounty keeps you separated from the love of God; for you are given the keys to the kingdom. You are given all that you need to be happy, and yet you know it not, for your eyes are dimmed and your senses see it not. Know indeed, Dear Ones, that the love of God for mankind is that awe-inspiring and most wonderful of all gifts given to man. It is the very blessings and the love of God which is your lifeline.

Open your eyes, O Sons and Daughters of man, and see and know the wonders all around you, for herein lies your power, your love, and your glory. Herein lies your power, and the love and the wisdom you seek. For in truth, it has been and will always be thine. Let not fear, and doubt, or worry come upon thee, and cause thee to be blinded. But instead, open your eyes and see and know that all is indeed made available to thee; for you are the children of God: loved, adored, and given all that you will ever need to be happy, and to know true bliss while here upon the Earth.

You are indeed the blessed of God, the Sons and Daughters of mankind, always invited to dine at the table of love; for it is your heritage, your right, your gift, given to you by your Mother Father God.

Let not your heart be troubled, but know, indeed, that you are the heirs to the throne. You have the gifts. You can see and taste the true bounty of God, and are able to feed as you need it.

The love of God is the very food you need, for with it all needs are met, and all wants are supplied. Let not fear and forgetfulness tell thee that you have been forgotten of God, and are lost and alone. For this is not so; for indeed, you have the gifts already, but fail to see and taste all that is there, made available to you.

Look on and know that the beauty of God is thine. The love, the peace, and the joy of God are all thine, given to you since the dawn of time; yours to take and to appreciate as you desire. Let not your faith be lost. Let not your hope fail to see that you are loved, treasured, and adored; for such is the bounty of God. You have all you will ever need and you will ever be provided for by your Mother Father God.

Open your hearts, and wipe away the fog and the shadows from your eyes, and see and know all your true blessings that await you; for indeed, they are already all around you. Open your arms and receive your bounty, for you are the heirs given all since the dawn of time. See the beauty, the love, the joy, the peace that is around you, and know that all will, indeed, always be well for thee.

May the peace and love of God continue to flow into your beingness always.

Adieu

23RD FEBRUARY 2012

Good morrow Dear One. Know indeed we are much happy to be here with thee and to answer your call. We are much happy indeed for great is the excitement with the beginning of this phase of our adventure. Know indeed that the love and the courage you show is indeed great, and happy are we to be able to join with thee once more to share the text.

Know, indeed, that the great and awe-inspiring love of God for mankind shows itself in the lives of mankind in a myriad of ways each and every day; for in truth, it is the very essence of life for mankind. For indeed without the love of God, mankind would be like a fledgling, wandering lost and alone in the wilderness. With the love of God, we see and know that man comes into his own, and is able to truly function and become that which he truly is. Know indeed, Dear Ones, that the love of God is that great and wonderful thing that allows man to come into his own beingness, and to truly develop and become that very spark of God which he is. For man, without the love of God, without the light and strength of God within him, would be naught: For indeed, the love of God is the essence of who and what has created man and put him upon the Earth.

Know therefore, Dear Ones that the love of God is at the core of the beingness of man; becoming, therefore, the essence of the life of man. Thus, Dear Ones, you come to know the power and the magnitude of this gift. For since it is the essence of the beingness of man which brought him into being; when man forgets his connection with God, when in human form upon the Earth, he is truly lost... for he has no purpose and thus can come the demise, and destruction of the Sons of Men. Know, Dear Ones, that the search to return to Mother Father God, and to find that which is missing or lost in the identity of man, is therefore at the core of his being. Thus like a magnet, searching for the opposite with which to be drawn, he wanders the Earth looking for his true self, and is desperate to find that connection that will make him whole and bring him life. For indeed we might say, that the love of God is like the very blood coursing through the veins of man. The shell or body is there but without the life's blood, there is no life and the body dies.

Know indeed, thus is the reason for the feelings of great emptiness and desolation, when man, in his search, realizes that something in his life is missing, and he would, in desperation, search to the very ends of the Earth to redeem that which he thinks has been lost. Know, Dear Ones, that the blood which is likened to the life source or the love of God can propel man to the very highest of highs, or the lowest depths of despair, when the meaning has been lost in his life. For indeed, the great and most powerful love of God for mankind, has and will ever cause him to search the very ends of the Earth in an effort to find this great and wonderful treasure. Know indeed, Dear Ones, that the love of God is life for the Children of Men, and so when man feels it is lost, he is likened to one in desperate need of oxygen: For he is panicked and is struggling to take in the life-giving air which will help him to live.

Know indeed, Dear Ones, that such is the nature and importance of the love of God in the life of mankind. Know, Dear Ones, that without the love and the beingness which is man's connection to, and with the divine, he is like a fish out of water that flaps and flips, and will eventually die. For, he cannot, in essence, survive without the life-giving source, which is the water. Thus, even as the water is the life-giving source for the fish, even so is the love of God the very oxygen, which when breathed into the lungs of man, will cause him to live. For the love of God is all that man needs to give him life. With the love of God, he has the strength and the resilience to find that which he truly needs, to make his life upon the Earth into a meaningful and love-filled experience. He can come to know that all his needs will be met, and all desires come to fruition; for his Mother Father God has provided all that is needed for him.

Thus, Dear Ones, you come to know, that without the life-giving source, which is the love of God, man dies. For he has nothing with which to be sustained, and he would wander the Earth lost and without hope, desperately searching for that which will make him whole. Know, Dear Ones that the love of God is thus truly all that man needs to know that he has; for with this knowledge, all things are possible. With the knowledge of the love of God as his true source, all of man's needs and desires are met. Without this knowledge he remains lost, in desolation, searching forever for that thing which will give him purpose, hope, and life. He thinks he has naught, and he lies down and dies; for he knows not that the gift that he has searched for has always been within him. It has always been a part of the very fabric and core of his beingness, but yet his forgetfulness would lead him to believe that he has no air, no life, no love, and so he dies.

Know, Dear Ones, that the hopelessness which is seen in the eyes of the Children of Men, when they search in desperation for Mother Father God, is the deepest pain, if such we can describe it, for Mother Father God. For indeed, we see and know that like a parent watching helplessly while their children destroy themselves, even so is the pain that is felt when the Sons of Men forget their connection, and the love that is their birthright, and wander upon the Earth, searching for that which is already thine.

Open your hearts, O Children of Men! And remember your true nature and your origin as children of the Mother Father God. Put on your remembrance, and come once more into that which you truly are... for you are so much more than you can ever imagine! You are so much more than you will ever know when in human form. For you are the very light and love of God! You have the life-source of God coursing through your veins, so live, Dear Ones! Breathe! Breathe in the love and light of God, and come into your true beingness for you are the children of God, the love of God, the light of God! Live out that true and most blessed of all creeds, and come to know that the life and the oxygen you strive to find is already coursing through you. For it has been yours since the dawn of time, when you were conceived in the mind of your Mother Father God. Know indeed,

Dear Ones, that such is the great and most wonderful love of God for mankind, that you are the favored of God! You have the life and love of God within you, so you can live, if such is your desire!

Remove the veil of forgetfulness and come out into the light, and feel once more the warmth and tenderness which is the love of God, given to you to give you life! Know, Dear Ones, that you are the beloved of God and that you are mighty beings. Throw off the cloak of helplessness and live!

Throw off the hunger and desolation of abandonment, and come once more into your true beingness, for you are always cradled in the arms and the bosom of God. For that is your true peace, Dear Ones; for like a shepherd, you are held and protected by God lest any harm will come to you. Know indeed, Dear Ones, that you are shielded, guided, loved, and protected at all times, by the loving power of Mother Father God. Thus you have no need to fear or worry, "What will I do, or who will take care of me?" Know, indeed, that you are in the arms of God always, and you need not fear, for you are eternally loved by your loving Mother Father God. Be at peace, Dear Ones, and know that you are indeed blessed! You are cherished, you are loved, and guided, if you will but turn your attention to the very things of God, and turn away from those distractions which are not of God— for therein will come your destruction. For without the memory and knowledge of this great love, you wander headlong into destruction and death: For your light is dimmed, and you do not the things of God, and you have no love for your brethren. You live in a world of hate, envy, greed, and pain and you forget your nature, which is one of love, happiness, peace, and joy.

Know, Dear Ones that the road of life can separate, and you are at the fork in the road. Choose therefore which way you will go, for one path leads to despair and desolation, with continued separation from Mother Father God, while the other path leads to the love, light, and the peace and joy of God.

Choose therefore this day, Dear Ones, and remember your purpose upon the Earth, which is love! Return to your very nature, and see and know the true joy, love, peace, and abundance of Mother Father God, for it will invigorate[112] thee and bring thee life. It will breathe new life into thee, and you will be filled with the love, peace, joy, and happiness, which is Mother Father God. Turn indeed, Dear Ones, and come to know the true blessing that is you!

Adieu, Dear Ones, we leave thee ever enveloped in the loving arms of God.

Adieu

---

[112]   To cause to feel fresh and vigorous: to give life and energy to

18ᵀᴴ MARCH 2012

Know indeed, Dear Ones, that the power and the love of God for mankind is indeed a blessing: For indeed, unlike those things that blossom and bear fruit in the mid-day sun, but then disappear at the close of the day; know indeed, Dear Ones, that the love of God for mankind is indeed endless, for it never wavers and is always to be seen and felt with the same intensity throughout all the ages. Know indeed, Dear Ones, that this love is of the most intense duration, and will never ebb[113]; for it is eternal in its intensity and its depth, for it never fades, never lessens, and never leaves thee: For indeed, it is always the same today, tomorrow, and always. It is never different. It is always constant, knowing no fluctuations. Know indeed, Dear Ones, such is the love of God for mankind; that it is given and remains with man until the end of time. There is no time or season when the love of God is not available. There is no power on Earth, or in the Heavens, that can cause the love of God to waver: for indeed it is unwavering, and unending, and so magnificent in its intensity

---

[113]   To flow backward or away: to return like the water of the tide toward the ocean

that there is nothing with which it can be compared, either upon the Earth or in the Heavens.

Thus is the love of God given to the Sons of Men, and lives within the soul of man, whether he is in spirit or incarnated upon the Earth. Know indeed, Dear Ones, there is nothing that you can do which can remove the love of God from the Children of Men. For even in your darkest hour, when you slaughter your brethren, and kill or maim, know indeed that your Mother Father God cannot and will not desert thee. For you are the Sons and Daughters of the Mother Father God, therefore you are known forever and loved forever by your parent, which is Mother Father God. Know indeed, Dear Ones that the love of God is thine forever, just as the trees are upon the Earth and the seas rush to shore. Know even so with the swelling and quelling of the tides, even so is the love of God for man consistent and never failing: For you are the beloved of God, and naught that you may do, can cause you to lose the love or favor of your Mother Father God.

Know indeed, Dear Ones, that you are not children of a lesser or unknown god. You are children of the only God; loved and protected beyond the limits of time —for indeed, in spirit it exists not—Know therefore that naught that men can do can ever take away the love of God from the Sons of Men. Know indeed, Dear Ones that the heavens would cry out on the day when this would transpire, for indeed it would be a day of days. Know, Dear Ones, you are loved and cherished by your parent, Mother Father God, and given the keys to the kingdom: So use this key to open the door. Know indeed, Dear Ones, this is not the key to an external door, but the very key to the heart and soul of man. For indeed, you have the key given to thee which will open the doors to your happiness, if you would but use the key to open the door to all that is good and worthy.

Know indeed, Dear Ones, that the love of God is that rarest of gifts given to all the children; yet given so long ago that you have forgotten that you possess this most wonderful of all gifts. Use it, Dear Ones, we say to unlock the golden gate to your soul, for you keep it locked away so none can find it… and now you have forgotten where you have placed the key. Know indeed, Dear Ones, that the key will fit the lock, if you will but remember where you have hidden it.

Know, indeed, it is the key to a great and glorious treasure given to you by Mother Father God. Search therefore no longer, Dear Ones, for you carry this key in plain sight. Look in the mirror, Dear Ones, and know that what you see is the face of God staring back at thee; for you are God upon the Earth walking as a man. You are emanations[114] of the Most High God, daily walking upon the Earth in search of the golden key. Know, Dear Ones, you search in vain for that which you think is lost. Know, Dear Ones, it is not lost to thee, and there is nothing you can do, however cruel you might be to your brethren that will remove the love of God from thee.

Know indeed, Dear Ones that you are the guardians of the Earth; the protectors of this wonderful and glorious garden given to you by Mother Father God to be your home. Know, indeed, you cannot ever leave this wonderful place, for this is your home. So we say live happy upon this place, and look into the mirror and once more come to know yourself, for this is your heritage, Dear Ones. This is your

---

[114]   Coming out from a source: coming from

peace, your happiness, and your joy. Be you always on point, and know that you are a beloved child of Mother Father God, loved since the dawn of time. You are ever loved, ever guided. Be you happy to know that your place at the table is guaranteed, even though others would have you believe that all are not welcome, and all would not have a place to sit and to dine in peace, love, and harmony. Know indeed, Dear Ones, that there is always room for all the Sons of Men; for this is the great and glorious promise of your parent, Mother Father God. Know indeed, Dear Ones, that you are loved and adored, and are always welcomed at this table which is covered with the bounty of God.

Know indeed, Dear Ones, you are the joy of God, the happiness, the peace, the love, and the hope of God. Go therefore into the world, Dear Ones, and proclaim the news of the great goodness of God and his bounty and benevolence: for such is your hope, such is your life, and such is your bounty. Know indeed, Dear Ones, that you are eternally blessed and ever held in the arms of God. Be you happy to know that the love of God will never leave thee, but will be with thee always, for this is your joy, your peace, and your blessings, Dear Ones.

Let none lead thee astray, and say you are forgotten of God, for this is foolish talk. Let none say you are not chosen of God, for they speak with idle lips! Know indeed, Dear Ones, that deep within your soul, you know the truth of your being and the depths of your relationship with Mother Father God. For even so are you always in the arms and the hands of God. Be of good courage, Dear Ones, and know that all will indeed be well for thee, for you are the beloved of God. Listen not to those who speak with false claims and false tales, that the love of God is not given to one such as thee, for even so is it given to the lowliest of all the Children of Men in equal portions. For there is no rank and authority in the eyes of God, for indeed all the children are seen in the exact same way. There is no differentiation for race, color, creed, religion, or any other devices or descriptions of man that would serve to separate the Sons of Men. Know indeed, Dear Ones, all the children are held in the same high esteem. All are held. All are valued beyond measure.

Hold up your heads, O Sons and Daughters of the Most High God! Remember your name, and know once more who you are, for you are the beloved children of the God of your being; loved since the dawn of time and throughout the ages. Be strong, Dear Ones, and know that you are made from God.

Know once more the words of our Dear Brother, Jesus, who said … "These things that I do and even more …..will you accomplish…. Dear Ones."[115] Know you are mighty beings! So cower[116] no more in the corner, but stand up in the light and claim once more your inheritance, for you are the heirs to the throne: The love of God's heart, and the very ones who can and must bring peace, hope, and joy, to this planet which is your home. Know indeed, Dear Ones, it is the great call to rise up and see and know, that great are the things which will happen to thee.

But you are the leaders, so take charge, Dear Ones, and know

---

[115]   John 14:12

[116]   To shrink away or crouch especially for shelter from something that menaces, domineers, or dismays

once more the joy, and peace, and love of God; for herein lies your strength, your peace, your joy, and your hope. Let all who would doubt these words and say that the Sons of Men are not chosen of God, be silent. For in that time, great would be the pain felt in the heart of God. Know indeed, Dear Ones, that all is indeed right with the world, and the Lord of Love and Light: For even so shall it be.

Arise! Greet the dawn of this new day, and know that a mighty change is come upon the Sons of Men; for indeed their memory fails them not, and their hearts are full of the love, peace, and joy of God. This is their truth. This is their hope. This is their fulfillment. For God is in his heaven, and all is right with the world! Be at peace and know that all is well!

Adieu

17ᵀᴴ JUNE 2012

Know, indeed, that the love of God for mankind is of the purest kind, and yet even gentlest kind, for it encompasses all the blessings in the known Universe. Know, Dear Ones that it is at the core of all that is known and yet even that which is unknown in the world, for it is the great passion of God to give to his children all that they need in order to survive upon the Earth. Know, Dear Ones that this love has been and will ever remain a part of the basic building block of the soul of man. Indeed, it might be well to describe it as part of the very DNA[117] of the soul of man. Know indeed, Dear Ones, we say that this love encompasses[118] all things, for indeed it is the thing on which the tenets[119]of the soul of man

---

[117] Substance carrying organism's genetic information: a nucleic acid molecule in the form of a twisted double strand double helix that is the major component of chromosomes and carries genetic information: Makeup of something: the combination of features that make something what it is.

[118] To include a wide or comprehensive range: to surround:

[119] Principle, belief, or doctrine generally held to be true; *especially* : one held in common by members of an organization, movement, or profession

is scaffolded[120]. Know indeed, Dear Ones, we say that it is likened to the foundation of the first of all the particles of the atom that is found in the construction of the soul.

Thus, Dear Ones, you come to know how we say that it is at the essence of the building block of the soul of man. Thus we say that it is at the core of the soul of man, and is therefore the core of who and what you are. For indeed, how can anything in creation that comes from a building block of pure love, not be love? Know indeed, Dear Ones, we say that this is why man is ever searching for God when in physical form upon the Earth. For, indeed, he is searching for that which allows him to feel the very essence of his parentage. Know indeed, Little One, this concept is indeed difficult to put into human terms, that might be easily understood... but yet, we say we will. Know indeed, Dear Ones that the search for God by mankind is a search that has been programmed into the very beingness of man; for indeed, man is ever looking for the way back to God. The love within him indeed is buried, but there are moments in the lives of all the Sons of Men when this great love is seen evidenced in the actions of man upon the Earth. For indeed, at the core of each, lives that which is ever trying to express itself as love.

That man when in human form, is clouded by the fog of forgetfulness is known, but yet even so, there still exists within him that spark of love which demands expression. Indeed, we say, that even in those who are bereft of any memory of Mother Father God when in the physical, even though they are so far away from all that would be considered as expressing evidence of God, will show moments

---

[120]   Supporting framework on which something is erected or constructed /built

of clarity— if such we may describe it— when indeed they will demonstrate acts of love to their brethren. Know indeed, Dear Ones, that even in ancient times when mankind was at its most barbaric, acts of love and kindness could be seen by the very conquerors who massacred their brethren.

Know, indeed, we say that the love of God was evidenced even so in them, who in their total forgetfulness, committed great acts of cruelty. Know indeed, that the love of God was theirs, and even though the fog of forgetfulness caused them to know not God, they indeed retained those elements of God within them: For indeed, it is ever present. Even though man may not, of self, know of its existence, know indeed that it is ever there, and will be shown in some form.

Thus, we say, that there has always been evidence of the love that is within the DNA of the soul, shown in evidence in the actions of men, even in the darkest of times. For indeed, Dear Ones, man cannot go anywhere where God is not and his actions, however cruel and unjust to his fellow man, can never cause him to lose the love of God: for once given, it is thine always. Once the soul is formed, the essence, at the core of its construction, cannot be removed, for the soul of man and the soul or essence of God is pure love. Thus, we say, that man in the physical form is only accessing a small portion of the soul, of who and what he is. Only a small essence of the entire soul is seen in evidence upon the Earth, and thus, this small essence— evidenced in isolation— cannot be fully understood by man. For it is at the core of the soul, but may not be seen in evidence upon the Earth. Know that the veil of forgetfulness robs the human of the memory of God in the conscious; but yet in his subconscious, there ever remains that knowledge of the true nature and beingness of man. Thus, Dear Ones, we say is the reason for the constant search of those upon the Earth, to find that elusive piece of himself which is God-love, in order to find peace.

Know indeed, Dear One, we say that the love which is God, is ever a part of thee and it is this which calls man ever to seek for that which he knows not. Thus, Dear Ones, we say that the love of God is thine always, and can never be taken away. For, indeed, it is in the construction of the very essence of the soul of man, and therefore cannot be removed. Even though the veil of forgetfulness would stifle it, and cause it to be hidden and forgotten, yet still it remains, for it cannot be removed. Know indeed, Dear Ones, we say that the love of God for thee is therefore eternal, and everlasting, so there is naught that man can do which will cause him to lose the love of God, for this is totally impossible to do: For it would be akin to removing the molecules from within the very construction of man. Know indeed, Dear One, we say that the great love of God for mankind is ever thine, for it is at the core of you, Dear Ones, and you are thus children of God. For you cannot go anywhere where God is not, and you can never remove this gift that is embedded into your own beingness. Be you ever in the knowledge that this love is freely given to you by Mother Father God, and thus is thine always.

Know that you are at the beingness of God, and thus you can go nowhere, where God is not. That you forget that you are part of God is part of the nature of man when in physical form... but know indeed, that a part of God is indeed who and what you are. Know indeed, that this great love will cause thee to know all that exists within the kingdom of God, which is likened to your heart; for it is ever within thee. It lives and breathes within thee, Dear Ones, and cannot be removed from thee.

When the incarnation[121] ends, at the time of death, and the soul leaves the physical body and returns once more to the arms of God, know indeed, Dear Ones, that the returning soul once more returns to its true nature, and is LOVE once more in its entirety and totality. Know, Dear Ones that is why each soul would then choose to return to Earth through the great desire to serve his fellow man upon the Earth. Thus, he returns to be of service to his brethren, and to enter the classroom of the physical existence, and to experience all the joys of the physical life upon the Earth. Know indeed, Dear Ones, we say that the love of God is like a great classroom that one enters in each incarnation, and works diligently to learn all that is presented: For indeed, he is the one who determines much of what will be experienced in each incarnation upon the Earth.

Be not afraid, Dear One, but know indeed that you are God expressing upon the Earth when you walk in human form. Thus, we say, awaken and shine your light of love on all those who are around you, and thus help them to awaken to the truth of their beingness. For that is the main reason for the sojourn here upon the Earth, Dear Ones. It is to find the love that is you, and to express it in all its many forms to those around you. For in so doing, you express God upon the Earth. Know, that you are the children of God, because you are all constructed— the soul— from the essence of God, and thus, we say, is why you are the expression of love, joy, and peace upon the Earth: For you are possessors of particles of God when in

---

[121]   The act of assuming flesh or taking on a human body

human form. When in spirit, Dear Ones, know that this is all of who and what you are, but the experience of becoming human, and the forgetfulness which is part of the human experience, leaves the Children of Men in a state of forgetfulness, searching for that which will allow him to be whole once more, and to know the totality of love which is at his core.

Know, Dear Ones, you are never separated from God, even though you forget who you are, and your very nature. This piece of love that resides in the soul is yet strong enough, to cause you to search for who and what you truly are. Even when all else is erased from you, this lives on, and controls your very growth and development when incarnated upon the Earth. Be not afraid, Dear Ones, but know that you return to God always when not in the physical, and thus are once more able to experience the totality of who and what you are. Be at peace, Dear Ones, and know that you are always loved by God and you are always LOVE, for it is who and what you are.

Adieu, in the love and peace of Mother Father God.

Adieu

Know indeed, Dear One, we say that the love of God is like an ever-spinning wheel, or indeed a circle, for in truth it has no beginning and no end, and is thus eternal. For so the love of God for mankind is seen by Mother Father God, for indeed, all that is needed by the Sons of Men are made available; that in truth, the many varied needs of the children may be met. Know indeed, Dear One that we say that this love which has no beginning and no end is ever available to the Sons of Men, for in truth, it allows him to move freely within the realm of man. For, indeed, since man is a child of the Most High God, he has the innate ability to move upon the Earth at will… and indeed if the mind takes him, to move into the cosmos at will: For such is the power of the Sons of Men that they have this ability, even though in truth, most know it not. For indeed, those who are aware of the gifts and the bounty of God know that all their needs will be supplied forever by their loving parent, Mother Father God. Know indeed, Dear One, that this love which asks for naught in return is that most selfless of all devotion, for indeed it asks for nothing except to be in service to Mother Father God, to rest always in the bosom of Mother Father God.

Know indeed, Dear One, that the love of God for humanity comes free as has been detailed, and no price is exacted. All that is needed, for it to be received, is for the Sons of Men to open his arms and receive it in love and humility, for this indeed is the way of God. Know indeed, Dear One, we say that the Children of Men are lost without the love of God and know not what to do, for all that they are is wrapped in the essence and beingness of God.

Know indeed, Dear One, that the love of God is never hidden under a bushel or hidden in a great cave, but is evident for all the Sons and Daughters of humanity to see and know of the vastness of the love of God for humanity. For indeed, we say that the love of God is that great shelter in the storm, and the bright light which leads those who are lost on stormy seas to find their way back to the safe shelter of home. Know indeed, Dear One, that the love of God enfolds thee and protects thee, and allows you to be that which you truly are: the Sons and Daughters of humanity. Know indeed, Dear Ones, that the love permeates all aspects of the life of man and is there made available to the Sons of Men whenever they would need to call upon the name and nature of God. For indeed, the Sons of Men need only to call upon the name of God to see and feel the great peace of God descend upon them. Know indeed, Dear Ones, that the love of God, like the great wheel, rolls ever onwards and is found wherever man is. For it is forever at the beckoning of the Sons of Men, ever available; and since there is no place, where God is not, know indeed that the love of God is everywhere found upon the Earth. For as God is everywhere, even so is the great and powerful love of God to be found in all the corners of the Earth.

For in truth, they must always have access to the loving power and nature of God. Even so are all the parts of God made available to the Sons of Men at all times and in all places upon the Earth. For if there were any corners where God was not, how could he support his children in their darkest hour of need? Know indeed, Dear Ones that this love is contingent upon nothing except the gentle and loving nature of man. For indeed, that man is able to contain the love of God is indeed evidence that deep within the heart and soul of man exists a place wherein the love of God can find a home and indeed flourish. Know, Dear Ones that the love of God finds a cherished home within the heart and soul of man, for this indeed is the home of the love of God.

For in as much as a glove is made to fit the dimensions of the hand, even so is the love of God the perfect fit for the heart and soul of man. Know indeed, Dear Ones, that the heart and soul of man, thirsts for the love of God and thus we see the reason why the soul of man will wander upon the Earth day and night for that which he knows not: For indeed, he knows it not by name, but only by nature, and the realization that this wonderful gift will give relief and peace to those who wait: For indeed, the wait is for the long expected prize which will bring peace to the weary soul, and joy and thanksgiving to all who are in attendance. For so powerful is this mighty force that man need not be the direct recipient to get the many blessings of God; for simply in being there, the effects of the power and peace of the love of God is felt by all.

For in truth, a great peace descends on all who are round about, and thus the children are all fed, even though they may have no awareness of all that has transpired. Know indeed, Dear One that the love of God, like the ever spinning wheel, continues to roll and as it does, it pulls the Children of Men into its path and all are blessed. Know, Dear One that the love, which is God, is endless in totality and in form; for by nature it cannot be weighed and no formal value can be placed upon it, for the true value rests only with the ones receiving the gifts. For without the value of the gift, the children cannot determine or sense that the miracle has truly happened and now all are blessed. Know indeed, Dear One, we say be you ever resting in the loving arms of God, in the safety and comfort of his breast, for thus will be your relief and your joy. For the pain of the great separation will be no more, and you will find yourself wrapped in the gentle arms of love.

Be never afraid, Dear One, to step out into the path of the wheel for with this decision will come your hope, your peace, and your joy. For the essence of the wheel will carry you along as though on the wings of eagles, that you might once more come to remember the loving and peaceful presence which is the love of God. Know indeed, Dear One that this love will ne'er leave thee, for it is ever thine. It will ne'er desert thee and surely will never cause thee pain, for it is the perpetual love of God that you cling to when you cling to the wheel which is the love of God. For in truth, your arms no longer are weary, and your legs wouldn't faint and collapse beneath you from tiredness and fatigue; for indeed, you grow not faint or weary for you are being cradled and caressed in the gentle, loving arms of God.

Know, Dear Ones, we say be ever alert and remember the mission of your life, for it is to one day return to the source and to know that you have discovered the greatest of all prizes possible upon the Earth. For with it come love, peace, joy, and contentment. With it comes the thoughts only of the love and light of God, for you are being reborn anew when you grasp this great wheel of life… for all that you desire is thine and all the very blessings you crave are thine.

Know indeed, Dear Ones that the love, which is God, was given to thee at the dawn of time and remains with thee always, even to the very end of time. For you are eternal beings, and thus the love of God is eternally thine; for being made of God, you are the perfect creations of Mother Father God, ever whole, ever perfect, ever loved of God. For this is your heritage, Dear Ones, so grasp this wonderful gift and be comforted to know that you will forever be blessed.

Know always that the light and love which is Mother Father God is given to thee in full measure, that you may never know want, or lack; yours that you may only know the love, peace, and blessings given to you— indeed, bestowed upon thee— since the dawn of time.

Know not fear, Dear One, but remember who you are. Remember your nature and your name, and come into the peace that is the love of God; for you are a beloved child of the Most High God and everything within the kingdom is at your disposal. Forget thoughts of lack or insufficiency, for there are no places in God's love where these things are measured or counted. All is given to thee in heaped portions, running over so that you might never know lack, Dear One. Throw away and forget the old ways with thoughts of inadequate portions, for the love of God is limitless and without end. It is thine now and forever, so claim your portion and enter into the gates of love and wonderment. For oh, how you are loved and adored, Dear One! Oh, how you are cherished by your loving, doting parent who has provided all that you will ever need for you upon the Earth!

Be not downcast and say that there is adequate for all except me, for I am bereft of love and unable to be loved. For indeed, every child of God has the love of God buried in his very DNA. He can be nowhere where God is not, and all his needs are met, if such is his desire. Look not to the four winds and search for your rescue, for indeed your rescue comes only from God. Know, indeed, that all your wants and needs are met in God, for this is the joy of your Mother Father God, to give you the keys to the kingdom.

Be not afraid to accept the key and speak of your unworthiness or your sinful ways; for behold, your Mother Father God sees and knows that you are his child and thus, like a loving parent, he can deny thee naught… especially his love, and protection, and guidance. Be you ever in the loving bosom and guidance of God and rest your weary head there, for therein will you find your solace and comfort, Dear One. For you are the beloved of God, and thus the ever-protected and loved recipient of all the blessings of God. Be never afraid, Dear One, but walk calmly into the light of God's love and know you are precious and wonderfully made, for this is your birthright and your gift from your loving Mother Father God. Be you always resting in the peace and abundance which is Mother Father God, and know that all is well. For you are the beloved of God: The chosen of God, and the favored of God. All the Children of Men are special and are held in the highest regard, for you are the joy, the peace, and the heart of God. Be at peace, Dear One, and know that the great wheel which is the love of God will cause you to know only the joy, peace, and love of God. Be you never afraid to come longingly into the arms of God, for you have been awaited and now it is time to join the feast.

For the table is indeed prepared, and the guest of honor is awaited. That is you, Dear One; be not shy, but step up and greet your beloved parent, for even so should it be. Know that all is in readiness, and all will be thine, if such is your choice. Open your eyes and see the love of God being given to you. Reach out and grasp it with both hands: for this is your destiny; this is your heritage. Look not around about thee expecting to see the guest, but know that all is indeed in readiness for you, Dear Ones, the Sons and Daughters of humanity, in unison.

Step into the light of God's love, and follow the ever-spinning wheel into the heart and soul of God, for this is indeed your peace, your home, and your rescue. Be never afraid, but know all is thine, if you should decide to accept it lovingly. Be always at peace, Dear One, and know how much you are loved, and once more return to the peace, joy, and love at the heart of God. Let the blessed of the Lord say Amen. And so it is!

Adieu, Dear Ones! For, you are loved beyond measure, if you would but remember this truth.

Adieu

Know indeed, Dear Ones, that the magnificent and most Holy of Holies is the love of God, which is here shared with the Sons of Men. For in truth, it is all things to all men upon the Earth, even though in reality, man may not be made completely aware of all the needs of the Sons of Men. For in truth, the Sons of Men know less of the truth of the beingness of the Sons of Men than they do of a myriad of other activities. Know, indeed, that the children began allowing others to become familiar with that which is a part of God, that is indeed buried deep within the soul of man. For in truth, man is able to see and know of many things but is not always able to see and know of all the blessings that are laid at the feet of the Sons of Men. For indeed, Dear Ones, the Children of Men all too quickly will forget all that is there made available to them daily through the love and benevolence of the love of God for man. For indeed the children will, indeed, take it upon themselves to become all that they should and could be. For therein lies your rescue, Dear Ones, so take the opportunity to plan for a quick review of all that is good and blessed upon the Earth. Know indeed, Dear Ones, that the Sons of Men will indeed take all the treasures and, in abject fear and worry, forget to give all the things that are required to God, who in his benevolence, has there poured all upon the people of the planet… for since, Dear Ones, there is very little that can be done, even so will mankind never waiver in his proclaimed love of thee.

Know indeed, Dear Ones, that the love of God for man is indeed a new understanding which thus allows all the Sons of Men to come into view, so that others might see the great works of God, and so come to know also his own entire and most bountiful group of friends, for indeed, they come bearing the most precious gifts—for indeed, listening to the Sons of Men is the main and most special of gifts given to God—but in vain, he has sought to find that most precious and darling of all blessings. For indeed it is time, Dear Ones, to see and know the truth and come into an awareness of the beingness of the love of God for mankind.

Know indeed, Dear Ones, that the very joy of God is that mankind would take it upon itself to do that which will bring it naught but peace and blessings, but in truth we say that the nature of man and the gift of free will prevents this from happening; for lo, there are those who would ever choose the path outside of the one that would call for peace and love. Know indeed, Dear Ones that the very blessings given to the Sons of Men are indeed given that all will know peace, if such is the desire. However, we see that the nature of man, when in the physical, leaves him bereft of the will or desire for a peaceful existence. Know indeed, Dear Ones that the love, which is Mother Father God in all its wisdom, still will not condemn the Sons of Men but will see this as simply another choice on the path of free will.

Know indeed, Dear Ones that the very nature of man continues to evolve, for since from ancient times when his innate needs and desires were barbaric in nature, mankind has truly progressed to that place where now he can look outside himself, and know that there are others who can and must be considered. So, in essence, the welfare of his brethren has come to the fore and he now moves away from the path of destruction to a place of contemplation, peace, and joy.

That love now flows throughout his beingness, is an echo to the new and wonderful truth of the nature of man. Thus, 'the great shift' is a shift, in essence, in the consciousness of man as well; for it allows him to see and know of others outside himself. For in truth, he sees and knows he is not all that exists in the world, and to be prosperous and happy, there is a great need to do for others, not just for self. Be you made aware, Dear Ones, that the changes coming into being in the hearts of men happen at the correct time so that man can, indeed, benefit from so much more in the kingdom of God. For in truth, when living in ignorance, fear, and anxiety, man indeed knows not of all his many blessings from his Mother Father God. Know indeed, Dear Ones, that the love, which is God, would see mankind live a joyful and peace-filled existence instead of living as he lives at this time upon the Earth. Know indeed, Dear Ones, that the love, which is Mother Father God, suffers much when his children are in pain and anguish... for it is difficult to sit and be silent while those you love are filled with naught but pain. Be you aware, Dear Ones that only the love, peace, and blessings of God can take man to that place of love, peace, and joy, and give him all that is required to be free and happy upon the Earth.

For indeed, the thoughts and actions of God, are those actions that would be expected by any loving parent. Be not dismayed and say, "But why should man be loved with such intensity?" For indeed, Dear Ones, we know that the love, which is God, is there in the Universe so that man might learn how to be the love, peace, and joy that lives within him; or how to be that joyous and peace-filled creature, that will be there for the brethren —he knows not when the times of fear and anguish will, indeed, come to an end—Be you happy to know, Dear Ones, that the love, which is Mother Father God, is ever present in the hearts and minds of men... but the veil of forgetfulness would cause him to forget all else and be the very cause of intense pain and suffering to all his brothers and sisters. Know indeed, Dear Ones, the vast and uncompromising love of God for man, yet allows mankind to do that which it desires but yet, still hold and know the vastness which is the love of God and the power and presence which is the love of God. For in so doing, mankind would be able to once more commune with his brethren and thus make a way for all upon the land. Be you in prayer, Dear Ones, and truly ask what you desire from your Father, for indeed, this would allow the Sons of Men to truly come into his own and come to know the love, peace, and joy which is God. Know indeed, Dear Ones, that the love of God is ever active, ever present in the lives of men, even though men may not yet come to realize all these very facets of God-beingness which they see daily expressed in the hearts and souls of mankind.

Know indeed, Dear Ones, that the love, which is God, is ever there, ever willing, and ever present in the lives of men; but the blindness to the truth of the beingness of God would lure the Sons of Men to the anxiety which is the reality of man. Know always we say, Dear Ones, that there will be other great opportunities for man to express his divinity always upon the Earth. For in looking all around himself, he can come to know that he is truly not all that exists in the world. For indeed, man, of self, contains the seed of God but in most instances knows not these truths. We say, indeed, that the time of the great awakening or 'the shift'[122] is upon you, Dear Ones, so that you may awaken to the truth of your magnificence as Beings of Light, and let go of the notion that the physical body is who and what you truly are

Be you ever content to know, Dear Ones that you are iridescent[123] beings of light, at your core as spiritual beings, for that is your true and most glorious nature. That here and now in the physical body you know not your true selves is part of the pain of God. For you are lost to the truth of your magnificence and know not yourself. Be you ever alert and know that you are the joy of God, the peace, the love, and the very heart of God, so become this in expression daily when you walk upon the road of life. Know in your heart that you are the beloved of God and that your Mother Father God calls thee daily to turn to love, peace, and joy, as your way of being in the world. Let go of the distractions and return once more to that which is the truth of your being, and become your true, magnificent self.

Let none say of thee that your light shines not brightly enough, but know, indeed, that your light radiates with the intensity of thousands of light emanations, so that your magnificence would be blinding to

---

[122] Shift in the consciousness of man

[123] Having rainbow colors: having rainbow colors that appear to move and change as the angle at which they are seen changes

the eyes of those who would look upon thee. Be you at peace, Dear Ones, and know that God is in his heaven, and all is right with the world. And so it is! Amen and Amen!

May the peace, love, and blessing which is Mother Father God, shine always within you, so that you feel its glow and radiate its truth in your daily life. Adieu, Dear Ones, in the name of Mother Father God and the Divine assembly of those who are here to assist thee in growth and love!

Amen & Amen

The Brotherhood

27TH JUNE 2012

Know indeed, Dear Ones that the wonder, which is the love of God, has served the hearts and minds of men for thousands of years. For indeed, from ancient times, man has always looked to the stars to find that entity that was responsible for putting in place the very foundations of the world. That, indeed, man was able, even with the limited knowledge of science and mathematics and of course, the physics, to come to conclusions about any naturally occurring events was not left to chance, Dear Ones; but know, indeed, that even in those times the inspiration to become so much more was given by Mother Father God to the Sons of Men. Know indeed, Dear Ones that those Ancients were very bereft of the knowledge of man today, yet in their ignorance they paid homage to the God of creation, and looked to the deity for all things. Thus, Dear Ones, we see and know that the love of God was recognized by the Sons of Men as being a major part of the relationship with man. That man has taken it upon self to pay no reverence[124] to the Mother Father God, in this great

---

[124] Feeling of deep respect and esteem mingled with affection: awe combined with respect

age when the science exists to confirm that all things are put in place by 'Intelligent Design'[125] is indeed a comment on the Sons of Men and the very thoughts of his heart, which say that man is supreme in the Universe and that the way of God is naught but idle fancy.

Know indeed, Dear Ones that the love of God for humanity, which is daily shown in the lives of men, now comes into view so that all can see and know the true and most powerful truths in the known Universe. That man now considers himself as being alone in the Universe shows a lack of realization of the vastness of the throne of God. For mankind is yet so very young in its development but would consider they are all that exists with intelligence is beyond the laws of logic to understand. For, indeed, the notion that God would create only one world and populate it with humans only, does not bear thinking. For indeed, there are millions of planets in the vastness of space, and the glorious place called Earth is but one of many places where life exists and can be considered advanced.

Know indeed, Dear Ones, that the light, which is the love of God, extends beyond the farthest reaches of space and beyond, for indeed it is endless in scope and nature, and all this was put in place by the mind of God. That God was so careful in planning the heritage of man and in populating the Earth shows to the very fullest extent the nature of the love of God for man. Know indeed, Dear Ones that this love which is given to mankind is of the most special and reverent kind, for in all things it was given freely along with all the other basic tenets of life that man would need for his survival upon the land.

---

[125] The theory that matter, the various forms of life, and the world were created by an "intelligent designer"

Know indeed, Dear Ones, that the love is indeed of the most intense and wonderful kind, so that it shows the full extent of the value of mankind in the heart and soul of God. For, indeed, it is known that man, and the Earth— as a garden—is but one of many places where the children of God are found. Know indeed, Dear Ones, that the love of God, which seeded this place, not only provides the place to live forever but also loves and supports his children daily in all things, so that he might know of the extent of the love of God for him, and come into his own beingness in the true nature of love and peace which are at the core of God-beingness.

Know indeed, Dear Ones that the love of God is given in abundance to the Sons of Men but as with all children, they forget their origin and take for granted all that has been given to them, so that now there are no words to describe the place of love for the Children of Men. Know indeed, Dear Ones, that the love and wonder, which is Mother Father God, is evident always in the lives of men... even though mankind may not look to see all the beauty and wonder which is God. Know, Dear Ones, that the love, which is God, is there made manifest in the lives of men, and the very Angels are put in place to support man when he falls and encourage him as he doubts his own divinity. Know indeed, Dear Ones, that the love, which is God, is ever present in the heart and soul of man; for indeed, it is the very love of God expressed upon the Earth. Know indeed, Dear Ones, that the soul which is God is ever in readiness to love, support, and protect his beloved children. For indeed, all is put in place to support the Children of Men, lest they should know pain and suffering. For indeed, this is the measure of the magnitude of the love of God for man.

Know indeed, Dear Ones, that the Sons of Men see not the wonder which is God, and know not the many blessings which are daily heaped upon them. For in truth, they consider it not and would instead believe that all is as it should be in the Universe, for man is the center of all things and reigns alone, supreme in the creation of God. That such thoughts exist are too humorous to discuss... but know indeed, Dear Ones, that you are indeed not the only planet that supports life, and indeed you are one of numerous places that mankind will come to know of in time. For indeed, being a warring clan, the great need to discover and to claim things for self will come into place and bring him naught but pain. Know indeed that the time will come, Dear Ones, when you will know of many things not known in this time, which demonstrate the magnitude of the love of God for mankind.

Know indeed, Dear Ones, that God in his magnificence is the great teacher and healer of mankind: For indeed, the supports that are available to the Sons of Men to guarantee success, love, and happiness are many. That man knows not of many things that are given to him for free, is also evident in his development; for in looking to the stars, man sees only the needs of men as conqueror. For God's love is there to support, cradle, and surround thee; to be the very foundation on which the very DNA of man was built. Know indeed, Dear Ones, that the love and wonder, which is God, is ever in the heart and soul of man... even though he would deny its very existence, and consider himself to be supreme ruler of all things. Know indeed, Dear Ones, that the love of God, given to man, is there for thee always, and is made available that man would come to know his importance in the heart of God.

Know indeed that the love, which is God, is ever present and is guarded and protected, that man can develop at his own pace and come to know the true and most blessed name and nature of God.

That man knows not of his place in the mind of God is the result of the distractions upon the Earth, and the vast expanse of knowledge of God which was invented by the mind of man, to explain the name and nature of God. For indeed, man is the child of God, loved and guided since the dawn of time, so that he might come to know his own divinity, and blossom as a child of God that he is. Know indeed that the nature of man causes much consternation in the mind of God, for indeed there is much doubt and fear of all the things that are unknown about the nature of God. Know, Dear Ones, that the love of God would ever be there to take man higher and to give him all that is there made available for him upon the Earth.

Be you ever humbled, Dear Children, and come to know that the true nature of God and the nature of men come from the same source: For ye are made from the same essence as the Father, creator of all things. Be you comforted to know that the love of God is given to thee freely, and will be thine forever; for this is the energy and love of God given to thee, Dear Ones. Know always of your true magnificence and learn the truth of your heritage and the very nature of God. For there are many truths still to be made known to thee, now that your hearts and minds are opening to the love, beauty, peace, and joy, which are at the core of the beingness of mankind since the dawn of time… but has been hidden from view by the failure of men to see and know all that has been given to the Sons of Men, that they might live abundantly in peace, love, joy, and happiness upon the Earth as children of the Most High God. Know indeed, Dear Ones, that you are loved beyond measure, and will come to know the true peace, love, and blessings which are thine, through the love and benevolence of Mother Father God, every day of your lives.

Be not afraid to say, "I am a child of God," for you are, indeed, children of a loving God. All the Sons of Men are indeed children of God, and are loved eternally. Know always, Dear Ones, that you are held and cradled in the arms of God: for this is the delight and wonder of God. Rest always in this peace and love, Dear Ones, and know how you are loved.

May God's grace and love continue to reign[126] upon thee, Dear Ones, as you come into your true beingness and realize your divinity as children of God.

Adieu & Amen

And so it is!

---

[126] Control or influence: the fact of being the dominant or controlling power or factor in something.

CHAPTER 4

THE SHADOW OF FEAR THAT HAUNTS MAN

...you are the creators of the illusion that says, "I am forgotten of God, and am alone in this desolate place." Know, Dear Ones, that the desolation and loneliness are felt only by the human mind, for the spirit within you indeed knows that you are given all that you need; and that indeed, you have all the keys to the kingdom within your grasp. Yet, you forget this and wander aimlessly looking for a way into the abundance of God.

For man must measure the length and breadth of his true knowledge in order to be able to measure his true worth. This is how the Children of Men assume their worth is measured, but it is clear that this is not the way of God, for in his wisdom; man does not need to measure anything that he does in order to know his true worth. The worthiness of man to enter into the kingdom of God is not dependent on anything that he can measure, since the value and worth of man is beyond any measurement that man can foster[127] or put into place. Man's knowledge and judgment is blurred and often not objective, so his worth as a yardstick is questionable.

To fully measure the worth and value of man, we must look inside his heart. For what lies there is the true and incorruptible measure of man. Our soul worth as Children of Men is beyond measure or compare; for each one of the Children of Men is of immeasurable worth in the eyes of God. (Eyes, we say; yes, for in essence, we mean the thought, or vision, or pleasure of God.) No man can comprehend

---

[127] To promote the growth or development of: to further: to encourage

the value or vision of what is being discussed here, in its entirety, without full knowledge of the redemptive power and source of God's love for man: For he is the way in which man sees and knows how truly he is loved by God. For man of himself is, of course, powerless to see and know anything of the full love and grace of God.

The Angels who live in the realm of man, and serve God's purpose here below, fully know how much value is placed on the souls of each and every mortal by the Eternal Spirit of the Most High God. Every soul is precious in the sight of God, and is of so much worth that a price cannot be exacted[128] to demonstrate its equivalent in the finest gold or precious metals known by man. For it is clear that God's love for each soul is so strong that in his wisdom, there is nothing that he would not do to protect each and every one from pain and suffering. Yet, for man, it seems that he will know pain and suffering for his life on Earth, or he does not feel that he can become worthy of God's grace and love. Man cannot see the truly redemptive nature of the love of God, which is able to move mountains, which display like peaks in the heart of man, and prevent his advancement into the grace of God, by causing him to think that the journey and the price of the ticket is much too much for him to afford. (All the time, of course, we find that the cost is free.) There is no charge. For the answer and the irony is that the love of God is available to all, simply through the acceptance of unconditional love for all. All you need is the love that is already rooted in the soul of man, in order to find the source of God, right here on Earth. Man doesn't need to pay any great price. Simply looking within himself will provide the answer to

---

128   Unable to set a price: unable to demand or require authoritatively: force or compel to be yielded

the question that has plagued him since the dawn of time: "How to enter into God's grace?" The path is easy and the road is simply laid out, for if man knows that love is the source of all redemption, then he can take advantage of this knowledge and utilize it to advance. "All you need is love." How simple is this concept? Yet, for man, this simplicity is, of itself, the most complex thing of all.

How can something so simple exact such pain and misery for the Children of Men? Simply by his innate nature, man is prone to the dangers of looking for the complex to find the answers to the mysteries of all creation.

By his nature, it is difficult to comprehend and/or accept that the answer he seeks can be so easily found and is so readily available to all, in this practice of loving.

Loving, of itself, is such a selfless act, for it sets as its goal the appreciation and recognition of someone outside of man himself. Man must be selfless to truly love. To love unconditionally, and to know and commune with the souls of others, he must go outside of himself and link with the souls of others. To love selflessly is to know God; to love is to become a part of God... to know the nature and being of God. The nature of humans, however, is and has been one of selfishness, for he has known with ease that the love of one person for another is not easy to attain, since we seek to love the outer trappings of what we see— and believe— is the true nature of man.

To demonstrate true love, however, is to love the soul and to connect with the soul of another being. When this is accomplished, we can truly say that we have loved. Only then, can we truly know how much man can know of another being. Only then can man see outside himself and his true nature, and move into the realm of God's grace.

To love is to know acceptance. To love is to know peace. To love is to know joy. To love is to know faith. To love is to know God; for in his mercy, all of these riches are tied to the glory and majesty of his kingdom. To attain the kingdom, man must know that he, of himself, is nothing, but God is all there is, and that through love, he can begin to savor the true magic when he discovers that love is all there is.

Adieu

To progress and to proceed in the knowledge and love of God is part of the sole purpose of man. His very being is created and his knowledge is perfected and increased, so that he can become a true disciple of God. His source and power come from the knowing of God, and his essence is to return to the love of God, and to the safety of his power and might. Man, of himself, is naught… but with the source of God's love pounding in his vein, he is able to do, be, and become all things. He is not able to become more than God, for this is not possible, but he is able to see and know all things that pertain to man on the face of the Earth. The trouble and strife that follows man and causes him to become less than his most powerful self and beingness is all part of the nature of man, which is constantly at odds with himself and his very nature.

The nature of man is to be that which God has charged him to be, but yet he finds he can wander aimlessly without any remorse or true knowledge of why he can lose himself, and forget all that is an innate part of his beingness. Man is a complex being but is yet simple in his very nature, for he constantly battles with himself and battles against himself, without any knowledge of why he is in this state of constant pain and turmoil. All man needs to do is to return to his true source, which is the love of God, in order for him to be able to make sense of his world, and become that true soul that nature intended. He cannot do this without fear, however; for he has learned that his nature is to go constantly against God. This, of course, causes him much strife, for deep in the innermost recesses of his soul is buried the memory of his true "raison d'etre," or the true reason for being: His connectedness with the love source, which is there to help him find the source of that which would bring him peace.

Man must learn to search deep within himself to find this source, which becomes buried each and every day as he moves about the Earth, and becomes more and more enchanted and enthralled by the wonders within the realm of man. The more he is charmed by the simple pleasures, the further away he drifts from his true source and the memory of his true course on Earth. The seekers on the road are those who have learned that there is more to life than is visible in the "natural eye" of man, and instead, seek to find and to return to the source while still in mortal form.

These beings find buried within themselves that spark of light, which causes the memory to stir and begins to open the door of consciousness to man. It is all predicated[129] on the fact that man must not be able to remember his true might while in human form, for fear that he will abuse his power and use it for ill.[130] Man is much like a child in his infancy, who must be protected from elements around himself, which would cause him to harm himself, if left unchecked. Vices[131] which plague man, such as lust for power, fame, and fortune,

---

[129]   Something that is affirmed or denied about something else

[130]   Opposite of good: wicked: wrong

[131]   Fault or defect: moral failing: form of wickedness or depravity

can help to propel him from the simplest of beings into the most complicated and fearful of all beings. This fear is what is, then, at the heart of his failure to find himself on the road, and to return to the path of love for which he is destined to return.

He lives his life in a selfish and mono-centered[132] existence, in which only he and his needs are the focus of his life. It is this that has caused all of the pain and the misery upon the Earth.

For it is when man forgets his nature and source, and is unable to connect with God and his true nature, that we find that he is at the core of the difficulties of this incarnation, and is the most wretched in the way that he must function. This, then, exacerbates[133] the quick sinking of his desires into the abyss of despair and hopelessness. He is lost and is unable to find his way to God. All that remains in his subconscious is a small spark of memory of the true nature, and the faint memory, of who he truly is.

To the children on the road[134], the veil of fear is lifted and they begin to see a faint glimmer of hope, and the memories return with more clarity, and these then can begin to stir in their hearts and they walk the tightrope of light, trying to find their way back to God whilst still here on Earth.

Adieu

---

[132] Alone: single: one: focus on the self only

[133] To make worse: increase the severity: to make an already bad or problematic situation worse

[134] Those searching for God

Yes God is Real – Morris, K.

Yes! God is real! The power and the purpose of God is to show man, in all his simple yet most precious ways, how special and wonderful he is to God. This is, of course, something that man has difficulty comprehending. He is unable to see and know, with the simplicity of a child in faith, that all needs will be met and that all burdens will be lifted simply by trusting in the ever present love and nature of God.

That God delights in all he does is apparent, and clearly God delights in man. His throne is prepared so that man can be exalted when the true nature and time for his excellence is come. Man cannot see or comprehend, however, that he is of such great value to God and continues to see himself as a lowly, abject[135] creature, shunned in sin from the face of God. How sad is this very thought, since this is as far from the truth as man can possibly move?

Yes, of course he is important to God. Of course he is special to God, and of course he is held in honor in God's eyes. His only thought, if such we can describe it, is to procure for man the best things in the

---

[135] Lowly: showing hopelessness: cast down in spirit

kingdom. His thoughts of love and protection for man are the first order, and only because man cannot comprehend this does he remain in the ignorance of pain and separation all his days. His kinship is set and his place is already prepared and ready, yet he is unable to take his place at the table of God's bounty because he continues to bask[136] in his unworthiness.

O children, why do you not open your eyes to see the vast treasures of boundless love that sit and wait for thee, only to open your hands in gratefulness and accept the wonderful bounty of God? The majesty, the love, the essence, of all that is God is available, and yet man is sitting with hands clasped tightly together, instead of opening his arms in acceptance to this gift so freely and easily given. O children, why cause thee to sojourn so long and hard in this valley of despair when relief is so easily obtained by reaching out to procure the gift so freely given by God? Love is the essence, the power, and might, of all that is attainable on God's Earth. All one must do is simply to open the arms in faith and know he will never be disappointed by God. The power and might and majesty of God are all established to assist man as he continues his journey of development and attainment throughout time. We know, however, that this task continues to baffle man regardless of how many prophets are sent to deliver and show him the way. He strives in abject pain and poverty, when relief is so easily at hand, if he will but see it. Turn, O children, and open your eyes to see the majesty, glory, and greatness of God's love. Open your eyes to the gifts given so freely and accept them readily, if you can. The palm is open, yet the gift slips out as if covered in oils, and cannot be grasped, try as you might. Know however, children, that

---

[136]   To take great pleasure or satisfaction in something

the oil exists only in the mind and that the closing of the palm, in faith, would be enough to secure the precious gift so freely given. We say indeed, O Daughters and Sons of the Most High God, that none but thee have caused such pain in the heart of God.

For sure, we know that in God's magnificence, pain cannot exist in reality, yet use this to express in metaphor how much anguish exists in the realm of God and Angels, when man continues to close his eyes and his palms to the gifts so freely given.

Love is the reason for being; the reason for knowing, the reason for growing. All must learn how to love and to love effortlessly, and with ease, all that is placed in his path. The nature of man must begin to allow for the expression of love with more ease, and the removal of doubt and pain from the knowledge and psyche of man. Man cannot continue on this path of self-destruction indefinitely, for he will perish. Why move you aimlessly in this path of destruction, when the alternative is so easily attained? Our very nature, of course must be changed, so that we can be able to see and to appreciate our oneness with each other and with God.

If we cannot achieve this oneness, we continue in poverty, and sin, and pain needlessly. O Sons and Daughters of Zion, open your hearts and hands and eyes to see the magnificence of God's love, and know that his heart is wider than any ocean, and deeper than anything fathomable in man's knowledge upon the Earth. Yes, of course love is all there is and all there will ever be. Without it, man cannot come into the bosom of God or see his true magnificence and essence. For through love, he is able to see and comprehend all the true beauty that is everywhere present, and come to know how greatly he is loved by God in his entirety.

Sons and Daughters of Zion, open your eyes to see the true love of God for his children, and to know you are precious beings created in love, for love, by love. Accept your birthright, and come into the powerful knowing of the true love of God for his children.

Adieu

Yes God is Real-Morris, K.

For the love of God is that special gift which can take man to the very highest pinnacle of a mountain, and there show him the true majesty of all that exists within that kingdom. Man, of himself, cannot reach the places that he can attain with the love and guidance of the Father God. Man must, therefore, avail himself of all that God is able to provide in order to take himself to the highest highs and not remain in the lowest lows of despair, without the love of God. The nature of man must not prevent him from moving forward or he will never be able to achieve all those attainable goals alone. Know, the very nature of his development can hold him at bay and he will fail to step forward into the golden city of God's love. We say, Dear Ones, that to avail oneself of all that actually exists, man must move forward without fear or trepidation[137] in order to achieve the prize.

As soon as man is able to do this, he will then be able to move forward into the kingdom and assume his true place of honor in the house of God. The Angels who dwell between heaven and earth are there to help man move forward and to guard him on his journey.

[137]   Involuntary trembling of the limbs: a state of terror: quaking with fear

They live in the realms of glory and support man in his pathway to God. They are there to provide the support and love that man needs, when doubt and fear would send him backwards.

Man must know that his task is not provided without support, but know that God gives him all he needs to be successful on his quest. Do not fear and do not believe you are ever alone, O Children of Men, but know that the love of God is ever-present, like a mantle covering around you as you travel the highways and byways of life. The mantle shall protect and keep you safe from anything that would cause thee harm, or prevent thee from entering into the ever-abiding love of God. Know that the safety of God's love shall shelter thee and keep thee warm, as a fire on a cold winter's night. Never fear that thou art alone, or conceive that thou art ever separated from God except in thy thoughts, for in truth thou art never separate from God, except of thine own choosing.

The love of God, so precious, is ever thine and is always there, present for you to utilize when in need all thy days. Never fear that thou hast been deserted, for how could God desert his children who he has loved since the dawn of time? Nothing can separate man from the love of God, for he has loved and cared for the Children of Men from their very infancy. To know God is to know true love and to become a part of God, for in loving God, man must move outside himself and take on the knowledge of something higher than himself. He must move outside himself and put on the mantle of unselfishness if he is to learn true love, and benefit from the grace of God which exists and is available to him at all times, if he will but reach out his hand and grasp that which is there prepared for him. As in days when the blindness of man caused him to stumble and fall, so even now, man cannot readily accept what is freely given, looking instead for those toys that would help him to grow... not ever knowing that he has always had what he needs within him already, and that he is provided with the very tools of success deep inside himself.

Man, O why seek ye the things of life outside thyself, when they are already so close at hand and are so easily attained through the mercy and love of God? Know thyself and remember thy greatness, and live in the love and wonder of God's grace, all the days of your life on Earth and in the heavens above. Cast off the fear that binds thee and move into the ever-reflecting pool of God's love and grace.

His pleasure is to give thee the kingdom and never to keep thee in darkness. Why choose ye to live in abject darkness and fear instead of stepping into the light of God's love? Move on, O Children of Men, and step into the light. Do not fear that the darkness will overwhelm thee, but know that the light is there within the darkness only because thou choosest not to see the light... but of fear is blinded to the true glory and magnificence of God's love.

Know every day, that man truly dwelleth in the highest places, and only the blindness and ignorance of man to his true glory and magnificence keeps him buried deep in despair. When man can open his eyes to the gifts so freely given of God, he can taste of the kingdom and inherit that which God wants to give him so freely without fear. Know your own magnificence, and how much you are treasured, O Children of Men, and come into the kingdom with ease. Open your eyes and see the ease with which you are given, all within the kingdom.

Never fear, for you are never alone; for God's love protects and defends thee at all times. He is ever-present in your darkest hour and in your shining moments. He is always there, if you would only open your hearts and hands to receive his grace and his love. Yes! God is so real, but if you cannot see these blessings, you will walk always in despair and longing, looking for that which you already possess... and hoping and searching for that which is already thine without asking. Open your eyes, your heart, and your hands, O Children of Men, and accept the grace of God, as a child accepting that most beloved toy he thought was lost to him. Feel the joy of the return, and nestle into the arms of God, and know the peace and joy that is thine, if only you will open yourself to the love of God.

Amen

13ᵀᴴ March 2010

Man's nature is determined; it seems, by those things around him and by the imprint of God upon his soul... but also, of course, we find that he is influenced by the soul group into which he enters the incarnation. For it seems that there is an abundance of evidence to suggest that the soul group helps him to grow or deteriorate in character. Each man enters the incarnation having been a member of the soul group prior to incarnation. Now on the Earth plane, he is heavily influenced by those around him, for good or ill. It is clear that he can make his own choices, but yet he spends much time doing things which may or may not be what he really wants to do. Why, then, does this happen? Simply because the nature of the soul group influence can be so strong that he becomes the very thing that surrounds him, and is the strongest influence there. He must learn to loosen himself from the bonds of this group while on Earth, or he will ever be in suffering if the negative forces of the group control his behavior, and his growth, as a soul.

Man must cast himself outside this group when and if he discovers that the effects upon his soul development are not helping him to grow. Thus, the nature vs. nurture[138] argument is born. From whence[139] comes the effects of 'evil' or negativity? It is unclear why this enters man's development so quickly but yet, enter it does. It takes him over and he becomes the epitome of what he should never be. Negativity is rampant and man begins to slide down into the abyss[140] of hate, anger, fear, and un-forgiveness. From this point, it is usually difficult to lift his soul, and he is drowning as one in sixty feet of water, with no hope of rescue. The nature of the love and things of God can be forgotten at such times, and he loses his way. Man is lost, and without the help of those around him to help him back to the path, he deteriorates into more and more negativity until he is lost without hope. It is here and now that the Diadem Band and Angel Band can come into being and help to bring him back to the path. For without this intervention on their part, his soul would surely perish.

Why, then, if they are there to help man, do so many seemingly negative things happen? Simple child! Because man is sometimes set on a course of self-destruction, and will not heed the guidance of the inner mind or 'Guides' to bring him out of the darkness into light. If man hears the voice and will do the work as he is directed, he can be saved... but when he becomes deaf and blind to guidance, he is truly lost and remains in that place of hell here on Earth. His

---

[138] The "nature" theory of human behavior believes that people behave as they do according to genetic predispositions or even 'animal instincts.' The "nurture" theory of human behavior believes that people think and behave in certain ways because they are taught to do so.

[139] From what or which source

[140] Bottomless gulf : anything profound and unfathomable

hope is lost as he sinks quicker and quicker into despair, pain, and loneliness, and enters into that place of unimagined horror where he conceives of ways to bring pain and suffering to other souls. This, then, is the nature of pain that enters man and whence he becomes the messenger of doom. His soul is masked in darkness, and no light can enter, so he descends even lower into the realms of darkness, pain, and despair. Man is now lost. He has forgotten who he is. He has no identity and with no memory of God, continues the long fall and descent into pain and agony. The soul is without hope at this point and will continue the incarnation on this path.

If he can be influenced to come out of the darkness, then there is hope… but if he cannot, then he will remain in this place of hell and continue the descent into that spiral from which he cannot return.

Jeffrey Dahmer[141] so exemplified this, where he was lost in despair and could not be brought back from the depths of despair into any light. He continued to go deeper and so was lost in this incarnation. Thus, we see that man's free will is the cause of much of his pain, since this allows him to make decisions about his actions. Whether he will heed the call and remember his divinity, or whether he will forget his true nature and live a life of pain and negativity, in which his main task is to hurt the others around him. If man cannot be brought to see the light, and continues to move in this downward spiral, there is little hope and he is lost in the fear, anger, hurt, and pain of this world, and is lost to the Angel Band.

---

[141] Jeffrey Lionel Dahmer was an American serial killer and sex offender, also known as the Milwaukee Cannibal, who committed the rape, murder and dismemberment of seventeen men and boys between 1978 and 1991.

Each loss is felt deeply by the Angel Band, for it is their task to keep man on the path and road back to his source. If he is lost to them, they suffer with him as they try to bring him back from the edge of despair, into the light of God's love and energy. The Angel Band works tirelessly trying to save all souls, but is sometimes unable to influence at all and the negativity wins out.

Listen to your inner voice, O Children of Men, and know this is truly the voice of God, trying to give you that which you so desperately crave. Know that God is with you each and every day, trying to bring you all things, especially his love and his light. Know you are never alone, especially in your darkest hour, and know your soul can be brought back from the edge of the abyss into God's light, if you so choose. There is hope for every soul, and there is redemption for all if man will allow it to happen. If he chooses to remain in pain, then so it is; but the Band will never desert him, for he is their charge. Every soul is in their care, and so they battle to keep them in the light of God's love and out of the darkness. Without the love of God, man cannot advance... but with it, he is able to enter into his true magnificence and take his rightful place as the child of God who he is.

Reclaim your birthright, O Children of Men, and see all that is before you. Enter into the grace and love of God, and remain there in that place of eternal bliss. Know peace, and find the true joy and love of God that is within you. Stay out of the darkness and know the light, love, and source of God's benevolence. Enter into the joy of God and live in that place, so that you can know peace and true joy.

Adieu

4ᵀᴴ MARCH 2011

Welcome, child of the sun, Daughter of the Royal House of Zion.[142] Know ye we are happy, indeed, to be here with thee. Happy, indeed, to see and to share the good works of God, for we see, indeed, the thoughts you possess and the deeds that would gladly help you fulfill your true task here on the Earth.

Know ye, Little One, that the times of change linger here with thee and that the changes, indeed, affect thee and thine in all ways. Know ye that the Lord of Hosts is with thee, and the God of Jacob remains your refuge. We see and know your heart and, indeed, we say blessed is the name of God, for the peace of God is truly dwelling within thee. Know ye that the Lord of Hosts is your refuge, and nothing can come nigh thee to harm thee.

Let not fear come nigh thee but know that all is as it should be. Let your heart and your love shine forth, Little One, and let all that is within thee come forth, for blessed is the name of the Lord. Let

---

[142]   Daughter of Jerusalem

not fear encompass thee, but know that the Son of God[143] himself protects and guides thee, Little One.

Know ye all these things; therefore, keep ye the faith, and be at peace, for only in this way can you truly live out your creed, and follow the plan for your life that was put in place when you decided to return in this incarnation. Look ye up and see all the magnificent works of God. Look ye up and see the true power and love of God for mankind. Know ye the fear that lurks in the hearts of men, but know, indeed, that there is no need for fear, for God is Lord of all and will shield thee and thine from harm.

Know ye that the Lord of Hosts will continue to protect thee and defend thee for all thy days. The days are here for the glory of God to shine forth in the lives and in the hearts of men. Look on, Little Princess, and see and know that the Lord of Hosts will protect mankind, and will deliver you from the snares and the wrath of those who would bring harm to thee. Let your light shine, Little One, and know that the days are here for the changes to come into the hearts of men. For from deep within the bowels of the earth will come the wisdom of the ages, and man will begin to see and know his true source... and find the golden key to learn his own strength and power.

O sons and daughters of the Most High God, look up, and see, and know your true strength, for such is your power and your destiny. Know your source, and see, and know your true magnificence. The God of Jacob is your God, and he is the only God, so be ye at peace and know that he is the same now and forever. For the throne of the Most High God is, indeed, the only one that can ever exist.

---

[143] God-Likeness : Spiritual relationship between God and a human being, based on love, respect and doing the will of the father (God).

Look on, Little One, and see the kingdom of earthly rulers as they tumble and fall. Look, and see, and know that there can be no true rulers here on Earth if truth, and justice, and peace, and love, do not readily flow from them to the people. All tyrants will fall in the reign of man, for such is the very nature of the establishment of man. If the Daughters and Sons of the Earth continue to bring pain to their brethren, know that there can be no peace for thee. For the eyes of the sleeping tiger are now open, and the Children of Men will now take hold of their destiny and move forward. The destiny of man is such that he must advance or perish. Look and see the devastation that is being brought in far lands.[144]

Know this will not last, for the people are a new people with a new heart, so the days of enslavement are truly past, as the 'shift' begins and man begins to see the light.

O Children of Men, come out of the darkness of the grave and into the sunlight of God's love. See all the magnificence and know that the days of change are upon us, and no more can the sleeping tiger be kept asleep. He must awaken and move upon the Earth... for such is the very nature and source of change.

The days of the dictators are past, for behold: a new day brings forth the new light that illuminates all things, and shows the very nature of the evil that has been in abundance for many moons.

Look on, Little One, and know that these are the times of change, and these, indeed, are the times that will try men's souls but yet will bring him, once again, into the light of God's love.

---

[144] The political crisis in Libya

Be brave, O Sons and Daughters of Zion, look on and know all is as it is written and should be; for the days of enlightenment are upon us and these are the works of man which must change. For love, and not hate and fear, must be established upon the Earth, and man must change and become what he truly is: that most loved of all God's creations. Not the mindless beasts of old, dwelling in ignorance, darkness, and fear, but walking in the light and love of God. Be at peace, Dear Ones, and know that the dark night will come to an end very soon, and liberation will follow for those who desire peace and freedom.

Let your light continue to shine, and know that you will continue to see the works of man multiply as you continue on your path. Continue to walk in the light, and know that the Lord of Hosts will be your strength and shield, and all will be right for thee. Be at peace and let all that is within thee shine forth, for such is the time, and the days that are ahead for thee. Live in the light and love of God, and know that all will transpire as it should. These are the days of awakening. Know that the lion sleeps no more. Look on in awe and see the works of God as they shine forth in the Sons of Men.

Adieu, in the light and Love of God. May peace continue to reign in your heart.

The Brotherhood

5ᵗʜ July 2011

Welcome, Child of Light, we say welcome, indeed. We are much happy to be here with thee at this most blessed of all times. Know, Sweet One, that much has been our learning of this time; for, indeed, we see much of this man from the East who carries such peace within his breast (His Holiness Sri Sri Ravi Shankar at the World Cultural Festival in Berlin.)[145] Know, Sweet One, that indeed his heart is of the purest nature and his intentions are only to spread the peace and love of the Divine to the Children of Men. Indeed, we see much sorrow in his heart for the deep pain existing still in the hearts of men, and the great separation that keeps mankind bound in pain. Know, Dear Ones, that this is the true sadness of the Divine, for to see the Children of Men suffering, brings naught but pain. Know, Dear Ones, that the light of God must be allowed to awaken those still in pain, and bring them the joy and happiness they so desperately need, to bring them back to the fold of God's love.

---

[145]   The author attended the World Culture Festival in Berlin, to celebrate the 30ᵗʰ Anniversary of the Art of Living Foundation - Celebrating one world family

Know we here are in much sadness too, but know that this is the plight of mankind, that until the hearts and eyes are fully opened; the Children of Men will continue to know pain and confusion. The pain and confusion of loss—the pain and confusion of children lost, without the guidance of the Mother Father God. For here indeed, we see that like sheep, they scatter to the four winds when the storms of life come upon them. They run with haste, this way and that way, searching for help but only this confusion keeps them running; for should they pause for a brief moment, they would know this confusion is naught but the thunder or the loud storms of life: for indeed no harm will come... if they hold fast.

Yet, without the great guidance of the love of God the Father, they run to the four winds, and in this panic, they lose their way and are, even so, lost once more. Know, Dear Ones, that when the storms of life are upon you, even then hold fast to all you know. This is the time to remember what you are; to remember your heritage and your birthright as the Sons and Daughters of the Most High God. This is the time to put on your armor, and to continue to hold fast. For, indeed, there is nothing to fear; for only the fear of that which is unknown takes thee by surprise, and causes the great plight. Know, Dear Ones, that the love of God is the anchor and the shepherd that can keep you grounded, even in the storm. It is that which will protect and defend thee. It is that which will give thee peace.

Open your hearts, O ye Sons and Daughters of the Most High God, and see, and know these truths; for ye are the keepers of the knowledge. Ye are the magnificent children of the Father, given all the love and the blessings of God at birth, and before the very dawn of time. Ye are the inheritors of the grace and love of God, given to thee at birth upon the Earth. Know, Dear Ones, you are spirit before you are flesh, and you are eternal beings from the realm of light, guided and loved by God: Protected and nourished by God, your Father. Why run in fear? Remember, these storms are naught but the trials you have asked for. These are the tests of courage and the great experiences you have sought, in order to help you to grow and to mature as Beings of Light. Know, Dear Ones, you need not fear the thunder and the storms of life, for it is naught but the sound of God calling to thee.

Fear not, Dear Ones; know that the noise will cause thee no harm. Stand your ground and face the storms of life, and know that no harm will come nigh thee, for you are the children of God: The Sons and Daughters of the Loving Almighty, who keeps thee and secures thee. For surely, the thunder cannot harm thee. There is no danger in the thunder. The only danger comes when we run with haste to the four winds, never remembering why we run, or even knowing where we run. We are in panic, and this panic causes great fear; so that the memory of the great and most powerful love of God is lost to thee.

Stand fast, O Children of Men, when the storms of life come upon thee! Stand fast and remember, you are protected. Stand fast and know you are shielded and guided. For you are the Sons and Daughters of the Most High God. Open your hearts, and know you need not run or cower from the storm, for you are fearless children. You are full of the knowledge and love of God, and as such, you cannot be harmed... for you are spirit, you are light, you are love.

Scatter not to the four winds but keep ye calm, and face the storms of life… and know that all will be well. For you are guided, you are loved, and you are protected by your Mother Father God. Remember these truths, and stand fast in the knowledge and love of God, for this will be your rescue, this will be your life, and this will be your joy. All must be tested in the storms of life. This is your calling, but yet it is not necessary for you to run in fear, for these are only minor trials and tribulations that would give thee strength and courage. Open your hearts, remember your mission and your heritage, and **know there is naught to fear but fear itself**: For these are the trials of life that would build thee up, and not tear thee down. Remember that these are your trials, chosen by you[146], to bring you back to the memory of God. REMEMBER and stand fast, for this will keep thee strong and cause thee to return to the fold of God's love. Be you at peace in times of storm, Dear Ones, and know that the love of God will keep thee safe. For you are eternal, you are light, you are love. You are the most blessed of God.

Open your hearts, and remember once more the great peace of God. Know that naught can harm thee. Naught can keep thee bound in chains but the fear of things unknown. Remember you are the beloved of God, given all the knowledge that you need, buried deep within you. Search your heart, and remember all that is the truth of God, for this will keep thee safe in the storm. This will keep thee from the rain, and shelter thee when the storm clouds gather above thee. God's love will protect, and keep thee warm and safe, so have no fear, Dear Ones, for you are not alone. You are never alone; you are always held in the arms of God; always protected by the love of

---

146   Chosen by you when you were in spirit to help to bring you back to God.

God, and always shielded by the power and presence of God. You are the children of God. You are ever loved and protected of God. Hold fast, Dear Ones, do not despair but know that your needs will be met, and you will be safely held and gently rocked in the arms of God. No harm can befall thee; for you are light, you are love, you are wisdom, and you are courage. You are the blessed Sons and Daughters of the Most High God. Rest in the knowledge of the love of God, and know sweet peace, Dear Ones, for you are the beloved.

Adieu Sweet Ones

Adieu

22NDJuly 2011

For, indeed, the path of fear, doubt, and worry can find no true place in the world of man. For as a spiritual being, the notion to live here cannot find peace. For there is much more that demands attention, and so fear, doubt, and worry cannot be encouraged to live within the heart of man permanently. For, indeed, these three emotions are among the most burdensome of all; for they strip the body and heart of the resolve to continue on. Instead, they have the great power to bring man to his knees in a crippling state of anxiety, worry, and the great inability to proceed with any task at any level. Thus, Dear Ones, we see and know the true strength of these emotions. For we have seen firsthand, the very heart of man brought to his knees from the fear, doubt, and worry in the heart of man.

Know, Dear Ones, we say to leave these thoughts behind, and begin to move, live, and have your beingness in the place of happiness, joy, and the full and complete knowledge of the love of God. For only this will allow man to proceed into the light of God's love with ease and with haste. Do not be consumed by the fear that grips the world; that dwells and multiplies, in the land of lack and anxiety.

For, indeed, this will bring thee nothing but multiplied amounts of fear, doubt, and worry. For like the weeds that cover the ground, even so are these three emotions able to grow, flourish, and nurture themselves with ease on the land (which is akin to the hearts of men). Know, Dear Ones, that naught can cause man to return to these states of unhappiness like the first emergence of the 'three sisters of defeat'—fear, doubt, and worry. For to know them, is to court destruction and ruin. For where they live and flourish, all other emotions are trampled and choked, and so get no chance to move on in the light of God's love.

Know, Dear Ones, we are happy for your triumphant return, and so see and know your heart. For in this great state, there are options as yet unimagined, or undelivered, which can help to repair the heart of man, so that he may be able to gain some insight into the lives of all others. For we, indeed, know your heart, and the magnificent heart that dwells beneath your robes. Know for sure, Sweet Ones, that you are well as you embark upon this quest, and know that many things will begin to flow inside the soul and body of man. For this is the path to enlightenment, so be firm-footed, and know that nothing can shake the resolve of man to live in happiness, and the love of God. For such is the heart of man, and such is the desire of the heart of man.

Know that the simplicity of the text is well known, but know also that we know that great is the work that is still yet ready to be, buried deep within the heart and soul of man. For such is your great concern, and indeed, so also is your area of focus. For you will succeed, and much will be the joy and exaltation in the discovery of these steps. Know, Dear Ones, that we are, indeed, much happy to be here with thee and to help to support thee as this great and most liberating task begins upon the Earth. For the great love of God for mankind is, indeed, seen each and every day, and can be measured by the many treasures provided for mankind that are now lying in the storehouse of God. For in truth, they can remain there until the very end of time, but naught will come of them, if they are not practiced and utilized each day as the blessings of the day. Know, Dear Ones, we see and know all that transpires, but realize that the most basic of creature comforts will be there, made available for you to partake of in the kingdom of men and of Angels.

Adieu

31ˢᵗ August 2011

For as much as the Lord of Light is the maker of all things pertaining to man, even so is the promise of God's love, perfected and made available to the Sons of Men. For indeed, Dear Ones, it is written that man should not eat bread alone but of everything that is found upon the Earth. Know, Dear Ones, that the benevolent Father Mother God has provided all things upon the Earth for the use of man. The wherewithal to feed, clothe, and shelter himself is provided for mankind. There is naught that man needs that he has not been provided with the great knowledge to secure. Thus, it is abundantly clear, that the Sons of Men have all that is needed in order to survive upon the Earth.

That mankind has taken this great ability and knowledge, and used it to hoard and to build up great storehouses, is most apparent. That some people starve, while others live in luxury, is the way of mankind and is the way in which man forgets his brother. Know, Dear Ones, that your Mother Father God has given man the knowledge and the gifts of survival upon the Earth, but yet man is unable to share the great wealth of Mother Earth with his brothers and sisters.

Why see your brother starving, and yet pretend you have no food, whilst all the time you waste that which is given so freely of God, or hoard all that was given in storehouses? Open the gates, O Children of Men, and share that life-giving substance with the weak and the poor. Let not your greed allow you to forget your Godhead. Remember that this is your brother, and open up the storehouses and share the great wealth of the world with one and all. Be you not selfish, but first instead becomes selfless, and swing open your hearts and show mercy to all those in need. Let not your greed and your selfishness continue to rule your hearts, but open up your eyes and your arms, and welcome in those who hunger and thirst. Let them know you care, and that you recognize them as your brothers and sisters: For indeed, you are ONE.

Become the lights that you are, and know that the God of your beingness is much pleased when we return to ourselves, and recognize that part of ourselves who sit in poverty and pain. Open your arms, O Sons and Daughters of Man, and see and know that the God of your beingness is there in front of you, waiting to be recognized, and to be seated at the table with you. Why hoard? For in your hearts, you know that you cannot ever hope to take on and consume all that you have hoarded? Let open the gates of your hearts, and help those in need, for herein lies your key to happiness.

Give to those in need, and know that more will be provided to you, for you live in an abundant universe: with all that is necessary for your survival. Share your wealth of knowledge with your brethren, and know that all your needs will be supplied, and all the needs of your brothers will be supplied with much to spare. Think and remember the story of the Loaves and the Fishes,[147] Dear Ones, and know that this was the tale of the act of sharing, which proved that alone, we have a small and meager existence: But yet, when we share our gifts with each other, there are abundant blessings from the storehouse of God, available for all.

Enough is there to share and much left over. For your Heavenly Father has provided all that you will need upon the Earth, so take ye not the path that says there is not enough, thus I must grab it and hoard, lest the supply is no more.

Open your hands, Dear Ones, and see and know that the Lord, the Giver of Life, has provided for thee, and will continue to provide for thee, all that is needed for your survival upon the Earth. Know, indeed, that the needs of man can be met with ease, and all needs can be supplied when man opens up his heart and his hands, and gives the love he holds with avarice also to those upon the Earth. Share the love, Dear Ones, and see the abundant blessings that are returned to thee. Know indeed, that as you give, even so shall you continue to receive. For the storehouses of God are ever filled to flowing over, with the many blessings of God. Give freely, and know that the measure you give will be the measure you receive. For the Lord, the Giver of All Things is a bountiful and generous God.

The Mother Father God has provided for mankind in his abundance. But, it is the heart of man which has caused the belief of lack upon the Earth. For, indeed, the belief that there is lack is the belief from the mind of man. Open your eyes, and see and know that this is no truth. For all is plentiful, all is provided, and all is there, made ready for

---

[147]   Matthew 14:13-21

mankind. Let not your fear or your greed lead thee astray. Know, Dear Ones, that you have been freely given of all that is needed upon the Earth. Even as you have been provided with the unconditional love of the Mother Father God, even so have you been given all that is necessary for your survival upon the Earth. Open your hearts and remember your beingness. Know that you are sons and daughters of the God of your beingness. Know, Dear Ones, that your loving parent would never leave you in need. Know that your loving parent would never deny you the right to survival upon this beautiful and glorious place.

Know, Dear Ones, that your greed and your forgetfulness have caused you to suffer. It is the decision of man that has caused, and will continue to bring, destruction and pain upon your fellow man. For indeed, as you have mistreated Mother Earth, even so now, you reap the rewards. For the devastation and the changes upon the Earth are the result of man's failure to give his love, and his recognition, to the source from which his life springs. Take care of your place of abode[148] O Children! And show it the love and caring you do to your houses and palaces. You strive to maintain them, and make them glorious, so that you may sit in splendor; even so, look you to Mother Earth and know that this will cause you to live happy and fulfilled lives. For in peace and joy, you may be able to sing and praise the God of your being. For when the heart is happy, all is right with the world. Look you not up and say, "We have need of this or that," but know, indeed, that all is supplied for thee, Dear Ones.

Know that your Mother Father God has provided all for thee. Be you full of the knowledge of the love of God and know that there is likewise enough of this to go around. There is an abundance of

---

[148]   Place of residence: dwelling

blessings for all the Children of Men upon the Earth… but yet, your minds tell you of scarcity and lack. Let not your eyes fool you, and cause you to believe there is not enough. Know, Dear Ones, you live in plenty, and that you have all you need.

Know that the love of God has already provided you with all you will ever need, and know that you have the power to see and taste the many blessings of the Mother Father God. Let not fear consume thee, and let not your eyes deceive thee. Know indeed, that you are the sons and daughters of the Most High God, and that all you need is ever present. If you are not to inherit the blessings and the gifts of the Mother Father God, then who will?

Be confident, and know that you are not orphans left to shelter in the doorways of a foreign place. You are the heirs of God, given all that is available. All your needs are met but your minds convince you that you live in a world of lack and limitation. Know, Dear Ones, that you are the children of God, and therefore are given all that you need in order to survive. Be you ever present, and know that you are loved and protected by God. All that you want and need is ever present. Open your arms, and receive your gifts freely given of God. Know, indeed, that nothing you need has been withheld.

That you believe in lack and limitation is the mind of man at work, trying to convince you that you are forgotten of God. Know, Dear Ones, you are never forgotten and can never be forgotten, for man is a part of God. How can your Mother Father forget his arms or his legs, or indeed his heart? For you are always with God, and a part of God; so how can God not provide for thee, Dear Ones? Know indeed, that you are the creators of the illusion that says, "I am forgotten of God, and am alone in this desolate place." Know, Dear Ones, that the desolation and loneliness are felt only by the human mind, for the spirit within you indeed knows that you are given all that you need, and that indeed, you have all the keys to the kingdom within your grasp. Yet you forget this, and wander aimlessly looking for a way into the abundance of God. Open your eyes, and open your hands, and see that the keys are there: freely given of God. All that you ever need is yours, Dear Ones. Know this truth and live.

Open your eyes, and remember your heritage and live! Open your hearts, and know that you are the Sons and Daughters of the Most High God, heirs to all that is given by God. Share and bask in the knowledge of the love of God, and live, Dear Ones! Let not the pain of the separation from your Mother Father God continue to keep thee bound in chains, for you are not separated, and can never be separated from the love of God... for you are gods. You are love, you are peace, you are joy, you are happiness. Open your heart, and know these truths, and know true happiness and joy, Dear Ones. Be at peace and know that all will indeed be well for thee, and that indeed all is well for thee. Be at peace, Dear Ones, and know that you are the sons and daughters of a loving and benevolent parent. All your needs are met, and all your wants are supplied. Share the love, the peace, and the blessings with all, and know that your life upon the Earth will be lived with happiness, and love, and joy.

May the peace, love, and blessings of God the Father continue to flow into your hearts, Dear Ones.

Adieu

For indeed, the love of God for man is a never-ending cycle of love and forgiveness. For man is ever able to return to the bosom of Mother Father God, who is ever able to allow man to make amends, if such we may refer to it. For the great and eternal love of God, knows no bounds, and is ever present; ever available to mankind. It is, however, mankind which prefers to believe that there are terms levied upon the forgiveness, and the love of God for man. For indeed, no such limit exists, for man is ever able to be with Mother Father God. For the love that is there available for man allows him always to return to God. Let not your heart be troubled, Dear Ones, and let not fear allow thee to say that man has run out of chances to return to God; for indeed, he is ever able to do so, without any kind of penalty.

Know, Dear Ones, that man is ever able when he can remember that the love of God is that thing which will bring him peace and joy: for to return to the source he must. For in no way does God keep count, and in no way can God choose to turn away from man, for this is not the way of God. For the eternal love that exists for man allows him to enter into the bosom of God and to find the love and peace that he has searched for throughout his life.

Know, Dear Ones, that the plight[149] of man upon the Earth would have him believe that naught exists but himself, and that he and his might are all that exists in the Universe. Know, Dear Ones, this is as far from the truth as it is possible to stray, for indeed mankind is not all the life form that exist in the heavens, and man is but one of the lesser beings that populate the stars. Know, Dear Ones, we say lesser, for indeed there are others in the Universe whose powers of cognition far outweigh that of man, and whose development is far superior to that of man. Let not fear come upon thee, Dear Ones, but know indeed, that none wish to bring harm upon the Earth so that you reside here in safety. Be you aware that the great and wonderful experiment that is man is allowed to flourish upon the Earth, and indeed is watched with great pride by those who work to protect the delicate balance that exists in the Universe.

Be at peace, Dear Ones, and know that life exists in many forms unknown to the mind of man, so that to comprehend it, would take much indeed. Be happy to know, that the presence of man upon the Earth will continue until— or unless— man turns upon Mother Earth, and in his greed and pain destroys this blessed place. Be at peace, Dear Ones, and know that since God is in his heaven, all is indeed right with the world; and the toil of mankind upon its shores, will continue on for eons.

---

[149] Condition : state :predicament: A risky or dangerous state

Know, Dear Ones, we know the pain that resides in the heart of man, and we indeed see that the level of understanding of man's connection to Mother Earth must change. For indeed, if no changes are made, then the Earth as it is known cannot continue to exist in this very form. For man must, indeed, be conscious of the life-force of the Earth, and the delicate balance that exists in this place.

Let none say that all is not connected, and the Earth is of no value. For indeed, such thinking will allow man to disappear from the Earth. For if care is not taken of this blessed place it will not exist for future generations of man to dwell upon. Be you at peace, Dear Ones, and know that the love of God for man can and will cause the eyes of man to open so that he might look outside himself, and see and know that he cannot continue on in this way. Be you full of peace, and come to know that the love of God will cause man to change.

For in being able to love his brother, he also is able to love all about him in his world, and to abide by the laws established in nature. For as things exist in this moment in time, we see, indeed, that great changes must come into being if the richness of the earth will be made available for future generations.

Open your hearts, O Sons and Daughters of Zion, and know that the days of selfish living must come to an end, for the days of reckless thoughts, and the selfish destruction, and wanton disregard of all about you, must end. Look to the seas, which no longer live and flourish as of old, because of the great and destructive force of man upon the seas. For in polluting the seas, you destroy those that dwell therein. Be you full of pain when the rivers run dry and the oceans no longer supply your needs? Be you happy, when the very life force is no longer evident in the seas? Be you able to survive, when you bring great and painful destruction upon the Earth?

Let not your heart be troubled, but know that man can control his urges, and can turn the tide of destruction... and halt the great and destructive force that can be mankind. Open your eyes, O Sons and Daughters of Earth, and see and know the truth of thy being. For you are a part of the earth as the Ancient Ones knew. Keep ye the sacred bond of brotherhood with all living things, and see and know great changes in your life. For the great and wonderful place that is the Earth can and will provide all that humankind needs for survival.

Listen not to the sound of the empty voices that say there is an unending supply of all things found here upon the Earth. For man in his wastefulness must deplete these supplies, and will, and must then find other sources to support life to (allow it to) exist upon the Earth.

Be at peace, and know that the time for change is truly upon you, O Sons and Daughters of Earth, and man must make the changes that are necessary for his survival. Know, Dear Ones, the time will indeed come, for changes to come into being, to bring about the new age of man; when with regard and reverence he sees the true and blessed nature of his world. Open your eyes, and see and know that the change must come into the hearts of men, so that greed is not the first and foremost emotion, but that love drives all things, becomes all things, and dictates all things. For only in so doing, can man know that the change in his heart will affect the very foundations of how he survives upon the Earth. Let not your heart be troubled, but know that a great change must come upon the hearts and minds of men, so that the Earth can survive, and be that most wonderful of places. Let all upon the Earth see and know that God is indeed in his heaven and all must be right with the world. For the destruction must cease, and the ravages and wanton destruction must come to an end. For the times of the seasons will indeed see great changes, and the things that were will be no more.

Turn, O Mankind! And look at the results of the greed, and neglect, of your home. Why allow it to fall into disrepair? Like your houses, where you maintain their structures, and keep them clean; you also must take heed and do this even so for Mother Earth, so that you may yet continue to enjoy her beauty, peace, and generosity to you, O Sons and Daughters of Mankind. Let not your souls tell thee tales that naught is affected by my actions, **but yet know that all is affected by your actions.** Be at peace, and know that this is the way of man upon the Earth; that must change, for the love of God for mankind caused him to provide this abode for thee.

Ever we say, take heed and be good stewards of the land so that it may indeed be a bountiful harvest for thee. For man must know, that in destroying his home, he destroys his hope and himself. Look on and know that there are other ways to be upon the Earth, in less destructive fashion. Be you inventive to find these things, and know that your life and your peace will know much promise, for the discoveries that come forth from the mind of man. Let all the world know that man is the child of God, and the keeper of his home, and the watchman on the tower who sounds the alarm to awaken the household, lest thieves break in to steal all that is within.

Know, Dear Ones, that the change must come, or the storehouses will be made bare, and man will know great need upon the Earth... as is evidenced already in some places upon the Earth, even now.

Let not the empty vessels[150] sound and say all is well, all is well; for the thief is indeed upon you, and will break in and plunder all the possessions, if care is not taken to secure that which is most precious. Know, Dear Ones, that the time is now, and the actions must be taken.

Be kind to your brethren, and to your world, for in so doing, you show kindness to yourselves, Dear Ones. Give love to all around you, and know the sweet peace of God. For the blessings and the abundance of the Earth will be thine to inherit.

Show love, and live! Show disregard, and know that the earth will not willingly give up her bounty to thee. For the pain, and destruction, and havoc[151] that is wreaked by man, must be repaid.

Be at peace, and know that this is thine to control, or to worsen, as thou choosest[152]. Let all who would bring about changes in the actions of men to bring about a more bountiful world, say that all is not as it should be, and take pains to address these truths: For even so, will the balance be returned to the place you call home.

Adieu

---

[150] Those people who have a little knowledge and usually talk the most

[151] Devastation: wide and general destruction

[152] Choose

1ˢᵗ February 2012

Arise! O Sons and Daughters of Zion, arise! And know it is time to greet the dawn. For the light and love of God for mankind is evidenced upon the Earth. Know indeed, Dear Ones, that the love of God for mankind is shown every day, in the many blessings and the love showered down upon the Sons and Daughters of Mankind: For indeed the children of God must be fed, and the love of God must be evidenced each day, so that mankind may know that it can never be forgotten of God. For you are, indeed, loved and adored by Mother Father God, Dear Ones. Know, indeed, that the love of God for mankind can be seen each day when the sun rises to bring thee light upon the Earth. For in truth, the sun is the very source of light and warmth upon the Earth. Know indeed, Dear Ones, it is the very source of life, for indeed without it the plants wither and fade, and the life's blood of man is left in the greatest of need. For indeed, the Sons of Men cannot live upon the Earth without the warmth of the sun.

Know, Dear Ones, that such is the vastness of the love of God for mankind; that all you need to survive upon the Earth is given to thee without question, or without the asking. For indeed, your Mother

Father God knows what you need before it is asked, and makes it available for and to thee. Know, Dear Ones, even as your Mother Father God anticipates your every need on such a grand scale, even so are all your smallest desires and needs made available to thee. Know, Dear Ones, only your failure to notice that you are provided with all you need keeps you ever in want. For indeed, all that you need is ever present and made available upon the Earth.

Only the doctrines, and teachings, and theories of man, would keep you ever in want and need. For teachings of lack and the inability to have all that is given has allowed mankind to believe in a teaching of inadequacy and insufficiency upon the Earth. That man believes all is rationed upon the Earth is evident in the unwillingness to share all the fruits and gifts of the Earth with his brethren. For indeed, if such teachings and beliefs existed not, man could share willingly with his brethren. Instead, Dear Ones, we see the hoarding and the denying of the basic tenets of life from his brother, in fear of lack. "For how can I share, when there will be none left for me?" Open your hearts and your eyes, O Sons of Men! And see and know that only your belief in lack and insufficiency would keep you a prisoner to such limited thinking. For, indeed, why would Mother Father God put you in a place without making adequate provisions for thee? Indeed, God would do no such thing, Dear Ones, for adequate supply is there given abundantly to the Sons of Men. That in greed, you refuse to believe it and exact a price upon it, so that some may possess it and others may not, is the belief and the evidence of the limited thinking of man. Know indeed, Dear Ones, that the love of God for mankind would prohibit such behaviors, for it would not encourage the fighting and the great inequalities seen upon the Earth.

Know indeed, Dear Ones, that the love of God for mankind is evidenced in the abundance of all things upon the Earth. Know that only the limited view of man has created a society in which all is not shared, but is kept in storehouses while the masses may starve for the want of it. Look Dear Ones, we say, to other ways and means to distribute the blessings and the abundance of God to all your brethren, instead of building storehouses to hold and to separate the blessings from your brothers. Know, Dear Ones that you are the heirs to the kingdom, and as such, all is made available for thee.

Look ye not to self alone, but share the abundance with your brethren... for therein lies your peace, your joy, your hope, and your destiny. For the great love of God for mankind is evidenced in the variety of foods and gifts made available upon the Earth, to meet your every need. Know indeed, Dear Ones, that you are the stewards of the gifts of God, given the ability to gather and to share this great abundance with all in need. Keep it not for thyself alone, but know indeed that your blessings lie in making it available to all around thee. For in keeping it to self alone, you go against the heart of God. You go against the teachings of God, and you go against the will of God.

For at no time does God say, "I will make you a gift, but will limit that which you may have." Does the fruit tree limit what it gives or does it provide a limitless supply for thee? Does the tree count out only what you should have in small quantities, or does it produce in great abundance for thee? Know indeed, it bears fruit abundantly, and it is only the thought and idea of man which would keep thee in want; that prevails upon the Earth, and causes man to erect storehouses and theories that bring wealth to one, and great need to his brother. Know, indeed, there is more than enough for all the Children of Men. More than enough to meet the desires of all upon the Earth... but only the hearts and minds of men would see inadequacy, insufficiency, and lack, upon the Earth.

Know, Dear Ones, that this limited view keeps thee ever in prison, and ever in bondage; for you fail to see and acknowledge the true greatness of the gifts of God. Know, Dear Ones, that when you share the wealth of the world with your brother, you indeed become richer: For the richness and the blessings flow with even greater abundance and all can be blessed.

Look to your brothers and sisters upon the Earth in need, in all the four corners of the world, and see that mankind has set up laws that breed the theory of lack and limitation as a way of living upon the Earth. For indeed, when you share, all are blessed. All are happy, and there can be happiness, peace, and joy upon the Earth instead of war, strife, famine, and want upon the Earth.

Know, Dear Ones, you are the creators of the disasters and famines upon the Earth, for your teachings and beliefs would rob your brother of his ability to survive, and attain the most basic of existences, while you store up wealth in storehouses and think not of your brethren in need. Be you aware, Dear Ones, that these are not the ways of God.

Remember your dear Brother, Jesus, who taught the sharing of all. Know ye not the story of the feeding of the multitude[153] was the teaching of the sharing of your gifts with each other? For in sharing, all are fed with the material food for the body... but also the spiritual food of God, which is evidenced in the love for one another.

---

[153]   Matthew 14:13-21

Know, Dear Ones, that the great love of God for mankind makes all (everything) available to all the sons and daughters of Earth, but only the Children of Men attach rules and limitations to the bounty of God. Know, Dear Ones, there are adequate blessings of God given to all. Only your belief in lack and limitation would keep thee bound in pain and imprisoned.

For your minds tell thee that there is not enough of anything, so you keep it hidden from view, lest you find there is none available for thee.

Know there will always be enough, so free your minds, and think and know that these thoughts and beliefs are no longer useful to mankind. For indeed, you are knowledgeable in the ways of the world, and you know in your hearts that there will be enough. Why hold you fast to the beliefs of a bygone age that limits you, and causes you naught but pain? Release yourselves! O Children! And know the true peace, love, joy, and freedom of abundant living. For when all are free to share in the abundance of the Earth, all will prosper. All will know that needs are met, and all will be able to survive upon the Earth. Know, Dear Ones, that with ease and with power, you can live lives of plenty in happiness, peace, and prosperity, when you change your hearts and give of your gifts to one another. Know, indeed, that the greed of man has caused you pain for eons, for it has allowed you to rob and pillage the wealth of others in the name of civilization.

For with thoughts, and dreams, and schemes of taking from the weak, you have pillaged the Earth and left your brothers in great need, starving in the corners of the Earth. Be ye mindful, Dear Ones, and remember you are, indeed, your "brother's keeper." Know indeed, the love of God teaches that you should care for the weak, and give aid and support to those in need. Be ye not selfish and say, "All is mine for I have earned it," but know, indeed, all have earned the grace, love, and blessings of God. Be you not God and say, "I will decide who should live or die." For this is not your way, this is not your charge upon the Earth. For indeed, your way is to learn, to share, to be love, and to show love to your brethren upon the Earth. Do these things, Dear Ones, and live. Do these things and know true peace, love, and blessings; for in showing these things, you show God upon the Earth. For these are the things of God. Know, Dear Ones, that when you open your hearts to your brethren, you inherit the true peace, love, and joy of God, for you see and taste the love of God, given to thee in the eyes of your brethren.

Know your blessings will overflow, and your lives will be full of happiness. For in this way, you taste the true joy of God. When you hoard and think selfishly only of self, you see and taste not the true love and joy of God. For in giving, you truly receive, and in showing love, you truly can be loved. Know, Dear Ones, that the love of God is thine without asking, and you are given all you need without charge from your Mother Father God.

Why, then, do you take these gifts freely given, and exact a charge upon them from your brethren? Know this is not the way of God, or how the love of God is shown to mankind upon the Earth. That the strong of heart or mind takes from the weak until he has naught, is not the way of God. Know that the ways of God are sharing, caring, loving, and being that example of goodness upon the Earth. Be a light upon the Earth, Dear Ones, and care for your brothers and sisters, and know happiness, peace, and love all the days of your lives. For it benefits thee not to hoard and to have all you would desire, when your brethren lie desolate and desperate in the streets. Be that light that you were meant to be, and share the wealth of the Earth and the wealth of your heart with all… and come to know, and be, the true peace, love, and joy of God upon the Earth. Be the shining examples of God upon the Earth, and live selflessly instead of selfishly upon the Earth.

Remember you are all a part of God, and know the true bliss of God when you join with your brothers, and share in the great bounty of God in your heart, and through your acts of love for your brothers.

Know, Dear Ones, that in this way you come to know true happiness, peace, love, and joy upon the Earth. For this is the way of God. This is the way of love. This is the way of God upon the Earth. Know always when you show love, you show God walking upon the earth. Be the LOVE of God upon the Earth, Dear Ones, and know true contentment. For your mission upon the Earth is to show love and caring for your brethren, not to show selfishness, greed, and avarice. For this is not the way of God. Be at peace and know all will continue to flow in abundance, when you can know and live these truths each day, and be the messengers of God upon the Earth.

Let all know that you are God, by your acts of love, and caring, and sharing, with your brothers and sisters: for you are ONE. Even as you share with your own family, remember and know you share with the family of God, for you are indeed ONE, all a part of God. Do this and know true bliss, happiness, joy, and peace, Dear Ones. Adieu in the love, peace, and abundance of God.

Adieu

26TH JULY 2012

Know, Dear One, that the love of God for man has always been available for the Sons of Men. For from ancient times, when man first became aware of the divinity within himself, he has always looked to the heavens to find his rescue, not realizing it was already living within his heart. Know, Dear One, that the Brotherhood of Light has been upon the Earth in many forms, taking on those roles that would help to enlighten the Sons of Men and teach them of the great love of God for mankind. For, indeed, that man has never fully comprehended the magnitude of the love of God for him is known.

For in its simplicity, man has never been able to comprehend that he could be loved and adored by God. Thus, man has always been content to see himself as a lowly worthless creature who could never willingly and easily walk into the very grace of God. For it is easier to consider the self as a lowly creature, rather than an exalted Son of the Most High God. For in truth, man sees himself as a sinful and wanton child. He sees not himself as in any way connected to that which is God, in the most tender of ways. For indeed, it is with ease that he has accepted, in many instances, that he is a worthless wretch. For indeed, there are many references upon the Earth that refer to the very nature of man as a sinner needing to be forgiven of God, for all the wrongful things he has done.

Know, Dear One, that the love which is God knows not this human who is described thus; for in truth, since the Sons of Men are held and nurtured in the very heart and soul of God, how can he ever be considered as a lowly abject creature to be forgotten and shunned? Know indeed, Dear One, that the love, which is God, knows not these words used to describe the Children of Men, for they do not share or reflect the thoughts or ideas of love, which is God. Thus, Dear Ones, we say blessed be the Sons of Men who, in their ignorance and forgetfulness, can still find their way to return to God. Know indeed, Dear One, that the love, which is Mother Father God, will always be available to love and surround thee, that you might never know lack or want, Dear One. For the nature of Mother Father God, being one of love, is ever willing to love, uphold, and support thee, that you might know only love, peace, happiness, and joy, Dear One. Be you ever happy to know that you are no sinner running from your Mother Father God, but a loved and adored child of God who is always loved and cradled in the arms of God. Be ye aware, Dear One, that the love and light of God will ever be around thee to uphold, comfort, and defend thee, that you might always know the love, peace, joy, and hope of God, for this is your rescue, Dear One.

You will want for nothing all the days of your lives, and you will forever know of the deep and abiding love which is God. Know, Dear One, that the love and beingness will ever be your home, for it will come to thee to be beside thee when necessary, and to carry you when your feet would falter and grow weary. Know that never are you separated from God, from his love or benevolence, because this is the only way of God: for such is the way, the hope, life, love, and the enduring kingdom, which dwells within thee. Know, indeed, that all is provided for thee, for this is the way of the love of God. Know indeed, Dear One, that the heart of God ever flows within the physical body, and thus you may find your rescue and your joy.

Know, indeed, that the love and light of God will encircle thee and bring you naught but sweet peace, and know, indeed, that the 'love of God is the hay-ride of the journey'[154].... But be mindful always that 'there are many ways to skin a cat,' for indeed all matters, and there are numerous ways to accomplish each task upon the Earth.

Know, Dear Ones, that the days are fast upon thee, that all might begin to see and know of your wonder and awe as children of a loving, and not an angry God. Know indeed, Dear Ones, that ye have much to do and to accomplish, that ye might willingly come to know the bounty of God. Know indeed, Dear One that the love of God, like the road, is thine to travel upon, if such is your desire. For indeed, you may choose which way you will go. For all is designed for us to allow your light to shine forth, that you might know of its greatest accomplishment. Know indeed, that all is indeed well for and within you, Dear One: For the love of God will find its way to you if you begin the search. For like the magnet to the post, it must, by all the laws.

Know, Dear One that the task of the Sons of Men will ever continue to be the source of light on whoever is close to his heart, for indeed that he sees not all of his own works, should be condemned. Let not

---

154   Most rewarding part: most enjoyable

your brethren give advice on the nature and impact upon the Sons of Men, for indeed that God is Lord of all is known throughout the Universe, and as such, he is ever there to love and guide those things which are not yet ready to go out into the world; to come to know all that is God which is in the firmament of possibilities, Dear One. Be ever alert and happy to know that God will forever be your parent, and your shield, and defender, that you might always know love and peace. Be you alert, and know, Dear One, that Mother Father God ever craves your attention, that you might know self and God once more, as you knew them in former times, so long ago. Know, Dear One, all is well, and the golden boughs of Mother Father God's arms will bow down to cradle and defend thee, that you might always know only God's peace, grace, and his love. Let the Blessed of the Lord say, and so it is.

For the love, which is God, is never removed from the Sons of Men, for God in his benevolence could never desert his sons and daughters, that they might find themselves alone and desolate upon the Earth. Know indeed, Dear One, that the love, which is God, will flow forever and remain forever with the Sons of Men. For in truth, the children would have nowhere to go but to wander aimlessly upon the Earth. Know, Dear One, that the love, which is God, is forever tied to the Sons of Men, that they might forever know the peace, love, and joy of God in their hearts: For to live without God is to live in desolation and fear. It is to know want and lack in your lives, Dear Ones. Know that you are children of Mother Father God; thus, you will always be held, and nourished, and nurtured in the arms of your loving parent, Mother Father God, that you might forever know love, peace, happiness, and the joys of God.

Be at peace, Dear Ones, and know that God is in his heaven, and all will, indeed, always be right with the world. Know that all will indeed be well for thee, Dear One. And so it is! Amen and Amen.

Adieu

CHAPTER 5

THE LOVE OF GOD WILL CARRY YOU HOME

The love of God will be there always to keep you strong, and to help thee to get home to the bosom of God's love. For it will be the guide, the shield, the protector, and the defender for you. It will be all that you require it to be when you require it. Know that it is never taken from you. It is never withheld, it is always there, always available to mankind. You must make the decision whether to utilize it or to steer your course in life alone.

5TH MAY 2011

Welcome, child of God. Welcome, indeed, for much are the words this day. We hail thy presence, and thank thee with many praises for all that has transpired... and will continue to be so. Look on and know that the great provider of the Universe, God the Father, doth lead and watch over all his children. Know, indeed, that the Sons of Men are the heart of the Father God; loved and adored by all in the Universe for the great works they perform. Lo, we say thank you, bold child of the Most High God, for your great willingness to serve in this most wonderful of ways. Know that the Lord of Hosts hails thee and thy request to serve mankind in this most marvelous of ways. Look on and know, Sweet One that the days are swiftly upon us when man must choose his path, for indeed, the days of change make it necessary for all to make the choice, and to move on and know that the practices of old can no longer be utilized.

For lo, there comes a day and time when man must make a great change in the ways of his life, or know that he can no longer sustain the life he has lived. "For behold, I will put a new song in your heart and cause a great peace to descend upon thee." Even so does the Lord of Hosts call his children to do that which will bring joy instead of pain. Bring happiness, instead of sadness and pain. Look on and know that the days of fear are erased from the hearts of men, and a new song is all that is heard, or is written in the hearts of men.

Know, Sweet One, we say indeed, much are the trials that do abound, but those who live in the light of God's love have no fear, no regret, and only joy in the happiness and love of God, which is found in their hearts. Look on and know that the Children of Men are free to choose whither they will go. For the four corners of the Earth are open to man, and he can yet choose where he will go and what he will do. Know, Sweet One, that he makes his choices, and then must live with that which he has chosen, until he decides to make more choices. Know, Sweet One, that the days of love and light upon the Earth are upon us, for mankind must know from whence he has come and know the great love of God for the Sons and Daughters of Mankind. Look on and know that God is in his heaven, and all is right with the world.

For truly, the Angels above, and here below, are much happy to see the great changes that begin to transpire for the Sons and Daughters of Mankind. Hail, Little One, we say hail, indeed, for such is the way and love of God. Look on and know that the light of God continues to shine on mankind, and begs him to open his heart to see, and know, and remember his true self. For such is his calling: the one and only true great calling and desire of man, to find his way back to God. Look on and know, brave Warrior Princess, that the light and love of God are the Sons and Daughters of Mankind. Make no mistake to think that God does not worry, if such we can call it, for the loss of one soul here on Earth, but know, indeed, that every soul is precious, and so he mourns the loss of each and every child who fails to remember his way back to God. Know, indeed, all is not lost, for the desire of man to return to his source will help to correct this great tragedy, if such we can call it, and return man back to the light and happiness he craves in the heart of God the Father. Look on and know, Sweet One, that the love of God that is so freely given to all alike, can help to bring man back to the true nature of his beingness, and allow him to return to his true source, to God the Father.

Look on and know, O Sons and Daughters of Mankind, that the days of strife must end upon the Earth, for man must return to peace in his heart, and to the knowing that love is all there truly is... and to the place of love for all mankind. For the way back to God is to love all thy brethren, for such ye are all brothers and sisters, O wonderful children of Earth. Know, indeed, we hail thee, and the works thou hast performed, but know, indeed, that the trials brought about by thy demands and through the very desires of your heart must now look to love and protection for all mankind.

For this is the way back to God. For God is LOVE. That is all that is required for man to remember. No vengeance, no retribution, no hate, no punishment... just LOVE, at its purest and best. **"Behold, I will put a new song in the hearts of men, and bring joy and happiness to the sons and daughters of humanity," says the Lord**. Look on and know that God is in his heaven, and all is right with the world. Let not fear come nigh thee, O Children of Men. Remember your birthright and forget not that ye are born of God, created of love, for love, in love.

No sin is ever part of thee, for SIN does not enter where God is, and God is within each and every being upon the Earth. All that is required is the memory of who and what you are, O ye magnificent beings of light. Remember thy heritage. Know thy lineage and return to the love of God, so freely given to all upon the Earth. Know that no cost is exacted. No fee is paid. It is freely given of all. All that is required is that man remembers his majesty and returns to God. Know thyself, O Sons and Daughters of the Earth. Remember who you are, look up and know ye are the Sons and Daughters of God. Look up and know that you are light, you are spirit, you are love. Remember your true self, and cast off the veil of forgetfulness which keeps thee bound in chains. Loosen the chains that bind thee to the darkness of forgetfulness, and the sin of hate and cruelty to your fellow man.

Remember you are brothers and sisters, and return to your true selves. Return, O Sons and Daughters of God. Let all know that you have found your way back to the source— Mother Father God— by the ways that you live in the world. Let love lead your way, and see the great peace and happiness that will descend upon you. Look on and know that you are divine Sons and Daughters of God. Cast not thy face to the dust and forget your birthright. Look on and know ye are all the blessed of God. No one is above the other, for all are one in God: All of equal value, all are precious in God.

All things are precious to God where mankind is concerned. Look on and know that the love of God is the great equalizer of mankind. Know that your souls are part of God, and must return to God when it leaves the physical incarnation upon the Earth. Remember, you are SPIRIT, you are eternal. You are light; you are love, born of God. Look up and know ye are Children of God and are the chosen. **All are chosen. No group, or sect, or color, are not of God. All are one in God, for God is the God of all.** Let your light shine, children, and know your true nature is to love. Return, O return to God, and the love of your beingness, and know true happiness while here on Earth.

THE LOVE OF GOD WILL CARRY YOU HOME

Wait not for the kingdom of God to come outside of thee, but know that it lives within thee, for ye are the Children of God, made from love and light, Eternal Spirit, one with the nature and love of God.

Fear not, and speak not of blasphemy, but know that God the Father is the one God of all mankind, called by many names and worshiped in many ways. Look on and know ye are the blessed. Ye are loved. When you forget your connection to God and to each other, we see pain upon the Earth.

Remember your love of each other, for ye are brothers and sisters born of the same parent: God. Look on and know, O Children of Men, that the love of God is that great gift you have been seeking for eons, only to learn that you have had it all along. Look no further for God outside of thee. Know he has always been within thee, throughout the ages. He is a part of you, buried in your innermost soul; part of the very beingness of you.

Look no more for God outside thee, but know he dwells within you, and that you are the most precious and wonderful child of the Most High God. Remember who you are and find true happiness... for love is all there is.

It's the only thing that is eternal. It is the creative fabric of the human, so return to who you are and know true happiness, O children. Let the blessed of the Earth say Amen, and so it is! Peace be upon you, child. We will leave thee now and return again.

Adieu Sweet One

7ᵗʰ May 2011

Behold the city of God, which stands on a hill and cannot be hid. Know, indeed, Little One, that much is there of God that, in truth, cannot be hid, for the love of God is so powerful and wonderful that it cannot be hidden. For the Lord of Hosts cannot, of himself, control or hide his love for mankind. Know, indeed, that the love is so powerful and awe-inspiring that it can never be hidden. This love is known and seen across the Universe, for such is its nature. All who know of this wonderful place called Earth can say of its inhabitants how much they are loved of God, for indeed it is so, Dear Ones. A love so wonderful that it causes one to bow down and worship at the feet of whomever one sees. Know, indeed, this love causes the receiver to know perfect peace, perfect joy, and perfect love. For such is its very nature, that the recipient cannot, of self, do anything but bow down in homage, and love, and grace, and be eternally happy.

Why, then, do we say that man is not able to do this? The truth, Dear Ones, is that man, of self, cannot remember or even recognize what has been given to him. Lo, he hides in the shadows and sits like one lost and alone, for he knows not the nature of the gift that is there available to him, for surely he would grasp it with open hands. Yet, this is not seen, for man is ignorant of the fact that the love is so powerful. He knows not that he has this gift and goes in search of trivial and mundane things to appease him, and to bring him joy. Try as he might, he searches for satisfaction only to find that there is nothing that can give him that most sacred of all truths and joy.

For, indeed, nothing that man can conjure can bring him the very thing he seeks most of all. The only thing capable of bringing him the eternal peace within himself is the love of God. For, indeed, from inception, man was built, if such we can say, to house and to recognize that eternal peace and joy can be attained by the love of God. Here on Earth, when the distractions of the world consume him, he forgets all, and is lost like a child who has lost his way home. He knows there is a place where love awaits, but he knows not of the address or, indeed, what or who it is he seeks. So, in vain, he stumbles on and on, looking and searching, for he knows not what.

In vain he searches, for he has forgotten why he began the search or how to find that most precious thing he seeks. Look on and know that man is desperate to find his heart, for such is the nature of that which is sought. He is desperate for it, but doesn't know it is already there, inside himself. So, he wanders on and on, ever searching for the elusive, precious jewel that will make him happy. Open your eyes, O Daughters and Sons of Mankind, and know you have that which you seek buried inside you. It is not lost, but simply needs to be remembered. The joy, the peace, and the happiness, are all there inside you. Look not outside thyself, but instead go deep within and find the jewel that is waiting to be discovered. Know that the discovery will set you free, and your life will change, for such is its power and might to remove mountains of pain, fear, and doubt. It can heal all wounds and help mankind to reach that most gracious and wonderful pinnacle of development.

Open your hearts and allow the love to flow, and see the magnificent and marvelous results that will benefit you, O Sons and Daughters of Mankind. For the love of God is all there is, and is like the medicine to a sick and dying man. Know it can heal you and make you well again. Well enough to taste the love and peace that is possible for the soul, and to give thee the love, and peace, and contentment, that will allow you to become your true selves: Remember the majesty of your true selves; your true power and your true joys that can be there for thee.

Open your hearts, and see and know your joy awaits and is available when you want to hold it. Open your eyes, and open your hands. See and taste the true peace that can be yours, O sons and daughters. Know, indeed, that all these treasures await, if only you will grasp that it is buried already within you. For you are the heirs of God. You are his children, made from God and given the keys to the kingdom, given access to the true and most powerful of all things, the love of God. For its power is outside of the grasp of man, and its scope is outside of the comprehension of man. Let yourselves be open to all that is within you. Let go of the mundane, and the worthless whims of fancy, and instead turn to this most valuable and wonderful of all things, and become your true selves. For this is the light that will heal you, and make you whole. It will bring you peace and joy, and eternal happiness.

It is all you really ever need in order to bring peace and joy to your soul. Accept it, O Sons and Daughters of Mankind, and see your glory. See your life change as you become the magnificent creatures you are destined to be. Be your true and wonderful selves and accept your birthright, for such it is. That most wonderful and truly blessed of all gifts that comes from your Mother Father God. Take it and see how you thrive, see how you grow. Open to the love, and see the wonders that cannot even be imagined. For such is its power to create that Shangri-La of all existences, right here on Earth. Like a small pea or grain of mustard seed, you will see how it can grow and blossom to be the greatest of all gifts, and can endow the owner with power, happiness, and joy beyond belief.

It will give thee that power to see and know how truly you are loved, how special and wonderful you are, and how much God cares for and wants thee to be at peace each day. Be you at peace when you receive it, for such is its nature to bring peace to your soul. Open yourself to remember the seed is inside of thee. Let it flourish and grow. Let it become that which it was meant to be, and know you will know no fear, no hate, no want, no hardship... for with it comes the wisdom to know you already possess these most desired of all things. Open your hearts, and know all you need is already within you, if you can but remember that it was given to thee by your Mother Father God.

Let your seed of love grow, and see the power and the happiness that can be yours. Let your heart soar with happiness. Know joy, know peace, and know contentment: for this is your heritage. End the searching that has haunted you. End the seeking for that most elusive of all things. End the wanting and the waiting. Look within, O children, and find that which you have always had: the love and the bounty of God, which has always been within you. Grasp it and see the light. Grasp it and know you are the chosen of God.

Grasp it and become your magnificent selves. Grasp it and know true peace, true happiness, and true joy. This is your birthright; grasp it and know the love and peace of God with all that you possess.

You are divine, you are loved, and you are the heirs to the kingdom. Take hold of your crown and place it upon your heads, for this is your mighty jewel. It is your treasure; wear it with pride and see all that will be there for thee. Be the peace, be the joy, be the love that you were meant to be. Cast away those things that serve thee not. Let them loose and find your peace, find your joy, and return to the love of your Mother Father God. Only in this way can you ever be happy, for this is the wellspring of your being. You are the Children of God. Mask not yourself in fear, doubt, and worry, but open yourself to the love, peace, and joy of God. For this is your destiny... this is your joy, this is your only path to peace.

Adieu, Sweet Sister, we leave thee now. May God's peace continue in your heart as you grow in the light of his love and grace. Blessings upon thee.

Adieu

9ᵗʰ MAY 2011

THE CITY OF GOD[155]

Welcome, Sister Sweet. Welcome, indeed, for we are much happy indeed to be here with thee. We say, indeed, much is the news this day, for indeed, many are we, and much do we have to share with thee, Sweet Princess of Light. For, indeed, the City of God does receive all the Children of Men. This is the love of God, and indeed we see and know that those who come to enter the City of God's love are never in need of anything, Dear One. Know, indeed, that the love of God carries and protects the Sons and Daughters of Mankind to the very heart of God. Know, indeed, that the heart of God is figurative language, for indeed, God does not possess a heart, such as you know of it, but know, indeed, that it goes to the core of the very essence of that which is God: That essence being the love and wonder of God.

For, indeed, we see and know that this most magnificent of all places is that very nature of God. For God is the essence of love, and so in going to the City of God, man is simply returning to that which he is, the love, and joy, and heart of the beingness of God. Know

---

[155] Awareness of the bountiful love of God: The beingness of God: The essence from which man is crafted and made (is the love of God)

indeed, Little One, that the City of God is that thing which brings man peace; for here, he can bask in the joy and essence of his own being, that which he truly is, the love essence of God.

Know, indeed, that the City of God is that most coveted of places, in that it is the awareness of the bountiful love of God. It is the very beingness of God: The essence from which man is crafted and made. That part of God which flows into the heart or essence of man. We know that the place of man in the kingdom of God, if such we may refer to it, is not easily understood, but know, indeed, that the City of God is, indeed, the love of God at its simplest form. For it is this that is the very source of the inception and central spark of man. It is the atom, which is the seed at the core of man. Without this love, man cannot be delivered to the knowing of the love of God.

For man must know and remember that he possesses this love in order for him to move on and claim his birthright. So thus, we say, that the seed or atom is that first building block, which allows man to remember his heritage and to eventually claim his birthright... and become who he is meant to be.

Know, O children, that the love of God is like that rose, which begins in such a tiny bud, but yet grows to open into that most beautiful of all flowers. For from its tiny path, it unfolds to spread forth and to open and display itself, in all its glory. (Imagine a flower opening.) Thus, we know that the love of God is like this rose that opens and unfolds, to be revealed into something so wonderful to and for the Children of Men. Know indeed, Little One, this love, once it is allowed to blossom and open, can be the most powerful source of light for the human soul. For with it mountains can be climbed, and the Children of God can do all things. For it brings them light and life itself, which can allow mankind to be that part of his true self, which God intended him to be.

Know, indeed, the memory of the love of God is the greatest joy for man, for it will allow him to open in the sunshine of God's love... and to bloom and to flourish, as man is able to bask in the joy, happiness, and peace of the love of God.

Know indeed, Little One, that the Children of Men who go to the City of God are simply returning to or finding that which was buried deep within them for so many eons. Know indeed, this love, when remembered, allows man to do and be all that he was destined to be: The miracle of God. For with the opening of the flower, comes the opening of the awareness or memory of the gift that is available to mankind each and every day. Without payment, without any price at all, the return to the nature of his beingness. This is the love of God. This is the joy of God, this is the wonder of God; for so is the way of God, and such is the joy and love of God. The seed and the bud that is within man, when it begins to grow and flourish, is that most precious of all gifts, O sons and daughters. For ye are the heirs to the kingdom, and the kingdom is the city, and the city is the love of God.

Know ye that the City of God, then, is the love of God. So all of mankind is forever welcomed into the City of God, and is ever to be returned to the City of God. For so is his nature to return to the source of his being. When man remembers that he knows the way to the City of God, he is remembering that he knows that he has the love of God within him and can return to that peace that lies deep within him.

Let us all go to the City, O Sons and Daughters of Mankind. Return to the City of God, for such is your beingness. Such is your nature, it is your home, your castle, your palace; your place of abode, for this is where you find the solace, the comfort, and the peace of God. It is all part of the love of God. The recognition of that peace, joy, and love, is the remembrance of the love of God.

It is (**like**) being at or outside the gates of the city, standing on a high place and seeing all that is within the city. For now, the Sons and Daughters of Mankind can survey the city and remember the splendor, and all the wonderful things that are possible in the City of God. Thus, the love of God and the City of God are one and the same. It is the essence of God, and the very essence of that which is part of man. For the love of God is within man, and man was created from this essence. Thus, when it is written, "Know your magnificence, remember your heritage, know who you are," this is a call to remember the magnificence of that city. For when standing in this high place, man can see all that is available within the city.

Claim your heritage, O Sons and Daughters of Mankind! Remember your birthright, and return to the City of God, for therein lies your peace, your joy, your happiness and your bliss. Return to the memory of the City of God, and understand that your nature is one of love. Forget your ways, which are not of love. Cast them off, and return to the City of God, for from this will come your refuge and your strength, your joy and your hope, and your peace. For you are made from the very essence of the brilliance of this city. For this city cannot be hidden. It must be seen from afar, and will shine like the diamond that it is within the hearts of men. For it is the true source of man. It is the very essence of man. So how and why do you hide yourself? Why do you fail to remember who you are? Shine on, O Sons and Daughters of Mankind; shine on like a wonderful city on a hill. You are the brilliance of God, and you possess the most precious gift that God can give: The love of God.

For you are the Children of God, given this gift without cost. It is freely given and was freely accepted. Now you have forgotten your place; forgotten your gift, and are wandering like lost sheep in the desert of despair, calling for and searching for that which you already possess.

Open your hearts, O Sons and Daughters of Mankind, and remember your gift. Remember who you are and return to the City of God. It is ever waiting for your return, for your memory to return.

Claim your heritage simply by remembering who you are. You are the heirs to the kingdom. You possess the keys to the gates of the city. Simply put in the key, and see how the gates will swing wide open to reveal all the glorious treasures that are waiting within the walls for thee. Know, indeed, the keys are in your hands, and in your heart. When you open your heart to God, you open your hands to receive the keys. All is waiting for you. Simply take the key, and open the gate to reveal the splendor and the magnificent gifts that are waiting inside the city for thee. You are the Sons and Daughters of God; who else can be given the keys, if not thee? Let your heart be open, let your hands grasp this key. Open the gate and enter the city. Come into your magnificence! Come into your beingness, and remember your birthright. This is your day, O Sons and Daughters of Mankind. Heed the call to remember, and so come into the City of God. For it is not, and cannot remain hidden from you. It is there within you, so open your heart and let the memory of the love of God flow through you.

You are the Children of God, blessed with this gift since the dawn of time. Use it to be who you are. Open your hearts and take hold of the keys of life and become your true selves. You are the magnificent heirs of God. Let your light shine. Let your peace flow from you; let your glory and magnificence become evident. Be who you are. Be the light you are. You are in the City of God, so bask in the light of the city. Take hold of the keys with both hands and remember your nature. Remember your source, remember your God, and remember the love you possess. You are in the City. Open your eyes, and know that the search is over. The long and difficult journey can come to an end, for you have traveled so far only to find you need not have struggled for so long… for the keys to the love of God.

The City of God has been in your pocket all along the way. The journey was fraught with needless pain and suffering, O Sons and Daughters of Mankind. You could have been spared this arduous journey and all its pain by opening your hands and looking within your pocket to find the keys. Search no longer, but know your journey can end, for you have the keys to the City and you can rest in the eternal love of God; the peace of God, the joy of God. The City of God is your refuge, your strength, your shield, your heart, and your soul. You have all that you need. Search no longer, but instead open the gates to find the peace, joy, and happiness you seek, Dear Ones.

Adieu

THE CITY OF GOD

For indeed, the City of God is waiting to receive the Sons and Daughters of Mankind... waiting until all is as it should be, and the sons and daughters of humanity awaken to the fact that the nature of God is one only of LOVE. For this great love is that which binds the physical with the nonphysical, and allows all to exist in that most ideal of ways, so that all who come nigh the city or love of God are enthralled by the vision and cannot avert their gaze. So all is set as it should be, and is prepared to meet the Children of God.

For so is the very reason for its existence. Its reason is to be there for the returning Sons and Daughters of Man, when they return to the fold of God's love. For behold, they awaken and are like sheep lost to the master or the shepherd. For they wander aimlessly to and fro and can find no peace or solace; for they desperately seek the peace and serenity of the comfort of home. Even so, Little Ones, we know that the return to the City of God is not an easy task for man. For in truth, he must have been dependent on the Father but then went astray. Now he is lost and alone, for he cannot find his way back to the arms of God, even though he knows it exists. It is as if the blindness had come upon him, and there is naught to be done but to wait and suffer until the Father comes to personally escort each one home again.

Know, Little One, that the personal invitation has been extended, and all is indeed in readiness for the welcome celebration. The chief guest has yet to arrive, even though myriad of others arrive; he is nowhere in sight and thus comes the despair of the host. But without the guest, how can the celebration begin? In truth, we see that they cannot begin without the guest's arrival. Thus we wait and wait in endless pain, looking for the arrival of the most cherished of all guests: the Children of Men. Why tarry ye here, O Sons, when all is in readiness? Why sit and cause thyself pain, O Daughters of Zion, when the jubilation is at hand? Know that you are the most honored of all guests, and it is only with thee that the celebration can begin, for all the preparations have been concluded and now the celebrations are able to proceed with flawless precision.

Know that the day and the hour is upon us, for man to be returned to the bosom of God, so that the party can begin. Know that the nature says no celebrations may begin unless the most beloved children of the Father are present. Thus we say, awake O Sons and Daughters of Zion, and see all that will come to pass. For such is the nature of the day and the magic of the hour, that we must begin the celebration so that all may see the great love of God demonstrated for his children.

Look on and know that this love will lead man to salvation, for such it is meant to do. Man must come willingly to the feast, for such is the nature of the requirement. He must, of self, know that each thing is set to happen at a certain date and time, and cannot be delayed or postponed for any reason. The hour is upon us and thus the celebration begins, and the party goes into the magical stages of celebration. For only in this way can we hope to celebrate the nature, love, and beingness of God. For man must enter the City freely if he is to truly taste and experience the majesty and magnificence of God.

His power, love, and might will become evident, and man will begin to grow in the event of the demise of participation. For Mother Father God is the creator of all and the master of all things. It is he who aligns the stars and allows man to see the many wonders of God. Without this access to the vast and glorious City of God, man would be like the orphaned blind child at a feast, unable to see with any true sight. Instead, he must imagine the splendor, love, and joy attributed to this great event, for it cannot be seen with his blind sight and thus is lost to man forever. For behold, the Sons and Daughters of Mankind must know and remember their lineage, and only then can they hope to return to the City of God. For the pathway to the city is hidden in the hearts of men. The journey, therefore, begins or ends based on the knowledge of the Sons and Daughters of Man.

Remembering your heritage is the way back. This truth can and will allow man to find his way to the City of God. For surely, without this knowledge, he remains lost upon the Earth, unable to decide or know his reason for being. He is alone, he feels, and is in true despair, for he feels abandoned by God. O awake, ye Sons and Daughters of Mankind, and remember your heritage, for you are not alone. You are always cradled in the love of God. You are always adored and loved by God. How else can you be? For you are the most beloved of God, that wonderful, most special child of God. Never, never, are you alone. Never, never, are you abandoned. Only in your mind and heart do you feel abandoned. Know that the love of God is thine and is ever with thee. You are always held in the love of God. Feel this love. Know this love and remember you are part of God... ever connected, ever living in the heart and soul of God. Open your hearts and remember this truth, for you are the beloved, you are the child; you are the prodigal son returned to the table of his father, given the best coat and the very best of everything the Father God has in store. You are the inheritor of the treasures of the Father. You are the light of his love, and you have all the gifts you will ever need, already provided by your Mother Father God. Know that nothing can take away these gifts, save you yourself, and your own failure to remember and know that you have them already. Know, Dear Ones, how precious you are. Know how much you are loved and held in highest esteem, for you are the Sons and Daughters of God. All are wonderful, all are special, all are loved.

Know your heritage, remember your destiny, and return to the path of God. Find yourselves; remember your reason for being upon the Earth. You are here to be love and to love... to know and to share the bonds of brotherhood, and to be the shining lights you are. You are not the sum of all the hate and the sum of all fears, for you are a powerful being, capable of giving and sharing unconditional love to all. This is your birthright, this is your destiny... so claim it and walk into the light. Claim it and walk upright with pride as you take your rightful place. You are the beloved of God. You are the Children of God. You are the beloved of God... you are the most valued of God. Know thyself and become who you were meant to be. Move out of the dust, out of the cloud of forgetfulness, and return to your true selves.

Look not at the things of this world and say "this defines me," for these are but physical things which will all fall away. For truly, all that matters is the love. This is all that lasts; this is all that can transcend the physical. All else is like grass upon the Earth that can be trampled and then is no more. All is vanity. All is nothingness, and will fall away. Only the love of God and the love for each other will last. Remember your truths, Dear Ones, and know this: kindness, love, and peace will be the way to God's heart.

Leave behind the thoughts of cruelty, hate, division, and separateness. All mankind are brothers: remember this truth. Love your brethren and see how wonderful your lives can and will be.

Think of and take care of your brethren, even when he cannot think of and take care of self. Extend a hand of love and show the blessings of God's love. This is your charge; this has always been your charge upon the Earth. The veil of forgetfulness has caused you to forget these truths and to live lives of separation, fear, and hate. Jealousy and envy has been your friend, when they should have been your enemy.

Take not fear into your bosom, but instead, cleave[156] love to your breast and know the true peace of God. For to give and share the love of God is that most sacred of all truths and gifts. Give what you have been freely given. Know that you are the magnificent Sons and Daughters of God, given every gift to be happy. Remember your truths. Remember your gifts, and share them gladly and willingly with your brethren. Be the peace. Be the love. Be the joy in this world, and see and feel the great peace of God descend upon your hearts. Know that there is no need to struggle and fight, for all that you need is freely given and is attainable within you. All is as it was meant to be, O Children of Men. Open your hearts! Let the light of God shine forth from you. Let the love of God shine in and through you, to all you meet. Be the peace, be the joy, be the love of God upon

---

[156] Attach physically

the Earth. Know that your very survival depends on this. Know that you have this great capacity within you, and you can unleash it at any time. Be the joy and the love that you are. Be the soul and life of God upon the Earth. Share your joys, your peace, and your love with those you meet, and see the true wonder of this age. For the time has come for the great change, and man must be able to move forward.

For the soul of man is like a man wandering in the desert in search of water. He is thirsty for the love of God, thirsty for the peace of God. Knowing not that he has the water at his arm's length, he continues to wander, dying of thirst… when all the time, the water was available. Hold out your hands, O Sons and Daughters of Mankind! Take the water of life into your physical bodies and live. Take the water and become the wonderful Children of God that you are. Take the water and be that which you are destined to be. Be the love and the peace of God. For you have that which you continually search for already.

Look no further outside thyself to find the happiness you desire so desperately. Know it is within you. It is there, waiting to be unleashed. Open your heart and know that you have the love you CRAVE; you have the PEACE, and the JOY you long for. It is already there within you. Unleash it and feel the eternal peace of God. Know the eternal joy of God, and be then in heaven, here on Earth. This joy can be yours, so take it and live. Take it and find the peace, love, and joy you have craved for eons. Know it is thine, take and be filled.

Open your hearts and remember you have the keys to the peace you seek, already given you by God. You are the Children of God, and every gift is given to you freely by God. Take and live an abundant life, for all is thine. Live in love, peace, and sharing in the bounty of God.

There is enough for all in this world. Take not from the weak and helpless. Help to build them up and make them strong. Let not your greed or the need for more, more, more, blind you to your true selves. Remember your birthright, and be the wonderful and most special brethren you can be... for ye are the blessed of God. Ye are the chosen of God. You are the delight of God. Be your true selves. Find the light and love within, and see the change that will then come upon you. For you will be able to see and know, and remember your true beingness, and live.

14ᵀᴴ JUNE 2011

Know, Little Ones, that the love of God knows no bounds and is not a love that teaches control or that seeks its own way. The love of God is there to guide the Sons and Daughters of Man to that greater power within themselves. It is the sail of the boat, and the anchor of the ship... but it does not criticize and it does not judge. For the Sons and Daughters of Mankind will be able to make all desires of their hearts come to fruition, whether they are aware of it or not. For the love of God is the anchor which grounds you, and keeps you focused. It is yet the sail, which uses the winds to help you on your way; pushing you and helping you to move as swiftly as you would go. Know that the love of God is always there, and can be used when you desire.

In most instances, we find that the sail is taken down, and then put back in place when it is needed. Know, Sweet Ones, that you control when it is utilized, for the sail is always there and always available. You must determine if and when you use it, to steer your course in life. For without the sail, there is much toil, and there is much work for the Sons and Daughters of Men... for the boat cannot move without the sail!

Likewise, the wind is the love of God. For like the boat with no sail and no wind, it is doomed to sit and waste away the time. For it is lost in a sea of despair and will sink to the very bottom of the ocean. Let the love of God take you to any destination, Dear Ones. Know it is ever available to mankind. Know that it can help to bring you safely to the shore, across the stormiest of seas. It will help you to navigate all the oceans of despair that life can toss your way. It can help you to find the peace and love you most desire in calm waters, and it can help you to chart unchartered lands when no one else will set sail. Such is the power of the sail: For it can and will save your life, if you use it. For without it, you are lost and deserted, waiting aimlessly; floating without direction, willing to go with the tide, going wherever you are tossed. Look on and know, Sweet Ones, that the love of God is that guide and that protection. It is that solace. It is the peace, the hope, and the joy of man. Without it you are alone, and in despair. But with it, you are renewed and are ready to approach the tumult and the pains of life. For there is always the resounding joy of knowing that you are held, guided, and protected by the Father God, the Most High protector and defender of mankind. Know that this love will help to steer and guide you in the storms of life[157]… to lead you through the perilous seas of life, and to take you safely into the peaceful seas of God's love.

Know, Dear Ones, you have the sail, but you must choose whether to use it, or to steer your course in life alone. Know that the choice is yours, and you only can determine your fate. For the love of God will always remain with you unconditionally at all times. It will guide and protect thee and it will keep thee focused in the storm.

---

[157] Life's challenges

The love of God will always be there for thee, and will always keep thee safe, Dear Ones. Know that you control your boat of life and you determine and chart your course. The love of God will be there always to keep you strong, and to help thee to get home to the bosom of God's love. For it will be the guide, the shield, the protector, and the defender for you. It will be all that you require it to be when you require it. Know that it is never taken from you. It is never withheld, it is always there, always available to mankind. You must make the decision whether to utilize it or to steer your course in life alone.

Know that it is the desire of God to be there for his children, to guide and protect, and love you all your days. Love you unconditionally, and to be always there when needed.

This is the nature of the love of God. This is the way of the love of God. For surely, the love of God is the anchor or the sail... but yet, know these things can be used, or not, as desired by the Sons and Daughters of Mankind. Know, Dear Ones, you must chart your course and you must decide whither you will go. Know that the love and support goes with you always, and will never be taken from you... even when you stray. For the love of God is freely given, and is always there for you, O Children of Men. Turn and see that which is given, and take it and live; live to find your way home. Take it and remember your truths. Take it and know that you are the chosen of God. You are the specially favored. You are the heart of God. Take the love and remember your birthright. Take the love and become the giants you are. Take the love and know that you are the Children of God: loved and guided forever. For this is your birthright, this is your choice, this is your life.

Take this most precious gift, and see how easily you navigate the storms of life. Take this most precious gift, and see, and know your path. See and know your truth, see and know your magnificence. Know, Dear Ones, that you are the captains of your ship, the Masters of your own fate. You have all you need. You have all you will ever need. For your Mother Father God is always with you. Know, Dear Ones, you are precious in his sight, precious and loved, so take the boat, and pull up your sails, and chart your course across any great ocean. Follow your heart, and know that the sails on your boat will bring you safely home. Will bring you to the arms of God, for the sails are the heart and love of God, which will help you get to the heart of God. They are the love, the joy, and the happiness you feel.

This is the love of God, Dear Ones. This is the nature of God. This is the joy of God: to love and protect his children and to bring you safely home. Take it and live, for without it, you die. Without it, you are wandering aimlessly, lost at sea, unable to chart a course, unable to find your way. This is the joy of God to be your sail; to be your anchor and to keep you safe and happy at all times. Remember your gifts, O Sons and Daughters of Men, remember your nature; remember your path, O Sons and Daughters of Men.

Remember and find peace, and know, Dear Ones, that you are never alone. Never lost except by choice, for you always have the love of God to help you find your way. You always have the peace of God to give you direction. Open your eyes and live. Open your eyes, and know that you are the joy, the peace, and the love of God. It is freely given… if you choose to take it, and to live. Unfurl your sails, and let the love take you home; home to the heart of God. Unfurl your sails, and let the winds carry you swiftly across the oceans and through the storms of life. Unfurl your sails, and let the love guide you back to God, for here is your refuge, your strength, and your hope.

Here is your joy, your love, and your peace. Here is your joy, your hope, and your happiness. Unfurl your sails and live, Dear Ones!

This is your choice. Keep them bound, and know not the joys of God. Keep them bound, and forget that you are the chosen. Unfurl your sails and fly over the oceans of life, and live as the happy Children of God you are meant to be.

Open your sails, and sail away in the sunset, knowing all is well, for you are guided by Mother Father God. Unfurl your sails, and become the captain of your ship. Unfurl your sails and live!

This is your charge. This is your only charge; to remember the love of God is given to all mankind: given to every son and daughter. Take the gift and live, or keep your sails tightly bound so you can never see its true glory. Keep it bound and allow yourselves to drift aimlessly on the seas of life. Allow yourselves to be the masters of your destiny, or the victim of the day. Unfurl your sails, and steer a path true and straight, to get you safely back to the arms of God. Be at peace, and know you have this great gift within you. Use it and live. Use it and grow. Use it and know you are the chosen of God, the most beloved children. All his children are there available... ready to call upon him for help, and willing to see and know his love. Know it is with you at all times, never to be taken away.

Know it is the heart of God to give you his kingdom. Be at peace and know that you are loved and guided by God, if you so choose. If not, live a life of forgetfulness and pain. The choices are yours.

THE LOVE OF GOD WILL CARRY YOU HOME

Choose well and live as you wish. Know that God will always be there for you; always available and ever present. He will be there when you need him, for such is the depth of his love for mankind. He will be there when you fail, when you fall, or are lost, and will uplift you on the wings of eagles when you call. This is the nature of the love of God. Claim it and live! Claim it and grow! Claim it and be at peace!

Adieu

THE FOOD OF GOD[158]

Know, Dear Ones, that the magnificent and all-encompassing love of God, will and can be all things to all people… for it can be like the very food from heaven. For like manna from heaven, it can serve to feed those that are hungry and thirsty. Know, Dear Ones, that this food can, indeed, feed and satisfy the soul. For such is the power and strength of the love of God for mankind; that he can feed them all with the essence of his love, joy, and peace, Dear Ones. Know, Sweet Children, that the love, peace, joy, and harmony of God can serve to be the very food of man, given by God to his children. For this food can help to bring man the peace and joy that he so desperately needs.

Know, Dear Ones, that this peace, and love, and harmony, serves as the food of God because it can help to fill the very places in the human heart and soul, that calls out for the love of God. Even so, Dear Ones, the love of God is able to feed every need of mankind, and provide man with all the nurturing and the sustenance he needs. Know, Dear Ones, that the food of God can take this form, and is

---

[158] The Love, peace and joy of God

able to give man all that is needed within his heart. Know that the love of God can and will help to lead man homeward to the arms of God. For in partaking of this food, the heart and nature of man is fed and nourished, and with the feeding, man is able to progress on to the very heights of love, and power, and wonder, and glory.

For so powerful is the food of love that is given by the Mother Father God, that in reality, man can gain all the nourishment that is needed to feed the hungry soul. Thus, Dear Ones, we see and know that the need for the physical food to nourish and to replenish the cells of the body can be diminished when the food of God is provided by spirit: The food of love, the food of service, and of peace. For so precious is this gift, that it meets all the needs of man, and can help to take him even higher when he partakes of the food. Like the ancient text,[159] which speaks of the eating of the fruit of the tree of knowledge, even so does this food help to meet all the spiritual needs of mankind. For so powerful and wonderful are the blessings which come forth from this food, that man is able to replenish his cells, and to generate new ones when he partakes of this food of God. For it is able to help him to grow, and to move on in the kingdom of God's love. For this is the reason for all things upon the Earth, Dear Ones, to allow mankind to advance in the knowledge and love of the Mother Father God. Know, Dear Ones, that the strength that is gained from partaking of this food, is likened to the strength of thousands; for so it is able to lift man into the highest of highs, and to take him beyond the very realms of this world. For so it can change the course of his life, and cause him to strive for only that which is great, and powerful, in the eyes of God. Thus we say, what food can offer such wonderful rewards, but the love

---

[159] The Old Testament Book of Genesis

and promise of God? The very food of the Mother Father God, which in true fashion, can allow mankind to know all of the unknown, and to be all the impossible, and to see the improbable.

For such is the reward of the food of God, when ingested by mankind. It can lift man into the heavens whilst still here on Earth and cause him to be all that he would be.

It will be the very life and love that flows within his breast, for such is the food of God.

Know, Dear Ones, that this food can penetrate the very soul of man, and cause him to be other than he would ever be. For with this food, man can be who and what he chooses, for his heart is strong and he can do all things through God who strengthens him. Know, Dear Ones, that all this and more can be given to man as the life energy of God, when mankind eats of the foods of God, and is nourished and fed. For such is the way of God, to give the Children of Men all that they desire, and all that is needed and more, from the arms of God. Know, Dear Ones, these then are the basic tenets of the rewards that flow from the food basket of God's love. Know, Dear Ones, that this magnificent love is there for all, and can give all the peace, love, joy, and beauty to mankind upon the Earth.

Be at peace and know, Dear Ones, that the light and love of God is the essence of the food of God, for it is this which allows man the great strength to move upon the Earth. For without this food or nectar of God, man will lie dormant like a seed on the forest floor, waiting for the sunshine of God's love to shine down upon him, and give him the life force and energy that is necessary to survive. Know, Dear Ones, that we are much happy to share this knowledge with thee, and to see and know the truly wonderful nature of the power of the love of God for mankind's awakening, whilst still upon the Earth.

The great awakening is upon us, Sweet Ones, and it is this that is stirring within the hearts of men, and causing the disarray upon the Earth at this time. For with the feeding comes the waking and the opening of the conscious streams, which let in the light, and repeats the whole cycle. The more food that is given to the body, the more growth becomes obvious… and the more food the body continues to crave, for it will not and cannot be satisfied with the crumbs from the table, when it needs the heaped plates with all the wonderful nourishment that will ensue. Look on and know, Dear Ones, that this food is the food of life itself, for each and every soul upon the Earth. For it is this which will provide all the nourishment that is needed for mankind upon the Earth. Be of good cheer, Dear Ones, and know that this food will feed all wants and nourish the soul of man, leaving naught to chance and leaving no one hungry, except by choice and free will. For if the spirit wants to be fed, it will gain all that is necessary from and through this great food of God. But, if the desires of the world keep man blinded to his true nature, he will never thirst or hunger for the food of God.

Thus, he leaves the table as though full, and can do nothing, for he has gained nothing about the love, peace, joy, and happiness of mankind. Be at peace and know, Dear Ones, that this food can feed every nerve and cell of the body, and cause thee to expand into consciousness. So be ye at peace, and know that all will be well for and with thee, once you have eaten of this magnificent food from the table of God's love. Be happy ,O Sons and Daughters of Mankind, and know that all your needs are met, and all your desires, and wants, and needs will be fulfilled; for such is the nature of the love of God, and the power of the promise of God's grace. For, indeed, the grace of God is naught but the knowledge of God, which is given to mankind by God the Father himself.

Know, Dear Ones, that such is the love of God for mankind, that he gives mankind this food with which to learn, and grow, and advance in the knowledge and love of God. For such is the nature and the beingness of God, that all these things are made manifest to the Sons of Men, and that they give him (men) the grace, love, and knowledge to be the heirs to the throne of God. For such is the great love of God for mankind, that they are denied nothing by Mother Father God. All their needs are met, and all their desires can be fulfilled, if and when they eat the food from the table of God's love

For it is the food of life, the food of grace, the food of compassion: The food of love, the food of peace, the food of light, and the food of love.

Look on and know, Dear Ones, that such is the food on which the soul of man can be fed daily when you eat at the table of God's love. For the goodness of God is abundant blessings, and is ever available to be poured out upon the souls of mankind, if he but chooses to come to the table, pull up a chair, and eat. Be at peace, O Sons and Daughters of the Earth, and know your needs are met when you can dine at the table of God, and you will be filled ever with the blessings of God, so that your soul wants for nothing, for you are the inheritors of the spirit and grace of God's love. All is at your disposal; come, eat, and be filled with the love, peace, and joy of God. Come, eat, and be filled, so that you may rest in the shade of God's love and want for nothing, Dear Ones. For such is the food of God; such is the grace of God that all needs will be met, and all desires fulfilled. For the food that is eaten at the table of God's love is the food that feeds the heart, the soul, and the spirit of man forever and ever, Dear Ones.

Be at peace and know that the food found at the table of God's love will feed the heart and soul of man forever, and give him the peace, love, and joy he searches for, each and every day. End the search when you eat at the table of God, and know that contentment, peace, love, and harmony will reign in your hearts, O Sons and Daughters of Mankind, and you will be filled with the grace and the great peace of God forever and ever, Dear Ones.

Your invitation has been sent and received. Come to your place at the table, and see and know the great peace of God. For this is your desire; this is your destiny; this is your path… if you will but venture forth and take your rightful place at the table. For you are the honored guest, you are the chosen, the beloved of God, given all the best dishes to taste and eat. Be full, and know that you will want for nothing once you sit at the table of God's love, and partake of his blessings, and his peace, and joy and happiness once more. Return to your Father Mother God, and eat as the honored guest, and know joy, and peace, happiness and love, for you are joyous. You are the peace and happiness of God, and you are the chosen.

Know that your seat is waiting. All you need to do is sit and be satisfied. Be happy and be fulfilled, Dear Ones. This is your birthright, this is your peace, your love, and your happiness, waiting to be eaten so it can nourish your body and give you strength and life.

Adieu

24TH JULY 2011

For unto us is born a child, unto us a son is given; even so was the Son of Man delivered to the sons of Earth to deliver the message of the love of God for mankind, and indeed, was there to preach and to deliver a way of living. But as was known and foretold, the Sons of Men have failed to follow the teachings and instead, has taken to worshiping the messenger. Know, Dear Ones, that the God of your Being, sent the one, our Dear Brother, Jesus, to deliver the message of the hope, love, peace, and joy available to all men through the love of brethren and the joy of God. In fear, the leaders of the world at the time, and in later times, held sway,[160] and used the words of the message to control the Sons of Men. Know, Dear Ones, that the time for truth is upon us, and man must know his true path to God. For only with this knowledge, can the true peace, love, and joy be established upon the Earth.

Know, Dear Ones, that the time for the great change is here, and man will, indeed, know that the love of God will be that great divining rod, which will help to bring man the love, peace, and joy that he so desperately needs. For without this love, this peace, this joy, he lives in turmoil and will

---

160   Have a controlling influence over

wither and die. Know, Dear Ones, the love of God can be that power and source that can pull man back from the brink of destruction and pain. For indeed, it is the pain of separation that brings the pain of the soul of man. For in his searching, he finds no peace, no love, no joy, and in loneliness, he wanders the Earth in search of a purpose and a path in life. Lift your voices and lift up your hearts, O Sons and Daughters of Mankind, and see and know the true peace, the true happiness, and the joys of the Father God. For this is the love that will indeed make thee whole. For, from ancient times, your Father God has loved and adored thee, and has given thee all the tools to make a happy and successful time upon the Earth. But indeed, with the veil of forgetfulness cast upon mankind, man has failed to remember his reason for being upon the Earth, and has been distracted by the things of the flesh… instead of looking for the things of the spirit within himself. For it is truly the spirit which will help to bring man the peace, love, and joy of God, and make him whole.

Know, Sweet Ones, that the peace of God will descend upon mankind, and will cause "The Great Shift"[161] or mankind will perish and die upon the Earth. For eons, man has spent his time in warring and hate, but that must come to an end, and the reign of peace, love, joy, and happiness must descend upon the Earth. For so it is written, that man must know strife, and will then move to that place of love, and happiness, and sharing with his brethren, so that he can advance in his knowledge of God.

Be aware, Dear Ones that God has never, and will never change. For He is the same yesterday, today, and forever. Because the past, present, and future happen in the same instant, so there can be no change. His

---

[161] The changes occurring in the world, ourselves, and the evolution of consciousness leading up to the year 2012

love is eternal and his peace is eternal, if man would but open his heart to see and know these truths. For the love of God is a way of living in the world. It is a way of being, and a way of growing in the world. For it teaches man that all are one and are part of God. So in loving one, we love all, and in so doing, love God the Father and Mother of our being. Know Dear Ones, that this is the way of man, and the only way which will cause him to grow and to change the destiny of mankind.

For to continue on the path, without the knowledge and love of God, is to continue on a path of fear, doubt, and pain… and in a place of wanting and lusting for those external things that can bring no peace to the hearts of men. Know, Dear Ones, that this is, indeed, the path of alienation and fear; so open up your hearts, Dear Ones, and see and know all the wonders of God's grace and love. See and know all the peace of God, for such is the very nature of man's being; that it will change his life of loneliness, and despair, and bring him the great peace that he seeks. Know, Dear Ones, that this is the way to happiness, and know that it cannot be achieved without a change and shift in the ways of man. For his heart must once more radiate the light and love of God, as was so at the inception of mankind… when God's light radiated within the hearts of men. Now, the light is growing dim, as man lets his light fade in the course of the distractions of the day. Know that without a return to the peace, love, and joy of God, there can be no great peace upon the Earth. For man is ever angry and impatient, ever anxious and in pain; so let go of these emotions that fail to serve thee, and return instead to the bosom of God… and see and know all the true joys that live and have their beingness in that peace. For this is the only hope: that mankind will find that which he has sought for so many generations, and once more bask in the peace and love of God. Be at peace, and know all these things are available, Dear Ones, and God will be the shield, comforter, and parent of the Sons of Men, who can help to heal the pain of loss he finds within himself, because he has forgotten his parentage.

Know, Sweet Ones, that this is the way and the truth, and none can, indeed, truly know and understand God without this knowledge and the feeling of the joys of God within himself. Understand, Dear Ones, that your Mother Father God wants nothing more than the happiness of mankind. For with it will come the great peace and joy that mankind needs, if he is to usher in a time of peace… and end all wars and strife upon the Earth. Know, Dear Ones, that this is the way of all happiness. For there can be no lasting truth if man is not aware of these simple truths. Be at peace and know that all is well, when man and God are joined once more on all levels, to bring about the return to the days of love, and cooperation, between and among the Sons of Men. Without this return to love, man will continue to be in pain, and to hurt his brethren, and to know only strife and pain in his heart. Open your hearts, O Sons and Daughters of Mankind, and know that all will be well when mankind can know that God is love, light, peace, joy, and happiness, and that there is a heaven that can exist upon the Earth, when man knows these truths. For with the recognition of these truths, comes the joy of the return. And then peace, and love, will indeed flow unceasing upon the Earth; for mankind will be at peace, and there will be no warring. For there will be brotherhood, love, peace, and joy unceasing upon the Earth. Know that this is the heaven on Earth that must come into the heart of man, if he is to survive upon the Earth.

Adieu

For the Son of Man, in all his glory, is naught but a child of the Most High God. Know, Dear Ones, that the Children of Men are always there upon the Earth to learn and to grow in the knowledge and the love of Mother Father God. Even so, Dear Ones, know, indeed, that the days of learning are much different now than in former times. For indeed, the times of old were full of suspicion, and superstition, and pain, and thus our messages given to mankind were cloaked in much secrecy, lest those in receipt were, indeed, harmed or put to death for the sharing of the news. Know, Dear Ones, that the facts of these times are much changed, and indeed, it is now with great ease that the words can be shared. For the souls of men, once dark and clouded with fear, are now opening to the light and love of God knowledge. For, indeed, that which once was so feared is now known in all its splendor.

Know, Little One, that indeed, much will be the changes that will continue to come upon the Sons of Men. Know, indeed, that with the 'great shift' will come the new and wonderful age of change for mankind. For, indeed, the joys and love of God can now become a wonderful truth for the throngs who sit and wait in pain and in darkness in this time. Know, Little One, that great, indeed, will be the change that will be evident in the heart of man. For the days of selfishness will begin to be no more, and the new dawn of love upon the Earth will arise: Love for self, love for others, love for God, and moreover, love for Mother Earth. For, indeed, the times must change if man is to survive upon the Earth. Know, Dear Ones, that this is the new destiny for mankind. That he will, indeed, take up the cross of responsibility and do that which must be done for his brothers... for this is the way of survival. This is the true way of love, and the true way of joy and peace upon the Earth. For the ways of pain, and anger, and selfishness, cannot continue.

Man must advance if he is to remain upon the Earth. Know, Dear Ones, that the light and love of God must prevail upon the Earth for man to move forward. He can no longer continue on his old path, for thus says the Lord of Hosts, **"I will make a new plan for mankind, and thus, it is written that a new age must be seen upon the Earth, if man is to survive upon these shores."**

Know, Dear Ones, that the times are indeed a-changing, and thus it is written that naught shall harm thee or bring thee pain. For the love of God will be your shield and defense against the storms of life that would strike fear into the hearts of men. Know, Dear Ones, that many, indeed, are the paths to God, but know that all paths end with God, for he is the source of all that is light, goodness, and love.

He is the Father and knower of all things, and the one who, like a parent will never abandon his children. Know, Dear Ones, that the love of God is always available to the Sons of Men, and will never be removed from them, for they are children of the Most High God, who in all his ways has provided for mankind and will continue to provide for him that love which is fathomless: without end and without borders. For this limitless love transcends all else, and will, indeed, never be taken from mankind, for it will be there at the dawn of each day, and even so at the close of each day, forever. For you are the Sons and Daughters of the Most High God, so know, indeed, that this is your charge upon the Earth: to love your brethren as yourself, and to always be there for those who sit in darkness... to help them find the light of God's love.

Know, Dear Ones, that this is the charge of each man: to bring peace, and light, and love upon the Earth, and to share these truths with his brethren. Be not dismayed to think that this is an impossible task, but know, indeed, that this very thing will come to pass upon the Earth, for only in this way can man survive upon the Earth. Let not fear and worry of the how or when come upon thee, Dear Ones, but know that it is coming. Behold, a great light is shining even now in the hearts of men as they begin to awaken to their true potential and move out of the darkness of fear and ignorance. Let not the darkness and separation consume thee, O Children of Men, but know instead that the love of God should be that which would consume thee. For, thus, will man be able to reach his true potential, and know peace, love, and joy, upon the Earth.

For the times are truly changing, and great is the exaltation throughout the Universe, Dear Ones. Know, indeed, that the pain of the separation from God, if such we may call it, must come to an end. For, in truth, man can never be separated from God, for he is an integral part of God Beingness. For he is a part of God, and thus, can never be separated from God, or the love of God. Be you comforted to know, Dear Ones, that there is never a separation from God, even though man, in his forgetfulness, will think there is no God. Know, indeed, that the link between God and man is eternal and can never be severed, for thus man is made, and even so will he always be, a part of God... always to be in his heart and always to possess his love.

For the plight of man, when upon the Earth, may cause him to forget his connection with God, but know that he can never be separated from the love of God. For it is given freely, NEVER removed. Know, Dear Ones, no wrongs can separate thee from the love of God. Only man himself can forget God and choose to live in darkness, but he is never separated and is never lost to God. For when he returns to spirit, he is once more in the bosom and the arms of God. Know, Dear Ones, that thus is the love of God given, and yet never taken away from the Children of Men. Love, therefore, and live in the light and love of God, for this is, indeed, your birthright and your heritage until the end of time, for you are a child of God, loved and adored by God. Look on and know that God is in his heaven, and all is right with the world.

Peace be with you all Dear Sisters and Brothers!

Adieu

For indeed, the love of God is like the very essence of life to man, for it flows from the well-stream of God and gives life to the Children of Men. Know indeed, Dear Ones, that the flowing of this well-stream is that most precious of all gifts, for it enables man to survive upon the Earth, and to be that most wonderful of all beings upon the land. For indeed, without the love of God in the lives of men, we know that there is much anguish and pain, and indeed, the Children of Men run upon the Earth to and fro like wild stallions chasing the wind. For they have no direction, and go where the liking takes them; thus they are without purpose and are lost to the world. For they know not whither they go and why they go there, so that all is chaos and all is without thought. For without God in the lives of men, they are truly lost upon the Earth and wander to and fro. With the love of God in the lives of men, know, indeed, that the Sons of Men are no longer lost, for they can now find their way home.

Know indeed, Dear Ones, that the love of God is like the taming of the wild stallion. For it becomes the very harness upon the animal, which will allow him to be guided and to be shown all the wonders of the kingdom here on Earth. For indeed, without the harness,[162] he runs too swiftly and without purpose. He spends no time taking in his surroundings, for indeed, he sees it not. For in his haste and hurry, all is a blur... all is merged into one and without form. With the love of God, he can walk slowly into the gardens and into the valleys, and can see and taste all the joys of life, which now come into view. Know, Dear Ones, that the love of God allows man to see, with his heart, all that is possible within his life; for indeed, without it, he sees nothing, and runs with the crowd... never knowing where he runs or why. Know, indeed, that thus is the wonder of the power of the love of God, for it allows the Sons of Men to calm their weary souls and to see the great and glorious dawn, and the magnificent sunsets of life. For herein lies the happiness of man, in seeing and tasting the glorious gifts of God. For indeed, Mother Father God has given to mankind all of these most bountiful gifts. Yet man, in his great haste and hurry to drink in the diversions of this world, is yet not able to see or notice and appreciate all of these most wonderful of all joys. For the cares of the world, would take the focus away from the things of God, and man loses his way.

Let not your heart be troubled, but know, indeed, that the Sons of Men must have the harness put upon them if they are to remember who they are... lest they continue to run from place to place without purpose. For in their haste and hurry, they would trample the weak and see not the suffering of those around them. Know, indeed, like cattle they run, without direction when the storms of life frighten them. For at the sound of the thunder and lightning, they run with no thought of where or why they run. Know, indeed, that they destroy the land and bring chaos to all around them, as they rush to and fro. For all is focused on naught, and

---

[162] The gear or tackle by which a horse or other animal is yoked and made to follow the desires of man.

the collective consciousness— if such we may call it— leads them to no port in the storm. For they run until they are weary, and in doing so, will trample all around them and even fall into despair and destruction. For they see not where they run... but simply follow the lead of the herd. Whither one goes, all chooses the same path, and so are lost with ease. For they think not, and see not that their doom is laid out before them in running quickly, this way and that.

Know, Dear Ones, that the storms of life will not cause thee harm, and the thunder and lightning will do thee no harm. Run not ceaselessly from place to place, but pause and live. For destruction awaits thee when you run with the herd aimlessly. Know indeed, that the dangers of life are not seen, and all rush unceasing in the same direction at great speed, even to their deaths. For indeed, the death of mankind happens when he is yet alive in the flesh; for without the knowledge of the love of God, he is dead inside. For like the cattle, he has no purpose; for he runs this way and that, following the herd from place to place, with no knowledge of whither he goes or why he goes there.

He takes on the desires of the herd, and becomes not himself; for all actions are not of the heart of God, but based on instinct. He runs and runs without purpose, until death. Thus, when he returns to Source at the point of death, he realizes that he has accomplished naught of his tasks, and is lost. For indeed, his time upon the Earth was full of distractions, and that indeed, he showed no love for his brethren, and his heart was not set upon the things of God. Know indeed, Dear Ones, we say open your hearts, and your eyes, and see and know the things of God, for herein lies your rescue and your hope. For the Sons of Men will perish and find not his way upon the Earth. Remember your heritage and know who you are, for you are the Sons and Daughters of the Most High God, given all the riches of this Earth to enjoy. Look to the sunset and see the beauty; look to the stars and know you are never alone.

Look not to the herd for rescue, for indeed, it cannot help thee. All it can do is to confuse and alarm thee, for it cannot find its way upon the Earth, when the storms of life come upon it. It runs in fear, and harms all around it without intent, for indeed, it is not conscious of the existence of anything but its own needs. Thus, it runs ceaselessly to and fro, and is lost to the God of its being, for indeed, it knows not God. All it knows is the need to run, and so continues upon this quest without reason, for eons. Lift your heads to the stars, Dear Ones, and see the gifts of God, and know that you are not alone. Remember in your hearts who you are, and taste the wonders of the Earth, for herein lays your help, herein lays your rescue. For this is the way to your survival upon the Earth.

Remember your nature, allow the harness to be placed upon you, for you will benefit. For without the harness and the calming influence it brings to thee, you will continue upon the Earth, running from place to place, and finding no rest. For you seek the peace, the love, and the joys of God, but will not find it. For you know not where you are, as you move with haste upon the Earth. Know indeed, Dear Ones, that the love of God will shield thee when the storms come upon you, and will cause you to remember that you can survive the storms... for, indeed, the thunder and the lightning will not harm thee, but hear the voice of God calling to thee. Know, Dear Ones, that the love of God will shield thee, and be the wind beneath your wings indeed, for it will guide thee to places new and allow thee to taste the joys of God upon the Earth.

Let not your heart be troubled but know, indeed, that all will be well. For the love of God is thine to keep all the days of your life. For indeed, it is the very food of men, for it gives thee life: the life force to continue upon the Earth. Know indeed, Dear Ones, that the love of God is the harness that can lead thee to safety and keep thee safe.

Be you willing to allow the memory of the love of God to enter your hearts, and know, indeed, that you will be enriched, for it is the source of all things for the Sons of Men: For it will bring you peace, and love, and happiness, and joy.

For therein lays your strength, your hope, your peace, and your joy. For you are the Sons of Men, but are also the Children of God, loved and adored by Mother Father God, ever in the care and protection of God, so you need not fear for anything that would cause you alarm. Know that you will always be loved and protected by Mother Father God, for this is your birthright. Open your hands, O Children of Men! And see and know the wonderful gifts of God, given to you since the dawn of time. Open your hands and see, and know the true peace, love, and happiness of God, for this will bring you life: For ye are not lost, alone, and unprotected. You are never alone, never abandoned.

You are always loved, always protected, and always in the arms of God. Remember your heritage, and know sweet peace, love, happiness, and joy upon the Earth: For Mother Father God has given you all you will ever need, if you would only remember it. Let not the cares of the physical world cause you to forget who you are. Know, indeed, that you are ever enfolded in the loving arms of God, and ever protected and loved. For you are most precious in the eyes of God: ever adored, ever loved. Be who you were meant to be upon the Earth. Create your destiny and live. Be the master of your destiny, and follow not those who would lead you astray. For you are the sons of God, the children of the Most

High God. Be the wonderful stars you were meant to be upon the Earth and shine in all your true glory. For this is your charge: to be wonderful examples of God in the flesh. When you show love, peace, and joy, you show God upon the Earth. When you help your brethren, you show God, for these are the things of God.

Be not happy to say, "My eyes are closed, so I see not the suffering of my brethren," for this is not the way of God. Share the great wealth of this Earth with those in need, and take not from the weak. Instead, give to those around you, and know that you are sharing the wealth and the abundance of God with your brethren; for this is truly the gift and the love of God in action. Lift up your eyes, O Sons and Daughters! And see and know the beauty, love, peace, and joy of God. For this is your true charge upon the Earth. Be who you were meant to be, and give help and love to all you can, for this is how you show God upon the Earth. Let your light shine, and know that you are the Sons and Daughters of the Most High God, given all you need: Loved of God, and adored in all your splendor, for you are the beloved Children of God. Be your marvelous selves upon the Earth, and know true happiness, peace, and joy. For therein lies your hope, your life, your peace, your joy. You are the beloved of God, so open your hearts and live, for you are the beloved of God. Take the time to wander slowly upon the face of the Earth, and taste the beauty, love, and peace of God, for this is thine, given freely by Mother Father God. You are ONE, you are the chosen, and you are the heart of God. Be who you were meant to be and live. You are the beloved. You are the Children of God. You are the joy of God. Live and be happy upon the Earth, for this is the gift to you from Mother Father God!

Adieu

A NEW AGE

For in truth, the days of man are short upon the Earth... but in his mercy, Mother Father God provides all that is needed by man to live in peace, love, and harmony upon the Earth. The nature of man is such, however, that he spends much time in warring and being in conflict with his neighbor. Know indeed, Dear Ones, that the warring must indeed cease, for the time of man upon the Earth is wasted in the warring between clans, and creeds, and religions, and no time is left for peaceful pursuits. Know, Dear Ones, that the nature and will of Mother Father God, is one only of peace; so therefore in warring, you go against the very will and nature of God. Know indeed, that God supports no side in a conflict, and whether you win or lose is based on might and your own skills. For in no way can Mother Father God condone the killing of any of his children; for indeed all are precious in his sight. Know, Dear Ones, that the essence of God is love, peace, happiness, and joy, and the thoughts of supporting one child against another cannot be tolerated— if such we may describe it— by God, for indeed, this goes against the very nature of God.

Know, indeed, that the God of love that is Mother Father God cannot harm his children, and it is the very nature of man that would harm his brothers. For indeed, man, of self, has the nature to destroy all that is about him in an effort to secure that which he most desires. Know indeed, Dear Ones, that the love of God can carry you safely to the shores of God's love... but yet, you strive daily to bring harm and pain to your brethren. Know, indeed, that the love within you has been pushed to the side, or in some cases completely hidden so that you turn upon your brethren, and commit hideous crimes against him. Know, Dear Ones, this is not the nature of God, and naught comes close to this ability of man to harm his brethren. For indeed, the love of God should prevent man from taking a life, yet he has established rules wherein it is called into being as a form of punishment.[163]

Know, Dear Ones, we see and know the great plight of man in deciding how to bring punishment on those who have taken a life, yet we know that the taking of that life in no way brings the desired pain to a halt. For indeed, all are still in pain and anguish when this is done. Know, Dear Ones, we say a return to love and the ways of love, would bring thee sweet peace, indeed. For the teachings of our Dear Brother, Jesus, reminds you that loving those who hate and persecute you is the way of being. Know, Dear Ones, that this may not seem practical, when faced with the pain and hurt of the loss of those we love. Yet in reality, we know that the darkness takes over the heart of men, and they forget their reason for being upon the Earth, and they bring naught but harm to those around them. Stirred on by what can be seen only as zealot behavior, they would

---

[163] Capital punishment or the death penalty is a legal process whereby a person is put to death by the state as a punishment for a crime.

wish to remove all from the Earth who do not act, think, or believe as they do. Indeed, this pain has been brought on to others because they do not look like you do. Know, Dear Ones, that the very nature of man must change, for it is time to realize that all upon the Earth are your brethren.

All are your neighbors, your family, and kin. All are ONE, for in the very creation of your souls, you are all one from the very spark of God, choosing to come to the Earth in a rainbow of hues to experience life upon the Earth. Know, Dear Ones that the Sons of Men must change their ways and look to help their brethren.

Instead of tearing down, take the time to build them up and know that your lives will be fuller and richer, for therein lies your victory: for to love is to know bliss and harmony. To love is to know peace and the true meaning of the Creed of God… and to know happiness, love, and joy.

For all are ONE, all are part of God, all are brethren, all are the Sons and Daughters of God. Know, indeed, that man has taught you to accept that killing the weak to take their possessions is acceptable, and indeed, this has been the way upon the Earth since the dawn of time. Know, Dear Children, that a new age is upon you and the time for change has come. For the love of God can, and must carry you to new heights, and into new and exalted places: For a time of justice, peace, love, and harmony must be established upon the Earth. For the warring and the pain of hatred for no reason other than race, color, and creed, must end. For the time of the great establishment of love, peace, joy, and harmony upon the Earth is here.

Know, Dear Ones, we say with much joy, that this time is here and it is now time to leave the brutal past behind, and to move to a place of enlightenment and love. For in loving, we forgive, and in loving we allow things to be different, and people to be and to think differently, without the need to bring them harm. Know, Dear Ones, we say that the love of God is the great equalizer, for even as it is given equally to all the Sons of Men, even so must the Sons of Men come to know that the love of God is their shield, and all that they need to be happy in the world. Know, Dear Ones, that the Children of Men must move to higher levels of consciousness, and let go of the avarice, greed, envy, and pain, that has been such a part of the human condition.

Know, indeed, that the time for change is even now upon you, Dear Children: To change your path, and to change your destiny, and to once more know the great peace of God. For this is the moment to LOVE and study war no more, for therein lies your rescue; therein lies your hope and your redemption. For indeed, you bring too much pain to all around you, including animals, for your neglect of Mother Earth is, indeed, a great war upon her shores. For indeed, we say that this is one war you will not win, for in all her glory and majesty, Mother Earth will exact her wrath upon the lands. For in your poor treatment of all that has been given, you are destroying your home. Know indeed, that once destroyed, you will have nothing, so take care of all that you have been so lovingly provided with by Mother Father God, and know true peace, love, happiness, and joy. For this is the only way for peace to return to the Earth.

For indeed, you have pillaged her, and given nothing in return. You have destroyed her rivers and great oceans, but yet you continue to dump toxic substances into her very soul. Know, Dear Ones, that you must return to the days of old, and pay homage to Mother Earth, and give her due respect, as done by the natives so very long ago. For in her nature and beauty, she has provided for mankind. She has given you food and shelter, and yet now man would turn upon her and cause waste and destruction to be part of her daily plight. Let not your hearts forget all you have is this place called Earth to live upon. When you destroy it through raping and pillaging of the land, you are destroying your own homes, for nature itself will call out to you in revolt, and much will be the desolation seen upon the Earth

For the floods and the natural forces of the Earth will result, Dear Ones. Know, indeed, your actions and great disregard for your home brings you naught but pain if you continue as you do now.

Let not the selfishness of mankind cause you to lose your only home. Know indeed, that the same way in which you pay attention to your own place of abode and give attention to your space, even so must you take pride in Mother Earth and discontinue the practice of bringing her pain and destruction. For she is part of your life-source and part of you. When you harm Mother Earth, you harm yourself.

Know indeed, Dear Ones, that the love you hold must be shared with Mother Earth, for she is, indeed, a part of you. Let not your greed and disregard of all that is around you destroy Mother Earth, for mankind will indeed suffer the pain of this war. Know indeed, Dear Ones, that you cannot win that war, for indeed, the Earth must win, for she is the very source of life for mankind upon the Earth.

Be at peace, and know that the road is set before you, and you must choose the path you will take, for the choice is yours, Dear Ones. Know that you hold the key, and all that will transpire can change, only if the Children of Men will change and return once more to paying homage to the beauty that is Mother Earth, your home.

Choose ye which way you will go, and know that you are the Children of Men... but that Mother Earth is your home, so be kind to her and know you will be provided with all that is needed for your survival.

Let your heart be at peace, and know all is in your hands, and all can be changed, if such is the will of men. Let go of greed, and know that the Earth must be protected, for indeed, it is your home and your castle. Let not any harm come to her, so that you might enjoy her wealth, her glory, and her gifts forever.

Peace be unto you, Dear Ones. Know that you have the power, and use it wisely to enjoy the benefits of Earth, and to live in harmony with her and not be at war against her. For you cannot ever hope to win that war. Know that you are the Children of Men, and your true nature is one of peace, for you are made of God, and as such you are peacemakers and not warmongers. Let not greed turn you away from the path. Protect and love Mother Earth, and know that all will be well for and with thee.

Adieu

Know indeed, that the great and all-encompassing love of God for mankind is daily demonstrated in the wind, the rain, and the flowers. Know indeed, Dear Ones, for of such is truly the love of God found and made. For indeed, this love is so great and awe-inspiring, that it demands that man, in his splendor, shall do all that must be done to show the majesty of his might, power, and love: For truly, the love of God is as wonderfully and most beautifully made as can be imagined. Know indeed, Dear Ones, that the love of God is demonstrated in the very variety of the flowers found upon the Earth. For in truth, even as there are human beings upon the Earth, even so are there many different varieties of flowers. For in truth, the very variety demonstrates the great love of God for mankind. For in providing this variety, God demonstrates the many aspects of beauty and shows how, in all her splendor, Mother Nature is to be worshipped. For even as she shows her true colors, and man marvels at the beauty found therein, even so are there myriad of different shades and hues of each and every flower.

Know, Dear Ones, that the great and awe-inspiring love of God is that most marvelous and awe-inspiring demonstration of love, truth, and beauty to be found upon the Earth. Know, Dear Ones, that the great God of life is even so able to demonstrate and provide the greatest of variety in all things. For his power is shown in the majesty and love of nature. Know indeed, that the joy and peace of God is seen in nature, for in all its magnificence, it radiates and glows with the majesty and love of God. Know indeed, Dear Ones, that the peace of God even so is found in the nature of all upon the Earth. For indeed, man, of self, cannot count the vast array of hues, and colors, and shades, of all that is here provided in abundance and love, for the Children of Men.

Know, Dear Ones, that the great love of God for the Children of Men is seen daily in the sunrise and the sunsets which echo the beauty of the Earth, and the magnificence of all that is given to the Children of Men. For indeed, who on Earth can re-create the rainbow, or re-create the early dawn light? Know indeed, Dear Ones, all these blessings and gifts are freely given to mankind to enjoy free of cost, but yet in his blindness, the Children of Men see not the marvels of nature in each day as they rush to and fro, taking on the business of the day. Stop! O Children of Men! And look up to the sky, and see all that is here, given to thee to enjoy and to view, for, indeed, it is freely given but you neither see nor appreciate its beauty. Take the time, O Sons and Daughters of Man, to sit and enjoy the very gifts of God, given to you to bring you naught but joy and pleasure of the highest degree. Know indeed, Dear Ones, that of such is the love of God made, for indeed, it is given freely to mankind in the beauty of Mother Earth, and in the wonder of the skies and the very stars that twinkle at night in the midnight sky. Know, Dear Ones, you forget the simple joys of life when you fail to look up, and to see and notice all that is around you. For indeed, you walk as if blind upon the Earth when you fail to see and to appreciate all the beauty that is here, made available and given to thee.

Know, indeed, that the depths of the love of God for man is shown in oh, so many ways, by the very beauty and joy of nature; for herein lies the joys of God. For the heart of God is seen in the things provided by Mother Father God, for the Children of Men.

Take the time, Dear Ones, to smell and view the complexity of a flower, the breadth and intensity of the fragrance, and the awe-inspiring nature of the beauty seen before thee. For man sees not the beauty around him, and takes not the time to give thanks... but instead, would destroy all upon the Earth in the name of greed. For this is the way of man, but know, Dear Ones, things must change and man must be able to stop and smell the roses, for therein lies your peace and your joy. Therein lies your way to God. For in its very simplest of demonstration is to be found the deepest and most profound examples of the love of God for mankind. Know indeed, Dear Ones, that this love, which encompasses all, is likened to the most precious of all gifts given to mankind, yet, so many fail to see and know its true beauty; for indeed, the love of God is the very essence of man. It is the very thing on which the foundation of man is sculpted. For indeed, if men could but see and know the true depths of this beauty, love, and grace, they would see and know of the depth of the love of God for man. Know indeed, Dear Ones, we say that the love of God is the greatest demonstration of love found anywhere in the Universe, for it outweighs and outshines all else.

For it is that eternal and blessed emotion that gives man his purpose upon the Earth: A purpose that is clearly given to all at birth, to find their way back to Mother Father God. Thus, Dear Ones, we see and know that the love of God is seen in the very beauty of nature, and the very landscape of the Earth. For in truth, this gift is freely given to mankind to daily drink in and be filled. For in truth, it shows the vastness of the depths of the love of God for mankind. Look ye from the highest mountain peaks, into the lowest valley below, and see and know the true wonder of God. For such is the nature and bliss of God, to give all of these many blessings to the Children of Men. For in the seeing and noticing of all the magnificence of nature, is man being shown the depths of the love of God. For who, but a loving and doting[164] God, would provide all this beauty for the Children of Men? Who, but a most loving Mother Father God, would give such great gifts to his children? For the love of God is seen in nature, and is therefore to be appreciated in its simplest form.

Ingest each moment of beauty, Dear Ones! Drink in the sunrise and the sunsets, and the beauty of the flowers, and the adornment of nature in each season, and see and know the true and abundant nature of the love of God for mankind. For when you are able to truly acknowledge all that is around you in nature, you will truly see the wonders of God. For in providing such beauty and bounty for mankind, God daily shows his great love for mankind. Know, Dear Ones, that the love and light of God can be daily seen in all the wonderful sights and sounds of nature. Open your eyes, O Sons of Men, and see and know your true worth in the eyes of God— if such we may describe it— for your worth is truly beyond measure, and even so is the joy of God and the love of God for mankind. For indeed, God provides your daily bread, and in likewise fashion, he gives all else to the Children of Men to drink in the beauty and love of Mother Nature. Take the time, O Sons and Daughters of Mankind, to know and to love Mother Earth, for in all her splendor, she is the

---

[164]   To love to excess or extravagance

demonstration of the love of God for mankind upon the Earth. For this great and all-encompassing love cannot truly be measured or appreciated by mankind, unless he opens his heart, his hands, and his eyes to taste the beauty that is here made available: To taste the complexity of the fruits and to drink in the shining beauty which is Mother Earth.

Look on and know, Dear Ones, all is freely given as a demonstration of the love of God for mankind. All is given freely, so take and eat and remember, that as Sons and Daughters of God, all is freely given to thee. Open your eyes and your heart, and be filled to the brim with the vastness of God's love for you, Dear Ones. Open your hands, and receive all that is here, made available for thee, for herein lies your hope, your rescue, and your peace. Rest in the knowledge of the love of God for mankind, when you can see and know the beauty that is all around you. Live in the moment! Take time from the hustle and bustle and sit and drink in the true wonders of the love of God. Taste the fruits, and drink in the flowers and all the sights and sounds of nature, and see and know God in all his magnificence. See and know the true nature of the love of God for mankind, for only in this way can you come to know the depths of the love of God for mankind. Look you to all that is freely given to thee, O Sons and Daughters of Mankind. And know that all is here made available for thee. For it is the way of God, to give freely to his children all that is here made available to thee, for these are the true joys and pleasures of this life.

Take the time to sit and view Mother Nature in all her splendor, and find your true peace and your true joy, Dear Ones: For this is your way on the Earth. This is where your true joys will be found. For these are the things of God, given freely to all mankind, as a token of the great love of God for his children. Know, Dear Ones, that the gifts of nature are God's way of showing the very depths of his love for the Children of Men. Look on and know all is given to thee, so take and eat, drink, and be filled with the peace, love, and joy of God... when you look to Mother Earth and her many gifts given to mankind.

Be at peace and know that herein lies the examples of the depths of God's love for mankind, and herein lies the deep and abiding passion of the love of God for his children. For like a loving parent, Mother Father God gives only the very best to his sons and daughters. Only the best of everything is fit for the Children of God, and thus, only the best can be given by a loving and most patient Mother Father God to his children. Know, Dear Ones, that the love of God is seen in the stars, the sands on the seashore, and the very night sky, or in the early light of dawn. Know, indeed, that you are truly loved and adored, O Sons and Daughters of Mankind, and know that all is, indeed, given to thee as a token of the depths of the love of God for mankind.

Take, eat, and be filled, for herein lies your joy, your love, your hope, and your blessings, for such is the beingness of God to provide these gifts for the Children of Men. Be at peace and know that all will indeed be well, and all will be right with the world. For mankind will open its eyes, and realize that God's love for mankind is daily demonstrated everywhere, if the Sons of Men would only open their hearts and look up. Be at peace, and know that you are the beloved of God, and you are the Children of God. You are the treasures, and the passion, and love of God, given daily.

Open your hands, and your hearts, and minds, and know the true bliss and blessings of God. Be at peace and know that all is right with the world, and all will be well for thee, Dear Ones. May the knowledge of the love of Mother Father God for mankind continue to shine in your hearts, and allow you to see and know the true happiness, peace, and joy of God. Be at peace, and know that all will be well for thee, Dear Ones, when you see and experience the bliss and the love of God for mankind. Adieu ...May God's peace, love, and grace continue to flow into your hearts as you awaken to the love of God that is you.

Adieu

3ʳᵈ January 2012

Know, indeed, that the Son of Man is the heir to the very throne of God, but as indeed, all of humankind are also sons and daughters of Mother Father God: even so, indeed, are they also heirs to the throne. For in truth, all that exists in the kingdom are part of the glory and bliss of God, and indeed, the Sons of Men are able to claim their place in the kingdom. Know indeed, Dear Ones, that the Sons of Men and the Children of God are one, in that their abilities and this very purpose are one. Know indeed, Dear Ones, that the Sons of Men have all that is ever needed, given to them by Mother Father God, but yet the children continue to bring pain and suffering to their brethren. For all that is necessary is that the Children of Men turn to Mother Father God and do that which is required or necessary for them to do, in order to inherit the kingdom.

In truth, we see that there is naught that mankind needs to do in order to be worthy, for as Sons of Men they are the first in line to receive the true bounty of God. Know, Dear Ones, that the love of God knows no bounds, and so in the truth of this expression, we see that man can yet turn to the love of God to find that peace, love, and surrender, that is needed there in the arms of God. Know, Dear Ones, that the love of God will carry you safely to the shore and deliver you upon the sacred sand of God's love. Be you happy to know, Dear Ones, that the love of God exists there in return for doing all that's required for Mother Father God.

Know, indeed, that there is no direct penance or payment, so that all can be covered for each of the moments of this life. Know, Dear Ones, that the love and beingness of God continues on and on endlessly, and that the pain and anguish of men will continue on until man can learn how to take his place as rightful heir to the kingdom. Be you happy to know that the love of God will take thee beyond the stars, and into the outer realms of the Universe that is known by man.

Know, Dear Ones, that indeed, all that man needs in order to know peace is to determine what is missing from the marriage as soon as possible. Know, Dear Ones, that this great masterful and wonderful of all truths is thine to describe, and to know intimately, Dear Ones. We say, indeed, that the love of God is the very Angel of all that is required, and can and will lead thee home, Dear Ones, into the very heart of God. For even as man considers himself to be all that is human in the known universe, know, indeed, that he has lived for thousands of years, nestled and cradled and, indeed, shows that this is but the truth given to the Sons of Men to help them describe their world and the place of God within that hierarchy.

Let not your hearts be saddened, but know, indeed, that the love of God will be there with thee forever and ever, until the end of time. Know, Dear Ones, that all your needs will be ever supplied, and all your wants will ever be within the constant love and caring of the Father. Know, Dear Ones, that you are the chosen of God, and your every need is uppermost in the mind— if such we may describe it— of God.

Be you happy to know that the love of God is thine always, and will forever be thine to know and hold, for such is the very nature of God, that you are ever given every blessing and every treasure. For you are loved and adored, and ever watched over and loved by God. Be you happy to know all happens as it should, and all will come upon each other when the time is right, because you are loved and adored by God. Be you attentive and know all the bounty of God is placed at your feet, and is yours to accept or reject. For indeed, you are ever being guided by God, and can never stray far from the love of God, for it is likened to the very air you breathe. Know that all is well and will continue to be so.

Adieu

25ᵀᴴ January 2012

Arise! O Sons and Daughters of Mankind! Know ye not that, indeed, this is the day that the Lord has made, and the Sons and Daughters of Zion should, indeed, arise and greet the dawn? For indeed, the great and awe-inspiring love of God for mankind is like a tree planted by a pool of water. For indeed, it is nourished and watered by the rains, and indeed brings forth much fruit.... but know, indeed, that the tree begins to wither and dies, for it is full of pestilence and there is naught to save it for it cannot be brought back.

Know indeed, O Sons and Daughters of Mankind, that the very nature of God is such that the very thought of God brings happiness and joy to the Sons of Men, and in due season, all are happy and cannot be contained. But yet, the day arrives when, indeed, there comes disease upon the land, and all withers and dies; for indeed it is found that the tree has become full of pestilence and so dies. Why, O Sons and Daughters of Mankind? Why, O Children of the Most High God do we find such pain? For while we danced and sang with delight, do we yet see that the Children of Men have no happiness and joy in their hearts? For indeed that which was once seen as great joy and reason for celebration, now turns to sorrow. For indeed, in the light of day, we know this is in no way the truth of what was truly in existence.

Know, Dear Ones, that the love of God is that very tree which one day is flourishing in the hearts of men, and they dance and sing with delight. Yet quickly, this celebration turns to weeping and mourning, for indeed, there is no reason for celebration. For we see, Dear Ones, that the very reason for the great celebration has been taken away. For mankind has lost its way, and what was once seen as the reason for the greatest of all joys, is now recognized in its entirety as the very sickness that will come to destroy it. For lo, in the light of day, we see there is no reason for celebration, for the Children of Men are not able to thrive on what they are being fed.

Know, Dear Ones, that the love of God is that very food which, when fed to the Children of Men, can and will bring them all the nourishment, and peace, and joy that is required. But when the exterior is pulled away, we find that if the water is polluted it cannot feed the children and they wither and die. Know indeed, that is the truth of the love of God for mankind, but the water must be pure and full of all that is good: for in truth, without this purity, the tree cannot survive. For when the water is fouled, that which once was a source of life now becomes the very reason for death. For the poison within the water will come to be the very reason for its destruction of the tree it once nourished.

Know, Dear Ones, that the love of God, given so freely to the Sons of Men, has been changed and poisoned by those who manipulate and manufacture their own truths within it, so that that which once was a source of life and strength turns upon itself and becomes the very reason for its destruction. Know indeed, Dear Ones, that the Word of God and the teachings of Mother Father God are lessons of love and peace, yet men, in their search for self, have turned these very truths upon themselves, and now that great love which teaches how to save and to protect mankind has been used to teach how to kill and maim the Children of Men.

Know, Dear Ones, that the very teachings of love have been manipulated and changed to meet the desires of man until now they are no longer words of love, but words of hate, which poison and condemn the very Sons of Men. Know, Dear Ones, that the Children of Men are being harmed by those who would kill and maim in the name of God. For God cannot kill. God cannot and will not harm, for he is a God of love. A God only of peace, happiness, and joy, and thus cannot kill his children. Know, Dear Ones, that the great and wonderful name of God has become synonymous with death and destruction, for the Sons of Men now turn to use it when they come to destroy their enemies. Why use you the name of God and say, "My God protects and delivers me from thee," and then kill thy enemies? Know ye not the God of love cannot and would not kill his children?

Know ye not the God of love cannot kill any of his children, for ye are all brothers and sisters in the family of God? All one family, one heart, one soul: All one, in the love and light of God. Know ye not that ye are brothers and sisters of the heart?

Look upon your brethren and see the great resemblance, and know that ye are one. Look upon your brethren and see and know that beneath the exterior covering, ye are one. Know ye not that ye are one?

THE LOVE OF GOD WILL CARRY YOU HOME

Why kill and maim your brethren and say you, come with the blessings of God? Know ye not the God of love cannot condone the killing of his children for any reason? Know ye not that the heart of God bleeds when his children are destroyed or are cast down? Know ye not the name and nature of God would not cause harm to come upon anyone? Would a parent kill his child whom he loves with the deepest love, and the most intense of all passions? Know ye not that the Lord of Hosts is that God of love who feeds and protects his children?

Know, Dear Ones, the killings done in the name of God must cease, for they are the very poison that infect the life source of the Children of Men, and cause them to die. For they feed upon it, willingly thinking and believing that they are being nourished, only to discover that it is not nourishment but poison that is being fed to the Sons of Men.

Seek the true path of God, and give the truth of the beingness of God to the Sons of Men, and know that they will live and flourish instead of dying from the poison of the teachings of hate and destruction. Turn, O Sons of Men! And know the truth of the love of God and live! Turn and once more see and know the truth of the love of God for mankind, and come to know the true and glorious peace of God! For God is now and always only a God of PEACE and LOVE. God is not a God of war, or hate, or division. God is a God of UNITY, LOVE, HOPE, PEACE, and JOY.

These things that heal and nourish are the things of God. Those things that would cause destruction and pain in the hearts of men are not the things of God. Turn away from the poisoned teachings of old, and look to a new and glorious truth, and live, Dear Ones! For there is a new dawn, a new day, and a new medicine that will cause thee to live, if you would but see and know these truths.

Drink no more from the fountain of hate and division, but drink instead from the well of unity, love, peace, and joy, and be nourished. Know, Dear Ones, that the teachings of hate and division would poison you and cause your destruction, if you drink only from this fountain

Turn away, Dear Ones, and see and know the truth of the love of God for ALL his children, and come to see and understand the truth of God. Come to know the way of peace, happiness, and prosperity upon the Earth. For the days of drinking in the poison, and expecting to survive upon the Earth are no more. For the poison will circulate within you as of old, and cause you to wither and die. For it is not life and nourishment that you drink in, but surely death and destruction.

Look on and know that your food that you take in to help you grow is naught but poison which will destroy you, Dear Ones. Turn away from that which you think is nourishment, and know, indeed, it is only disguised as nourishment but yet, is the strongest of all poisons. For indeed, you drink it in with vigor, thinking you are doing what is good and right, and all the time you are poisoning yourself. For the hatred will kill thee, Dear Ones, and you will fall away from the Earth… for you are destroying yourselves while expecting to flourish and live. Know, Dear Ones, that the day of change is upon you, when your eyes are opened and you come to know that you cannot drink the poison and expect to be nourished, for surely poison will and must kill thee.

Know, Dear Ones, that the true and awe-inspiring love of God will not cause thee to be destroyed, for this is a message of unity, peace, love, and joy between brothers. It is a message of sharing and of love between brothers. Know, Dear Ones, that it can only bring you nourishment and strength, for when you drink in that which is good, it will serve to strengthen you, Dear Ones, and to build you up, not cause you to die.

Know, Dear Ones, that the greed and envy of your brethren must end, for theirs is the very poison which seeps into the life-giving springs from which you drink. How can you expect to live and flourish, when you daily drink in the poison of separation, hate, division, fear, and anger? How can you expect to thrive when you would turn upon your brethren, and kill and maim in the name of God?

Use you not the name of God to justify the slaying of your brethren and say, "We kill in the name of God," for this cannot be so, for the name of God supports only LOVE. Not hate or WAR. Know ye not that the name and nature of God should only be used when in reference to love, peace, sharing, and caring? For to use it with reference to war is to go against the things of God, and to poison the hearts of men. For in so doing, you poison their hearts and they die. For in believing in the poisonous teachings, you kill and maim your brethren, and you die within your hearts. For you will never know the true peace, love, and joy of God, when you carry and teach war, pain, vengeance, and hate of others. Let go of the poison, and find the sweet nectar of peace, love, and happiness, and drink in this glorious food and thrive!

Open your hearts, O Children! And see and know that this is your salvation. This is your hope, to turn away from the self-destruction and to move, instead, to the love and beingness of your Mother Father God, which will save you, and cause you to know true peace, happiness, joy, and love upon the Earth. **For you cannot expect to drink poison and to thrive and grow, for your body was built to thrive on love and not on hate.**

The hate will kill you, Dear Ones, for it seeps into your very veins and circulates throughout your body, and it dies. It cannot survive on hate, when it was built to thrive on LOVE and peace. It cannot survive on ENVY and cruelty, when it was built to survive on the things of God, which are joy, caring, and sharing.

Know, Dear Ones, that this is the true and only way of God, the true and only way of survival for mankind upon the Earth. For to drink poison[165] and expect not to die is madness, Dear Ones. The poison will kill thee, for that is its purpose. It is meant to destroy, and cannot serve to build thee up, and to strengthen, and nourish thee. For that is not the true sustenance of men, for man cannot live when he is poisoned. He suffers and dies from within, and naught can save him, for he is infected with the very toxins that destroy who and what he is. The toxins cannot cure thee or build thee up! They are designed only to destroy!

Know, Dear Ones, that the poison cannot cure thee, cannot build thee up, or strengthen thee. It can only destroy thee. Look not at the poison and say, "See how it strengthens me and gives me life, for it is good." Know this is only an illusion, Dear Ones, and know that when you drink this water, it will cause you to die, for it is not the life-giving water you would think that it is. It is death that you drink

[165]   Pain, fear, envy ,war, vengeance and hate are poison to the soul of man

in, Dear Ones, for indeed, it will destroy thee! Open your hearts, and see, and know that the days of illusion are past! Open your eyes! Remove the covering that would mask them, and see that the water you drink in is, indeed, poison and naught else.

Close not your eyes, and believe, "If I do not look, I can imagine that it will not harm me." Fool thee not yourselves, Dear Ones, and believe you can live, when all you live on is hate, and fear, and anger, and vengeance. For in truth, this cannot help you to survive. Turn to a new thought, a new day, and a new knowing that the love of God is all that can truly strengthen thee. For it is that which contains the very source of life for the Sons of Men. It is that which contains all that is needed to give you life. It is that, which is the energy-giving source for man upon the Earth.

Turn away from the pool of poison! Do not go willingly to your death! Pull away your roots from the poisons of life, and know that you will live, grow, and flourish, Dear Ones! For you are the Children of God, loved and adored by God. See your brother, and know the joys of brotherhood and love, and know that this is your strength. For together, you can do all things: For you are powerful beings when you harness your strength and wisdom for the accomplishment of good upon the Earth. When you drink the poison, you see only death and destruction, and you wither and die… for you feed the heart and soul with poison, yet you expect to live, flourish, and grow.

Be at peace, Dear Ones, and know that the days of change are upon you. For the time is here for a new learning and a new remembrance of who and what you are, and what you truly need in order to survive and thrive upon the Earth. Know, Dear Ones, that the day of, and for, change is upon you. You must either drink the poison and die, or turn away and live.

Choose you this day who you will serve, Dear Ones! God or Mammon?[166] For indeed, one path leads you to destruction, and the other to life everlasting. For you are the Children of God, loved and adored by God. Turn away and live, grow, and flourish upon the Earth. Continue on your path, and know only death can follow you, for you travel the path of destruction. Drink in the true food of life, and see how you are nourished, Dear Ones.

Drink in the poison of hatred, fear, division, anger, rejection, envy, greed, and separation, and know you die, for these are the very poisons of the hearts and souls of men. Drink in love, Dear Ones, and know true peace, happiness, joy, contentment, and love: for this is the true way of God.

Let not the eyes or lips deceive you, so you think you drink in nourishment any longer, when in truth, you drink in the death of the soul. For the love, which is God, is all that can strengthen thee and give thee life. All other substances will bring you only death, for they are not the things or the teachings of God. Be at peace and know, Dear Ones, that you can put your roots into the water of life, and live and grow in love, peace, harmony, joy, and contentment... or you can drink in sure death, and perish upon the Earth. Know, Dear Ones, you are loved by Mother Father God all the days of your lives, and know that the choice is thine, so choose this day what you will do. Know that your choice will determine your survival or demise upon the Earth.

Be at peace and know that you are loved beyond measure, Dear Ones, and that your Mother Father God will never desert thee... but choose ye your path carefully, Dear Ones, and know that you

---

166   Material wealth, avarice or greed, most often personified as a false deity.

cannot drink poison and expect to thrive, for only the life-giving nourishment, which is the love of God, can strengthen and uphold thee. Hate, fear, anger, envy, and jealousy cannot uphold thee. Only the greatest of all these things— LOVE— can cause thee to come to know the true peace, LOVE, and joy of God.

Adieu, Dear Ones! May you continue to grow and thrive in the love and beingness of Mother Father God. May you always have the discernment to know, and to do that which is right and just upon the Earth. God's peace and blessings are yours, Dear Ones.

Adieu

The Brotherhood

4ᵀᴴ APRIL 2012

Know, Dear Ones, that the heart and soul of God, and the heart and soul of man are united. For being a part of God, the body and mind of man is ever united with the Lord, the Giver of Life. Know indeed, Dear One, that the shell of man, which is that covering which is seen by the naked eye, is that of the exterior only, for the true nature of man can only be seen in the love and peace of God. Know indeed, Dear Ones, that the nature of man emanates from God, but when in human form, the love that is God and the love that is man is forgotten, and cannot be seen or imagined by the eyes or heart of man. Know, Dear Ones, that this vast expanse which is man exists outside of the realm of man, and there in the ether lives the true heart and soul of man which is the God source, which gives him life and all the most basic elements of life. Know indeed, Dear Ones, that the love of God encircles the body which is man, and shields, guides, and protects thee each and every day.

Know indeed, Dear Ones, that this most blessed of all love and beingness is that most sacred part of God and man, for it carries the soul of man. Know that the love, which is man, is ever encircled by that great love and beingness, which is God. For indeed, this allows man and God to commune in wonderful ways, even though in the naked light of day, man knows not that he has communed with God. For to gain this knowledge would indeed cause him to express great pangs of unworthiness. For indeed, he understands and knows not of his magnificence, or the depth of the love of God for him. Thus, he sees himself as a lowly creature in the eyes and face of God.

Know always that you are held in the highest esteem by your Mother Father God, and thus you can and must always look to your Mother Father God for love, guidance, and all the things that you will ever need upon the Earth. Know, Dear Ones, that all you need to do is to call upon the name of your Father Mother God, and ask for the guidance you seek, and all will be made available to thee. Know indeed, Dear Ones, that you are loved and adored, and thus given all that is your Father God's to bestow. Be not amazed to know how you are blessed, but come to understand, Dear Ones, that you are the special children of a loving parent. Be you never afraid to claim your parentage, and to tell the world that you are a beloved child of the God of Love, Father of your heart, and the joyful seeker of all that is most precious for his children. Know, Dear Ones, that your parent ever cares for and adores thee. He lifts thee up when the storms of life would pummel thee and drive thee into the ground.

For indeed, without love, the forces outside of man that are present upon the Earth are ever pressing upon thee, trying to push thee under the ground. Know, Dear Ones, that the love of God would never cause thee to be downtrodden, and to be cast down, for that is not the way of God. Your loving parent is ever with thee, cradling thee in his arms so that you know not the dangers that fly around thee day and night. Know, Dear Ones, that you are the chosen, the love, and the heart of God. Be you always in the loving bosom of your parent, and know that all will be well for thee. Let all know of the love and beingness of God, for in his love and mercy, he keeps and protects thee ever in his bosom. Know indeed, Dear Ones, that all is well, for the face of God ever smiles on thee, and the heart of God ever loves thee: For you are the love of the heart of God. Be you ever in the lives and loving kinship with your brethren, and know that all will be well.

See and know, Dear Ones, that the task of God is to love thee, and he (man) ever wants to be held there in the arms and outstretched hands of God. Be you ever in the tender and loving place where God dwells within you, for even so shall you find your rest and your rescue. For you are magnificent beings, held and cradled in the arms of God. Be you happy to know that the Master of all Beingness is thy comforter and friend, your hope, your peace, and your joy. Be ever uplifted and know that the great love of God is there for thee always, and will take thee onto the shores and safety of God's love.

Be advised and know, Dear Ones, that your shield, your rock, and your fortress is your Mother Father God. He is all you will ever need, and he will ever sustain and uphold thee, for such is the way and life of God. Fear not of what you would eat or drink to sustain your physical body, but know that the love of God will always be enough to sustain and uphold thee and carry you to those places where none else may travel. Know, indeed, that the love and light will embrace thee, and keep thee constant and safe... for this is your hope, your rock, your fortress. Cling to him, Dear Ones, and live in the peace, love, and light always. Be not afraid when the storms howl around your door and say, "All is lost, for I am doomed." Know always you will ever be with your Mother Father God, and will be encircled always in the most deep and intense of all loves possible upon the Earth or in heaven, for you are a child of God. Drink in your partnership with the Divine, and become who you are meant to be. Eat voraciously, as though this was ever your last meal, but always know much more will be provided for thee. For you are loved! Oh, how you are loved!

Be happy and sing songs of great joy, for you are the chosen of God, and the hope of all upon the Earth: For even as it happens to one, it happens to all upon the Earth. Let the Children of God say, and so it is!

Amen & Amen

9TH MAY 2012

Know, indeed, that the blessed of God will always know peace and joy, for therein lives your strength, your peace, and your hope. For indeed, Dear Ones the love of God for mankind is like the flowering of the garden on a hot summer day. For indeed, the sunshine falls gently on the flowers, and they smile with great happiness and bliss at the warmth of the golden rays of the sun. The wind blows gently through the trees, and perfection is seen upon the Earth. Thus is the love of God: all that is happiness and light in the lives of the Sons of Men. Know indeed, Dear Ones, that even when the sun departs upon the horizon at the end of the day, the memory of her warmth and love ever remains with the flowers she has kissed. For the memory can never fade from view, for she brought so much love, peace, and happiness to those she touched.

Know, Dear Ones, that the love of God for mankind will forever be held in the minds and hearts of the Sons of Men, for even so have they been kissed by the warmth of the love of God. Know that the remnant of the glow and the bliss will ever remain etched upon the memory of all she touched.

Be like the flowers, Dear Ones, and drink in the warmth of the radiance of God's love and know the sweet peace and bliss that can be thine. For indeed, you are denied nothing, and want for nothing in the garden of God. Your every need is supplied, and you can bask in the glow of the love of God, which is there made available for thee. Be you ever happy to know that you will ever be supplied with all that would bring thee happiness, peace, joy, and contentment, for such is the love of God for mankind, that nothing is ever denied the Sons of Men.

For all things in the garden of God are ever at the disposal of man. All is available, all is given, all is presented to meet his needs. Only the pain of forgetfulness would rob man of this most blessed memory, so that he knows not his parentage or his home. Thus, he wanders to and fro, searching daily for his parents and those who can love and comfort him.

Know you not, Dear One, that you are ever held and cradled in the arms of God, ever protected, shielded, and guided by Mother Father God? Know you not that you are the beloved child of the Most High God? Remember your name, Dear One! Remember your heritage, and reach your true potential, for you are the beloved Sons and Daughters of God. Be you ever held and cared for by God. Be you ever nourished and nurtured by Mother Father God, for therein lies your hope. You are the beloved Children of God and the heart of God. Be you ever happy to know that your home is with your Mother Father God, and until you are in the arms of your parents, you will ever know pain and anguish; for this is but the pain and anguish of the great separation, which keeps thee bound in chains and wrapped in the darkness of forgetfulness. For the darkness will envelop thee, and cause thee to forget your name and nature, and cause thee to wander like one lost upon the Earth.

Be you ever happy to know that although you may forget your name and your identity, know that all that is you rests always comfortably in the arms of Mother Father God. Be you ever happy to know that when you finally remember your name, all other facets of that which is you will come flooding back to you, and your golden light will shine forth, Dear Ones.

Be you always at peace and know that you are never lost upon the Earth, even though your human mind would convince thee that you are lost and alone. Know always, you are never alone and cannot be lost, for buried deep within you is the guidance, which when activated, can take you back to the arms of your Father Mother God. Be you never lost or unable to be consoled when fear would overtake thee, but know that you will always be guided, loved, and protected by the arms of God. For even so, will you always find the peace for which you have searched, waiting for thee in the loving arms of God. Be you ever at peace, Dear Ones, and know that the garden will always provide food for thee and the warmth of God's love will always be that very thing which will bring thee sweet peace.

Know no harm can come to thee there, for you are held, loved, and protected by God. All will be well for thee, for the garden is owned by Mother Father God, so that you may always be at peace. Release all thoughts of doubt or fear from your thoughts, Dear Ones, and know that all will be well for thee, for you are a precious flower in the garden of God... and you will be fed, and watered, and nurtured, all the days of your life so that you may glow, and blossom, and bloom, and bring love and happiness to all those who would look upon thee. Be at peace and know that all will be well, for such is the gift given to all the Sons of Men by Mother Father God. Be happy, and bask in the glow of the sun, which is the love of God for thee. Know you are ever loved and ever adored, Dear Ones. So, live, laugh and be happy, for such is your task upon the Earth. Let the Blessed of the Lord say, and so it is.

Amen & Amen

Know, indeed, that the love of God for humanity is such that it is like the howling wind outside the door. Know indeed, Dear One, it howls night and day, and is ever constant. For indeed, it is a cold and windy night. Know that as the wind rages around the door, the door remains constant, and those inside are kept safe and secure. Even so, Dear Ones is the love of God for humanity. For lo, it is that ever-constant thing which is always there, keeping out the storms and the dangers of life that, if allowed in, would ravage those who dwell within the house. Know indeed, Dear Ones, that the love of God is that shield and protection that enables mankind to rest safely within the dwelling, knowing nothing of all that is occurring outside. Know, Dear Ones, that those who dwell within, are in no way conscious of all that is being done to keep them safe. For indeed, they are shielded from all that would come nigh them. Thus, they know not of the true nature of all that is being done to keep them safe and warm. Know that the great and wonderful love of God for humanity is likened to the door, for it keeps all that would hurt or harm the Sons of Men at bay; and thus, those who rest within are safely held in the bosom of Mother Father God and are well.

Be comforted to know that this love, which allows all those forces to be held at bay, keeps the Sons of Men in safety. For indeed, they are loved with such depth and intensity that there is naught that Mother Father God would not do to protect his beloved children. Be ye aware, Dear Ones, that the door, once closed, keeps all at bay, and none is allowed within to disturb the peace of those who rest within. Know, Dear Ones, that you are precious in the eyes of God and as such, you are ever held and wrapped in the arms of God— if such we may use this term, for indeed, God has no arms. Know that the love, which is Mother Father God, is that possession which allows all to see and know how deeply they are loved: For indeed, they cannot exist upon the Earth without this great blessing becoming evident in their life. Indeed, Dear Ones, since man searches endlessly, day and night, for that which he knows not, it is evident that he knows that his blessing and this great gift will bring him sustenance, and thus he searches for it day and night.

In turmoil, he walks the Earth searching, ever searching for that which will give him peace. Know indeed, Dear One, that the love, which is Mother Father God, is that force which calms the weary soul, and brings the bliss and happiness of God into the vision of man. Know, Dear One, that you are the heart and soul of God, and the benefactor of all the gifts of God. For indeed, all that is available in the kingdom is laid at the feet of mankind for him to use and enjoy at his leisure. Know that all is given in total love from your Father God, and is thine to keep always. For, indeed, nothing is denied mankind upon the Earth, and, all that dwells therein was made and provided for man that he might live in love, peace, joy, and happiness always.

Know indeed, Dear One, that the love, peace, and joy of God are ever thine. It is ever available, ever there for thee, and none can take away this great gift, for it is freely given of God to the Sons of Men. Know, Dear Ones, that only the forgetfulness of man would cause the door not to withstand the winds that howl around the door. For man would run in fear and open the door, that he might escape this great travail, instead of knowing deep within him, that safety lays in staying within the shelter. For in leaving the shelter of God's arms, man is now bereft of safety, and runs in panic to the four winds seeking refuge and shelter when he was safe all the time.

The great panic of his life has caused him great pain, for now, indeed, he has lost his safety and he feels abandoned and alone. He longs for the safety which he had formerly known, but knows not how to find this and return to it once more. Know, Dear Ones, that when the storms of life would rage around your door, be not alarmed, but remain where you are within, for you are safely wrapped in the arms of God where naught can harm thee. Why leave thee the comfort and safety of home to rush to the four winds, when you are held and loved where you have dwelt? Be not anxious to leave for fear of your safety, but know always that you are loved by Mother Father God always. Leave not the arms of God and try to find safety and happiness elsewhere, for there exists no place where you will feel this joy, love, peace and happiness that you love, Dear Ones, except in the arms of God.

Know that in running, you are running away from God— if such we can use this term— for indeed you can go nowhere where God is not. But indeed, in running, you leave the safety and security you have known and loved, and are running to the four winds searching for shelter, when there is nothing comparable to be found. For the love of God is that most precious of all gifts which is priceless, and is above the true knowing of man. For, indeed, man knows not the depths of the love of God for him. For, indeed, he sees only that the door to the shelter is in place, and keeps out the wind and rain. He knows not of all the other elements that are shielded from his knowing. For, like a child, he is safe within and is without knowledge of all that the door has done to keep out the wind, and rain, and the storms, and those who would come nigh thee to keep thee from the safety you have always known. For indeed, the great door keeps out the distractions of the world, and keeps thee ever safe and secure, so that no harm would come nigh thee. Know, Dear Ones, that the love of God keeps thee ever safe from all around about thee, but to the knowing of man, it is merely that which is there. He knows not of its power to keep him safe, and to protect him from harm. For indeed, it is that thing, which is always there, and thus is unknown to man, in its intensity. Know that you are shielded, guided, loved, and protected by Mother Father God every day of your lives. So, hold fast when the storms of life come upon thee, and know that all your needs will be met, and your protection and continued peace is assured.

Rest always knowing the peace, love, and light of God is ever thine, and you are ever cradled in the loving arms of Mother Father God and in need of nothing, for all is provided for thee. Be you ever held and loved in this safety, for without the love of God, the storms of life would ravage thee and bring thee naught but pain. For, indeed, you would see lack and limitation, instead of knowing the bounty and abundance of God. Be ever content to remain within the sheltering arms of God, for there is no safety to be had anywhere else upon the Earth. For naught of the external world can bring thee peace, happiness, and joy. Naught else can bring thee safety, and naught else can keep thee ever secure. Let not the world come to thee and say we will show thee the way to safety. For indeed, God is your way to safety, and only he can keep thee ever protected, loved, and guided.

Be not fooled by those who would say that they know of other ways to achieve peace, contentment, and joy, for there is only one way to achieve these great prizes and that is by resting in the ever-loving arms of God always. Be you ever happy to know that no danger can come nigh thee when you rest in the loving arms of your Mother Father God. For you are truly loved and protected from all those elements that would remove your peace and your joy.

Let none come to thee and say we have another shelter that would protect thee, for this is indeed folly. For there is no protection or safety better than the love of God. For truly, with the love of God in the lives of men, there is naught that is needed.

Be at peace, Dear Ones, and rest always in the peaceful, loving arms of Mother Father God and know true peace, joy, and happiness. For therein lies your hope. Know always that your Mother Father God keeps thee ever secure, ever loved, and ever protected, if such is your desire. When you fail to recognize your gifts, or would search for safety elsewhere, know indeed that you walk away from the very peace, love, and happiness you seek, when you would leave the safety of your dwelling in search of that which you already possess. Know always, Dear Ones, how you are loved and adored, and keep thee ever constant. For thus is your hope, your joy, and your happiness found in the love of God, and only in the love of God. May you always know the peace, love, and joy of God, Dear Ones. And so we say, amen and amen!

Adieu Dear Ones

Know indeed, Dear One, that that the love of God for mankind can be likened to a great wheel which spins eternally. It is constant in its spinning, and moves around and around, much like the water wheels of ancient times. Know indeed, Dear Ones, that within this great wheel, are the tenets of its formation, for indeed, there are spokes and channels which assist the wheel in turning as it is required. Know indeed, Dear Ones, that the wheel turns endlessly, and as it turns, it generates much force, for indeed, it allows mankind to do that which is necessary to move water from one place to another. This is the love of God for humanity, since in its entirety, the focus of Mother Father God is to help mankind along his path and give him the strength and love that he needs in order to complete his tasks and to find his way back to Mother Father God. Know indeed, Dear Ones, that this wheel is constantly in motion and it serves its function night and day, moving the water as it is necessary. Thus, Dear Ones, mankind can carry out the tasks with ease, for he has the assistance of that which makes all tasks easy, within his reach.

Know, Dear Ones, that the wheel is that source of light and love for the Sons of Men, for it allows them to proceed along all paths and in all endeavors. For indeed, they have the love and light of God with them, to provide them with the most basic of needs. Let not the ease of the task make you forget your way, Dear Ones, or allow you to forget your path, for indeed, there are many things along the journey and the path that would make you forget your life before the wheel. For indeed, it was a time full of pain and drudgery. For without the presence of the wheel, your task was to daily move the water upon your back, without the help of any device. Thus, Dear Ones, the pain was much as you carried the water and moved it from place to place, making sure it was delivered to each one in his turn.

Remember the days of hardship, Dear Ones, and know those days are no longer a part of your life, for indeed, the days of toil are past. For now, you may spend your time engrossed in things of leisure, knowing that those tasks of drudgery and of pain are past. Now, you may turn your eyes to the things that are not of pain but of pleasure, for indeed your Mother Father God has allowed you to learn of other things and to give you paths of smooth sailing. Your needs are met, so you can focus on other things. You need to break your backs no longer to do those most basic of all tasks, and thus your lives are lived in gratitude and love.

Move out of the darkness, Dear Ones, and remember that the days of pain are past, and live instead in the new age, where your tasks for gaining water are now so simplified. Look to your Father's love, which allows you to partake of all the many blessings available upon the Earth. Turn away from those distractions, but remember once more the love of your Mother Father God, which even now allows you all the bounty of the Earth without toil or struggle. For indeed, the days of the water wheel are long past, and your Mother Father God, continues to provide for the most basic tenets of life for the Sons of Men. For indeed, although your needs for toil are no more, in order to gain the life-giving substance— water— know indeed, Dear Ones, that your brothers in many lands toil that same hard and difficult toil for the same life-giving substance.

Turn, we say, Dear Ones, and look to your brethren and know that you can bestow this gentle gift upon your brethren, for it will, indeed, give them life. For indeed, it gave you life and allowed you to live; yet now you would close your eyes to the plight of those in faraway places and say, "This is not my brother and this is not my cause." Know, Dear Ones, that even as your basic needs are met, even so your brethren can be saved. For indeed, if water is the source of all life, how much can you help your brethren if you turn and look upon him with love and caring?

Know indeed, Dear One, that the wheel is the wheel of life, and it can give life to all the Sons of Men in equal portions. Be the keeper of the wheel, and turn to help your brethren. For even so will your lot be increased upon the Earth, for to love and support your brethren is to love and support God. For as our Dear Brother Jesus taught, "As you do this for the least of them, you do it for me." Know that the love of God is the wheel of life, and turn to your brethren and share all the gifts you have been given. For in this way, will your bounty be increased, Dear Ones.

Turn not away as if blind, and say, "I have all I need, and there is none for thee." Know that in sharing and caring, you show love and compassion. You show joy and hope in the lives of your brethren. Be not selfish, and claim all as your own, but know that this abundant Universe will always provide more than is needed for the Sons of Men.

Be not the one who owns the wheel and says, "The water is mine and you must gather yours in buckets, and bring them one by one to do the work that is needed." Know, indeed, Dear Ones, that the love of God will allow thee to partake in the bounty of God and yet still have enough to share with your brethren. Know indeed, Dear Ones that the love and light of God is all that you need to remind thee of the great abundance that is available to thee always. Let not your greed and your jealousy cause thee to turn from the ways of God, and once more begin to hoard and take from those in need. For these are not the ways of God. Remember that loving, caring, and sharing these are the things of God. Selfishness, greed, envy, and avarice are not the ways of God.

Know, Dear Ones, that you are all loved and cherished by God, and as such have been given the keys to the kingdom. Be not full of pain when you see your brethren but instead, show love and compassion, for these, indeed, are the things of God. Be you full of the joys and the peace of God, and see how your bounty will increase for, indeed, great will be your abundance when you remember and demonstrate the things of God. Know indeed, Dear Ones, that the great water wheel can give water to all in equal portions, but if you keep it separated for thee only, you do not the things of God... and you would try to separate the love of God from your brethren. For lo, the water can benefit all within this place, if you would share this great gift with the world and use it to bring love and joy into the lives of others, instead of hiding it within your corner of the world, and keeping its whereabouts hidden from all those who would benefit.

Know, indeed, that the love of God is the life-giving substance which can change the hearts and minds of all those who would recognize its existence. Be the light, Dear Ones, and share this great gift with those around you. Keep it not hidden. Bring it into the light of day, that all might see it and know of its magnificence. For truly, the love of God is given in equal portions to all the Sons of Men, so to deny them knowledge of this great gift is beneath thee, Dear Ones.

Turn not away and keep the secret, for in truth, you would cause great pain to all. Instead, call for a celebration, and make ready to celebrate the finding of this great treasure, which will serve to bring joy, contentment, and happiness to all. Be the loving brother or sister who shares with those around him, for in truth, since all men are your brethren, to share this gift, which is the love of God, with your brothers and sisters, is to share the love of God upon the Earth.

No more look you on and say, "He is of a different race, or creed, or clan, so therefore I will not share with him." Know indeed, that to share the blessings of Mother Father God is to bring multitudes of blessings within your life. For in truth, the abundance of God should be shared with all. The love, peace, and joy should be shared with all your brethren, for in sharing, you are sharing the abundance of God upon the Earth. Be you full of the peace, love, and joy of God, and know that the wheel of life is made available to all. Know that all can benefit from this great gift, for from it will come the blessings of God.

Be not ashamed to call your brethren your brethren, even though others may encourage you to see differences between you. Know indeed, Dear One, that all are one in God and as such, there are no differences, for you are one: One in the same, with the same parent, Mother Father God, loved the same by your parent always. Always cradled in the same way by God, for you are all one in the mind of God. Be not downcast, but be happy to share the love, light, and blessings of Mother Father God with your brothers and sisters, for it will give you comfort. It will give thee peace, hope, joy, and the heart of God when you remember once more your brethren, and call them by name and acknowledge their lineage. For you are all children of the same Father Mother God.

Be humble, Dear Ones, and walk in the humility and love, which is God, for this will bring thee the sweet peace of God. When you share the bounty of God with all, and acknowledge the love of God, which is that thing which allows thee to know the love and joy, which is God. Be you ever in the arms of God, sharing in the bounty of God with your brothers and sisters, Dear Ones. For this is the demonstration of God upon the Earth— when the Children of Men see not color or creed, race or religion— but know within their hearts that all are ONE in God.

Be you ever constant, Dear Ones, and know the great peace and joy of God always in your hearts. Let the blessed of the Lord say, and so it is!

Amen

14TH JUNE 2012

Know indeed, Dear Ones, that the love of God for humanity flows like a mighty rushing river, pushing its way to the sea... for indeed, the force of the water would affect the banks of this river and cause it to change its course, Dear Ones. Know indeed, Dear Ones, that the might of the water is underestimated when one sees the gentle flowing of the river in its daily course to the sea. Know, however, that when the rains have come and the swell of the river turns to rage, we see the pounding and the relentless nature of the water. For indeed, there is no way in which the water can be contained, for it rushes headlong down the mountainside and into the path it has always traveled, only to find that it can no longer follow its old and well-worn path. For, indeed, it must make a new way on its journey down this steep and winding path. For indeed, the water rushes with such rage that it cannot be controlled and curtailed, for it must go its own way and determine its way in life. It must make its own path and create its own way in the world, setting out in new paths, with an unknown destination. For although it must find its way to the great sea, even so it knows not how to get there, for it can no longer follow the path.

Thus, Dear Ones, we say look ye no more to the old, for that which is old has passed and the new things must come into being. For the new ways must replace the old, for even so must the Children of Men no longer hold fast to the ancient ways, or to things of the past, for they no longer serve thee, Dear Ones. Look instead to the new, and the change in the laws of the world of man, for indeed, his consciousness has shifted and he must move on or die spiritually. For to survive, a new path and a new way must be found, so that others might, indeed, follow this course.

Know indeed, that the love of God is that great urge that pushes man forward and allows him to find his way to the table of love and into the arms of God. Know indeed, Dear Ones, that the message tells of the great and magnificent ways that are still to be brought into view. Know indeed, Dear Ones, that even as the mighty river rushes, even so does the love of God coursing in the veins of mankind to call him to action. For indeed, this is the time for action: That very action which can help to turn the tide and change the course of mankind upon the Earth. For indeed, mankind can no longer follow the paths of old but must now turn to find the love of God, and see that the old energy is dead, and a new way must be found for man upon the Earth... so that he might live with his brethren in peace and harmony, all the days of his life.

Know indeed, Dear Ones, that the mighty river flowing is the soul of man, who must harness the true strength that lives within him and move boldly into a new direction, carving out a new path where none has existed before. Be not afraid and say, "I must return to the old path, for there is safety there, while this new path may be fraught with dangers." Let God be the guide and shield. Let God be your compass, and know, Dear Ones, that He will guide thee through this great uncharted place, for you are never alone and the love of God is ever thine to keep these flowing waters safe and comforting. For indeed, he that is stronger than Mother Father God might wish to stand and be counted. Know indeed, Dear One, that the waters rush endlessly to the sea, and there is naught to separate thee but much to unite and bind thee.

Be bold, Dear Ones, and go headlong into the unknown, for the love of God is there behind thee, pushing and encouraging thee ever forward. Know indeed, that the arm of God is ever surrounding thee, guiding thee— if that is your desire— on the path that you would go. Know indeed, Dear Ones, that this powerful love has been thine since the dawn of time— for indeed, it has grown in all aspects of thee— and will never fail to swell. For indeed, you are that divine, sweet child of the Most High God. Be at peace and know that all is indeed well, for indeed, there is much joy in the hearts of men who would daily try to make thee try another way. Know indeed, Dear Ones, that the love of God can be seen in the very nature of the water, which on its most wonderful journey, pushes its way through all obstacles in order to find its way to the desired destination. Know indeed, Dear Ones, that the love of God is that magical elixir which gives thee the strength of many and the desires of all who would remain behind to cloak himself in invisibility.

For indeed, naught can stop or delay the rolling river, for her task is to get to the sea and to become a part of that great and mighty ocean. Let not your heart say it is time to slow down, for indeed this is not so. "It is time to move to the shores of Galilee," said Mary, but know that all you need on this journey will adhere itself to thee and thus will travel with thee until the journey is over. Know, Dear Ones, that the journey is undertaken, and know, indeed, that like the mighty river rushing to the sea, the love of God cannot be halted... for it is a force unknown to mankind, which can change the very heart and soul of those who would cower in the shadows, fearing the great adventure ahead.

Open your heart, Dear Ones, and know, indeed, that the love of God will accompany thee wherever you would go. For, indeed, it is the very stream of life for the Sons of Men. Be not full of fear but step out into the light and join in, Dear Ones, for together you will become a mighty force. For you are tiny drops of water when alone but a mighty river when combined. Be not surprised to know that the love of God will guide and uphold thee, for such is its power upon the Sons of Men, so that you might succeed upon this great quest and come to know that you are a light upon the Earth for the Sons of Men. For you carry the divine spark within thee, and thus you must glow and show your true colors.

Be never sad and remain on the banks... but instead, become a part of this great quest and run your true course upon the Earth. For your charge as children of the Most High God is to live, love, laugh, and to show the light of God upon your heart, and on your face each day, so that all might know thee.

Be alert always, and know that the love of God will ever be thine. May the grace, love, and blessings of God shine upon thee. Adieu, Dear Ones, in the love, light, and beingness which is Mother Father God. And so it is!

Amen

Know indeed, Dear One, that the love of God for mankind is like the flowers growing in the garden of God, for in truth, all are watered and fed abundantly by the loving arms of Mother Father God. Know indeed, Dear One, that indeed, each day the sunshine and the life-giving rains are made available and the flowers thrive, and bloom, and grow. Know indeed, Dear One, that they turn their buds to the sun and daily drink in the life-giving rain, and sense the strong and beautiful buds that they have given to man. For in truth, they do not look to say we are too beautiful to give you thanks and blessings, but indeed, they know that the food comes from the rain and the sunshine, and thus they enjoy the benefits of all that is there, made available to them. They enjoy each day with happiness as they drink in the love and bounty of God... but in no way do they take it for granted, for they know that these blessings are theirs to enjoy, but they do not know from whence they come. They drink in the energy of the Earth, and take the water to meet their very needs... but yet, they know not its source but are indeed grateful, Dear One.

Know, indeed, that as the days go by, their strength and size increase as they look to the sun and the rain for all their needs. They are, indeed, in the sheltering arms of all around them, for they know only that their task is to drink in and enjoy all that is given to them by Mother Earth.

Thus, they live in happiness and fulfillment, for indeed, all their needs are met. Thus, Dear Ones, they daily smile and know that, indeed, all is well, for it is the very nature of their beingness to be a source of joy and love upon the Earth. They bring pleasure to the Sons of Men, and thus their task is accomplished, for that is the very reason for their existence upon the Earth— to live that others might gain happiness and the life source from their being in the world. Thus, Dear Ones, we say the flowers in the garden of God are planted there to bring joy to all who would look upon them. For they bestow upon those who would gaze upon them the most blessed of all prizes, that of happiness and joy. For indeed, the Sons of Men take great pride in the giving and receiving of the flowers, and indeed, in the sharing of this simple thing, much happiness is shared upon the Earth.

Thus, Dear Ones, we say to live your lives like the flowers in the garden of God, for indeed it is their task to simply be and to bring joy to those around them, by being who and what they are. For in truth, when the eyes of man looks upon the flowers, he comes into contact with the most precious gifts of God, which delight the heart and soul of man.

Know indeed, Dear Ones, that the Children of Men are like the flowers in the garden of God, for their task is to bring happiness to all by being and expressing their very nature as children of the Most High God each and every day. For it is their task to be love and to show love, and to become the very expression of love upon the Earth. For like the flowers, whose task is simply to be that which they were created to be, even so must the Sons of Men become that which they are meant to be, as expressions of the joy, peace, love, and beingness of God.

Dear Ones, you come in many colors, hues, and shapes and sizes, but in your fine raiment you are resplendent children of the Most High God, whose task is simply to be God in expression upon the Earth. Your task is simply to be who you are meant to be, and to express love, and be love upon the Earth.

For, like the flowers, when man looks upon you, they should see the face of God, for that is who and what you are meant to be. For you are the Sons and Daughters of Mother Father God, and thus are the emissaries of God upon the Earth. Your task— if such we may describe it— is to be and to show love upon the Earth: for this is your purpose, this is your calling, this is your very reason for being upon the Earth: to love and to be love upon the Earth, to bring joy, peace, and happiness to all you meet, and to be the joy and the expression of love upon the Earth. Know indeed, Dear Ones, that you are the emissary of God upon the Earth; the ones who would show how to live in the world with peace, joy, love, and happiness, as a way of being in the world.

Know indeed, Dear Ones, that this love is who and what you are, for you are the very expressions of God upon the Earth. Know indeed, Dear Ones, that you are the very heart and soul of God… the peace, love, and joy of God upon the Earth, so be who you are and smile, smile, smile. Smile at the sun and dance in the rain. Drink in the gifts and grow with the love and wonder, which is God. Be always the truth and beingness of God upon the Earth, so that when men look upon you, they see only the truth of God. For in your petals are the joy and hope of love, the peace and beauty of God.

When men gaze upon you, they see the beauty deep within your heart, and know of your true magnificence... for you are the true emanations of God, the evidence of the depth and scope of the bounty of God. Be you ever in the love and the beingness of God, and accept all that is readily given to you, free of cost, for this is your gift from your loving and most benevolent Father, who in his love provides for thee all the gifts that are needed. For in this way, all those who look upon you will know by your fragrance, and your color, and your beauty that you are a wonderful gift, given to the Earth by your Mother Father God.

Know, indeed, that you are the bringer of the evidence of the love of God to the Sons of Men. In seeing you, they see the depth of the love of God, and in drinking in your beauty; they drink in all the very beauty and love, which is God. Know, Dear Ones, that you are the evidence of the love of God for mankind upon the Earth. You are the expression of the passion of God, for in giving you to the Earth and placing you in the magnificent garden of God; all may see and taste the beauty that is you.

All may gaze upon you, and know once more of all that is possible upon the Earth, for in seeing you and all the perfection that is within your nature, they come to see and know of the true majesty of God, who is able to create something so wonderfully delicate yet stunningly beautiful. For your beauty cannot be reproduced by man, try as he might, for only the creator, Mother Father God, can make a flower and only God can create the beingness which is individually you, Dear Ones.

Know, indeed, that the love, which is God, is given to all to share in this wonderful bounty of God, and the abundance of God, that you might know how deeply you are loved. For this is the way and beingness of God, Dear One, so live, and bloom, and grow in the garden of God, and know that all will, indeed, be well. For this is your charge, as a flower in the garden of God: to live, and bloom, and grow, and become that expression of love, joy, beauty and happiness upon the Earth. That, Dear Ones, is your only charge.

To be and know happiness, love, and joy when upon the Earth, that you might remember always that you are the Children of God, heirs to the very throne and the expressions of God's love upon the Earth.

Know always, Dear Ones, how much pleasure you give to God when you live and grow in his garden. For in bringing joy to others, you bring joy to the heart of God. Know always, Dear Ones, that all the flowers in the garden are loved with the same intensity. All are special; all are adored, for none is more exalted than the next, for all are loved by God. All are nurtured and fed by God, for this is the nature of God to take care of the things he loves. Thus, Dear Ones, know you are loved beyond compare with the deepest of all love, and you will never be where God is not. For there is no place where you can be where God is not, so know always you are loved and adored by God, and are always cradled in the arms of God. For this is the nature of God, to show his love to his children. Be at peace and know that you are the stars in the heavens as viewed by God, for such is your worth and value to God.

You are the evidence of love and beauty upon the Earth, so never fear that you will be removed from the garden; for indeed the grace and love of God will never be removed from thee, for this is not the way of God. Be not ashamed to show and to tell the world that you are a flower in the garden of God, loved and adored by God. Know always you will be at home in this garden, and all your needs will be met... for this is the heart and soul of God, and the very intention of God: to protect and to keep thee ever safe, for this is the nature of God and the very way of God.

Be always like the flowers in the garden, and hold up your heads in the sun Dear Ones. Be proud and hold your faces to the sun, for this is your life, your hope, and your rescue. For without the sun and rain of God's love, you will wither and die, so remember always to be the evidence of God upon the Earth, that you will know the true peace, love, and joy of God... as you daily show your beauty and perfection to the world. Live in happiness, Dear Ones, and know the abundance, love, and joy of God always! Let the blessed of the Lord say and so it is. Amen and Amen!

The Brotherhood

Know, indeed, that the love of God for mankind glows with the light of each new dawn, for indeed, it is that brilliant light which lights up the hearts of men and allows the heavens to shine in all her glory. Know, Dear One, that this love is so powerful that it can allow all that comes into contact with it to glow like an eternal and brilliant flame. Know, Dear One, that the light, which is the love of God, shines forth in the hearts of men and radiates outward upon the Earth, that all might see the brilliance and realize the wonderful and awesome nature, which is God. Know, Dear One, that the love, which is God, is not easily housed within the soul of man, for indeed, it glows that all might see and know that it lives within the heart and soul of the Sons of Men.

That some men do not recognize its glow, is, in truth, explained by the fact that they are buried so deep in the forgetfulness, which is the physical world; that indeed, they see not that very thing which is in front of them. That man knows not of his own magnificence is likewise attributed to this forgetfulness, which would have him believe that he is lost and alone upon the Earth.

Know, Dear Ones, that when the light shines forth from the Sons of Men, they become a beacon in the night and cannot hide their light, try as they might. For in truth, the light and love of God shines forth from the face of man, and others may see and know of the special nature of this being, but yet not fully understand why. Know, Dear One, that the truth, which is the love of God for man, cannot lay hidden when the light and heart of man recognizes that within him glows the love and peace of God. For in truth, he walks and talks with love and looks upon his brethren with the eyes and the heart of God. For that love, which is God, is oozing from his very pores and he is recognized as a child of the Most High God.

Know, Dear One, that the love, which is Mother Father God, has the power to calm the very tempest that would cause man to think that all is lost and he is alone upon the Earth, with none to give him that comfort and solace that is the love and beingness of God. Know, Dear One, that the days of wine and roses are upon the Sons of Men, for in truth, these are the days of the dawning of the awareness of the Sons of Men, that a new day is dawning upon the Earth: A day and time when man must learn that the love within him burns bright, and that he is, indeed, the child of the Most High God.

Know, Dear One, that you, as Children of God, are being called to open your hearts and to look within to find that which is the source and fountain of your strength. For this is, indeed, the path that will lead thee home to the peace and love which is Mother Father God. Know, Dear One, that this peace of God, which shines within you— as light in a window of a dark house— can become your very rescue; for this light, which not only burns outwardly also burns within thee, that you might come to know that you have the light of God within thee.

Know, Dear Ones, that you are forever the Children of God, and you are ever held and cradled in the loving arms of God. Thus, you are ever in contact with your parent. All that is God is contained within thee, for you are, indeed, the masters of the Earth, given dominion over all things.

That you know not of your true power or your true magnificence is indeed the pain of the heart of God— if such we can use this term— for indeed, we know that God, being spirit, feels no pain as is felt by the Sons of Men. Suffice it to say that the pain that would be felt by God is likened to the pain of a human parent forced to watch his children suffer. Know, Dear Ones, that while your parent watches you as you live in forgetfulness and isolation— you think— he knows that all that transpires, happens so that you might grow and advance as souls.

Know, Dear Ones, that the journey back to God is a love-filled journey and undertaking, for indeed, it is filled with rejoicing and happiness... for indeed, like the 'Prodigal Son,' one who was lost and had forgotten his heritage and his beingness, has now, once more, returned to the fold and is being reunited once more with his loving parent, that he might once more come to know and remember all the happiness, the peace, and the love, which is God: All the joy and the ecstasy, which is communion once more with his beloved parent.

Know indeed, Dear One, that the love, which is God, is that great compass which will point the way home, back to the loving arms of God. That the Children of Men lose their way, and lose the compass which would guide them, is caused by the distractions of life which pull them this way and that, so that they become weary and lost upon the road of life.

That he is then full of pain and bereft of home becomes the very way of man upon the Earth, so that he knows not the reason for the great sojourn upon the Earth, and understands not that he is a child in the great classroom of life, learning the very lessons that would help him to grow and allow him, once more, to return to that very place of peace, happiness, love and contentment that he barely remembers when he was in spirit. For lo, he cannot make the connections which would allow him to know that he is oh, so much more than he would ever consider himself to be.

Know indeed, Dear One, that this great love, which is God, can envelop thee if you would but open your arms and welcome the peace, love, and joy of God into your heart and your life. For indeed, in doing this you welcome that which is whole, beautiful, and powerful into your very beingness. Know, Dear Ones, that the ways of God lend themselves only to love, peace, joy and happiness, that the Sons of Men might know the contentment, which is God. For when the Sons of Men begin to remember the reason for the journey upon the Earth, and can understand who and what they truly are— Children of God lost upon the Earth, trying to return to their parent— their hearts are jubilant and they are at peace. For indeed, the great peace and contentment of God, which descends upon them, causes them to see and know, once more, their true nature and worth as children of the Most High God.

Know indeed, Dear One, that the joyous and triumphant rejoicing of the Sons of Men returning to the fold of God's love is the most wondrous of all things known to the Children of God. For, indeed, it means the ending of the great separation from their loving parent, and a great reunion with the heart of God, from which they do not like to be separated. That their prolonged separation from Mother Father

God has caused great pain to the Sons of Men is apparent, for indeed, they are happy to be once more held in the loving arms of God.

Know always, Dear One, that the return to Mother Father God is like the return of the iron filling to the magnet, for, indeed, they are a part of each other and long always to be together. For this is part of the very nature and essence of the one for the other that they might forever be joined: for their nature and their origin are one. One is a particle of the other, thus they are forever searching for that part of the self which will make it whole. For without the return, they are splintered and scattered upon the Earth, and long for the time when they can, once more, become whole. Know, Dear One, that the love of God is that very glue which causes you to feel whole, and loved, and adored, for indeed, this is your natural state.

For this is as natural to you as the sun is to the day, and the moon is seen at night. For indeed, that the Children of Men feel lost and alone when upon the Earth is because they feel fragmented and know not why. They search for that glue which will allow them to be ONE once more, but know not that this is what they search for. Know indeed, Dear One, that the love, which is God, is the glue that binds the Sons of Men together that they feel that they are no longer lost and alone, but can now have focus and purpose upon the Earth. Know always, Dear One, that the journey home to your Mother Father God is the return of the love and support of the parent to the child. You are being held and cradled, Dear One, and you will come to know, once more, the peace, love, joy, and warmth, which are the arms of God.

Know, Dear One, that you will forever be held and cradled, and will know no wants or needs, for all your needs will finally be fulfilled and your soul will want for nothing. For emptiness and the feeling of loss is no more, for you are filled with the love, passion, hope, joy, and peace of God. Be never afraid, Dear One, that you must suffer always upon the Earth, but know that the great peace of God is already given to thee. Look in your pocket and see the many treasures that hide within. Know that you were given all the gifts and talents you would need upon your journey when you entered the physical body. Look no longer outside yourself for your treasure, but remember that your treasure lies deep within your heart. Look no more to the four winds to find your rescue, but remember, Dear One, that your peace, your hope, and your rescue resides within your heart, where it was placed by your loving parent.

Think not that your gifts were given to another, for you see them not but know that, indeed, you were given all you will ever need to survive upon the Earth. Be always at peace, Dear One, and come to know the joy, which is God, within your heart. For where you are, God is, and love, peace, and contentment reigns. For this is the promise and the hope of God. This is the nature and the beingness of God. Open your hearts, Dear Ones, and remember your true nature as Children of God, and become your true selves once more.

Be at peace, Dear Ones, and enjoy this wonderful journey home, back to the loving arms of God. For you have always been there, cradled and loved. Only your physical mind would cause you to forget these truths, that you might forget your nature and your name as Children of God. Remember always that you are loved, cradled, and adored by God, for this is your truth, your joy, and your rescue,

THE LOVE OF GOD WILL CARRY YOU HOME

Dear Ones. Shake off the veil of forgetfulness, and return once more to the knowledge of the love of God and be at peace.

Let the blessed of the Lord say, "And so it is, now and forever, for this is the will of Mother Father God."

Adieu, Dear Ones!

Know always you are loved and adored, for this is the will of your parent that you might know only love, happiness, peace, and contentment throughout your journey and your lives upon the Earth. And so it is.

Amen & Amen!

The Brotherhood of Light